Defining an AI-Based K-12 Education System

Syed Far Abid Hossain
https://orcid.org/0000-0003-0729-1456
BRAC University, Bangladesh

Walton Wider
INTI International University, Malaysia

IGI Global
Scientific Publishing
Publishing Tomorrow's Research Today

Vice President of Editorial	Melissa Wagner
Director of Acquisitions	Mikaela Felty
Director of Book Development	Jocelynn Hessler
Production Manager	Mike Brehm
Cover Design	Jose Rosado

Published in the United States of America by
IGI Global Scientific Publishing
701 East Chocolate Avenue
Hershey, PA, 17033, USA
Tel: 717-533-8845 | Fax: 717-533-7115
Website: https://www.igi-global.com E-mail: cust@igi-global.com

Library of Congress Cataloging-in-Publication Data

(CIP Data Pending)
ISBN13: 979-8-3693-6346-1
Isbn13Softcover: 979-8-3693-6347-8
EISBN13: 979-8-3693-6348-5
British Cataloguing in Publication Data
A Cataloguing in Publication record for this book is available from the British Library.

Table of Contents

Detailed Table of Contents

Recently, Artificial intelligence (AI) has become more prevalent in the educational context and garnered substantial attention, among its several applications the integration of AI into K-12 education is underscored where it upholds the promise to reshape the conventional teaching and learning approaches and experiences. Despite the enticing prospect of technological advancement, it is necessary to investigate the implications of AI when integrated into the education sector, particularly in K-12 education. This chapter critically examines the threats and opportunities of AI in K12 education, by reviewing studies that have been conducted during the timeframe of the year 2021-2024. The methodology of the study consists of a thorough analysis of a wide-ranging corpus of research regarding the numerous ways in which artificial intelligence is being utilized in K–12 education. A comprehensive search has been conducted using relevant keywords across numerous academic databases and only relevant and contemporary journals have been chosen.

The adoption of Artificial Intelligence in Education (AIED) in K-12 has embedded the curiosity and understanding that lean to accelerate the students towards being the right fit for the data-driven world of industrialization. This secondary literature review-based chapter strives to address the ongoing trends, significant challenges, and opportunities of AIED. The findings state that Massive Open Online Courses (MOOC), Intelligent Tutoring Systems (ITS), Dialogue Based-Tutoring Systems (DBTS), Learning Management Systems (LMS), Exploratory Learning Environments (ELE), Interactive Learning Environments (ILE), and STEM program are the leading preferences of the students and teachers heeded by organizational, methodological, technological, and psychological challenges for effective integration. Additionally,

As AI grows more significant across businesses, educators must understand technology to educate kids for the future. This study will create a K-12 AI teacher training course that seamlessly blends AI literacy and ethics. The study discusses ethical education and the best AI literacy teaching methods and resources for teacher training. The best methods were found by qualitative literature review. A comprehensive AI literacy and ethical education method boosts educators' confidence and proficiency. Success requires AI initiatives, ethical exploration, and professional development. Interactive workshops, real-world AI applications, and collaborative learning are essential for education. The study reveals a well-planned AI teacher training course can prepare K-12 teachers to teach AI literacy and ethics. Teachers may include AI by using hands-on projects, emphasizing ethics, and promoting growth. This method prepares pupils for a tech-driven future by explaining AI and its morality.

Artificial intelligence is, in particular, one of the fastest-developing areas within the education sector, especially at the K–12 levels. From personalized learning experiences to efficient processes for various administrative tasks, AI has massive potential, which could hugely affect teaching and learning. However, before that, educators need proper training in AI technology. The integration of AI into education exceeds just the boundaries of technical tools; it requires a more detailed cognition of how the technology can improve performance, further equity, and personalize experiences in an environment of inclusivity. This chapter delves into some basics of training AI teachers, the capabilities expected of a teacher, and some real-world examples of AI in the classroom. We will look with equal interest at how quality educator preparation can help resolve the challenges brought about through AI integration for the success of both instructors and students in an educational setup supported by AI.

The Ministry of Education Malaysia aims to promote digital education in schools. However, a disparity between government initiatives and educators' competency has been identified. Past studies suggest that educators' perspectives play an important role in integrating technology in education. This qualitative research explored educators' perceptions of Artificial Intelligence (AI) use in education and the necessary strategies for AI-integrated education. A total of 11 educators from diverse backgrounds participated in the study, sharing their perceptions and experiences regarding AI-integrated education. The interviews covered three primary areas: experiences with technology use in teaching and learning, perceptions toward AI-integrated education, and suggested strategies. Thematic analysis identified the main themes related to these areas. The current findings not only contribute to the literature by presenting Malaysian educators' perspectives but also provide insights into designing effective training programs to facilitate AI-integrated education in Malaysia.

This chapter addresses AI's potential, difficulties, and effects on learning utilization in research and implementation. AI's rapid expansion offers individualized learning, adaptive training, and AI-driven assessments, but it also raises ethical issues, especially in India. Data privacy, biased algorithms, the digital divide, and education equity are matters of concern in K–12 education. The study explores Indian primary, secondary, and high school AI integration, its potential, obstacles, and socio-cultural effects. Methods emphasize ethics, education, and assessment. How educators and schools can employ AI responsibly has been examined. AI affects Indian education's ethics, learning, and culture. The study assesses AI-powered education's efficacy, and inclusion. Teachers, politicians, scholars, and technologists must work on data privacy and algorithmic bias. Student growth depends on ethical AI use, pedagogical congruence, and fair access to high-quality education.

The integration of Artificial Intelligence (AI) into FinTech education is transforming financial services and academic programs, bridging the gap between traditional learning and industrial expectations. This chapter focuses on how AI-driven FinTech education improves financial literacy, financial management, and FinTech adoption. It explores fundamental concerns about AI's role in FinTech education, its implementation, and its impact on learners and institutions, with a focus on educators, students, and industry professionals. The findings emphasise the possibilities of AI-powered FinTech solutions to customise learning, give market insights, and optimise financial decision-making to increase student engagement. The topic emphasises the importance of a multidisciplinary curriculum, regulatory constraints, and ethical concerns associated with AI integration in education. Finally, FinTech education boosted by AI is critical for equipping graduates with skills and encouraging financial inclusion.

This chapter focuses on the underlying concept paradigms, and best practices for integrating AI into elementary, middle, and high school curricula. This chapter aims to educate teachers, lawmakers, and stakeholders how AI might improve training, administrative efficiency, and critical thinking. As AI technologies grow, K-12 AI education must prepare kids for employment changes. AI advances are transforming science, economics, law, farming, food security, and health in industry and government. K-12 education will soon transform in the “Age of AI”. AI will change employment, training, and procedures. AI will work with humans in several fields. Teaching artificial intelligence (AI) in grades K-12 is a significant issue in the world of teaching research, especially because schools and instructors are having a hard time incorporating AI into their lessons. Research into the testing, training, development, and implementation of AI learning systems by humans is very lacking. This is especially true for elementary and secondary schools.

This chapter explores the potential of Large Language Models (LLMs) like ChatGPT in creating inclusive and adaptive K-12 curricula that effectively integrate the needs of students with special needs. Using Generative AI technologies like LLMs, this chapter presents innovative strategies for designing and implementing curricula that cater to diverse learning needs with an inclusive approach for special needs that ensures equal opportunities for students' academic success. Case studies and examples are further discussed to help reader towards implementing AI supported curriculum integration in educational settings.

Besides fulfilling its preceding objectives through AI-oriented tutoring techniques, multifarious chatbots have been introduced to assist students with their academic assignments. This qualitative review has been performed to answer whether the integration of artificial intelligence in education is a blessing or a curse for students' academic integrity, as not everyone is a wise user of innovation. The findings state that AI education techniques have both optimistic and pessimistic impacts on students' academic integrity. Whether a student will adopt unfair means entirely depends on cognitive abilities and behavioral components. The future might be jeopardized if such practices persist, which creates doubts and prognostication about the ample scope of malpractices in the educational community. Thus, this chapter aims to make academicians and future researchers aware of the perception and consequences of academic integrity in the presence of AI learning modules.

This research aims to explore the integration of artificial intelligence (AI) technologies into traditional classroom settings, assess their impact on teaching and learning practices, and address concerns related to ethics, equity, and pedagogical effectiveness. Through conducting a comprehensive review of existing literature, case studies, and empirical data, this research seeks to provide insights into the transformative potential of AI-enabled classrooms. Additionally, it will propose recommendations for effective implementation and address ethical considerations to ensure equitable and effective AI integration in education. This study also aims to identify best practices and highlight successful models of AI adoption in various educational contexts, providing a roadmap for policymakers, educators, and technologists to navigate both the challenges and opportunities presented by AI in education. By understanding AI's multifaceted impact, the research hopes to contribute to developing an inclusive and forward-thinking educational ecosystem in India.

Preface

INTRODUCTION

The rapid evolution of Artificial Intelligence (AI) has ushered in transformative possibilities across industries, and education stands at the forefront of this change. In this edited volume, *Defining an AI-Based K–12 Education System*, we seek to explore the role of AI in the contemporary era, with a particular focus on its implications for K–12 educational development. At a time when societies and governments bear increasing responsibility for developing, forecasting, and ensuring equitable access to education, it is imperative to critically examine how AI can support—and responsibly shape—this mission.

Ensuring education for all remains one of the most pressing global commitments. To cope with this challenging task, policymakers must cultivate a sufficient understanding of Artificial Intelligence—its tools, systems, opportunities, and limitations. AI-driven technologies are not merely technical innovations; they are instruments that can influence curriculum design, assessment systems, personalized learning pathways, administrative efficiency, and inclusive practices. When thoughtfully implemented, they offer the potential to strengthen educational access, quality, and equity.

Teachers, as skilled professionals in the academic arena, play a central role in this transformation. AI-generated tools, techniques, software applications, and intelligent systems can significantly reduce administrative burdens, streamline instructional planning, and enhance pedagogical effectiveness. However, technology alone does not guarantee improvement. Meaningful integration requires professional readiness, ethical awareness, and pedagogical insight. When educators are empowered to engage critically and creatively with AI, they can foster more adaptive, responsive, and learner-centered environments. In doing so, education systems move closer to achieving broader sustainable development goals by reinforcing the commitment to inclusive and equitable quality education.

The chapters in this volume collectively examine key issues emerging from K–12 education in the age of AI. Contributors analyze conceptual frameworks, pedagogical innovations, technological infrastructures, ethical considerations, policy implications, and practical case studies. Together, these perspectives illuminate both the promises and the complexities of designing AI-enabled education systems. Importantly, the book does not approach AI as a panacea; rather, it encourages critical inquiry, balanced evaluation, and solution-oriented thinking.

By identifying current challenges and presenting possible solutions, this volume aims to prepare stakeholders to anticipate and address emerging concerns. From digital divides and algorithmic bias to teacher preparedness and governance frameworks, the discussions herein broaden the scope of expertise required in contemporary educational leadership. Our goal is to foster informed dialogue that bridges theory, research, policy, and practice.

This book is intended for academicians, educators, researchers, policymakers, administrators, and other stakeholders invested in the future of K–12 education. We also believe it will be valuable to professionals across the academic and policy landscape who seek to analyze complex educational problems while exploring practical and forward-looking solutions.

As editors, we hope this collection stimulates thoughtful engagement, responsible innovation, and collaborative action in shaping AI-based K–12 education systems that are equitable, ethical, and sustainable.

ORGANIZATION OF THE BOOK

The chapters in this volume collectively examine the evolving architecture of AI-based K–12 education systems from critical, pedagogical, technological, ethical, and contextual perspectives. Each contribution advances the broader dialogue on how artificial intelligence can be responsibly and effectively integrated into school education while addressing pressing concerns of equity, governance, and sustainability.

In **Chapter 1**, Sayada Mollika and Rezuana Tabassum provide a timely and critical review of AI's threats and opportunities in K–12 education. Drawing upon studies published between 2021 and 2024, the authors systematically analyze contemporary research to evaluate how AI is reshaping traditional teaching and learning models. Their review balances optimism with caution, carefully interrogating both the transformative potential of AI and the structural, ethical, and pedagogical risks that accompany its rapid adoption. This chapter lays a strong conceptual foundation for the volume by situating AI integration within evidence-based scholarship.

Chapter 2, authored by Anika Zarin Chowdhury and colleagues, expands the discussion by examining trends, challenges, and opportunities in Artificial Intelligence in Education (AIED). Through a comprehensive secondary literature review, the chapter maps key AI-enabled learning environments—such as MOOCs, Intelligent Tutoring Systems, Dialogue-Based Tutoring Systems, and STEM initiatives—while identifying organizational, methodological, technological, and psychological barriers to implementation. The authors situate these developments within the broader vision of Education 4.0, arguing that AI can move schooling beyond conventional paradigms toward more innovative and future-ready models.

In **Chapter 3**, Aarzoo and Ruhi Lal explore the intersection of AI-driven innovation and brand promotion within K–12 educational start-ups. This chapter uniquely integrates perspectives from digital marketing, entrepreneurship, and educational technology. Through literature review, industry insights, and case analyses, the authors highlight how AI-powered digitization enhances operations, personalization, and stakeholder engagement, while also acknowledging persistent challenges such as data privacy concerns and implementation costs. Their work demonstrates that strategic branding and AI innovation are increasingly intertwined in shaping the competitive landscape of educational enterprises.

Chapter 4, by Chengen Li and Huimin Wangwan, provides a comprehensive framework for defining an AI-based K–12 education system. The chapter synthesizes current trends, evaluates AI tools such as adaptive learning platforms and intelligent tutoring systems, and examines their implications for curriculum integration and personalized learning. Importantly, the authors address ethical challenges, data governance, teacher preparedness, and policy considerations, offering forward-looking perspectives on how education systems can evolve responsibly in an AI-driven era.

The focus shifts to educator capacity-building in **Chapter 5**, where Ruhi Lal and Aarzoo design a teacher training program centered on AI literacy and ethics. Recognizing that technological advancement must be accompanied by pedagogical preparedness, the authors propose interactive, practice-oriented professional development models. By emphasizing ethical awareness, real-world applications, and collaborative learning, the chapter outlines how structured training can empower teachers to integrate AI confidently and responsibly into classroom practice.

Complementing this, **Chapter 6**, authored by Sheneen Hossain, further elaborates on educator training within AI-based education systems. The chapter highlights the competencies required for teachers operating in AI-enhanced environments and presents real-world classroom applications. It underscores that AI integration extends beyond technical familiarity; it demands inclusive thinking, equity-oriented design, and performance enhancement strategies. The discussion positions educator preparation as central to the long-term success of AI adoption.

In **Chapter 7**, Anna Wen Huey Ong and her co-authors present empirical insights into educators' perceptions and experiences with AI integration in Malaysia. Through qualitative thematic analysis of interviews with practicing educators, the chapter reveals the gap between national digital initiatives and on-the-ground competency levels. The authors offer contextually grounded strategies for bridging this divide, contributing valuable practitioner perspectives that inform both training design and policy formulation.

Chapter 8, by Nandini Deb, Ruhi Lal, and Deep Gogoi, turns to ethical considerations in the Indian context. The authors examine pressing concerns such as data privacy, algorithmic bias, digital divides, and socio-cultural implications of AI adoption across primary and secondary education. By foregrounding equity and responsible governance, this chapter reinforces the necessity of ethical alignment in AI-supported learning systems and calls for collaborative engagement among educators, policymakers, and technologists.

Broadening the scope of AI integration, **Chapter 9**, authored by Arif Ahsan and colleagues, explores AI-driven FinTech education. The chapter demonstrates how AI can enhance financial literacy, decision-making, and industry alignment within educational programs. By advocating for multidisciplinary curricula and ethical regulatory awareness, the authors highlight the importance of preparing students for emerging financial ecosystems shaped by intelligent technologies.

In **Chapter 10**, Tahsin Mallik and co-authors examine the conceptual paradigms and best practices for integrating AI across elementary, middle, and high school curricula. The chapter emphasizes AI's transformative impact across industries and argues that K–12 education must proactively respond to workforce shifts and technological disruption. By identifying implementation gaps and research shortages—particularly at foundational schooling levels—the authors call for systematic innovation and research-informed practice.

The commitment to inclusion is further advanced in **Chapter 11**, where Yusuf Mshelia and colleagues investigate Large Language Model (LLM)-driven curriculum design that integrates special needs education. By presenting adaptive strategies and illustrative case examples, the chapter demonstrates how generative AI tools can support differentiated instruction and equitable academic opportunities. This contribution underscores AI's potential to foster inclusive education when guided by intentional design.

Academic integrity becomes the focal point in **Chapter 12**, authored by Anika Chowdhury and collaborators. Through a qualitative review, the chapter interrogates whether AI-enhanced tutoring and chatbot technologies strengthen or compromise academic honesty. The authors present a balanced perspective, recognizing both constructive and detrimental impacts, and caution against misuse that may undermine cognitive development and ethical standards within academic communities.

Finally, **Chapter 13**, by Aashish Jain and Rohit Khokher, presents a comprehensive review of AI-enabled classroom transformation in India. The chapter evaluates pedagogical shifts, ethical considerations, and successful adoption models, offering practical recommendations for policymakers and practitioners. By mapping both opportunities and challenges, the authors provide a roadmap for building inclusive, forward-thinking educational ecosystems aligned with 21st-century demands.

Together, these chapters form a cohesive and multidimensional exploration of AI in K–12 education. They move beyond technological enthusiasm to address governance, ethics, pedagogy, entrepreneurship, inclusion, academic integrity, and contextual adaptation. As editors, we believe this collective scholarship offers both critical reflection and actionable guidance for shaping equitable, sustainable, and future-ready AI-based education systems.

CONCLUSION

As we bring this volume to a close, we are reminded that Artificial Intelligence in K–12 education is neither a distant prospect nor a passing trend—it is an unfolding reality. The chapters in this book collectively demonstrate that AI is reshaping how we conceptualize teaching, learning, assessment, administration, curriculum design, professional development, inclusion, and governance. Yet, as emphasized throughout this collection, the true transformation lies not in the technology itself, but in how thoughtfully and ethically it is integrated into educational ecosystems.

This volume has intentionally brought together diverse scholarly voices from multiple countries and contexts. The contributors have explored AI from critical, pedagogical, entrepreneurial, ethical, technological, and policy-oriented perspectives. They have examined both optimism and apprehension, highlighting opportunities for personalization, innovation, efficiency, and inclusion, while equally interrogating concerns related to data privacy, algorithmic bias, academic integrity, digital divides, teacher preparedness, and systemic inequities. Such balanced inquiry is essential if AI-based K–12 education systems are to remain human-centered and equitable.

A recurring insight across the chapters is that educators stand at the heart of meaningful AI integration. No intelligent system can substitute for professional judgment, ethical discernment, and pedagogical wisdom. Teacher training, AI literacy, and ethical awareness emerge as foundational pillars for sustainable implementation. Likewise, policymakers and institutional leaders must adopt forward-thinking yet cautious strategies, ensuring regulatory clarity, infrastructure readiness, and inclusive access.

Another important theme running through this volume is inclusivity. Whether through adaptive learning platforms, LLM-driven curriculum design for special needs learners, AI-enabled financial literacy education, or context-specific transformations in countries such as India and Malaysia, the contributors consistently highlight the necessity of equitable access. AI must not widen existing disparities; instead, it should serve as a bridge to expand educational opportunities for diverse learners.

As editors, we believe that defining an AI-based K–12 education system requires more than technological deployment—it requires vision, collaboration, and responsibility. It demands interdisciplinary dialogue among educators, technologists, researchers, entrepreneurs, regulators, and communities. It calls for ongoing research that evaluates long-term impacts rather than short-term efficiency gains. Most importantly, it requires a steadfast commitment to the fundamental purpose of education: nurturing critical thinking, creativity, ethical reasoning, and human development.

We hope this volume serves as both a scholarly reference and a catalyst for further inquiry. May it encourage informed debate, inspire innovative practice, and guide responsible policymaking. The "Age of AI" in education is already underway; the question before us is not whether AI will shape K–12 education, but how we will shape AI to serve the collective good.

With this book, we invite readers to participate actively in that shaping process—thoughtfully, critically, and collaboratively—so that AI-enabled education systems remain inclusive, ethical, and future-ready for generations to come.

Chapter 1

A Critical Review of AI's Threats and Opportunities in K-12 Education.

Sayada Mollika
http://orcid.org/0009-0005-9826-4980
BRAC University, Bangladesh

Rezuana Tabassum
BRAC University, Bangladesh

ABSTRACT

Recently, Artificial intelligence (AI) has become more prevalent in the educational context and garnered substantial attention, among its several applications the integration of AI into K-12 education is underscored where it upholds the promise to reshape the conventional teaching and learning approaches and experiences. Despite the enticing prospect of technological advancement, it is necessary to investigate the implications of AI when integrated into the education sector, particularly in K-12 education. This chapter critically examines the threats and opportunities of AI in K12 education, by reviewing studies that have been conducted during the timeframe of the year 2021-2024. The methodology of the study consists of a thorough analysis of a wide-ranging corpus of research regarding the numerous ways in which artificial intelligence is being utilized in K–12 education. A comprehensive search has been conducted using relevant keywords across numerous academic databases and only relevant and contemporary journals have been chosen.

DOI: 10.4018/979-8-3693-6346-1.ch001

1 INTRODUCTION

"Artificial intelligence and generative AI may be the most important technology of any lifetime." - Marc Benioff.

Artificial intelligence (AI) is the capability of computer systems or algorithms to imitate intelligent human behavior, alternatively, it is a branch of computer science dealing with the simulation of intelligent behavior in computers, as defined by the Merriam-Webster dictionary. Naqvi, (2020) identified artificial intelligence (AI) as the area of computer science concerned with simulating intelligent behavior in computers and their potential to emulate—and hopefully surpass—human behavior. The COVID-19 pandemic and its aftermath have brought attention to our reliance on AI systems and our need for assistance. AI systems are becoming more and more prevalent in various industries including education, healthcare, manufacturing, retail e-commerce, finance and banking, energy and utilities, communication and media, transportation and logistics, public safety and security, legal service, tourism and hospitality, and agriculture and so on. Right now if we look at the surroundings of our house or our office we will see Ai powered smart devices like smart thermostats, smart acoustic, smart desks, Amazon Echo, AI quality monitors, robotic vacuums, smart lighting and so on that are capable to learning our preferences and habits to control the environment of our soundings. Living in today's world and beyond is practically difficult without encountering AI-powered applications, as we continually use search systems, seek virtual assistance to receive recommendations for personalized music and films that we are interested in, and use real-time location instructions.

With artificial intelligence (AI) advancing at an accelerated rate and permeating many aspects of our daily lives, important questions about AI's role and impact in the field of education have arisen. Recent advances in artificial intelligence (AI), such as machine learning algorithms, natural language processing, and data analytics, have demonstrated significant benefits for supporting students in their academic pursuits. An increased educational, societal, and political interest has sparked in teaching citizens to be adept in AI. Education institutions have started to prepare children in grades K-12 to live in a world that requires them to deal with AI. Thus, the conventional academic atmosphere has been profoundly transformed by the presence of these tools.

The many algorithmic applications that artificial intelligence (AI) offers to educators and students include virtual classrooms, interactive textbooks, collaborative, adaptive, and gamified learning tools, personalized multilingual learning, automated assessments, emotional AI, and so on, these AI-enhanced tools enable connection among teachers students from anywhere in the world, teachers can deliver live lectures and students can attend and participate in spontaneous classroom discussions.

AI-powered textbooks make learning more dynamic and engaging by offering interactive audio-video learning materials along with type-in, drag-and-drop quizzes, and simulations. Students can benefit from AI-powered teaching systems that adapt the pace and level of difficulty of instruction based on their prior knowledge and development. AI-enhanced platforms can also facilitate collaborative learning through the monitoring and tracking of group activities, peer contributions, and teacher feedback. Additionally, students can connect with peers to gain insight into complex concepts. Finally, learning can be made more enjoyable by gamifying traditional educational components into engaging activities that award points, badges, and leaderboards to successfully complete tasks. Students who struggle with stress, anxiety, and other emotional issues can benefit from emotional AI. Despite the opportunities of AI applications in education, there are societal and ethical concerns or threats.

> *"Everything that civilization has to offer is a product of human intelligence... success in creating AI would be the biggest event in human history. Unfortunately, it might also be the last, unless we learn how to avoid the risks." - Stephen Hawking.*

Therefore, it is necessary to investigate the implications of AI when integrated into the education sector, particularly in K-12 education. As noted by renowned physicist Stephen Hawking, assessing these threats is critical to humanity's survival. This study first identifies the existing benefits or potential for integrating these artificial intelligent algorithms in K-12 contexts, as well as the concerns, before highlighting how to capitalise on these opportunities and manage the threats.

2 METHODOLOGY OF THE RESEARCH

This chapter was written using the SLR (Systematic Literature Review) technique. To further arrange search processes, quality assessment (QA) (Okoli & Schabram, 2015), and article rating (Kitchenham et al., 2009), several approaches recommended by various research have been adapted to prepare this study.

2.1 Research Question

For this systematic literature paper, the researchers have developed two research questions. These are given below:

1. What are the threats associated with AI education in the K–12 setting? How do educators mitigate threats and challenges associated with AI?

2. What opportunities do AI technologies offer for enhancing teaching and learning processes in K–12 education? How to avail those opportunities for better teaching and learning outcomes?

2.2 Research procedure

The diagram of research procedure is given below:

Figure 1. Process of research (Silaban et al., 2022)

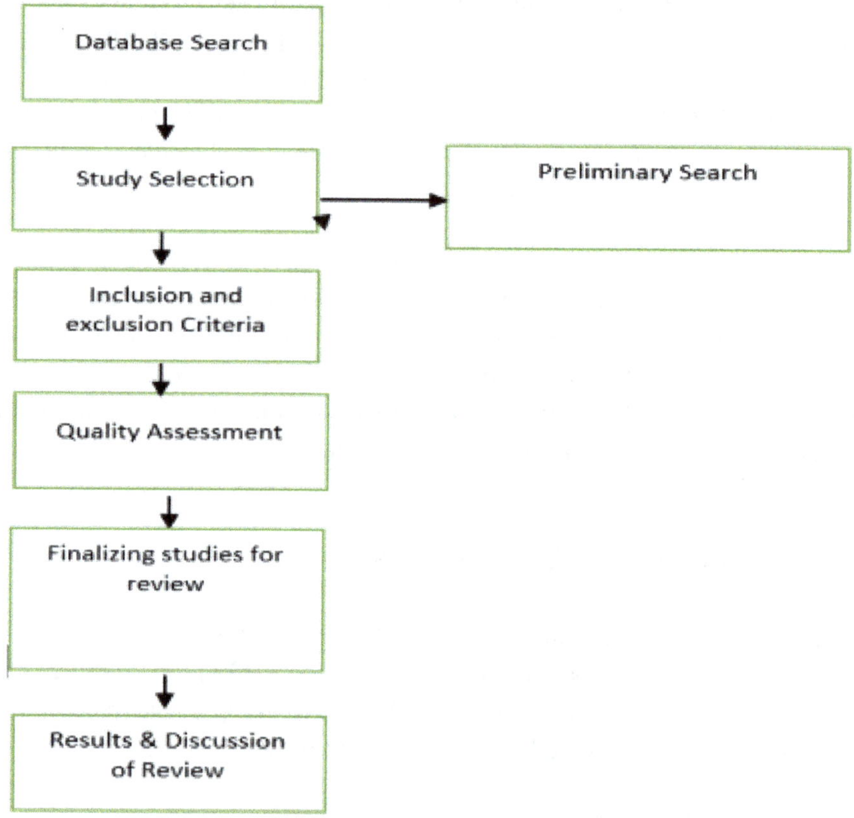

2.3 Search Procedure

This research aims to explore the field of AI in K-12 education and find out the threats and opportunities that Artificial Intelligence has in educational curricula. This research strategically evaluates strategies for mitigating threats by preventing biases, teaching proper ethical and data security policies, ensuring access and equity to everyone, developing an AI-based curriculum to engage students in the class, reducing pedagogical difficulties and technical issues, and providing training to teachers. Also, this paper states ways to avail opportunities such as motivating learners through career opportunities, implementing curriculum from the early stage, introducing workshops to teachers, promoting hands-on activities, partnering with high-tech companies to develop an AI-based curriculum, and many more.

The study makes use of popular search engines like Google Scholar, Research-Gate, Science Direct, SpringerLink, Wiley Online Library, JSTOR, Scopus, Elsevier, Emerald Insight, and Web of Science, to extract data in the timeframe of January 2021 to June 2024. Articles filtered by search terms such as "Threats and AI in K-12 education," "Threats in AI-based K-12 education", "opportunities and AI in K-12 education," "Opportunities in AI-based K-12 education", "Threats in K-12 education", "Mitigating threats of AI and curriculum ", "availing opportunity and AI education", "Opportunities in AI-based curriculum", "grabbing opportunities in AI and K-12 education "AI in K-12 education". Table (1, 2, 3, 4, 5, 6, 7) displays the results of the search method. The objective is to extract beneficial insight that is pertinent to the development of AI-based education in K-12 settings.

2.4 Study Selection

Initially, 25 results have been found for this research. Then, the following sections of inclusion criteria, exclusion criteria and quality assessment have been followed to assess further by selecting the most relevant pieces of literature.

2.5 Inclusion Criteria

1. Included studies focused on AI education in K–12 education.
2. Included studies involving primary data.
3. Included studies mentioning various threats and opportunities in AI education in K–12 education.
4. Included quantitative, qualitative, and mixed-method studies published from 2021 to 2024 in English.
5. Included articles that are free and accessible.

2.6 Exclusion criteria

1. Excluded studies focused on only AI education but not K–12 education
2. Excluded studies focused on only K–12 education but not AI education.
3. Excluded studies involving only secondary data.

4. Excluded studies that do not include threats and opportunities in AI education in K–12 education.
5. Excluded studies published before 2021.
6. Excluded articles that are not free and inaccessible.
7. Exclude publications in languages other than English

2.7 Quality Assessment Criteria

QA1: Does the study include AI applications in K–12 education?
QA2: Do appropriate primary data support the findings?
QA3: Is the research methodology clearly described and appropriately designed?
QA4: Are ethical guidelines and standards followed in the research?

The modified scoring method is based on the inclusion of required elements in research articles which can be found by answering QA1, QA2, QA3, and Q4.

'Y' (YES)=1, full inclusion
'P' (Partial)=0.5, partial inclusion
'N' (No)=0, no inclusion (Kitchenham et al.,2009)

Each article must achieve a minimum total score of 3.5 to qualify for inclusion in the discussion section. Those scoring less are excluded.

2.8. Search Result

After going through a quality assessment, the researchers could include only 8 studies among 25. Then all 8 studies were critically analyzed to extract findings and organize them in the table for critical discussion. The studies are organized in Table 1 of section 3.

2.9 Quality Evaluation

5 studies could score 4 out of 4 and 3 scored 3.5. The studies that scored more or equal to 3.5 were selected for this SLR paper (See Table 7 of section 4). Studies scored less than 3.5 were excluded.

3. FINDINGS AND DISCUSSION

Table 1. Geography & references

	Geography	References
1.	China	Chai, C. S., Lin, P.-Y., Jong, M. S.-Y., Dai, Y., Chiu, T. K. F., & Qin, J. (2021). Perceptions of and behavioral intentions towards learning artificial intelligence in primary school students. Educational Technology & Society, 24(3), 89–101. https://www.jstor.org/stable/28032858
2.	Hongkong	Chiu, T. K. F. (2021). A holistic approach to the design of artificial intelligence (AI) education for K-12 schools. TechTrends, 75(5), 897–808. https://doi.org/10.1008/s11528-021-00738-1
3.	USA	Dwivedi, U. (2021, June 24). Introducing children to machine learning through machine teaching. In Interaction Design and Children. IDC '21: Interaction Design and Children, Athens, Greece. https://doi.org/10.1145/3459990.3473394
4.	Spain	Fernández-Martínez, C., Hernán-Losada, I., & Fernández, A. (2021). Early introduction of AI in Spanish middle schools. A motivational study. KI. Künstliche Intelligenz/KI - Künstliche Intelligenz, 35(2), 173–180. https://doi.org/10.1008/s13218-021-00835-5
5	Korea	Omae, Y., Furuya, T., Matsushita, M., Mizukoshi, K., Yatsushiro, K., & Takahashi, H. (2023). Artificial intelligence education in an elementary school and its evaluation by career development, motivation, and rubrics. Information and Technology in Education and Learning, 3(1), Trans-p002. https://doi.org/10.12938/itel.3.1.trans.p002
6	India	Priya, S., Bhadra, S., Chimalakonda, S., & Venigalla, A. S. M. (2022). ML-Quest: a game for introducing machine learning concepts to K-12 students. *Interactive Learning Environments*, *32*(1), 229–244. https://doi.org/10.1080/10494820.2022.2084115
7.	Turkey	Topal, A. D., Eren, C. D., & Geçer, A. K. (2021). Chatbot application in a 5th grade science course. Education and Information Technologies, 27(5), 7241–7275. https://doi.org/10.1008/s10739-021-10728-8
8	Massachusetts - US	Van Brummelen, J., Heng, T., & Tabunshchyk, V. (2021). Teaching Tech to Talk: K-12 Conversational Artificial intelligence literacy curriculum and development tools. In Proceedings of the . . . AAAI Conference on Artificial Intelligence (Vol. 35, Issue 18, pp. 15755–15773). https://doi.org/10.1709/aaai.v35i18.18844

It is visible in Table no 1 that 'Asia' is the most active region, conducting research on Artificial Intelligence in k-12 education. Also, many primary data-driven types of research have been done from 2021 to 2024 within this region. Studies from Hong Kong, Turkey, China, Korea, and India are included in this SLR paper. From specific applications like chatbots or games to holistic curriculum design, these countries are exploring various aspects of AI education at different levels of schools. Moreover, studies are also focusing on students' motivation as well as career development.

In Europe, Spain is focusing on the motivational aspects of early AI-based education and North America has representation from the USA, which is contributing significantly to the field of studies that examine curriculum development and practical applications related to AI knowledge in K-12 education.

This distribution of research highlights the global nature of educational technology, specifically emphasizing innovative approaches and applications in countries of Asia.

However, there are contradictory ideas that reflect different approaches and priorities in integrating AI into K-12 education. While some studies emphasize early introduction and specific applications, others support general AI literacy and holistic integration of Artificial Intelligence. These are given below,

Early Introduction Versus Holistic Integration

A. Early Introduction (Spain)

Fernández-Martínez et al. (2021), advocated for introducing AI early in middle schools and emphasized motivational benefits. The approach their paper took, suggested starting AI education at an early age to build foundational skills and evoke students' interest.

B. Holistic Integration (Hong Kong)

Chui (2021) proposes a holistic approach to AI education by integrating concepts of AI across the whole curriculum of K-12. Here, this method focuses on a comprehensive understanding of Artificial intelligence rather than emphasising an early introduction. It does not synchronize with the idea of a targeted early start by supporting integrated and continuous exposure throughout education.

General AI Literacy Versus Specific Application

. A.General AI Literacy (Massachusetts, USA)

The study of Van Brummelen et al. (2021) came up with a curriculum for conversational AI literacy to emphasise the importance of understanding AI across cross-disciplinary subjects. In this approach, they try to fill learners with the skills and knowledge of AI instead of aiming for specific applications within individual subjects.

B. Specific Application (Turkey)

A study by Topal et al. (2021) suse of stated that the use of chatbots in (5th grade) science courses on the practical application of tools related to AI by highlighting the use of AI to enhance experiences regarding subject-specific learning.

Focus on Educational outcomes versus student perceptions

A.Educational Outcomes (Korea)

Omae et al. (2023) assessed AI education based on motivation, rubric assessment, and career development, focusing on quantifiable learning outcomes. This study highlights the impact of AI-based education on students' academic achievement and future career prospects.

B.Student Perceptions (China)

Chai et al. investigated primary school students' behavioural intentions and perceptions of AI that emphasise the significance of understanding students' views as well as motivation to engage with AI.

Table 2. Methodology & level of participants

	Method	Level of Participants
1	Quantitative - Survey questionnaire	Primary School - Students
2	Qualitative-Thematic analysis	Middle School - Teachers
3	Qualitative	Primary School - Students
4	Quantitative - using Situational Motivational Scale, quiz, and evaluation tools	Middle School - students
5	Mixed method	Primary School - students
6	Quantitative	High School - Students
7	Mixed method	Secondary School - Students
8	Mixed method	K-12 - Students and Teachers

An overview of the methodology and level of participants in AI education and a k-12 setting is observed in Table 2 which highlights the strengths, lackings, and potential gaps of this study field.

The positive aspects and advantages (Strengths) in the studies on AI education include diverse methodologies such as qualitative, quantitative, and mixed methods. Also, there is a focus on both teacher and student experiences which is essential for developing effective AI-based teaching strategies and curricula and a wide range of participants like primary to high school students and teachers ensures that the findings are comprehensive as well as relevant across different stages of k-12 education that can inform policy-making and curriculum development for a wide range of audiences.

However, there are some notable gaps. For instance, due to the emphasis on quantitative data collection methods, nuanced insights might have been overlooked in this case as a quantitative method can generalize findings and is valuable for its objectivity; a need for more qualitative studies to explore attitudes along with subjective experiences of teachers and students regarding AI education. Also, there is a lack of longitudinal studies which is crucial to track the long-term impact of AI on k-12 students' learning outcomes, skill development, and career aspiration.

Moreover, Table 2 shows a limited focus on the primary level of education compared to middle and high school students. Therefore, more research is needed to understand the ways young children perceive AI-based learning and engage with curriculum activities that integrate Artificial Intelligence. Also, there is a lack of focus on training and professional development for teachers in AI though the table includes research that involves teachers. Thus, effective AI-based education requires educators who are trained in pedagogical strategies and AI concepts. Further researches on AI in k-12 education needs to be explored to understand how to design and implement teachers' training programs to benefit overall educators.

Therefore, some recommendations are to increase qualitative and mixed-method research, focus more on the primary level of students and early education, conduct longitudinal research, broaden the geographical scope of studies, and enhance teacher training research for a more comprehensive understanding of AI-based curriculum, and implementing policy in various stages of k-12 education.

Table 3. Database, data resource & year

	Database	Data resource	Year
1.	Journal - JSTOR	Primary	2021
2.	Journal - Springer	Primary	2021
3.	Conference paper - Google Scholar	Primary	2021
4.	Journal - Springer	Primary	2021
5	Journal - Google Scholar	Primary	2023
6	Journal - Google Scholar	Primary	2024
7.	Journal - Springer	Primary	2021
8	Conference proceedings - Google Scholar	Primary	2021

Table 3 is derived from the studies, collected by following the inclusion and exclusion criteria of this Systematic Literature Review (SLR) on AI in k-12 education. Hence this table provides several important aspects that add credibility and depth to this review:

The above table is crucial to this review and illustrates the quality and range of sources analyzed. This range includes research articles from prominent databases such as Google Scholar, Springer, and JSTOR. According to the inclusion criteria 1, this table demonstrates only concentration on primary data sources. This ensures credibility through direct evidence.

The research selected for this study continues from 2021 to 2024 and covers the most recent positive aspects and trends in AI education. Different Journal articles and conference papers, having distinct geographical contexts ensure a current and comprehensive understanding of AI's role in K-12 education that reflects on well-established findings and emerging research. These broaden the analysis of opportunities and threats of this Systematic Literature Review.

Table 4. Research findings on threats & mitigation strategy of AI in K-12 education

	Threats	Mitigation Strategy
2, 4	Digital Divide	Provide funding and resources to under-resourced schools Invest in necessary IT infrastructure to support AI initiatives.
1, 2, 3, 4	Ethical Concerns & Data Privacy	Incorporate AI ethics into the curriculum Implement strict data protection policies to safeguard student privacy Making students understand the societal impact of the ethical aspect of AI and the importance of data privacy as they lack those. Approval of parents is needed. Developing and implementing a strong data protection policy is a must to ensure the security of students' and children's data. Teachers and students should be informed about the data privacy policy that must be created and implemented by data protection regulations.
8	Slow pacing of workshops reducing engagement for some students	Offer written tutorials for advanced students and create extension opportunities
5	Sustainability of impact over time	Continuously evaluate and refine AI educational practices based on student feedback and learning outcomes.
5	Diverse learning outcomes among students	Personalize AI educational approaches to cater to different learning styles and abilities
5	Difficulty in measuring the effectiveness of AI practices	Implement robust assessment methodologies that go beyond initial scores to track long-term impact.
3	Challenges in maintaining children's interest and engagement	Create engaging and exploratory game-based learning experiences that integrate machine learning issues and challenges. Utilize interactive and hands-on approaches to sustain interest.

continued on following page

Table 4. Continued

	Threats	Mitigation Strategy
3	Lack of accessibility for blind and visually impaired children	Design inclusive interfaces following Universal Design principles to accommodate all users, regardless of physical, cognitive, or developmental issues.
1, 7	Reliance on technology (Over-reliance)	Combining traditional educational methods with AI-based learning and ensuring a balance between them is required to maintain diverse learning experiences for students and teachers.
1	Anxiety Towards AI	Provide resources to help students manage anxiety, such as counseling, workshops, and anxiety-reduction techniques. Include AI-related content gradually to build comfort and familiarity.
2	Student Learning Diversity	Use modular and level-up approaches to cater to different learning abilities and backgrounds.
1, 2, 4	Preparing Teachers	For teachers, implementing developmental programs on AI knowledge such as comprehensive professional developmental programs is necessary Provide time-to-time professional development opportunities for teachers and encourage environments that support collaborative learning where teachers can share best practices and learn from each other.
2	Lack of Appropriate Content	Develop standardized, accessible AI curriculum content tailored for K-12 education.
1, 4, 7	Resistance to Change	Build confidence in educators through support and training, addressing fears of job displacement.
4	Training Needs	Provide adequate and ongoing training for educators
2, 3, 5, 8	Technological complexity	To adjust children's level of knowledge with their learning process, co-design strategies need to be applied. A simple and engaging interface is necessary which can be used without any prior x knowledge in programming. Generation of simple ideas on AI with the help of standardized language, practical activities, and graphical representation of it. Teaching materials (AI-based) need to be developed by considering learners' age and education level along with clear explanations and interactive tools.
1	Infrastructure Needs	Upgrade and maintain robust IT infrastructure.
1, 2, 4, 7	Resource Disparities	Ensure equality in terms of access to AI technologies across all schools, provide educational institutions with necessary AI tools and resources Offer flexibility in curriculum design to match available resources.
1, 2, 3, 4, 7, 8	Fairness & Bias	AI systems need to be managed and monitored properly. Monitoring is required while using various datasets to train AI systems. AI algorithms need to be checked regularly to fix bias. Make ethical choices while developing AI. Students should be taught the value of training data via games.

Table 4 shows collective threats and mitigating ways derived from the studies. Thematic analysis of threats and mitigation strategies in AI for k-12 education are given below:

Access and Equity

In integrating AI into K-12 education, many concerns can be seen and one of the crucial concerns is the digital divide. This digital divide means that students from different socioeconomic backgrounds do not have equal access to technology. This inequality can lead to differences in learning outcomes as they are not getting similar learning opportunities. Therefore, it is mandatory to provide funds to schools that lack resources. In order to support AI initiatives, investing in necessary IT infrastructure is a requirement.

Similarly, inconsistent access to AI technologies and resources throughout different schools can be mitigated by providing and ensuring equal access to all technological tools and resources. Moreover, the curriculum needs to be designed flexibly so that it can match the available resources in the school. Also, designing inclusive interfaces are essential for students with disabilities especially students who are visually impaired. These are essential to ensure collective benefit to all who use AI-based educational tools.

Student Engagement in AI-based Curriculum and Learning Outcomes

First of all, engaging students with the curriculum and getting successful learning outcomes are crucial areas to focus on because providing every student with similar kinds of facilities is challenging due to their mixed backgrounds and various learning abilities. This problem can be mitigated by using modular and level-up approaches. As many students have anxiety towards implementation of AI, so counseling, techniques (anxiety reduction), and gradual inclusion of AI-based material can improve familiarity which will help to reduce AI-related anxiety among students.

Again, keeping students interested and engaged in AI topics is a challenging task. Game-based learning which is engaging and exploratory can mitigate this challenge as this interactive approach can play a crucial role in sustaining students' interest. Another challenge is assessing the long-term impact of AI in the education sector. This challenge can be reduced by implementing robust assessment techniques. It is necessary for tracking long-term impact. Also, a personalized AI educational approach is required for students with different learning styles and outcomes. Additionally, continuous evaluation is mandatory for a sustainable positive impact. Lastly, slow-paced workshops can slow or hinder the progress of advanced students. Therefore, creating opportunities for extension and written tutorials can add to maintaining learners' attention and interest.

Pedagogical Difficulties and Technical Issues

Implementing AI in education is challenging because of its ancient IT infrastructure and technological complexity. Simplifying concepts, ideas and terminology can help to overcome these difficulties. Adapting educational material specific to age level and clear explanations can help to mitigate as well. Moreover, continuous upgrading, and maintaining robust technological infrastructure is mandatory for mitigating IT infrastructure-related issues. For maintaining different learning experiences, limited screen time, critical thinking skills, and balance between AI and traditional teaching methods is essential.

Overreliance on technology is a concern as it will hinder critical thinking ability therefore, developing policies related to limited screen time and offline activities are crucial to maintain a holistic learning experience.

Training Teachers and Prepare them for AI-based Curriculum

Most of the teachers lack knowledge and skills regarding the effective integration of AI into their classroom teaching. To mitigate this significant threat, providing opportunities such as ongoing professional development programs. These are effective as these developmental programs will keep them updated with recent pedagogical practices related to AI. Collaborative learning environments are also beneficial as they allow teachers to share practices among themselves. It helps them to learn from each other.

Concern Over Ethics and Privacy

Ethical and privacy concerns in AI education are for those students who do not have an appropriate understanding of the ethics related to AI and its societal impact which is a significant concern in education related to AI, so these concerns can be mitigated by implementing firm data protection policies along with including ethics of using AI in the curriculum. Again, data privacy is another crucial issue in the field of AI education among students because there is a risk of misusing the data of students which is a significant threat that requires prompt solutions. Therefore, educating teachers and students on proper data privacy practices, data protection policies, and security measures is important to mitigate challenges. In addition to this, acquiring consent from parents regarding data usage ensures trust and transparency. Another issue is bias and unfair practices in AI which can be mitigated by monitoring and frequently auditing AI algorithms along with managing AI-related technologies carefully.

Table 5. Research findings on opportunities of AI in K-12 education and ways to grasp them

	Opportunity	Ways to Grasp Opportunities
4	Future STEM Careers	Spark interest in STEM careers by showcasing real-world AI applications.
1, 4, 7	Enhanced Learning Outcomes by Collaborative Learning and Communication	By implementing AI-driven adaptive assessments To enhance learning outcomes, communication and collaborative projects need to be encouraged between students and teachers. Use AI, To gamify learning experiences (through AI-driven educational games) To adjust the pace of learning and provide immediate feedback. To personalize educational experiences.
4, 7	Personalized Learning	Tailor educational experiences to meet individual student needs.
1, 2, 4	Skill Development	To develop critical thinking, engage learners in AI-based projects, and provide hands-on experience with programming and AI tools. To develop practical AI skills, offer hands-on coding activities and projects by including AI literacy as a fundamental part of the curriculum.
4, 8	Leveraging Technology	Utilize AI-powered interactive tools for engaging and personalized learning experiences. Implement virtual labs for safe and controlled experimentation with AI technologies. Personalize learning experiences by allowing students to choose project topics and explore areas of personal interest.
2, 4	Adaptive Assessments & Flexibility in Curriculum Design	Based on learners' performance, adjust difficulty level and provide immediate feedback. To fit teachers' school's unique environment and students' needs and interests, allow teachers to adapt the curriculum.
3	Fostering AI literacy without the need for programming skills	Emphasize image and audio-based inputs to provide various accessibility needs and preferences for learning. Create and implement machines that are teachable and allow children to test and train algorithms interactively.
4	Community and Industry Partnerships	Partner with tech companies to expose students to the latest AI advancements. Involve the local community in AI education initiatives.
2	Global and Local Understanding	Combine local examples with global perspectives to give students a well-rounded understanding of AI's impact.
2	Preparation for Future Workforce	Equip students with AI knowledge and increasingly relevant skills in the modern workforce.
3	Social Good and Ethical AI Usage	Encourage students to develop AI solutions that address societal challenges. Highlight examples of AI being used for social good and sustainability.

continued on following page

Table 5. Continued

	Opportunity	Ways to Grasp Opportunities
5	Enhance creativity and confidence in AI	Encourage students to propose and develop their own AI applications or projects related to real-world problems.
5	Raise awareness of AI's societal importance	Organize seminars or workshops that showcase AI's impact on various industries and societal challenges.
8	High student engagement through hands-on, interactive activities	Incorporate more hands-on projects and interactive activities like coding tutorials and group brainstorming sessions.
8	Teachers seeking to bring AI workshops into their classrooms	Provide accessible and adaptable workshop materials for teachers to integrate into regular classroom activities.
1, 2, 4	Curriculum Integration	Applying AI concepts to real-world problems, use project-based learning. Integrate AI education into various subjects. Design AI curriculum in a way that integrates various subjects which promotes interdisciplinary skills and knowledge.
8	Teachers reporting a better grasp of AI concepts and how to teach AI	Teachers reporting a better grasp of AI concepts and how to teach AI
3	Enhancing accessibility through AI, particularly for children with disabilities	Built an AI education technology that is inclusive from the beginning by utilizing AI's features of accessibility, for instance, personal speech recognizers for students with ALS and object recognizers for blind people.
2, 3	Early exposure to AI and machine learning concepts for children/students	To spark interest, introduce concepts of AI at an early age, and inspire future career aspects in AI and technology. Introduce fundamental AI concepts in a child-friendly manner by using accessible and interactive tools such as Google's teachable machines. Machine teaching curriculum needs to be integrated into the early school curriculum.
8	Teachers seeking to bring AI workshops into their classrooms	To integrate workshop materials into regular classroom activities, teachers need to get access to an adequate amount of adaptable workshop materials.
2, 5	Increase students' intrinsic value, Inspiration, and Motivation	Make the curriculum engaging by incorporating AI into it. For example, including problem-solving tasks and interactive simulations. Use engaging and real-world applications to inspire and motivate students to pursue careers and further studies.

Future STEM Careers and Personalized Learning

The aforementioned table (table 5) comprises the Findings on Opportunities of AI in K-12 Education and Ways to Grasp them. Since choosing a career is crucial and can be achieved when a person picks his career in line with the personality and surroundings, AI can ignite interest in STEM careers among students if educators can illustrate how AI is entangled in real-world pioneering industries. Normally, this would result in a strong job orientation. When someone is passionate about their career, they will put in more effort to obtain the position they are interested in. Additionally, the pupils will have a greater desire to learn.

AI maximises student learning results by providing a variety of tools to support peer collaboration in the classroom, allowing teachers to lead group and peer activities and enabling students to engage with one another to better understand complex concepts. AI-driven adaptive tests enable students to quickly receive feedback on assignments. Instructors can oversee their work from a distance, and AI-powered learning programmes provide points and badges for tasks successfully completed. This encourages and motivates students, which ultimately improves learning results.

A growing number of artificial intelligence (AI)-driven educational games have arranged learning materials into game formats that allow students to play and learn at the same time. Students find this gamification of learning engaging. Artificial intelligence (AI)-powered learning tools adjust automatically to the speed and needs of the student. They use the student's current proficiency to determine the difficulty level of a question and provide immediate, personalised feedback. This kind of personalised learning makes a classroom full of dry lectures into one that is engaging and dynamic. For instance, Platforms like DreamBox Learning and Khan Academy employ AI-powered algorithm and can be used in teaching, applications like Duolingo also employ AI and provides lessons based on the students' needs and progress.

Curriculum Integration and Flexibility

The curriculum needs to be designed in a way so that teachers can adapt the curriculum to fit in an AI-based unique environment. Professional developmental workshops will increase opportunities for teachers to successfully learn about teaching strategies. Also, diverse learning needs can be addressed through teachers' and learners' proper access to the resources.

Another opportunity is creating interdisciplinary approaches to AI education that can be achieved by integrating concepts of AI in various subjects. Introducing project-based learning is a must to apply AI to real-world issues.

Early Exposer to AI Education and its Long-Term Impact

Introducing AI in the early stages of education opens a great opportunity for students as it sparks interest in them. Learners become interested in future career aspects in AI and technology. Therefore, fundamentals of AI concepts need to be introduced in a child-friendly manner through interactive and accessible tools such as Google's teachable machines so that students find it easy to comprehend. To get access, the best way is to integrate machine learning into the curriculum in the early stages.

4 QUALITY ASSESSMENT TABLE

Table 7. Quality Assessment

No	Q1	Q2	Q3	Q4	Score
1	1	1	1	.5	3.5
2	1	1	1	1	4
3	1	.5	1	1	3.5
4	1	1	1	1	4
5	1	1	1	1	4
6	1	1	.5	1	3.5
7	1	1	1	1	4
8	1	1	1	1	4

5. DIRECTION FOR FUTURE RESEARCH

The following Table 6 offers a critical view of the future directions in the research field related to AI education entailing comparative studies across various regions to comprehend the implications of AI-enhanced learning including the psychological factors like anxiety and stress that come with such teaching and learning experience. According to the reviewed studies, teachers' inclusion and adaptability improve when they practise or test AI courses in K-12 educational environments; additionally, teachers achieve professional excellence during this process. These affirmative findings provide educators with a great lead for future endeavors. Moreover, integrating interactive AI technologies into the curriculum from the outset can help all students become more accessible, literate in AI, and adept at solving problems, this is important information for stakeholders, as they can begin considering how to incorporate AI-infused technology from the start of a learner's academic journey. Research on ethical issues and long-term effects can also be used to create frameworks that are sustainable and boost learners' comprehension of AI-powered tools and their applications. By prioritizing ethical and real-world learning environments, learners can engage in AI education to the fullest extent possible.

No research has been done in the Bangladeshi context. Therefore, there is an opportunity for future research that can look at the suitability of including AI in K-12 education in Bangladesh.

1. examine and compare K-12 students' AI learning from other cities or countries and levels of students, consider adverse psychological factors such as anxiety towards AI, investigate subjective norms as a potential facilitating condition, and explore the influence of control items on perceived behavioral control.
2. testing the proposed AI curriculum model in diverse school settings, incorporating student and societal perspectives, and investigating the impact of teacher professional development in AI on curriculum design and implementation.
3. Future opportunities include integrating inclusive and interactive AI education technologies into early school curricula to enhance AI literacy, foster problem-solving skills, and support accessibility for children with and without disabilities.
4. Investigating the long-term impacts of AI on student outcomes and teacher practices, exploring integration methods in diverse and under-resourced educational contexts, examining ethical implications, assessing effective teacher training approaches, and addressing equity in access to AI technologies.
5. AI educational practices have the potential to significantly enhance students' intrinsic value, attainment utility value, expectancies for success, and career development, thereby fostering greater interest and confidence in AI-related career paths in K-12 education.
6. ML-Quest seeks to further develop its capabilities by including more levels and enhanced visualizations.
7.. Future research should focus on creatinging and implementing equitable, bias-free AI systems that enhance personalized learning, improve teacher efficiency, and ensure data privacy and security in K-12 education.
8. Should focus on developing scalable, interactive AI education curricula that emphasize ethical considerations, hands-on learning, and collaboration between educators and researchers to enhance student understanding and engagement.

6 CONCLUSION

To conclude it can be said that AI in K-12 education is a significant shift from traditional teaching and learning methods in school In the past, getting information was not easy because teachers and students needed to refer to or search for every piece of information in books and were required to perform time-consuming data analysis research work on their own. However, now due to Artificial Intelligence research work has become easy. Many classrooms are now equipped with artificial intelligence which is making teaching and learning interactive. Even though teachers and students are facing challenges to implement and adapt AI in education. To mitigate all these threats and challenges, teachers and learners need to follow certain ways and approaches, and the most prominent way is to develop a curriculum that complements AI technology.

AI in K-12 also has opportunities for teachers as well as students. Early inclusion will give students future opportunities that can be achieved through continuous assessment and the collaborative help of teachers. Therefore, this integration of AI in K-12 education will open a new dimension in our education as well.

REFERENCES

Chai, C. S., Lin, P.-Y., Jong, M. S.-Y., Dai, Y., Chiu, T. K. F., & Qin, J. (2021). Perceptions of and behavioral intentions towards learning artificial intelligence in primary school students. *Journal of Educational Technology & Society*, *24*(3), 89–101. https://www.jstor.org/stable/27032858

Chiu, T. K. F. (2021). A holistic approach to the design of artificial intelligence (AI) education for K-12 schools. *TechTrends*, *65*(5), 796–807. DOI: 10.1007/s11528-021-00637-1

Design and Children, Athens, Greece. DOI: 10.1145/3459990.3463394

Dwivedi, U. (2021, June 24). Introducing children to machine learning through machine teaching. In *Interaction Design and Children*. IDC '21: Interaction DOI: 10.1145/3459990.3463394

Fernández-Martínez, C., Hernán-Losada, I., & Fernández, A. (2021). Early introduction of AI in Spanish middle schools. A motivational study. *KI. Künstliche Intelligenz/ KI - Künstliche Intelligenz, 35*(2), 163–170. DOI: 10.1007/s13218-021-00735-5

Kitchenham, B., Brereton, O. P., Budgen, D., Turner, M., & Bailey, J. (2009). Systematic literature reviews in software engineering – A systematic literature review. *Information &amp. Information and Software Technology*, *51*(1), 7–15. DOI: 10.1016/j.infsof.2008.09.009

Naqvi, A. (2020). *Artificial intelligence for audit, forensic accounting, and valuation: a strategic perspective*. John Wiley & Sons. DOI: 10.1002/9781119601906

Okoli, C., & Schabram, K. (2015). A guide to conducting a systematic literature review of information systems research.

Omae, Y., Furuya, T., Matsushita, M., Mizukoshi, K., Yatsushiro, K., & Takahashi, H. (2023). Artificial intelligence education in an elementary school and its evaluation by career development, motivation and rubrics. *Information and Technology in Education and Learning, 3*(1), Trans-p002. DOI: 10.12937/itel.3.1.Trans.p002

Priya, S., Bhadra, S., Chimalakonda, S., & Venigalla, A. S. M. (2022). ML-Quest: A game for introducing machine learning concepts to K-12 students. *Interactive Learning Environments*, *32*(1), 229–244. DOI: 10.1080/10494820.2022.2084115

Topal, A. D., Eren, C. D., & Geçer, A. K. (2021). Chatbot application in a 5th grade science course. *Education and Information Technologies*, *26*(5), 6241–6265. DOI: 10.1007/s10639-021-10627-8 PMID: 34177344

Van Brummelen, J., Heng, T., & Tabunshchyk, V. (2021). Teaching Tech to Talk: K-12 Conversational Artificial intelligence literacy curriculum and development tools. In *Proceedings of the . . . AAAI Conference on Artificial Intelligence* (Vol. 35, Issue 17, pp. 15655–15663). DOI: 10.1609/aaai.v35i17.17844

Chapter 2
AI Education for All: Trends, Challenges, and Opportunities

Anika Zarin Chowdhury
http://orcid.org/0009-0005-4710-7141
BRAC University, Bangladesh

Khaled Arafat
http://orcid.org/0009-0002-6509-9112
BRAC University, Bangladesh

Iffat Sahira Ramisha
http://orcid.org/0009-0001-1211-3390
BRAC University, Bangladesh

Khadijatul Labannya
http://orcid.org/0009-0008-2117-7661
BRAC University, Bangladesh

ABSTRACT

The adoption of Artificial Intelligence in Education (AIED) in K-12 has embedded the curiosity and understanding that lean to accelerate the students towards being the right fit for the data-driven world of industrialization. This secondary literature review-based chapter strives to address the ongoing trends, significant challenges, and opportunities of AIED. The findings state that Massive Open Online Courses (MOOC), Intelligent Tutoring Systems (ITS), Dialogue Based-Tutoring Systems (DBTS), Learning Management Systems (LMS), Exploratory Learning Environments (ELE), Interactive Learning Environments (ILE), and STEM program are the leading preferences of the students and teachers heeded by organizational, methodological, technological, and psychological challenges for effective integration. Additionally,

DOI: 10.4018/979-8-3693-6346-1.ch002

Education 4.0 has vast opportunities to shift conventional education to the unexplored dimensions of knowledge, evolution, and development. Hence, this review will benefit academicians and future researchers by acknowledging the significance of AI in envisioning a promising future.

1. INTRODUCTION

Education is one of the fundamental rights of every human being. Receiving quality education is a must when revolutionization has knocked on the doors of educational institutions of all levels. Artificial Intelligence (AI) is still rapidly evolving, and that evolution will have significant consequences for society (Li et al., 2024). This brings us to the question of how AI is being used in education, but first, a brief understanding of this revolutionary technology is vital. Artificial intelligence can be explained as the capability of a computer system or a smart machine to do what would normally require human intelligence.

Many programs and devices implemented utilizing AI capabilities can include decision-making, problem-solving, and the understanding and reproduction of natural language, as well as the interpretation of unorganized data (Hamilton, 2024). With the enhancement of AI technology in most aspects of our existence, there is growing awareness of the need to introduce AI literacy to students. In the past, the major focus of AI education was to socialize future specialists who would further develop their knowledge in this area. However, understanding the role of early AI exposure in students' preparation, educational interventions have shifted to the K-12 level (Li et al., 2024). To this effect, this shift seeks to ensure that the younger generation has basic knowledge and understanding of AI to prepare for the future, with AI as an essential component in many fields and numerous activities. The integration of AI knowledge in all the courses also calls for the development of a society with technological literacy to be able to operate and participate in an AI world (Li et al., 2024).

The trends show that assessment and instructions are the key areas of concern in AI education, primarily through the use of Intelligent Tutoring Systems (ITS) and other AI-assisted applications. According to ITS, there are hardware and software systems for education that have their databases or knowledge bases or content knowledge base for educational content as well as the teaching-learning strategies and try to make conclusions about the capabilities of the learner to understand the content and identify his strengths and weaknesses to make changes in the learning process in respect to the content and the methods (Alrakhawi et al., 2023). The transformation of the learning agenda that requires help for every learner can be optimized using AI. Technological advancements such as the mobile internet and cloud computing help offer learning content for various students. Various new types of web-based chatbots or humanoid robots, which are introduced because of AI, are also ways it help foster the student in every step (Saputra et al., 2021).

When it comes to putting into practice the idea of AI education for the student, it can be a complex affair since school and college teachers may sometimes have a digital skills deficit in many areas. A study also reveals that a vast majority of such technical skills are necessary with advancement in the use of technology in teaching, and to use them, and also to learn to cope with yearly advancing technologies, educators have to become accustomed to it. Nevertheless, they are robust to encounter several limitations such as organizational constraints, technological difficulties, methodological concerns, and psychological factors. Therefore, enhancing the competencies in the digital literacy of higher education educators is a significant step. As these skills are interrelated, working collaboratively in improving, developing, and adopting these areas will facilitate a smooth shift toward digital education and improve the learning process's efficiency (Knyazeva et al., 2022).

In the use of AI in education, there are many opportunities to be explored. AI promotes diversity since it enables learning organizations to avail resources or strategies that meet diverse learning requirements. For instance, language translation facilitates the breaking of communication barriers, while speech-to-text services help students who might encounter challenges with conventional techniques. Furthermore, there are AI assistance tools that help students learn, especially students with disabilities, to achieve greater results because of the individualization of the course content (Majorana et al., 2022). These tools not only benefit students with learning disabilities but also make education fair and inclusive for every learner.

When AI is used in education, certain drawbacks always come with the facility. Nonetheless, the opportunity that comes with the use of AI in education is very enormous. AI can bring improvements in adopting teaching methodologies and tailored approaches by creating effective educational content for each student according to their learning abilities and preferences. This can lead to higher learning outcomes and also keep the students more engaged than when they sit to read at their own pace. Furthermore, it is worth considering that AI tools can also enhance a learner-centered approach to education by accommodating learners with different learning styles, preferences, and needs. The appropriate use of AI calls for investment in technology and the professional development of educators. It will, therefore, be important to continue to research and study the difference between creating new and innovative methods in research and development of the ethical consequences of such methods. In this way, it is possible to guarantee that artificial intelligence will be useful for improving education, and it can become available for all people as more personal and effective. On balance, the path to the adoption of AI in education is binomial and replete with challenges, but the opportunities offered by this process are worth striving for.

2. LEARNING OBJECTIVES

After reading this chapter, you will be competent to:

1. Comprehend the transformation of Education 4.0 from Education 1.0 and its vital features to K-12.
2. Pinpoint the emerging, globally accepted trends of Artificial Intelligence in Education (AIED).
3. Address the challenges encountered by the students, teachers, and the institution itself to ensure a smooth transition.
4. Scrutinize the opportunities of AI in education, which is dedicated to shaping future endeavors of the students and educators.

3. EDUCATION 4.0 AND K-12: TRANSFORMING LEARNING FOR THE FUTURE

The term "Education 4.0" broaches a paradigm change in education and learning that is being pushed by the necessities and demands of the Fourth Industrial Revolution (4IR) alongside a rapid leap and breakthrough in terms of technological advancement (Chituc, 2021). It emphasizes an approach that prioritizes learners that makes use of cutting-edge contemporary technology, nurtures and stimulates critical thinking, and prepares students for a future that calls for creativity, adaptability, versatility, and problem-solving (Chituc, 2021). Henceforth, the ultimate objective of Education 4.0 is to transform current K–12 educational establishments to better serve the needs of a dynamic, networked community.

3.1 The Evolution to Education 4.0

Education 4.0 is an advancement from the previous educational models and approaches that were often more inflexible, standardized, and predictable (Chituc, 2021). Previously, Education 2.0 brought out more communicative, engaging, and cooperative parts in the education sector. In the following days, Education 3.0 employed technological advances to enhance acquiring knowledge, while Education 1.0 concentrated more on memorization and rote learning (Figure 1).

Figure 1. Phases of education (Paul, 2022)

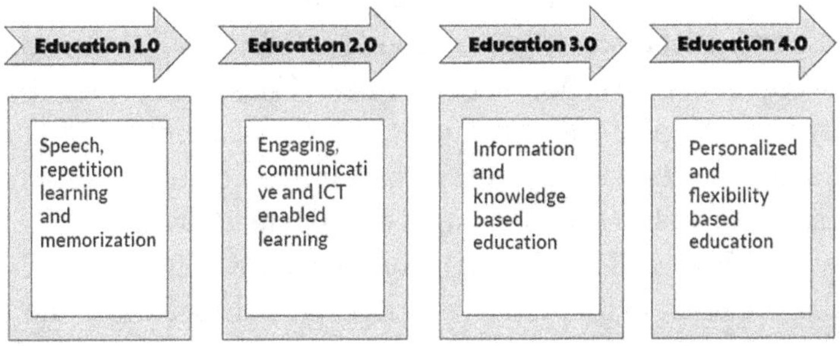

Nevertheless, Education 4.0 modified and customized, student-centered learning experiences integrating tech into every facet of the educational process, going beyond straightforward technological consumption (Moraes et al., 2022).

4. COMMON TRENDS

AI is the future. Artificial Intelligence is the answer to almost anything in this tech-driven 21st century. On the other hand, education is the most powerful tool of a human being. When two powerful tools are taken together and used to each other's advantage, exciting things happen.

A rather holistic and conventional method of approach was proposed by 24 teachers (Chiu, 2021), where every one of the teachers wanted to introduce AI to their syllabus. The structural curriculum can be quite challenging when they introduce AI to the curriculum. Many factors are to be taken into heed, like quality assurance, quite a bit interaction, interactive courses, and the most important factor, to see the recipients are grasping and getting the knowledge. After a careful and brief analysis, six key components are seen: AI knowledge, AI processing, the relevance of student and teacher, a communication bridge between a student and a teacher are a few (Chiu, 2021), and all these are taken after a careful test at 12 K-12 schools. Thus, a holistic approach is seen (Chiu, 2021). Furthermore, this is not the first study, nor will this study be the last. Another study has been conducted in order to restore the trust and faith of the teachers in implementing AI-powered tools in AI-EdTech (AI Powered Educational Technology) (Nazaretsky et al., 2022), where the main motive is an ice-breaker and gaining their trust and easing them into implementing technology in education.

AI-powered education will reshape the pathway of education. Four areas are explored, and as such, more student-lecturer interaction, creative teaching strategies, technology-enhanced evaluation, and customized content (Chassignol et al., 2018) are seen, which brings a revolutionary change in the education system.

One of the trends that essentially play a vital role in mass education is a system called Massive Open Online Courses, or MOOCs (Chassignol et al., 2018), mainly contributed by free and paid websites, like Coursera, Udemy, 10 Minutes School, and so on. Not only are these courses free, but one can complete different courses from these respective websites and obtain a certificate; they can also learn various things through AI, Virtual Reality (VR), Augmented Reality (AR), and so on. In ABC's popular medical series, The Good Doctor, it is seen that the doctors go through a warmup round every time they perform a surgery, massively done by VR. This shows their flaws and points out their mistakes.

The most important part of any education is communication. Without communication, teachers will not know what the student wants, and in return, no constructive criticism can be given to the student. If a student works on a paper, and any criticism over the work he has done will result in a long-lasting effect, and it is something that many educators follow on. In this case, ITS (Intelligent Tutoring System) works like a charm (Chassignol et al., 2018). The system is integrated at such that it communicates with the student at any level, based on the answers they write on their script. Not only does the system give constructive criticism to the students, it gives explanations based on what they write. The responsiveness is not always limited.

AI is the yin-yang of education. We are quickly moving away from conventional teaching methods and toward more contemporary ones. Education and AI are inextricably connected (Kaur et al., 2020). Many students can achieve academic success thanks to AI technology. Instructors already spend a significant amount of their valuable time on tedious tasks like answering student-related queries, handing out homework, keeping track of attendance, and so on. These labor-intensive duties can be handled by technological Artificial Intelligence, allowing teachers to spend more time with their students. Classification and database development are made more accessible by Artificial Intelligence (Kaur et al., 2020). Textbooks that are appropriate for a range of courses are being created thanks to AI technologies. In the field of education, an instructor's role is crucial. Choosing what is to be taught is a prerequisite to providing precise instructions. When a student is having difficulty in learning, the traditional classroom environment is essential. The primary objective of digitalization in education is to facilitate the analysis and assessment of learning obstacles (Kaur et al., 2020). The current AI system has many flaws, and to overcome that, success in conducting that research has to be ensured.

Furthermore, the education sector will be significantly impacted by research done in a wide range of areas, both directly and indirectly. Although their importance in education will never diminish, teachers' roles may shift when new technologies are incorporated into the infrastructure of smart computing systems (Kaur et al., 2020).

In the long run, Artificial Intelligence has the potential to replace human teachers in many real-world situations by taking over duties like grading, attendance, and many more. However, there are a lot of educational domains where the application of AI could be helpful.

After the use of ITS (Chassignol et al., 2018), the use of DBTS (Dialogue Based Tutoring System), where the system analyses the answer given by the student and answers it back according to the level and understanding of the student (Paek & Kim, 2021), this not only clarifies the misconceptions and confusion of the user but also gives an accurate answer and a clear idea. The University of Memphis developed a system based on DBTS, known as Autotutor, which analyses responses and helps the user understand better and more explicitly (Paek & Kim, 2021). Perhaps the most hands-on learning approach would be the Exploratory Learning Environment, or ELE, where the learner is encouraged to have their own understanding and apply their thoughts through a well constructive approach (Paek & Kim, 2021). However, all these systems are well renowned and used all across the world, with a high success rate and an assured quality check.

In a classroom full of students, especially when the issue is regarding many global students, many educators cannot give their constructive criticisms individually, so that is where ILE (Interactive Learning Environment) comes in (Chassignol et al., 2018). It is a system that combines technologies and techniques of e-learning (like Learning Management Systems, or LMS) with the aid of interactive learning (Chassignol et al., 2018) for a fully-fledged understanding of the students. This system ensures that the student will not only learn but will also never cease to gain knowledge and facts. Many other learning tools are there, like Knewton, where the students are recommended different platforms catering to their needs and understanding, or Highlight, where the system actually tracks a student's progress and their materials. There is also the Watson Education classroom, where the teacher gives personalized criticism and study materials for a better understanding of the students, i.e., giving exactly what he or she needs.

The new generation is living in a world where smartphones are as common as pebbles. Loading that up with an internet connection will make that device an AI-enabled device (Chiu, 2021). However, when used right, it will throw that device into a learning curve. Likewise, here, robotics will play an effective role. Kids can learn different things from Cubelets, a set of robots teaching children the basics and fundamentals of robotics, or the Ozorobot STEM program, teaching programming languages, fundamental science and math, and so on (Chiu, 2021). The goal here is never to coerce the student, rather it is to instill the joys of AI-enabled systems and services and how it plays an important role.

Many other topics were seen being taught, like incorporating Machine Learning (ML) in elections (Lee & Kwon, 2024), data-driven ML systems and their usage in everyday life (Lee & Kwon, 2024), and so on. Instructional techniques for teaching AI refer to the methods and strategies used in AI education. The examined research used a variety of ways to facilitate major educational possibilities while taking into account learning objectives and the potential of artificial intelligence technology (Lee & Kwon, 2024).

As the first generation to grow up and study in the midst of AI and its endless possibilities, the students can easily depict results and decisions from automated systems. In a study conducted, twenty-eight students created machine learning models (Jiang et al., 2023) that used text data to distinguish between positive and negative ice cream shop ratings. There were nine data modeling strategies that pointed out how students explore, construct, and test models around data technology-driven automated decision-making (Jiang et al., 2023). The findings have implications for both the role and responsibilities of data modeling users alike in the advancement of artificial intelligence systems, as well as for providing accessible data modeling experiences that help students understand data justice (Jiang et al., 2023).

Learning the definitive uses of AI and ML has shown various positive result-bearing events, and as such, students were seen honing their imaginative creativity. 3 types of AI are seen; mostly Narrow AI, General AI, and Artificial Superintelligence. While Artificial Superintelligence (Marrone et al., 2022) is seen to exceed the capabilities of Homo Sapiens, stating their advanced capabilities compared to humans (Marrone et al., 2022). Narrow AI is seen to be in use almost all the time, having been a goal-oriented system and assisting in various life-altering fields, like image recognition, speech recognition, AR/VR, blockchain, ML, and many more (Marrone et al., 2022). The possibility of AI is that it supports creativity, mainly problem-solving, but it aids in the favor of the students very much (Marrone et al., 2022). The same has been tested in South Korea, conducting research in a free semester in middle school to develop an educational program with the use of AI, and not only to develop but also to test its effectiveness (Park & Kwon, 2023). After building the program, the effectiveness of the program is seen, emphasizing on the ethical use of AI, AI's physical computing, and so on (Park & Kwon, 2023). The end results showed the main objectives of the free semester, job discovery, and technological education, which they created AI software facilitated, according to the study's findings. It was also noted that the AI education curriculum, which prioritized technical problem-solving, was significant from a technological education standpoint. These findings will have a big influence on how artificial intelligence is used in technology (Park & Kwon, 2023).

5. SIGNIFICANT CHALLENGES

For years, students have received education in a classroom setting, and academic institutions have provided training to their teachers about how to conduct and interact with students in person; thus, the transformation from physical classrooms to online learning modules which is quite formidable to execute (Shet, 2024). The roadmap to incorporate the curriculum of Education 4.0 from Education 1.0 not only alters the pattern of teaching but calls to address challenges such as organizational, methodological, technological, and psychological of both teachers and students (Olari & Romeike, 2024). Hence, a brief overview of the challenges is as follows:

5.1 Organizational Constraints

In the school management practice, principals and school leaders should develop their leadership abilities by acknowledging digital literacy. The school leaders tend to incorporate AI in their decision-making process and guidelines and commence the cultivation of AI-human cooperation; outdated school leadership practices after the integration of AI curriculum are not only the cause of the dearth of crucial specialized infrastructure but also identify the shortcomings of the teachers to discourse their digital literacy subsidies and problems internally (Karakose & Tulubas, 2024). In brief, obsolete leadership practices are incompetent in aligning with AI transformation.

Figure 2. TPACK framework (O'Dea & O'Dea, 2023)

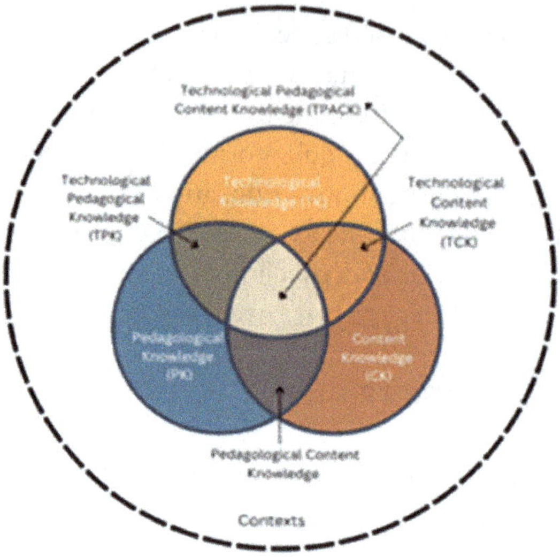

Through a survey, it was discovered that for AI-based education system, academicians, primarily administrative authority, and the teachers have minimal adoption mindset towards Education 4.0 and holistic endorsement as they lack dexterities, have an attitude to withstand change, absence of guiding and reinforcement strategies, obsolete academic procedures and do not have adequate addressable communities to intercommunicate their unease and affliction (Li et al. 2023; Velander et al., 2023). In addition, inflexible budgets, impaired training facilities or workshops for the teachers, and deficient literacy in the e-learning environment inhibit the pathway of acquiring innovative education (Liu & Yu, 2022). Numerous schools provide Teachers' with AI-related technological, pedagogical, and content knowledge (TPACK), an intelligent focus group practicum to help teachers to be competent in managing AI issues promptly, but the training module is insufficient to cover AI as a whole for teaching to the students as AI is comprised with various comprehensive conceptualizations that led the teachers to sometimes back to square one due to the delinquency to pinpoint substantial inquiries to scrutinize, analyze and decipher (Velander et al., 2023). Figure 2 illustrates the TPACK Framework designed by Punya Mishra and Matthew J. Koehler in 2006 (O'Dea & O'Dea, 2023). For providing K12 with quality and standard education, the institutional policy and the methodology to engage the teachers in AI literacy, which are supposed to be designed dynamically rather than the alignment of the teacher's training and the AI curriculum, appear vague and underdeveloped. Further, the mythology of teachers about judging a limited digital knowledge and understanding of the students with limitless access to devices such as mobile phones and computers is concerning because either some teacher overestimates the profoundness or underestimate it.

Correspondingly, the table of figure 3explains the surveillance of online education mechanisms requires profound attention, such as the management of the contents, which requires strategic and systematic organization and a spectrum of flexibility to draft innovative engagement methods for both motivated and unmotivated learners (Hakimi et al., 2024; Mukhamediev et al. 2022).

Table 1. Internal constraints of AI technology

Data	Learning Process	Results	Technology
1. Complications in data assemblage and prior processing. 2. Prerequisite of comprehensive quantities of data. 3. Absence and time-consuming data labeling. 4. Solitariness, prejudice, and data protection.	1. Imperceptive teaching procedure. 2. Required substantial computing capabilities. 3. Insufficiency of significant image processing technologies.	1. Scarcity of interpretability and translucence.	1. Acquired instability of the current answers due to machine learning and their reliance on noise. 2. Single-tasking element of the contemporary machine learning models and biased associatively. 3. Ought to devise renewed machine learning models for bizarre circumstances of application and explicit data. 4. Necessity for cyber-infrastructure for industrial AI and ML applications.

(Mukhamediev et al. 2022)

The emphasis should not be confined to revolutionizing the education system but should address the organizational school infrastructure. Administrators are required to address the reasons for the under-developed building infrastructure and components to be an intelligent center of education (Dhakshan et al., 2024). Education 4.0 deserves an intelligent setting, so the building infrastructure with inferior networks, conveyance management, and monitoring would not be competent to align with the expected purposes.

5.2 Methodological Concerns

To accelerate learning in K12, it is paramount to consider the strategy of integrating the model. In organizational school structure, horizontal and vertical integration are the most discernible curriculums worldwide. In the traditional setting, the focus used to be on cognitive development, but AI is supposed to broaden the development factors for students from early education. Transformational evolutions happen sometimes, preserving the essence of the curriculum intact. Suppose an educational institution opts for vertical integration of technology in its curriculum. In that case, it strives for the incremental involvement of students with digital literacy at a specific level, bottom to top, age-based, resulting in a lifelong and sustainable learning module (Huk, 2021). Sustainable learning modules in the AI curriculum could be more consistent, but they question the authority over a longer period. The vertical integration tends to backfire, threatening the academic freedom of the students and the critical thinking pedagogies as the modification in the curriculum is costly and time-consuming for an enormous number of students (Vargas et al., 2020). That is why vertical integration is adequate but a wicked and tricky strategy to maintain as a whole.

In the case of horizontal integration, the curriculum establishes the involvement of students at a given interval of the educational stage to commence (Huk, 2021). This type of curriculum is what students experience from secondary school onwards. Horizontal integration in education provides a scope in addressing curriculum differentiation where a student can select the subject to pursue for future education based on their interest and dreams (Teichler, 2020). For example, a student may have an interest in pursuing business management and a desire to be a business analyst; in this case, curriculum differentiation is the immaculate module for studying business management in-depth.

The pool for specialization in the knowledge economy is particularly demanding, which makes the integration of innovative and collaborative learning challenging due to the lack of consistent research and development, AI-oriented learning material, and insufficient class duration to properly use technology for better understanding (Li et al., 2023). The research and development of continuous intelligent learning modules is costly to maintain. Again, Intelligent Tutoring Systems (ITS) is the most complicated technology to work with as the integration faces crucial challenges of understanding because Artificial Intelligence tools because of limited language options It has the option to select for translations but many researchers addressed that language translation results in challenges, such as spelling mistakes, changes in the verbs, and others (Injadat et al., 2021). Similarly, the Learning Management System (LMS) has its drawbacks too. In a study, it has been discovered that the integration of LMS challenges skills, such as pronunciation, grammar, vocabulary, writing, reading, speaking, and listening (Nasim et al., 2024). The main victims of these LMS methods are the weak and introverted students of the class. Whether it is vertical or horizontal integration, designing the new course pedagogy and cognitive development approaches are the most critical parts of the AI curriculum.

5.3 Technological Difficulties

Artificial intelligence learning tools have intricate algorithms and infrastructures that require instantaneous assistance and training to make the materials efficiently grasped by the little learners, K12. In terms of grading, the AI application utilizes a matter-of-fact technique to grade essays, where a large number of essays are required to be fed earlier so that AI can acknowledge the standard characteristics of the grading system. However, the teacher follows the subjective method for grading, and this leads to a comparison of humans-generated grading with machine ones (Injadat et al., 2021). Even though it is said that machines cannot read human emotions or interact as humanly as teachers, that ushers to addressing the societal loopholes caused by technological instruments. There is a filtering option that decreases the workload of the teachers, but the question of societal consequences remains in its place. The menace of algorithmic nonobjective or obscure datasets raises the odds of being subject to the digital divide as the AI mechanism is furnished on a data-driven practice module, which looms to recast the everyday preferences of human beings (Velander et al., 2023).

When there was onsite or traditional education in full swing all over the world, dropout rates were not exceptionally high. However, the emergence of online learning and blended learning indeed attempted to diminish the illiteracy rate but has drawn a line of discrimination as technological equipment, which is required to perceive education as expensive (Injadat et al., 2021). Almost two-thirds of children all around the world have suffered from the digital divide, and more than 90% of the languages have been excluded from the mechanism that degrades inclusion (Douse, 2024). For the costly nature of the integration, the dropout rate of K12 is higher. As online learning is mainly a self-driven learning pedagogy that slows down the speed of the smart knowledge economy for unmotivated and average students.

Additionally, the solitude of data is a concern to academicians. Platforms like Zoom and Microsoft Teams have end-to-end encryption to secure data privacy, but for writing essays, for example, students need to surf the internet and download numerous articles, and this could lead to the threshold of any harmful viruses that impede the privacy of students (Liu & Yu, 2022). Cyber threats are caused by storing unprotected data for a long time and establishing an unprotected network between the cloud and the physical environment (Dhakshan et al., 2024). AI applications require users' data to modify their system more appropriately, and here, the data plays the game of tension as the user's data is preserved in an unencrypted way that triggers the hackers or third parties to intrude, and exposure of data gets misused in a vulnerable way.

Cloud computing is quite famous for storing data, but these are more vulnerable to getting hacked, and many studies have found traces of cloud hampering users' privacy and data. In addition, the studies reveal that acknowledging three essential steps, which are keeping backup in an encrypted platform, constantly updating the device's system and privacy software, and assessing and monitoring the cookies. Unfortunately, not all students are well aware of the proper technique for maintaining devices, software, and the Internet of Things (IoT), which could enhance the longevity of data and devices and lessen the pathway of cyberattacks.

5.4 Psychological Factors

While integrating AI into education, proper addressing of the psychological factors cannot be ignored at all. The transformation from the traditional to Education 4.0 lead many students to acquire negative attitudes or mindsets toward the adoption of innovative and collaborative AI-oriented teaching methods and a lack of motivation due to cultural differences (Li et al., 2023). Due to their extended exposure to screens, students experience elevated stress, frustration, apprehension, bafflement, a feeling of greater accountability and inhibition, lessened peer interactions, and unpredictable network disturbances during examinations (Bal, 2024). Education and psychology are closely related to each other.

Figure 3. Mechanism of brain-computer interface (BCL) (Balderas et al., 2021)

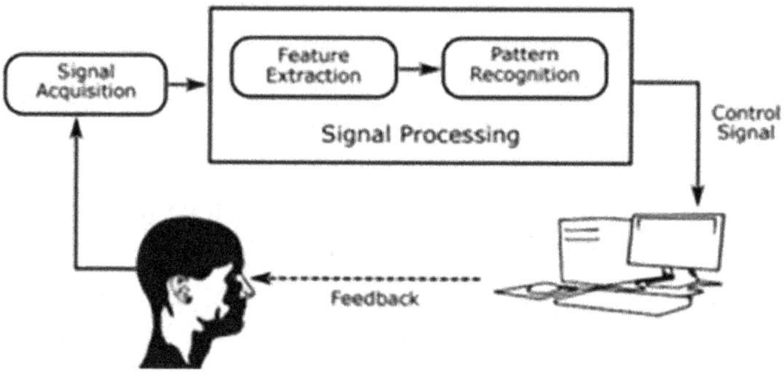

The early stages of child brain development are crucial, and the educational environment and learning modules impact cognitive factors either positively or negatively. The emerging technology, which acts as a mediator for communication between the human brain and technology, poses threats that question the principles of humanity. Figure 4 explains the mechanism of how the Brain-computer interface (BCL) works, and BCL is also misused in educational platforms when students are stigmatized based on the performance level of their brain activity, which results from exercising the right to equitable access for all students (Pandey & Prasad, 2024; Maiseli et al., 2023). Further, to obtain Artificial Intelligence in Education (AIED), the usage of devices like smartphones or pc is a must; hence, there is the question arises whether AIED is negatively impacting children's brain cognitive development and behavioral components such as attention span or attention problems and increasing of being attacked with health risks (Nasim et al., 2024).

With the blooming speed of the adoption of AI, student ethics is an alarming matter of threat for academicians. UN fears that the integration of AIED might threaten the right to human dignity, and autonomy, be heard, experience the digital divide, data privacy and data protection, and transparency and explainability (Holmes & Tuomi, 2022). The AIED model of ethics is vital but not sufficient with the radical technological changes that enter into the realm of teaching and learning now and then. Moreover, research pinpointed that no matter what method is integrated, academic misconduct and plagiarism are notwithstanding (Nasim et al., 2024).

6. OPPORTUNITIES OF AI IN THE EDUCATION SECTOR

As artificial intelligence advances in many domains, there is a growing emphasis on preparing students for a world where highly skilled technology will shape virtually every aspect of human life. Schools and other educational centers are continuously including AI-related topics in curricula, understanding the need to equip students for the future. It is also not limited to just the classroom training of students in the area of AI, but rather education in general, and its improvement with the help of AI tools is also considered in this approach. The integration of AI technologies into education promises to address some of the field's most enduring difficulties while also opening up new avenues for innovation as it evolves. Below are the key opportunities AI presents in the education sector, discussed in detail.

6.1 Personalized Learning

Among the most significant opportunities is the potential to offer individualized learning experiences. AI offers education. Since the one-method-fits-all model aids in presenting only conventional knowledge, educators have recently been paying attention to the significance of increasing differentiation in teaching approaches. AI is able to customize instructional materials to every student's unique needs so that they can adjust in real time to their learning preferences, style, and speed (Tapalova & Zhiyenbayeva, 2022). AI-powered tools may evaluate an individual student's capabilities and shortcomings and design individualized learning lessons that concentrate on their areas of greatest need for development (Tapalova & Zhiyenbayeva, 2022). For example, Artificial intelligence-driven learning platforms can give advanced materials to students who pick up topics fast or extra tasks for students who are having trouble understanding a concept in particular. AI technology holds the ability to support and implement a fully differentiated approach to learning by incorporating the learner's preferences, as well as strengths and weaknesses. With high precision, Artificial intelligence ensures that the content and support the learners receive are personalized according to their abilities and learning needs. This cycle of learning engulfs every student, and based on their interests and the kind of human being the student is, the approach to teaching is modified, which revolutionizes the education system by addressing the most significant and universal issue of how to make learners be interested and motivated in learning (Ananyi, 2023). One of the most critical advantages of AI systems is their ability to forecast, analyze, and comprehend based on massive loads of data. In the context of learning analytics, these aspects promise an opportunity to gain highly detailed insights into learners (Figure 4). In other words, AI can point out recurring features that may be associated with the student's learning profile or weaknesses. It can further lead to the creation of highly individualized instructional material, which would enable addressing individual learner needs as required (Omar Jian, 2023). This degree of customization has an opportunity to boost student engagement and yield more impactful learning results.

Figure 4. Personalized learning (Tapalova & Zhiyenbayeva, 2022)

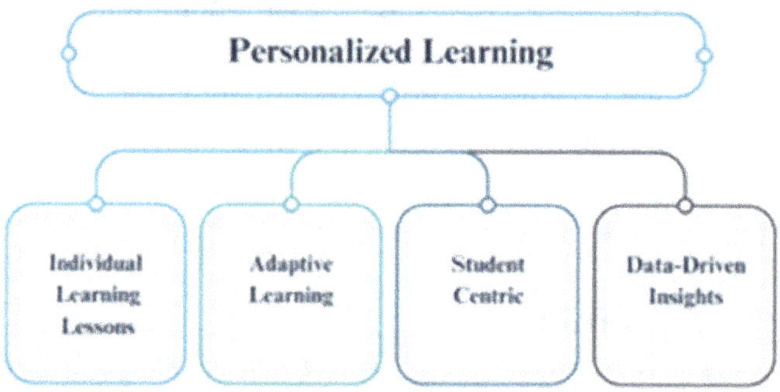

During the first twenty years of a person's life, students study for approximately 15,000 hours (Pataranutaporn et al., 2021). Thus, the environment and learning circumstances have a significant influence on the individual and, by extension, on society. AI characters may be used to provide interesting instructional resources for students of all ages and sorts, from content dissemination in the classroom to content engagement. In order to help students understand any topic more easily, cutting-edge algorithms can be used to bring well-known historical, fictional, or contemporary characters to life. These "lived" experiences can include scientists sharing their findings, historical figures recounting battles, or painters discussing their processes and sources of inspiration (Ahmad et al., 2024). Character appearance in a learning environment has been shown in several studies to positively impact students' motivation, attitudes, and actions. Additionally, it has been shown that learning activities, including made-up narratives and characters, increase concentration and involvement (Ahmad et al., 2024). Therefore, the integration of the current approach towards the development of personalized learning is benefiting the students as well as other user requirements.

6.2 Automated Grading and Assessment

AI has got the capability to drastically reduce the workload of educators by automating the grading process. Traditionally, grading can be time-consuming, especially with large classes. AI algorithms can grade multiple-choice tests, short-answer questions, and even essays with a high degree of accuracy, which will eventually allow teachers to prioritize offering instructions more and less on administrative work in due course (Figure 5). Feedback is a concept that is related to cybernetics, control, and system theory, and it is the main source of AI because it is the easiest and most uncomplicated way to understand the connection and transmission between humans and machines (González-Calatayud et al., 2021). Artificial intelligence is an attempt to imitate human natural intelligence in computers so that these robots may learn from past events or results and make judgments based on those experiences (Hooda et al., 2022).

Figure 5. Automated grading and assessment (González-Calatayud et al., 2021)

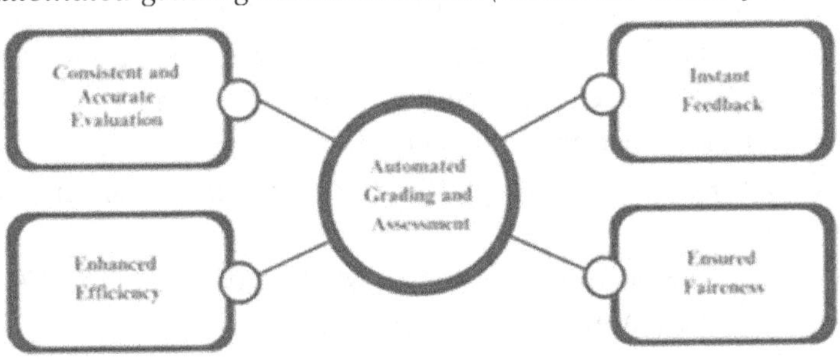

Artificial intelligence is finding a greater extent of usage in various fields, especially in education. With the help of machine learning, which is one of the parts of AI, they are taking proactive steps to support students who are struggling, and also the algorithms of it assist the teachers in evaluating student performance in a systematic manner. Research indicates that artificial intelligence enhances educational quality by optimizing students' ultimate performance (Hooda et al., 2022). Moreover, AI-powered assessment tools can analyze their performance over time, identifying trends and providing insights that can inform instructional strategies.

6.3 Enhancing Accessibility

AI has the potential to significantly increase and improve the accessibility of learning for students with impairments or disabilities. For students who are hard of hearing or deaf, artificial intelligence voice recognition and natural language processing technologies can transcribe lectures. In a similar manner, text-to-speech programs can offer assistance to children with visual impairments or blindness by reading digital information verbally aloud (Hooda et al., 2022). Additionally, AI can help create more inclusive learning environments by providing language translation services for non-native speakers, which is more specifically valuable in diverse classrooms where students may speak myriad languages. By breaking down linguistic barriers or monolingualism, AI can make certain that every single student has the equivalent opportunity and access to all the educational resources (Alam, 2023).

6.4 Adaptive Learning Platforms

Adaptive learning platforms are AI-driven systems that dynamically adjust the difficulty level and type of content presented to students based on their performance. The aforementioned platforms use data analytics and machine learning to continuously assess student progress and adapt lessons accordingly (Alam, 2022). For instance, if a student is struggling with a specific topic, the platform may offer additional resources, practice problems, or alternative explanations (Kabudi et al., 2021). Conversely, if a student is excelling, the platform might introduce more challenging materials to keep them engaged. This adaptive approach ensures that students are always working at the appropriate level, which can improve learning efficiency and outcomes.

China's one of the first adaptive learning systems is called Squirrel AI Learning. Individualized adaptive learning training provided in the classroom is compared to large-group teaching in one research and to small-group instruction in another (Wang et al., 2020). Compared to students randomly assigned to whole-class or small-group teaching led by experienced teachers, Chinese eighth-grade pupils from two provinces who were randomly assigned to utilize Squirrel AI Learning demonstrated higher improvements on a mathematics test (Wang et al., 2020).

6.5 AI-Enhanced Content Creation

AI can help teachers produce excellent instructional content more quickly, for instance, using the content taught in a course, AI technologies may create quizzes, examinations and assignments without any hassle very quickly (Singha & Singha, 2024). These resources may also be used to produce interactive visualizations and simulations that simplify difficult ideas. Additionally, it can allow for virtual laboratories, which offer practical learning opportunities in areas like science and technology (Liang et al., 2021).

One example of how AI is being used in language learning apps is the generation of adaptive grammar exercises and tailored vocabulary lists by AI algorithms, which increases instructional efficiency and student engagement (Liang et al., 2021). Additionally, educational games and virtual reality experiences delivering fully immersive learning environments may be created using AI. Learning may be made more enjoyable and engaging with the help of such technologies, which is especially beneficial for younger pupils or those who find it difficult to learn using traditional techniques (Singha & Singha, 2024).

6.6 Global Classroom and Learning Networks

With time, the phrase "smart classroom" has changed to better represent the modern technology used in classrooms because smart courses that integrate artificial intelligence and smart technologies are a result of the rapid advancements in technology and the need to design more inventive and efficient learning environments that facilitate both in-person and remote learning (Dimitriadou & Lanitis, 2023). AI can facilitate the creation of global classrooms where students from different parts of the world can learn together in a virtual environment, and through AI-powered platforms, students can learn, ally, and join forces on different projects, participate of any discussions, lot of resources and give their ideas, regardless of where they are in the world (Lee & Perret, 2022).

This transnational approach to teaching encourages cross-cultural dialogue and gives pupils a range of viewpoints on different subjects. It also eradicates geographical and time zone constraints, enabling educational institutions to present and deliver courses to a wider audience (Dimitriadou & Lanitis, 2023). According to Mr. Chandan Kumar Dubey (2024), there has been a specific consideration in AI education for inclusive learning. Inclusive learning can be described as a concept of imparting education to every learner who wants to get an education and has faced learning difficulties. The adopted method of personalized learning, the methods of assistive technologies, and the ones regarding the use of tutoring systems all significantly change the model of the learner or teacher when learning and making it more suitable. Further, the use of AI is even more inclusive because of some of its functions, which include speech recognition and text-to-speech recognition for students with disabilities. In this regard, AI may be described as comprehensive learning for the many who need to be looked after by others on their behalf.

6.7 The Future of AI in Education

The role of AI in education is likely to expand further as technology continues to advance. Future developments may include more sophisticated AI-driven tutors who are capable enough to understand and respond to the complexity of learners' emotions, fully immersive virtual classrooms powered by AI and augmented reality, and AI systems that can predict and adapt to future educational needs (Grassini, 2023). Not only that, but AI can identify the skills that are in demand and help create customized learning paths for reskilling and upskilling, particularly in industries undergoing technological transformation (Grassini, 2023).

To make sure that all technological advancements are utilized in ways that improve learning while upholding ethical norms, educators, legislators, and technology developers must collaborate as artificial intelligence becomes more deeply ingrained in the framework of educational curriculum (Grassini, 2023). In addition, teachers will require continual training in order to adjust to the evolving nature of education and successfully incorporate AI into their lesson plans. When they work together, AI technologies that are not just efficient but also fair and available to all students may be developed.

From better and more widespread accessibility and data-driven insights to individualized learning and intelligent tutoring systems, artificial intelligence has a plethora of chances to fundamentally reinvent or upend the education industry (Alam, 2023). Even if there are lots of barriers still to overcome, artificial intelligence has enormous potential to improve education. Educational institutions may design more inclusive, dynamic, and productive learning environments that better prepare students for the future by utilizing AI (Alam, 2023). It is essential to give ethical issues top priority as we investigate and develop AI technologies and make sure that these resources are applied to support fair access to excellent and high-end educational opportunities for all students.

7. CONCLUSION

The Education 4.0 system, a precise route towards a radical transformation of education delivery and experience, is packed with digital teaching competence, elements to enhance students' soft and hard skills, generative technological driving passions, organizational approaches, and visionary pedagogy (Oliveira & Souza, 2021). To a contemporary extent, AIED is in the spotlight because different advancements in technology are gradually shaping the intelligent teaching module to be more aligned so that the students have more generous accessibility and partake in customized, individualized learning environments. Based on extensive prerequisites of data acquired from the users and the academicians, the AIED system has developed and familiarized numerous intelligent learning modules, programs, and software with continuous updates and upgrades. Though COVID-19 took away many lives, it also uplifted the popularity of K12 and the usage of AI applications and tools. It augmented the swiftness of the involvement of students and academicians to provide cost and time-effective and pragmatic innovative education through digital learning and transformation (Beke & Tick, 2024). In addition, augmentation has constantly driven the trends of AIED to evolve rapidly, making the students eligible to settle down in the domain of Industry 4.0. AI, the automated and data-driven technology, has nurtured students to experience flipped classrooms, cloud computing, education using AR/VR tools, E-textbooks, and many more. This research has scrutinized the multiple trending learning Ed-Tech platforms that allow students and teachers to enjoy developing their cognitive skills and interpersonal skills. Many educators are ecstatic to see the use of AI in education (Grassini, 2023), stating that the implementation will make their jobs easier. AI is seen to be an essential tool in grading different essays and course works, judging the work done by the student, and also passing on helpful feedback to work on. Not only that, the usage of an AI-powered automatic grader has, in many cases, been a teaching aid for many of the students.

However, it cannot be said that AIED of K12 is charmed with optimistic outcomes merely. Academia, in order to bridge the gap between Education 4.0 and Industry 4.0, encounters significant challenges categorized into four parts, which have already been discussed in the chapter. The most crucial difficulty is the high dropout rate due to the cost and lack of technical infrastructural assistance, which is contributing to the increase in thein the illiteracy rate globally. In this case, affirmative and collaborative action from the government, academicians, and the industry could make a valuable contribution to the reduction of prices to allow students to engage in inclusive study. AI is, in the end, just a program. It has no human judgment of its own, so when a user unethically approaches it, it will have no judgment of its own (Kooli, 2023), especially in educational institutions, where the students will most likely take undue advantage. Although there are shortcomings, there is a future scope for AI in implementation in the field of education, where in the field of Information, Technology, Learning, Education, and Training (ITLET), different ethical approaches are seen, where many systems are introduced for the hosting and bonding between AI and humans, like Adaptive Instructional Systems (AIS), creating a more learning experience (Mason et al., 2020). Therefore, the integration of artificial intelligence in K-12 education will make students and academicians more reliable digital citizens who behave constructively.

REFERENCES

Ahmad, K., Iqbal, W., El-Hassan, A., Qadir, J., Benhaddou, D., Ayyash, M., & Al-Fuqaha, A. (2024). Data-Driven Artificial Intelligence in Education: A Comprehensive review. *IEEE Transactions on Learning Technologies*, *17*, 12–31. DOI: 10.1109/TLT.2023.3314610

Alam, A. (2022). Employing adaptive learning and intelligent tutoring robots for virtual classrooms and smart campuses: Reforming Education in the age of Artificial Intelligence. In *Lecture notes in electrical engineering* (pp. 395–406). DOI: 10.1007/978-981-19-2980-9_32

Alam, A. (2023). Harnessing the power of AI to create intelligent tutoring systems for enhanced classroom experience and improved learning outcomes. In *Lecture notes on data engineering and communications technologies* (pp. 571–591). DOI: 10.1007/978-981-99-1767-9_42

Alrakhawi, H. A., Jamiat, N., & Abu-Naser, S. S. (2023). Intelligent Tutoring Systems In Education: A Systematic Review Of Usage, Tools, Effects And Evaluation. *Journal of Theoretical and Applied Information Technology*, *101*(4), 1992–8645. https://www.researchgate.net/publication/369019319_INTELLIGENT_TUTORING_SYSTEMS_IN_EDUCATION_A_SYSTEMATIC_REVIEW_OF_USAGE_TOOLS_EFFECTS_AND_EVALUATION

Ananyi, S. O. (2023). COST-BENEFIT ANALYSIS OF ARTIFICIAL INTELLIGENCE INTEGRATION IN EDUCATION MANAGEMENT: LEADERSHIP PERSPECTIVES. Researchgate, ISSN: 2992-5614. https://www.researchgate.net/publication/375609860_COST-BENEFIT_ANALYSIS_OF_ARTIFICIAL_INTELLIGENCE_INTEGRATION_IN_EDUCATION_MANAGEMENT_LEADERSHIP_PERSPECTIVES

Bal, N. G. (2024). Unlocking online language education: Opportunities, challenges, and recommendations. *Turkish Journal of Education*, 158–179. DOI: 10.19128/turje.1379149

Balderas, D., Ponce, P., Lopez-Bernal, D., & Molina, A. (2021). Education 4.0: Teaching The Basis of Motor Imagery Classification Algorithms for Brain-Computer Interfaces. *Future Internet*, *13*(8), 202. DOI: 10.3390/fi13080202

Beke, E., & Tick, A. (2024). Applicability of education 4.0 in higher education: Engineering students' survey. *Journal of Technology and Science Education*, *14*(2), 529. DOI: 10.3926/jotse.1845

Chassignol, M., Khoroshavin, A., Klimova, A., & Bilyatdinova, A. (2018). Artificial Intelligence trends in education: A narrative overview. *Procedia Computer Science, 136*, 16–24. DOI: 10.1016/j.procs.2018.08.233

Chituc, C. (2021). A framework for Education 4.0 in digital education ecosystems. In *IFIP advances in information and communication technology* (pp. 702–709). DOI: 10.1007/978-3-030-85969-5_66

Chiu, T. K. F. (2021). A holistic approach to the design of artificial intelligence (AI) education for K-12 schools. *TechTrends, 65*(5), 796–807. DOI: 10.1007/s11528-021-00637-1

Dhakshan, S., Balamurugan, G., Mohan, J. S. S., & Tyagi, A. K. (2024). Role of Emerging Technologies in Education 4.0: Challenges and future research directions. In *Role of Emerging Technologies in Education 4.0*. IGI Global., DOI: 10.4018/978-1-6684-9285-7.ch006

Dimitriadou, E., & Lanitis, A. (2023). A critical evaluation, challenges, and future perspectives of using artificial intelligence and emerging technologies in smart classrooms. *Smart Learning Environments, 10*(1), 12. Advance online publication. DOI: 10.1186/s40561-023-00231-3 PMID: 40478141

Douse, M. (2024). Educational planning and artificial intelligence. *Educational Planning, 31*(2), ISSN-1537-873X. https://files.eric.ed.gov/fulltext/EJ1425308.pdf

Dubey, Mr. C. K. (2024). Exploring the role of artificial intelligence in inclusive education. Researchgate. https://www.researchgate.net/publication/378907681_Exploring_the_Role_of_Artificial_Intelligence_in_Inclusive_Education

González-Calatayud, V., Prendes-Espinosa, P., & Roig-Vila, R. (2021). Artificial Intelligence for Student Assessment: A Systematic review. *Applied Sciences (Basel, Switzerland), 11*(12), 5467. DOI: 10.3390/app11125467

Grassini, S. (2023). Shaping the Future of Education: Exploring the potential and consequences of AI and ChatGPT in educational settings. *Education Sciences, 13*(7), 692. DOI: 10.3390/educsci13070692

Hakimi, M., Katebzadah, S., & Fazil, A. W. (2024). Comprehensive Insights into E-Learning in contemporary Education: Analyzing trends, challenges, and best practices. [JETL]. *Journal of Education and Teaching Learning, 6*(1), 86–105. DOI: 10.51178/jetl.v6i1.1720

Hamilton, I. (2024, June 6). Artificial intelligence in Education: Teachers' opinions on AI in the classroom. Forbes Advisor. https://www.forbes.com/advisor/education/it-and-tech/artificial-intelligence-in-school/

Holmes, W., & Tuomi, I. (2022). State of the art and practice in AI in education. *European Journal of Education*, *57*(4), 542–570. DOI: 10.1111/ejed.12533

Hooda, M., Rana, C., Dahiya, O., Rizwan, A., & Hossain, M. S. (2022). Artificial intelligence for assessment and feedback to enhance student success in higher education. *Mathematical Problems in Engineering*, *2022*, 1–19. DOI: 10.1155/2022/5215722

Huk, T. (2021). From Education 1.0 to Education 4.0 - Challenges for the Contemporary School. opus.us.edu.pl. https://doi.org/DOI: 10.15804/tner.2021.66.4.03

Injadat, M., Moubayed, A., Nassif, A. B., & Shami, A. (2021). Machine learning towards intelligent Systems: applications, challenges, and opportunities. *Artificial Intelligence Review*. https://arxiv.org/pdf/2101.03655

Jiang, S., Tang, H., Tatar, C., Rosé, C. P., & Chao, J. (2023). High school students' data modeling practices and processes: From modeling unstructured data to evaluating automated decisions. *Learning, Media and Technology*, *48*(2), 350–368. DOI: 10.1080/17439884.2023.2189735

Kabudi, T., Pappas, I. O., & Olsen, D. H. (2021). AI-enabled adaptive learning systems: A systematic mapping of the literature. *Computers and Education Artificial Intelligence*, *2*, 100017. DOI: 10.1016/j.caeai.2021.100017

Karakose, T., & Tulubas, T. (2024). School leadership and management in the age of Artificial intelligence (AI): Recent developments and future prospects. *Educational Process International Journal*, *13*(1). Advance online publication. DOI: 10.22521/edupij.2024.131.1

Kaur, S., Tandon, N., & Matharou, G. S. (2020). Contemporary Trends in education transformation using Artificial Intelligence. In *CRC Press eBooks* (pp. 89–103). DOI: 10.1201/9781003032410-7

Knyazeva, N., Mikhailova, I., Usmanova, N., & Shindina, T. (2022). Overcoming barriers in developing digital skills for higher education teachers: Challenges and solutions. Review of Artificial Intelligence in Education, 3, e024. Researchgate. https://www.researchgate.net/publication/378165747_Overcoming_Barriers_in_Developing_Digital_Skills_for_Higher_Education_Teachers_Challenges_and_Solutions

Kooli, C. (2023). Chatbots in Education and Research: A Critical Examination of ethical implications and solutions. *Sustainability (Basel)*, *15*(7), 5614. DOI: 10.3390/su15075614

Lee, I., & Perret, B. (2022). Preparing High School Teachers to Integrate AI Methods into STEM Classrooms. *Proceedings of the AAAI Conference on Artificial Intelligence, 36*(11), 12783–12791. DOI: 10.1609/aaai.v36i11.21557

Lee, S. J., & Kwon, K. (2024). A systematic review of AI education in K-12 classrooms from 2018 to 2023: Topics, strategies, and learning outcomes. *Computers and Education Artificial Intelligence, 100211*, 100211. Advance online publication. DOI: 10.1016/j.caeai.2024.100211

Li, L., Fengchao, Y., & Zhang, E. (2024). A systematic review of learning task design for K-12 AI education: Trends, challenges, and opportunities. *Computers and Education Artificial Intelligence, 6*, 100217. DOI: 10.1016/j.caeai.2024.100217

Li, X., Chen, W., & Alrasheedi, M. (2023). Challenges of the collaborative innovation system in public higher education in the era of industry 4.0 using an integrated framework. *Journal of Innovation & Knowledge, 8*(4), 100430. DOI: 10.1016/j.jik.2023.100430

Liang, X., Haiping, L., Liu, J., & Lin, L. (2021). Reform of English interactive teaching mode based on cloud computing artificial intelligence – a practice analysis. *Journal of Intelligent & Fuzzy Systems, 40*(2), 3617–3629. DOI: 10.3233/JIFS-189397

Liu, M., & Yu, D. (2022). Towards intelligent E-learning systems. *Education and Information Technologies, 28*(7), 7845–7876. DOI: 10.1007/s10639-022-11479-6 PMID: 36532790

Maiseli, B., Abdalla, A. T., Massawe, L. V., Mbise, M., Mkocha, K., Nassor, N. A., Ismail, M., Michael, J., & Kimambo, S. (2023). Brain–computer interface: Trend, challenges, and threats. *Brain Informatics, 10*(1), 20. Advance online publication. DOI: 10.1186/s40708-023-00199-3 PMID: 37540385

Majorana, C. D. B., Gonçalves, R. B., Neto, F. L. A., & Camargo, R. Z. (2022). Enhancing Administrative Efficiency in Higher Education with AI: A Chatbot Solution. Review of Artificial Intelligence in Education, 3, e023. Researchgate. https://www.researchgate.net/publication/378170981_Enhancing_Administrative_Efficiency_in_Higher_Education_with_AI_A_Chatbot_Solution

Marrone, R., Taddeo, V., & Hill, G. (2022). Creativity and Artificial Intelligence—A student perspective. *Journal of Intelligence, 10*(3), 65. DOI: 10.3390/jintelligence10030065 PMID: 36135606

Mason, J., Peoples, B. E., & Lee, J. (2020). Questioning the scope of AI standardization in learning, education, and training. *Journal of ICT Standardisation*, •••, 107–122. DOI: 10.13052/jicts2245-800X.822

Moraes, E. B., Kipper, L. M., Kellermann, A. C. H., Austria, L., Leivas, P., Moraes, J. R., & Witczak, M. (2022). Integration of Industry 4.0 technologies with Education 4.0: Advantages for improvements in learning. *Interactive Technology and Smart Education, 20*(2), 271–287. DOI: 10.1108/ITSE-11-2021-0201

Mukhamediev, R. I., Popova, Y., Kuchin, Y., Zaitseva, E., Kalimoldayev, A., Symagulov, A., Levashenko, V., Abdoldina, F., Gopejenko, V., Yakunin, K., Muhamedijeva, E., & Yelis, M. (2022). Review of artificial intelligence and machine learning technologies: Classification, restrictions, opportunities and challenges. *Mathematics, 10*(15), 2552. DOI: 10.3390/math10152552

Nasim, S. M., Mujeeba, S., AlShraah, S. M., Khan, I. A., Amir, N., & Ali, Z. (2024). Exploring pedagogical perspectives of EFL instructors: Advantages, disadvantages, and implications of Blackboard as an LMS for language instruction. *Cogent Social Sciences, 10*(1), 2312659. Advance online publication. DOI: 10.1080/23311886.2024.2312659

Nazaretsky, T., Ariely, M., Cukurova, M., & Alexandron, G. (2022, July). Teachers' trust in AI -powered educational technology and a professional development program to improve it. *British Journal of Educational Technology, 53*(4), 914–931. Advance online publication. DOI: 10.1111/bjet.13232

O'Dea, X., & O'Dea, M. (2023). Is artificial intelligence really the next big thing in learning and teaching in higher education? A conceptual paper. *Journal of University Teaching & Learning Practice, 20*(5). Advance online publication. DOI: 10.53761/1.20.5.06

Olari, V., & Romeike, R. (2024). Data-related concepts for Artificial Intelligence education in K-12. *Computers and Education Open, 100196*, 100196. Advance online publication. DOI: 10.1016/j.caeo.2024.100196

Oliveira, K. K. D. S., & Souza, R. C. (2021). *Digital Transformation towards Education 4.0*. Informatics in Education., DOI: 10.15388/infedu.2022.13

Omar Jian, M. J. K. (2023). Personalized learning through AI. Researchgate. https://www.researchgate.net/publication/376814707_Personalized_learning_through_AI

Paek, S., & Kim, N. (2021). Analysis of worldwide research trends on the impact of artificial intelligence in education. *Sustainability (Basel), 13*(14), 7941. DOI: 10.3390/su13147941

Pandey, B., & Prasad, S. (2024). USING BRAIN-COMPUTER INTERFACES (BCI) IN EDUCATION. In *THE FUTURE OF EDUCATION IN THE DIGITAL AGE*. IMRF INTERNATIONAL PUBLICATIONS.

Park, W., & Kwon, H. (2023). Implementing artificial intelligence education for middle school technology education in Republic of Korea. *International Journal of Technology and Design Education*, *34*(1), 109–135. DOI: 10.1007/s10798-023-09812-2 PMID: 36844448

Pataranutaporn, P., Danry, V., Leong, J., Punpongsanon, P., Novy, D., Maes, P., & Sra, M. (2021). AI-generated characters for supporting personalized learning and well-being. *Nature Machine Intelligence*, *3*(12), 1013–1022. DOI: 10.1038/s42256-021-00417-9

Paul, P. (2022). Digital Education: The Aspects and Growth in Socio-Economic Development—Towards sophisticated Education 4.0 Practice. *Economic Affairs*, *67*(5). Advance online publication. DOI: 10.46852/0424-2513.5.2022.32

Saputra, I., Astuti, M., Sayuti, M., & Kusumastuti, D. (2021). Integration of Artificial intelligence in Education: Opportunities, Challenges, Threats and obstacles. A literature review. Researchgate. https://www.researchgate.net/publication/373530759_Integration_of_Artificial_Intelligence_in_Education_Opportunities_Challenges_Threats_and_Obstacles_A_Literature_Review

Shet, A. (2024). Transforming traditional education with PHP: Building an Online classroom. *Amit Shet Al. International Journal of Recent Research Aspects*, *11*(2). https://ijrra.net/Vol11issue2/IJRRA-11-02-01.pdf

Singha, S., & Singha, R. (2024). Revolutionizing content creation and curriculum development through generative AI. In *Advances in educational technologies and instructional design book series* (pp. 261–280). DOI: 10.4018/979-8-3693-1351-0.ch013

Tapalova, O., & Zhiyenbayeva, N. (2022). *Artificial Intelligence in Education: AIED for Personalised Learning Pathways.* https://eric.ed.gov/?id=EJ1373006

Teichler, U. (2020). Higher education system differentiation, horizontal and vertical. In *Springer eBooks* (pp. 772–778). DOI: 10.1007/978-94-017-8905-9_36

Vargas, V. R., Lawthom, R., Prowse, A., Randles, S., & Tzoulas, K. (2020). Implications of vertical policy integration for sustainable development implementation in higher education institutions. *Journal of Cleaner Production*, *235*, 733–740. DOI: 10.1016/j.jclepro.2019.07.022

Velander, J., Taiye, M. A., Otero, N., & Milrad, M. (2023). Artificial Intelligence in K-12 Education: Eliciting and reflecting on Swedish teachers' understanding of AI and its implications for teaching & learning. *Education and Information Technologies*, *29*(4), 4085–4105. DOI: 10.1007/s10639-023-11990-4

Wang, S., Christensen, C., Cui, W., Tong, R., Yarnall, L., Shear, L., & Feng, M. (2020). When adaptive learning is effective learning: Comparison of an adaptive learning system to teacher-led instruction. *Interactive Learning Environments, 31*(2), 793–803. DOI: 10.1080/10494820.2020.1808794

Williams, A. R., Windle, R., & Wharrad, H. (2020c). How will Education 4.0 influence learning in higher education? *Journal of Learning Development in Higher Education, 17*(17). Advance online publication. DOI: 10.47408/jldhe.vi17.572

Zawacki-Richter, O., Marín, V. I., Bond, M., & Gouverneur, F. (2019). Systematic review of research on artificial intelligence applications in higher education – where are the educators? *International Journal of Educational Technology in Higher Education, 16*(1), 39. Advance online publication. DOI: 10.1186/s41239-019-0171-0

Chapter 3

Brand Promotion and AI-Driven Innovation in K-12 Educational Start-Ups

Aarzoo
http://orcid.org/0009-0006-7604-2583
Manav Rachna International Institute of Research and Studies, India

Ruhi Lal
Manav Rachna International Institute of Research and Studies, India

ABSTRACT

AI improves K-12 learning. Digital innovation affects K-12 educational institutions using AI and brand marketing. Know startup challenges and growth prospects. This study discovered pros and downsides of brand marketing, digital innovation, and AI. We examined branding. Included are literature reviews, founder and marketing expert interviews, industry polls, and successful startup assessments. Branding benefits from social and focused learning. AI-driven digitization boosted operations and education. New methodology criticism, data privacy problems, and exorbitant implementation costs persist. AI-powered brand marketing and innovation can be profitable despite challenges. These skills include student-specific education, massive data and user management, and trend analysis. K-12 educational enterprises can flourish, study shows. Need unique branding and AI-powered digital innovation. Stakeholder engagement and strategic planning improve operations and personalize education to solve challenges. Results suggest K-12 education needs AI, innovation, and branding.

DOI: 10.4018/979-8-3693-6346-1.ch003

INTRODUCTION

Education start-ups face potential problems due to the convergence of AI-driven innovation and brand promotion techniques in the quickly changing K–12 classroom. This study examines how brand marketing tactics and digital innovation abilities can be applied to AI-driven K–12 educational start-ups to better understand this intersection (Baker, Smith, & Anissa, 2019). The researchers attempt to comprehend how these methods are utilised in the competitive educational technology industry by looking at various start-up approaches, including partnerships, social media marketing, content development, and their expertise in digital innovation. In addition, the researchers want to investigate, in the context of AI integration, the interaction between digital innovation skills and K–12 educational start-ups (Kajiwara, Matsuoka, & Shinbo, 2023). This entails learning how startups create and use digital innovation capabilities to include AI into their educational programmes, improving their goods and services to match the changing demands of K–12 students. This study also aims to determine the potential and difficulties that K–12 educational start-ups encounter when putting brand promotion and AI-driven innovation into practice (Danniels & Pyle, 2023). These observations were ultimately support start-ups' success and long-term viability by assisting them in overcoming challenges and seizing new opportunities in the educational technology sector. With these goals, the research hopes to offer K–12 educational start-ups insightful advice on navigating the ever-changing world of AI-driven innovation and brand promotion.

Research Objectives

1. To explore the applicability of brand promotion strategies and digital innovation skills in AI-driven K-12 educational start-ups
2. To investigate the relationship between K-12 educational start-ups and digital innovation skills in the context of AI integration.
3. Identify the challenges and opportunities faced by K-12 educational start-ups when implementing brand promotion and AI-driven innovation.

Research Question

RQ1 What branding strategies work best for K-12 educational start-ups?
RQ2 How does digital innovation influence the effectiveness of K-12 educational start-ups?
RQ3 What are the main challenges faced by K-12 educational start-ups when integrating AI technologies?

RQ4 What are the potential benefits of integrating lean brand promotion, digital innovation, and AI technologies in K-12 educational start-ups?

Relevance of the Study

The relevance of this research, "Brand Promotion and AI-Driven Innovation in K-12 Educational Start-ups," is in its examination of how educational technology is developing and how it affects start-ups aimed at K–12 schooling. Recognizing how start-ups market their brands in this industry is crucial to their survival and expansion, given the growing application of AI in education. Credibility and trust are critical in the fiercely competitive K-–12 education sector, and this study helped in clarify successful brand promotion tactics. Furthermore, investigating how AI-driven innovations affect consumer behaviour and brand perception in educational start-ups might yield insightful information for investors and entrepreneurs. By looking at these areas, the study hopes to advance our understanding of marketing and innovation in educational technology and provide helpful advice for educators, marketers, and policymakers.

Significance of the Study

This study is significant because it looks at how two critical aspects that shaped education and entrepreneurship in the future intersect. It is crucial to start-ups' success to comprehend how they market their brands in the K–12 educational space, particularly when incorporating AI-driven advancements. By looking into this subject, the study can provide insights into successful marketing tactics designed to help educational start-ups stand out in a crowded industry. Moreover, as AI increasingly becomes a central component of educational technology, examining its influence on brand promotion in this context can provide valuable guidance for both start-up founders and educators. Ultimately, the findings of this study can contribute to developing more targeted and impactful branding and marketing approaches for K–12 educational start-ups, fostering innovation and improvement in the education sector.

Conceptual Framework

Figure 1. Conceptual framework

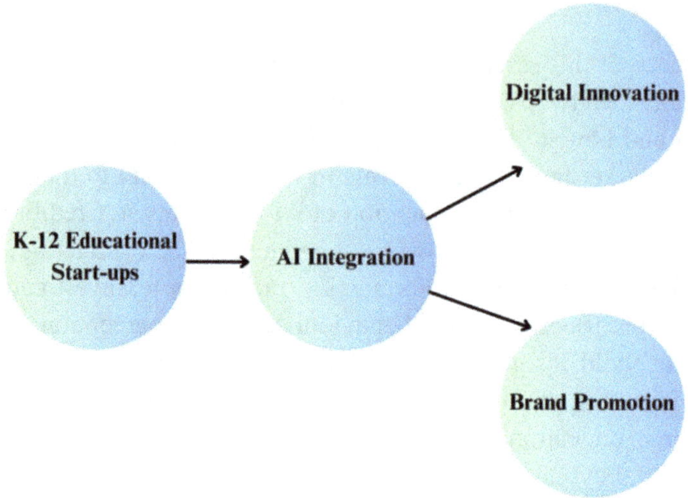

Brand Promotion and AI-Driven Innovation in K-12 Educational Start-ups" provides a conceptual framework that clarifies the relationship between brand promotion tactics and the uptake and performance of AI-driven innovations in the K–12 education space. To comprehend how strong branding improves the adoption of AI-driven solutions in educational start-ups, it emphasises the relationship between branding and the integration of AI technologies.

The Rationale of the Study

The goal of this study was to better understand how new educational start-ups handle brand promotion in a rapidly evolving environment. It's critical to investigate how these advances affect branding tactics in K–12 start-ups, given the growing integration of AI technologies in education. This research attempts to close this gap by investigating the connection between AI-driven innovation and brand marketing in K–12 educational start-ups. Through research on this subject, the researchers can learn about the best strategies for startups looking to build and market their brands in the education sector while accounting for the impact of artificial intelligence (AI) technologies. Start-up owners, marketers, and educators found great assistance in this research when creating tactics that improve brand awareness, legitimacy, and efficacy in addressing K–12 audiences.

Scope and Utility of the Study

The primary goal of this study is to investigate the marketing tactics used by K–12 educational start-ups to establish their brands, especially in light of AI-driven advancements in the field. Examining how the incorporation of AI technologies affects other brand promotion strategies, like content marketing, social media marketing, and partnerships, is part of the scope of the study. The influence that consumer behaviour and the acceptance of AI-driven educational products and services are subject to is another area that the project were investigated. This research is useful because it offers takeaways that entrepreneurs, marketers, and educators can use to create branding plans that work in K–12 education and take advantage of artificial intelligence advancements. It eventually encouraged innovation and improvement in the educational offerings for K–12 students by increasing brand visibility, legitimacy, and market competitiveness.

REVIEW OF LITERATURE

Digital Innovation in K-12 Educational Start-ups

Digital Innovation in K-12 Educational Start-ups" explores the transformative impact of digital technologies on educational entrepreneurship. This study investigates how start-ups in the K-12 sector leverage digital innovations to enhance learning experiences and educational outcomes. Digital innovation has been utilized and heavily advertised in education as a set of tools and services that enhance student learning by providing more interesting courses (Cavanagh, 2013). It facilitates individualised instruction and also lowers total school spending by facilitating more effective teaching and administration (Danniels & Pyle, 2023). Edtech companies use a variety of marketing techniques, such as placing advertisements in teacher journals, providing schools and individual instructors with "free" software items, and supporting trade exhibitions (Player-Koro et al., 2018), where educators can get information about the benefits and products of edtech (Kandlhofer et al., 2016). According to Noonoo (2018), the annual conference of the International Society for Technology in Education in 2018 brought 6,000 representatives from tech businesses in addition to over 18,000 guests from 87 countries. Edtech is changing education in ways that can put teachers in a less controllable position (Singer, 2015, 2017; Singer and Ivory, 2017). How a lesson is delivered and how students interact with the content are influenced by the software program that is used. Applications for personalised learning could steer pupils in various directions other than those that the teacher would have anticipated 1002 Policy Futures in Education, 17(8) (Roberts-

Mahoney et al., 2016). Since schools are in charge of safeguarding student and teacher data, edtech involves the transfer of such data to private enterprises, which raises privacy issues and potential legal ramifications (Peterson, 2016; Reidenberg et al., 2013; Zeide, 2017). Ultimately, the use of this data to improve edtech products means modifying instructors less and students more in the process. With the hope that this beta testing enhanced the products and, consequently, student learning, ed-tech companies frequently collaborate with educational institutions to evaluate new products. However, these businesses are also using instructors and students to test their products simultaneously (Cavanagh, 2013).

Algorithms are used by tech programmes, which adapt them based on student usage and make changes. An analysis of the business variables driving ed-tech seems warranted given the enormous effects that ed-tech is poised to have on K–12 education and the political support for technology in the classroom. Four major actor groups have played a significant role in edtech advocacy (Rahman, Lal, & Ratna, 2022). There are well-off foundations that feel that technology provides instruments to enhance children's educational experiences and are worried about the status of the US educational system as the most important first group (Baltodano, 2017; Hess and Henig, 2015; Reckhow, 2013). These benevolent capitalists include the Chan Zuckerberg Initiative, the Carnegie Foundation, and the Bill & Melinda Gates Foundation. The digital giants themselves, such as Google, Facebook, Microsoft, and Apple, represent the second group. They are the ones creating and promoting products meant for use in K–12 schools (Singer, 2015, 2017; Singer and Ivory, 2017). Education publishers like Pearson and McGraw Hill are the third group; they provide software and online resources that are adapted from their print materials. Lastly, venture capitalists (VCs) are making investments in tech start-ups because they perceive growth potential in the education industry. This study focused on analysing the latter category, which has gotten less attention than the other three (Hogan et al., 2016). There has been a rise in investment in tech goods and activities across all education categories, including K–12, business, adult, and postsecondary education. Initially, funding for edtech was mostly directed towards massive open online courses (MOOCs) in higher education. Before 2000, the education industry had a rough start, with many businesses collapsing during the 2001 stock market crisis. However, by 2010, patterns indicated that an increasing number of investors and entrepreneurs were revisiting K–12 education. K–12 tech firms have received unprecedented amounts of funding in terms of cash and transactions over the past six years.

Applicability of Brand Promotional Strategies in K-12 Educational Start-ups

An analysis of the application of brand promotional strategies in K–12 educational start-ups looks at how marketing strategies are used by educational start-ups focusing on K–12 education. In the competitive field of educational entrepreneurship, this study investigates the efficacy of several brand promotion techniques. Building a brand and its promotion is crucial for every start-up (Rahman, Lal, & Rena, 2024). When multiple products with identical features are offered, it facilitates the customers' ability to identify and decide which one to buy. According to a research study by Allen et al., (2018) nine out of ten consumers prefer to buy from well-known brands. They are also well-known because their emblems and insignia can be seen on a variety of prominent platforms, like Byju's and many others, or because customers watch their advertising multiple times a day (Lal, 2023). In the views of Allen et al., (2018) although branding makes the goods easier to identify, brand marketing helps consumers form a strong, favourable opinion of the company. Furthermore, advertising a brand helps consumers believe that its goods and services are the best available for whatever need they may have while also fostering customer trust. People frequently select that brand while making purchases as a result. Moreover, Kapoor (2021) suggested that by reaching audiences who have never heard of a brand, marketers may extend their target market, lower the cost of acquiring new customers, raise brand awareness, and do much more. Using brand promotion to boost sales and revenue during the Indian Premier League (IPL), which has a high brand value and a global viewership, has several advantages. Web 2.0 has emerged in the last ten years, particularly in the social network space. A lot of sectors have been drawn to use the social network as a marketing tool because of its vast user base (Lal & Sharma, 2021). Additionally, there are free services available, and the creation of income is reliant on both the marketing and the content. Web 2.0 helps websites and users exchange information, and social media platforms are drawing interest from academics because they help define individual profiles, make social media information about users accessible, and provide information that helps understand user behaviour (Mata & Quesada, 2014). Chua and Parackal (2009) stated in the survey that blogs are mostly utilised to comprehend the leadership philosophies of the leaders; yet, in this day of fierce competition, Facebook, Twitter, and Instagram have emerged as essential branding tools. Twitter and Facebook have been essential in helping firms stay in close contact with their customers and create a feeling of community among them. By engaging with the brand they already use, they satisfy the human need for interaction (Mata & Quesada, 2014). Lipsman et al. (2012) examined the influence of social media advertising on branding, researchers hypothesised that social media can assist in carrying out several tasks from a brand's point of view, including “sponsored stories,” a Facebook advertisement unit, and connections re-sharing material. Within Facebook's new feed category, branded content is heavily utilised. Fans and their connections make up the two main audience types that it focuses on. Brands may use the potential of unexplored market niches through the Facebook platform.

Challenges and Opportunities for K-12 Educational Start-ups

Even while technologies are being used more and more in practically every industry, there are still major obstacles standing in the way of their successful integration in educational settings. Chokhani (2017) discussed the traditional system of schools being weakened by administrative problems involving teachers, pupils, and school administrators, which are a result of the various demographics and large school landscape. Furthermore, parents are not as involved as they may be and the classroom lacks personalisation for the diverse group of students. Indian startups first have to deal with the fundamentals: finding and managing employees, handling customers, and creating a marketing plan. A large number of Indian entrepreneurs lack commercial acumen and come from non-technical backgrounds. Aggarwal, (2017) although skilled labour is not in short supply in India, entrepreneurs are not always able to afford them. Nonetheless, it is frequently quite challenging to locate the multiskill required to produce start-up success stories. A start-up requires a large sum of working cash to operate. Many start-ups, especially those in their early stages, are bootstrapped, meaning that their founders support the business entirely from their resources or by taking out loans from friends and family. Tests can yield a range of questions, the solutions that are vitally needed by all companies. However, because of response times or budgetary limitations, they are often disregarded or stagnant. Startups need outside funding, and many of them start their hunt for backers as soon as they decide to grow. Even if they have received positive feedback on their product and have some evidence of market validation, it can be challenging to find the proper investor and raise money. Establishing a company in India adds additional obstacles to getting products on the market because Indian marketplaces are difficult to break into. Iwasiuk, (2016) one element is the competitive climate, which is characterised by a large number of enterprises that are either already established or are entering the market, including copycats. The disadvantages faced by startups in comparison to more established companies constitute a second element. The rationale for this is that governments like to enter into contracts with well-established enterprises, public procurement is perceived as weak, and huge market actors are more adept at adhering to administrative regulations. The time and work necessary for maintaining contact and client retention make up a third factor. Indian consumers could be difficult to convince, especially if the start-up produces unique products and focuses on untapped market sectors. Aggarwal (2017) suggested that the developing demand for their products and services can sometimes be difficult for entrepreneurs. Even if earnings are improving, the Indian consumer base is still price-sensitive and has a low willingness to pay for goods and services Aggarwal(2017). Startups often struggle to balance affordability with quality while developing solutions (Teece, 2017). Many startups have low earnings and are motivated by volume for this reason. Obtaining and guaranteeing timely payment may present a challenge for startups that do not charge customers using digital payment methods (Burton & Basiliere, 2016).

Integration of AI for Digital Innovation Strategies

According to Burton & Basiliere (2016), a business-driven structure known as a "digital platform" enables a network of suppliers, partners, and clients to exchange and improve digital capabilities and processes or to expand them for mutual gain. Organizations must drive their businesses to adopt an outside-in, data-driven approach to develop a digital business platform (Evans & Gawer, 2016). Interactive and adaptable digital business exchanges are enabled by digital business platforms. These kinds of platforms allow for the disruption of multifaceted marketplaces by using digital resources, channels, and capabilities. Diffuse platform network effects, or externalities, are thus produced by digital business innovation. Leiblein (2018) defined platform innovation as being used to describe modifications to support systems that improve the efficiency with which a set of tasks may be carried out on a platform. Innovation in product platforms involves making adjustments to a shared part or body of knowledge that might be applied to several products (Hogan et al., 2016).

Innovation in industry platforms involves adjusting the laws, regulations, and infrastructure to facilitate interactions between different companies (Burton & Basiliere, 2016). Applications and business capability elements of the business platform technology stack that digital technology platforms provide are used to characterise these platforms (Yablonsky, 2018ab, 2020). Through the above-described viewpoint, which involves the applications and business capability components of a digital business platform and the technological stack they enable, AI-driven platform innovation can be generated. It aims to give a high-level summary of the essential competencies required to put together an AI-driven platform innovation in the stack of digital business platforms. Platform capabilities are more closely linked to the business model, leadership, and talent platforms (Teece, 2017). A company's affiliates having access to a larger ecosystem or ecosystem communities of actors with professional, academic, or experiential knowledge in a variety of geographical and disciplinary fields using these organisations, which aim to facilitate knowledge exchange in business model and leadership environments (Boudreau, 2010; Boudreau et al., 2011; Colombo et al., 2013; Colombo et al., 2015; Evans & Gawer, 2016). A business model's and a leadership platform's main functions are to gather information from disparate sources, reassemble it, support management and creativity, and adapt it to new organisational and technological contexts. To allow, support, and manage a digital business, new capabilities are needed for the delivery of a digital platform business (Burton & Basiliere, 2016). The variations in a company's digital business performance may stem from variations in the resources and capabilities of its platform when compared to competitors in the market. Some articles discussed how AI can be used in conjunction with business strategy to create new goods and services. Feldmann et al., (2013) thought of using AI to facilitate machine-to-machine communication in new organisational opportunities, but their proposals were rejected. On the other hand, some academics concluded that companies have benefited from the creation of new products and the provision of new services. The most significant impact of intelligent technologies is their capacity to direct innovation straight into the industrial sector. AI is quickly rebuilding services, carrying out new tasks, emerging as a major source of innovation, and creating chances for creative human-machine interaction (Kohler et al., 2014).

RESEARCH METHODOLOGY

Research Design

The research applies a qualitative design to thoroughly examine the brand marketing methods, potential for digital innovation, and integration of artificial intelligence (AI) in K-12 educational start-ups. The qualitative component were included conducting in-depth interviews, which were then used to develop case studies. This approach guarantees a strong grasp of both the intricate, situational aspects of the subject and the wider, applicable patterns.

Research Frame

The research frame centres around educational start-ups that utilise AI technology and cater to students in grades K-12. This frame covers start-ups that use AI to improve educational outcomes, create innovative digital learning experiences, and implement unique brand marketing strategies. The study aims to capture the unique challenges and opportunities faced by these start-ups in a rapidly evolving technological landscape by focusing on this specific segment.

Sampling Technique

To ensure a cohesive and logical approach, the researchers used purposive sampling to select educational start-ups that are making significant use of AI for their operations and marketing. This technique guarantees that the chosen participants possess pertinent and valuable information that aligns with the study objectives. To ensure a comprehensive representation of various subgroups within the educational start-up ecosystem, the quantitative component was employ a stratified random sampling technique. This technique encompassed start-ups at different stages of growth and with varying levels of AI integration.

Sampling Criteria

The qualitative sample consisted of educational start-ups operating in the K-12 sector that utilise AI in their educational or operational processes and have an active brand marketing strategy. Start-ups that have been registered and operational within the past five years, showcasing a certain level of AI implementation and actively participating in digital innovation practices.

Sample Size

The qualitative sample included 25 in-depth interviews with founders or key executives from selected start-ups, along with 3 detailed case studies. The aim is to ensure a cohesive and logical approach to gathering information.

Context

The research was carried out within the framework of the ever-changing landscape of educational technology, with a specific emphasis on the incorporation of AI and digital innovation in K-12 education. The study examined the interplay between socio-economic and technological factors in start-ups, specifically focusing on their effects on brand marketing strategies and educational outcomes.

Reflexivity

Throughout the research process, we made sure to maintain reflexivity to acknowledge and address any biases that the researchers may have had. The researchers were committed to maintaining a high level of coherence and logical flow in their work. They diligently engaged in continuous self-reflection and kept a reflexive journal to document their decisions, assumptions, and potential biases. By ensuring that the research findings are cohesive and logically presented, the credibility and authenticity of the study greatly enhanced.

Research Phases

The research was conducted in several phases:

Table 1. Phases of case analysis

S.No	Phase	Description	Case Study 1: WitBlox	Case Study 2:Schooglink	Case Study 3: EdCalibre
1.	Foundation Phase	Determine the purpose, scope, and objectives of the case study. Identify the essential metrics and objectives.	Discover brand promotion strategies, digital innovation, and AI integration in K-12 EdTech start-ups. Metrics: measuring levels of engagement, customer loyalty, and student performance.	Ensure rural K-12 students in India get high-quality, accessible education. The impact of education, the scope of educational efforts, and student involvement are measured.	Transform maths education by incorporating practical situations and engaging narratives. Metrics: Student engagement, learning outcomes, scalability.
2.	Pre-feild Phase	Collect the required background information and historical data. Establishing key performance indicators and setting targets is crucial for measuring success and progress.	Background: A start-up based in Mumbai that focuses on K-12 EdTech. Goals-Explore brand promotion, digital innovation, and the integration of AI. Key performance indicators: engagement and customer loyalty.	Background: Utilizing a tech-driven blended learning approach based in Bangalore. Goals-Improve educational opportunities in underserved communities through the use of technology. Metrics to consider: learning outcomes and educational reach.	Ahmedabad-based, focusing on practical math education. Goals-Enhance math education through the use of engaging stories and innovative digital resources. Metrics to consider: Student engagement and learning outcomes.
3.	Field Phase	Gather information, examine trends, and implement techniques. Utilize advanced tools, such as AI, to enhance predictive analytics.	Approaches: engaging content, fostering a sense of community, and utilizing AI to tailor learning experiences. Findings: increased levels of interaction, enhanced academic achievement, and the ability to expand.	Approaches: blended learning (online and offline), vernacular content, personalised learning paths. Findings: Enhanced academic achievements, expanded educational access, and increased empowerment of students in rural areas.	Approaches: incorporating storytelling into mathematical exercises, and developing educational applications for web and mobile platforms. Findings: increased ease of understanding abstract concepts and heightened student interest in involvement.
4.	Reporting Phase	Record the discoveries, outcomes, and influence of the case study. Discuss the difficulties and possible resolutions. Guide effective strategies.	Discoveries: digital breakthroughs, client loyalty, and technological triumphs. Community involvement could grow. Challenges: Data accuracy and expertise are required.	Educational gaps closed, and rural students' tech use improved. Opportunities: regional increase. Troubles with connectivity and resources.	Discoveries: math education breakthroughs, patent potential, student involvement. Potential: expanding narrative strategies. Financial backing and assembling a skilled crew are challenges.

Source: (Stake, 2013) Author's Compilation

Qualitative Data Analysis Techniques

The researchers used thematic analysis to analyse the qualitative data gathered from interviews and case studies. This technique requires coding the data to identify recurring themes, patterns, and insights cohesively and logically. The process involved becoming acquainted with the data, creating initial codes, identifying themes, evaluating themes, defining and labelling themes, and ultimately producing the final report.

Analysis Process in Detail

Table 2. Analysis process

S.no	Analysis Process	Description
1.	Knowledge of data	Transcribed interviews and studied qualitative data several times to learn it. Made first notes and observations.
2.	Initial Coding	Utilized open coding to categorise major components of the data, emphasising patterns and noteworthy aspects.
3.	Development of themes	Organized codes into possible themes, collecting all relevant data excerpts for each theme.
4.	Examining Themes	Streamlined the themes to ensure they accurately reflect the data, combining or dividing themes as needed.
5.	Establishing Themes	Provided a clear definition of each theme and explained its relevance to the research questions.
6.	Concluding Evaluation	Created a narrative that effectively connects the themes and demonstrates their relevance to the research objectives.
7.	Reporting	Organized the themes and findings in a well-structured report, backing them up with data to strengthen their validity.

Source: (Stake,2013) Author's Compilation

The research aims to provide a comprehensive understanding of AI-driven educational start-ups, their brand marketing strategies, digital innovation capacities, and the associated challenges and opportunities. Following organized methodologies helped with this.

Case Study Development Process

The process of developing a case study to investigate AI-driven innovation and brand promotion in K-12 educational start-ups follows a systematic approach to ensure thorough data collection and gain deep insights into each case.

Case Selection

To develop a case study, it is important to carefully choose cases that are representative and relevant. To ensure a cohesive and logically structured approach, it is important to establish specific criteria for inclusion. This may include factors such as actively incorporating AI into educational services, implementing unique brand promotion strategies, and having access to comprehensive performance and marketing data. We identify potential start-ups by analysing industry reports, and academic articles, and conducting in-depth interviews with experts. The candidates are carefully evaluated against the established criteria to create a shortlist of start-ups that align with the research objectives.

Data Collection

After selecting the cases, the next crucial step involves gathering comprehensive and detailed data from various sources. Conducting in-depth interviews with key stakeholders, including founders, marketing managers, and technology officers, offers valuable insights into the strategies and experiences of start-ups. To gain a comprehensive understanding of the start-ups, we gather internal documents, marketing materials, strategic plans, and performance reports. This allows us to delve into both the operational and strategic aspects of the business. Wherever possible, we conduct observations of the start-ups' operations, marketing activities, and AI applications to ensure a cohesive and logical understanding. Data on key performance indicators, such as click-through rates (CTR), conversion rates, and return on advertising spend (ROAS), are collected to offer a comprehensive perspective on each case.

Data Organization

Following the completion of data collection, the information is meticulously arranged to facilitate a comprehensive analysis. The data is sorted into categories based on themes like AI integration, brand promotion strategies, challenges, and outcomes. Comprehensive case files are generated for every start-up, which encompasses interview transcripts, document copies, and observation records. NVivo, a software for qualitative data analysis, enables efficient storage, management, and analysis of data.

Data Analysis

Now, we need to carefully examine the structured data to uncover any recurring patterns, themes, or valuable insights that directly relate to the research questions at hand. To ensure a cohesive and logical approach, it is important to start by thoroughly reviewing all collected materials multiple times to familiarise oneself with the data. The data is analysed using open coding to identify patterns and key points, allowing for a cohesive and logical labelling of significant parts. The codes are organised into themes, with corresponding data excerpts for each theme. The themes have been carefully refined to accurately represent the data, with any necessary collapsing or splitting of themes. The themes are well-defined and connected to the research questions, resulting in a logical and cohesive narrative for each case. The themes are integrated and tied to the research objectives.

Cross-Case Analysis

After examining individual cases, a cross-case analysis is performed to compare and contrast the findings across different cases. This helps to identify common patterns and unique variations. This requires analysing themes across cases to find similarities and differences, as well as identifying patterns that arise across multiple cases. It also involves highlighting the factors that impact the success of AI integration and brand promotion. Each case is carefully analysed to determine how different conditions affect the final results.

Synthesis and Reporting

Now, let's bring together all the findings and create a report that is comprehensive and provides actionable insights, addressing all the research questions. This requires bringing together the findings from individual cases to form a logical understanding of larger patterns and insights. The findings of the study are thoroughly discussed, highlighting their implications for theory, practice, and future research. Additionally, practical recommendations are offered for start-ups and policymakers, drawing upon the study's findings. The final research report is crafted to provide comprehensive descriptions of each case, thorough cross-case analysis, and synthesised insights.

Through a well-organized case study development process, the research seeks to offer a detailed and thorough insight into how K-12 educational start-ups utilise AI to drive innovation and enhance their brand visibility. The approach used in this study ensures that the findings are based on real-life examples, providing valuable insights for practitioners and scholars in the field of educational technology.

Case Study 1

Founded in 2017, WitBlox is a Mumbai-based K-12 EdTech start-up that specialises in offering robotics and technology education. With the support of the Mumbai Angels Network, WitBlox offers a unique educational experience that emphasises social e-commerce and captivating content like comic stories and DIY videos. This creates a thriving community for aspiring tech enthusiasts. The research explores the effectiveness of brand promotion strategies, digital innovation, and AI integration in start-ups. By implementing interactive content and cultivating a sense of community, WitBlox effectively enhances engagement and cultivates unwavering customer loyalty. By successfully overcoming technical barriers, AI-driven personalised learning has significantly improved student performance and scalability, demonstrating effective digital innovation in education.

Case Study 2

Schooling Private Limited, founded in 2016, is committed to providing accessible and high-quality education to K–12 students in rural India. Schooling, based in Bangalore, employs a technology-driven blended learning approach that seamlessly integrates online platforms with offline smart classrooms. This groundbreaking model strives to ensure that education is readily available to the vast majority of Indian schools located in rural areas, encompassing around 85% of them. Schooling is committed to addressing the educational requirements of 225 million rural students through the provision of localised vernacular content. Their app, Pathyacharya, has become a well-known educational tool, enhancing learning outcomes through its captivating content and personalised learning paths. Schooglink's efforts in rural India have been highly effective in bridging educational gaps and empowering students, thanks to the generous support of numerous angel investors.

Case Study 3

Founded in 2021 in Ahmedabad, India, EdCalibre Inc. is revolutionising mathematics education with its cutting-edge practice application that focuses on real-world scenarios and captivating stories. The platform seamlessly integrates educational web and mobile applications to provide students with an engaging and practical learning experience. By seamlessly incorporating narratives into maths practice, EdCalibre breathes life into abstract concepts, enhancing their accessibility and leaving a lasting impression on students. The company is currently working on securing funds and recruiting a team of skilled professionals to improve and expand its range of services. With the support of investors like Carleton University, EdCalibre is working diligently to obtain a patent for its innovative approach, positioning itself as a frontrunner in the educational technology industry.

Table 3. Challenges and strategies

S.No.	Case Story	Challenges Faced	Strategies Implemented
1.	Founded in 2017, WitBlox is a Mumbai-based K-12 EdTech start-up that leverages AI and digital innovation to offer robotics and technology education. Thanks to the Mumbai Angels Network, WitBlox creates an engaging community and improves student performance through captivating content like comic stories and DIY videos.	Addressing technical challenges and ensuring the accuracy and proficiency needed to successfully incorporate AI into educational materials.	Utilized engaging content and fostered a sense of community through the use of comic stories and do-it-yourself videos. Utilized cutting-edge AI technology to enhance individualised learning and boost student achievement on a larger scale.
2.	In 2016, Bangalore-based Schooling Private Limited began providing high-quality K–12 education to rural Indian kids. Our distinctive combination of traditional and online teaching offers a well-rounded education. For 225 million rural students, Pathyacharya provides a localized vernacular curriculum to improve learning and close educational gaps. Angel investors backed it.	We are working towards providing accessible and high-quality education for students in rural India. Focusing on resolving connectivity challenges and delivering content in local languages.	Utilized a combination of online platforms and smart classrooms to create a blended learning environment. Created the Pathyacharya app to enhance educational experiences for students in rural areas, offering tailored content and personalised learning paths.
3.	EdCalibre Inc., founded in 2021 in Ahmedabad, offers unique maths practice software with real-world settings and fascinating stories. This solution simplifies complicated ideas and engages users by seamlessly merging web and mobile apps. Investors like Carleton University are helping acquire finance, hire competent people, and obtain a patent.	Securing funding and recruiting highly skilled professionals to enhance and broaden services. Ensuring the preservation and expansion of an innovative approach to math education.	Utilized educational web and mobile apps to incorporate real-world scenarios and engaging stories into math practice. Collaborated with a renowned academic and institution to secure a patent and enhance our offerings through the backing of esteemed investors.
4.	Common Challenges	Technical barriers, skill requirements, connectivity issues, and scalability are all important factors to consider.	Utilized cutting-edge methods such as innovative content delivery, AI integration, personalised learning, and blended learning approaches. Dedicated to securing backing from investors and guaranteeing the ongoing enhancement and expandability of services.

Source: (Stake,2013) Author's Compilation

Prioritizing data organisation is crucial for ensuring high accuracy and consistency during the cleaning and preprocessing stages. To improve the reliability of the data for analysis, any unnecessary information and irrelevant entries were eliminated. By carefully selecting specific variables, parameters were established for examination.

Table 4. Framework of case study consideration

S.No.	Philosophical Consideration	Research Logic Consideration	Ethical Consideration
1.	Highlights the game-changing possibilities of AI and digital innovation in education.	Uses a combination of qualitative and quantitative data to evaluate the effects of interactive content and personalised learning driven by AI.	Places a strong emphasis on maintaining data privacy and security in AI applications. Ensures open and honest communication with stakeholders.
2.	Emphasizes the importance of making education accessible to all and reducing educational disparities in remote regions using technology.	Blends insights from user experiences with data on learning outcomes and engagement levels.	Places a strong emphasis on ensuring accessibility and inclusivity. Ensures that the content is sensitive to local cultures and respects local sensitivities.
3.	Leaders need new methods to enhance accessibility and engagement in education, particularly for abstract concepts.	Utilizes a combination of research methods, blending storytelling techniques with numerical analysis of student achievement.	Promotes the responsible and moral utilisation of narratives in educational materials. Obtains informed consent from participants.

Source: (Stake,2013) Author's Compilation

DATA ANALYSIS AND INTERPRETATION

The study employs a qualitative approach to examine the integration of AI, digital innovation, and brand marketing in K–12 educational start-ups. The researchers achieved this by conducting thorough interviews and carefully analysing case studies. When selecting participants for this study, a purposive sampling approach is employed (Kumar & Lal, 2023). The focus is on start-ups that have been utilising AI technology for the past five years. By carefully choosing participants, we aim to gather valuable qualitative insights. Additionally, a stratified random sampling technique is utilised to guarantee a comprehensive and varied representation. The sample includes 25 interviews and 3 detailed case studies to capture a wide range of data cohesively and logically. Conducted in the dynamic ed-tech sector, the study delves into the impact of AI and digital innovation on educational outcomes and marketing strategies. The researchers were thorough in their efforts to maintain objectivity, minimize any potential bias, and ensure that their findings were logically consistent. Building a strong foundation is the first step in the research process, which then moves smoothly into pre-field work, fieldwork, and reporting. It encompasses different elements like data collection, trend analysis, and finding documentation. Case studies on WitBlox, Schooglink, and EdCalibre highlight innovative educational approaches and the seamless incorporation of artificial intelligence. The process of thematic analysis involves identifying recurring themes and patterns through a series of steps, starting with initial coding and ending with final reporting. We take great care in developing case studies to ensure thorough data collection, organisation, and analysis. This results in valuable insights and practical recommendations by comparing different cases. This methodology aims to provide a comprehensive understanding of AI-driven educational start-ups, emphasising their innovative approaches and addressing sector-specific challenges cohesively and logically.

CONCLUSION

The study employs a qualitative approach to examine the integration of AI, digital innovation, and brand marketing in K-12 educational start-ups. The researchers achieved the results by conducting thorough interviews and carefully analysing case studies. When selecting participants for this study, a purposive sampling approach is employed. The focus is on start-ups that have been utilising AI technology for the past five years. By carefully choosing participants, we aim to gather a valuable study, "Brand Promotion and AI-Driven Innovation in K-12 Educational Start-ups" that delves into the integration of artificial intelligence (AI) and digital innovation in educational start-ups, emphasizing brand marketing's role in enhancing these efforts. Through qualitative analysis, including interviews and case studies, the research examines the impact of AI on operational efficiency and educational outcomes, identifying both challenges and benefits. The study finds that AI-driven innovation significantly improves educational customization, operational efficiency, and data management. However, challenges such as data privacy concerns, resistance to new methodologies, and high implementation costs persist. Despite these obstacles, AI integration in K-12 education shows promise for substantial rewards, including personalized learning experiences tailored to individual student needs and enhanced analytical capabilities for tracking learning patterns and trends. Brand promotion is crucial in this context, as effective branding strategies can drive the adoption and success of AI-powered educational solutions. The research identifies that active community participation and tailored learning approaches significantly boost branding efforts. By leveraging social media marketing, content development, and strategic partnerships, educational start-ups can enhance their visibility and credibility in the competitive ed-tech market. The research highlights the need for a holistic approach combining AI, digital innovation, and branding to transform K-12 education. Successful implementation of these strategies requires thorough strategic planning and active stakeholder engagement to navigate and overcome the inherent challenges. The case studies of start-ups like WitBlox, Schooglink, and EdCalibre illustrate innovative educational methods and the seamless integration of AI. These examples underscore the potential for AI-driven start-ups to revolutionize K-12 education by providing tailored, efficient, and scalable solutions. In conclusion, AI and brand promotion synergistically enhance the capabilities and market reach of K-12 educational start-ups. Addressing data privacy issues, cost barriers, and resistance to innovation is critical. Ultimately, a comprehensive strategy that merges AI technology, digital innovation, and effective branding can lead to significant advancements and growth opportunities in the educational technology sector.

REFERENCES

Allen, C. T., Fournier, S., & Miller, F. (2018). Brands and their meaning makers. In *Handbook of consumer psychology* (pp. 773–814).

Baker, T., Smith, L., & Anissa, N. (2019). *Educ-AI-tion rebooted? Exploring the future of artificial intelligence in schools and colleges*. Nesta Foundation.

Baltodano, M. P. (2017). The power brokers of neoliberalism: Philanthrocapitalists and public education. *Policy Futures in Education, 15*(2), 141–156. DOI: 10.1177/1478210316652008

Burton, B., & Basiliere, P. (2016). *Architect digital platforms to deliver business value and outcomes* (Gartner Report No. G00318861). Gartner.

Cavanagh, S. (2013, April 22). Beta testing ed. products can get tricky for schools. *Education Week*. https://www.edweek.org/ew/articles/2013/04/24/29ii-betatest.h32.html

Chokhani, R. (2017). Challenges and opportunities for Indian start-ups: Key points to note.

Danniels, E., & Pyle, A. (2023). Inclusive play-based learning: Approaches from enacting kindergarten teachers. *Early Childhood Education Journal, 51*(7), 1169–1179. DOI: 10.1007/s10643-022-01369-4 PMID: 35755935

Evans, P. C., & Gawer, A. (2016). *The rise of the platform enterprise: A global survey*. Center for Global Enterprise.

Feldmann, N., Kohler, M., Kimbrough, S. O., & Fromm, H. (2013). Service innovation analytics: Towards an approach for validating frameworks for service innovation capabilities via text mining. In Falcão e Cunha, J., Snene, M., & Nóvoa, H. (Eds.), *Exploring services science (IESS 2013)*. Springer. DOI: 10.1007/978-3-642-36356-6_6

Hess, F. M., & Henig, J. R. (Eds.). (2015). *The new education philanthropy: Politics, policy, and reform*. Harvard Education Press.

Hogan, A., Sellar, S., & Lingard, B. (2016). Commercialising comparison: Pearson puts the TLC in soft capitalism. *Journal of Education Policy, 31*(3), 243–258. DOI: 10.1080/02680939.2015.1112922

Iwasiuk, D. (2016). Key challenges, opportunities for tech startups in emerging markets. *Moneycontrol.com*.

Kajiwara, Y., Matsuoka, A., & Shinbo, F. (2023). Machine learning role-playing game: Instructional design of AI education for age-appropriate in K–12 and beyond. *Computers and Education: Artificial Intelligence*, *5*, 100162. DOI: 10.1016/j.caeai.2023.100162

Kandlhofer, M., Steinbauer, G., Hirschmugl-Gaisch, S., & Huber, P. (2016). Artificial intelligence and computer science in education: From kindergarten to university. In *2016 IEEE Frontiers in Education Conference (FIE)* (pp. 1–9). IEEE.

Kapoor, N. (2021). *Principles of marketing*. PHI Learning Pvt. Ltd.

Kohler, M., Feldmann, N., Kimbrough, S. O., & Fromm, H. (2014). Service innovation analytics: Leveraging existing unstructured data to assess service innovation capability. *International Journal of Information System Modeling and Design*, *5*(2), 1–21. DOI: 10.4018/ijismd.2014040101

Kumar, D., & Lal, R. (2023). Technological advancements in the media industry and the current job market in India. In Naim, A. (Ed.), *Accreditation processes and frameworks in higher education* (pp. 289–314). Nova Science Publishers.

Lal, R. (2023). New measures of teaching, learning, and evaluating with changing technology. In Naim, A. (Ed.), *Accreditation processes and frameworks in higher education* (pp. 267–287). Nova Science Publishers.

Lal, R., & Sharma, G. (2021). Social media influencers for online purchase behaviour: Mediation by brand consciousness. *Journal of Content. Community & Communication*, *13*(7), 83–94.

Leiblein, M. J. (2018). Platform innovation. In Augier, M., & Teece, D. J. (Eds.), *The Palgrave encyclopedia of strategic management*. DOI: 10.1057/978-1-137-00772-8_363

Mata, F. J., & Quesada, A. (2014). Web 2.0, social networks and e-commerce as marketing tools. *Journal of Theoretical and Applied Electronic Commerce Research*, *9*(1), 56–69. DOI: 10.4067/S0718-18762014000100006

Noonoo, S. (2018, June 28). All the upgrades and updates from Apple, Google and more at ISTE 2018. *EdSurge*. https://www.edsurge.com/news/2018-06-28-all-the-upgrades-and-updates-from-apple-google-and-more-at-iste-2018

Peterson, D. (2016). Edtech and student privacy: California law as a model. *Berkeley Technology Law Journal*, *31*(2).

Player-Koro, C., Rensfeldt, A. B., & Selwyn, N. (2018). Selling tech to teachers: Education trade shows as policy events. *Journal of Education Policy, 33*(5), 682–703. DOI: 10.1080/02680939.2017.1380232

Rahman, Z. T., Lal, R., & Ratna, R. (2022). An analytical study on the significance of folk and fairytales on the psychology of young children. *International Journal of Early Childhood Special Education, 14*(5).

Rahman, Z. T., Lal, R., & Rena, R. (2024). Challenges of communication with Gen-Z in the era of artificial intelligence-interceded digital economy. In *AI-oriented competency framework for talent management in the digital economy* (pp. 76–94). CRC Press. DOI: 10.1201/9781003440901-5

Reckhow, S. (2013). *Follow the money: How foundation dollars change public school politics*. Oxford University Press.

Reidenberg, J., Russell, N. C., Kovnot, J., et al. (2013). *Privacy and cloud computing in public schools*. Fordham Law School, Center on Law and Information Policy.

Roberts-Mahoney, H., Means, A. J., & Garrison, M. J. (2016). Netflixing human capital development: Personalized learning technology and the corporatization of K–12 education. *Journal of Education Policy, 31*(4), 405–420. DOI: 10.1080/02680939.2015.1132774

Singer, N. (2015, January 11). Silicon Valley turns its eye to education. *The New York Times*. https://www.nytimes.com/2015/01/12/technology/silicon-valley-turns-its-eye-to-education.html

Singer, N., & Ivory, D. (2017). How Silicon Valley plans to conquer the classroom. *The New York Times*.

Teece, D. J. (2017). Dynamic capabilities and (digital) platform lifecycles. In *Entrepreneurship, innovation, and platforms*.

Wikipedia contributors. (n.d.). Start-up company. In *Wikipedia*. https://en.wikipedia.org/wiki/Start-up_company

Yablonsky, S. (2018a). A multidimensional framework for digital platform innovation and management: From business to technological platforms. *Systems Research and Behavioral Science, 35*(4), 485–501. DOI: 10.1002/sres.2544

Yablonsky, S. (2018b). *Multi-sided platforms (MSPs) and sharing strategies in the digital economy: Emerging research and opportunities*.

Zeide, E. (2017). The limits of student purpose limitations. *University of Miami Law Review, 71*(2).

Chapter 4

Defining an AI-Based K-12 Education System

Chengen Li
INTI International University, Malaysia

Huimin Wangwan
http://orcid.org/0009-0007-5393-296X
Yunnan College of Finance and Economics, China

ABSTRACT

This chapter provides a comprehensive analysis of the current trends and emerging perspectives on the application of Artificial Intelligence (AI) within K-12 education. It explores how AI technologies are integrated into educational systems, evaluating their effectiveness and impact on teaching and learning processes. The chapter delves into various AI tools, such as adaptive learning platforms and intelligent tutoring systems, and their role in personalized learning and curriculum integration. Additionally, it addresses key challenges, including ethical concerns, data privacy issues, and teacher preparedness, offering strategies to overcome these barriers. Future perspectives on AI's role in education, potential innovations, and policy frameworks are also discussed, providing valuable insights for educators, policymakers, and researchers.

1. INTRODUCTION

Artificial Intelligence (AI) is revolutionizing various sectors, and education is no exception. In K-12 education, AI is being leveraged to enhance learning experiences, personalize education, and improve educational outcomes. This chapter provides a comprehensive analysis of the current trends and emerging perspectives

DOI: 10.4018/979-8-3693-6346-1.ch004

on the application of AI within K-12 education. It explores how AI technologies are integrated into educational systems, evaluates their effectiveness, and discusses the challenges and future prospects of AI in this field.

AI technologies are transforming the educational landscape by providing innovative solutions to long-standing challenges. For instance, AI can offer personalized learning experiences tailored to the individual needs of students, thereby helping them to learn at their own pace and in their preferred style. Adaptive learning platforms, for example, use AI algorithms to analyze student performance and provide customized feedback and resources, which can significantly enhance learning outcomes (Holstein et al., 2019).

Moreover, AI-driven tools are being used to automate administrative tasks, thus allowing teachers to focus more on instruction and student engagement. For instance, AI can handle grading and provide detailed analytics on student performance, which helps teachers to identify areas where students need additional support (Luckin et al., 2016). This shift not only improves efficiency but also contributes to a more personalized and effective educational experience for students.

The integration of AI in education also extends to intelligent tutoring systems that provide one-on-one tutoring experiences similar to human tutors. These systems are capable of understanding and responding to the unique learning needs of each student, thereby offering targeted instruction and support (Burns et al., 2020). Such personalized attention can be particularly beneficial in addressing learning gaps and promoting deeper understanding of subject matter.

However, the deployment of AI in K-12 education is not without challenges. Ethical concerns, such as data privacy and the potential for bias in AI algorithms, must be carefully managed to ensure that AI tools are used responsibly and equitably. Additionally, there is a need for adequate teacher training and support to enable educators to effectively integrate AI technologies into their teaching practices (Gardner-McCune & Touretzky, 2021).

Despite these challenges, the future of AI in K-12 education looks promising. Emerging trends suggest that AI will play an increasingly significant role in various aspects of education, from curriculum development to student assessment and teacher training. By harnessing the power of AI, educators can create more engaging, efficient, and personalized learning environments that better meet the needs of all students (Zawacki-Richter et al., 2019).

2. OVERVIEW OF AI IN K-12 EDUCATION

(1) Definition and Applications of AI

Artificial Intelligence (AI) refers to the simulation of human intelligence in machines programmed to think and learn like humans. In the context of K-12 education, AI encompasses various technologies designed to improve teaching and learning processes. These include intelligent tutoring systems, adaptive learning platforms, AI-driven assessment tools, and more. The integration of AI in education aims to enhance the learning experience by providing personalized, efficient, and effective educational solutions (Holstein et al., 2019).

(2) AI Technologies in K-12 Education

AI technologies are increasingly being adopted in K-12 education, with several applications demonstrating significant potential to transform traditional educational practices:

a. Adaptive Learning Platforms: These platforms use AI algorithms to analyze student performance and learning behaviors, providing customized exercises and real-time feedback tailored to individual student needs. This personalization helps students learn at their own pace and style, ultimately enhancing learning outcomes (Luckin et al., 2016).
b. Intelligent Tutoring Systems: Intelligent tutoring systems (ITS) offer one-on-one tutoring experiences similar to human tutors. These systems can adapt to the unique learning needs of each student, providing targeted instruction and support. ITS have been shown to improve student understanding and retention of subject matter, making them a valuable tool in the classroom (Burns et al., 2020).
c. AI-Based Assessment Tools: AI-driven assessment tools facilitate automated grading and provide detailed analytics on student performance. These tools can identify learning gaps and provide insights into areas where students need additional support. This not only saves time for teachers but also ensures that students receive timely and accurate feedback (Holstein et al., 2019).
d. Chatbots and Virtual Assistants: Chatbots and virtual assistants are used to provide administrative support and assist students with queries. These AI tools can answer common questions, guide students through learning resources, and even help with homework, thereby reducing the administrative burden on teachers and enhancing student engagement (Zawacki-Richter et al., 2019).

e. AI in Classroom Management: AI technologies are also being utilized to manage classroom activities more efficiently. For instance, AI can help in scheduling, attendance tracking, and managing student behavior. By automating these tasks, teachers can focus more on instruction and interaction with students (Gardner-McCune & Touretzky, 2021).
f. AI for Special Education: AI is playing a crucial role in special education by providing personalized learning experiences for students with disabilities. AI-powered tools can adapt learning materials to meet the specific needs of these students, offering a more inclusive educational environment (Kali et al., 2020).

(3) Benefits of AI in K-12 Education

The integration of AI in K-12 education offers numerous benefits:

a. Personalized Learning: AI technologies enable personalized learning experiences by adapting to the unique needs of each student. This helps in addressing individual learning gaps and promoting better understanding of the subject matter (Luckin et al., 2016).
b. Enhanced Student Engagement: AI tools can make learning more interactive and engaging. By incorporating elements such as gamification and virtual reality, AI can create immersive learning experiences that motivate students to participate actively in their education (Burns et al., 2020).
c. Data-Driven Insights: AI provides valuable data-driven insights that can inform teaching strategies and curriculum development. By analyzing student performance data, AI can help educators identify trends and patterns, enabling them to make informed decisions to improve educational outcomes (Holstein et al., 2019).
d. Improved Efficiency: AI can automate routine administrative tasks, allowing teachers to focus more on instruction and student support. This not only enhances efficiency but also reduces the workload of teachers, enabling them to provide more personalized attention to students (Gardner-McCune & Touretzky, 2021).
e. Support for Teachers: AI tools can assist teachers in developing lesson plans, creating assessments, and tracking student progress. This support enables teachers to deliver more effective and targeted instruction, ultimately improving the quality of education (Zawacki-Richter et al., 2019).

(3) Challenges and Considerations

While the benefits of AI in K-12 education are significant, there are also challenges and considerations that need to be addressed:

a. Ethical Concerns: The use of AI in education raises ethical concerns, particularly regarding data privacy and security. It is crucial to ensure that student data is protected and used responsibly (Luckin et al., 2016).
b. Equity and Access: Not all students have equal access to AI technologies and reliable internet connections. Efforts must be made to bridge the digital divide and ensure that all students can benefit from AI-enhanced education (Zawacki-Richter et al., 2019).
c. Teacher Training: Teachers need adequate training and support to effectively integrate AI tools into their teaching practices. Professional development programs focusing on AI literacy and its applications in education are essential for successful implementation (Holstein et al., 2019).
d. Bias in AI Algorithms: AI algorithms can sometimes exhibit biases that may affect their effectiveness. It is important to continuously monitor and address any biases to ensure that AI tools are fair and equitable (Gardner-McCune & Touretzky, 2021).

3. TRENDS IN AI DEPLOYMENT IN K-12 EDUCATION

(1) Global Adoption Rates

The adoption of AI in K-12 education varies significantly across different regions of the world. Developed countries, such as the United States, China, and several European nations, have been at the forefront of integrating AI technologies into their educational systems. These countries benefit from advanced technological infrastructures, significant investments in education technology, and supportive government policies that facilitate the adoption of AI in schools (Gardner-McCune & Touretzky, 2021).

In contrast, developing countries face numerous challenges, including limited access to technology, inadequate funding, and a lack of trained personnel, which hinder the widespread adoption of AI in education. However, there are notable exceptions where targeted efforts and international collaborations have enabled significant advancements in AI education. For example, in some regions of Africa and South Asia, pilot programs and partnerships with technology firms have led to the successful implementation of AI tools in classrooms, albeit on a smaller scale (Holstein et al., 2019).

(2) Variations in AI Implementation

The implementation of AI in K-12 education varies not only by region but also by the specific educational goals and challenges that different schools and districts face. A case study of the Qibin District of Hebi City in China illustrates how local contexts influence AI deployment (Case Study Analysis, 2024). In Qibin District, significant investments in AI education have been made, resulting in the establishment of AI laboratories, the integration of AI into the curriculum, and extensive teacher training programs.

(3) Literature Review

The literature on AI in K-12 education highlights several key trends and insights that have shaped current practices and inform future directions. There are Results and discussion as follow:

Figure 1. Number of publications and citations on AI usage in K-12 education

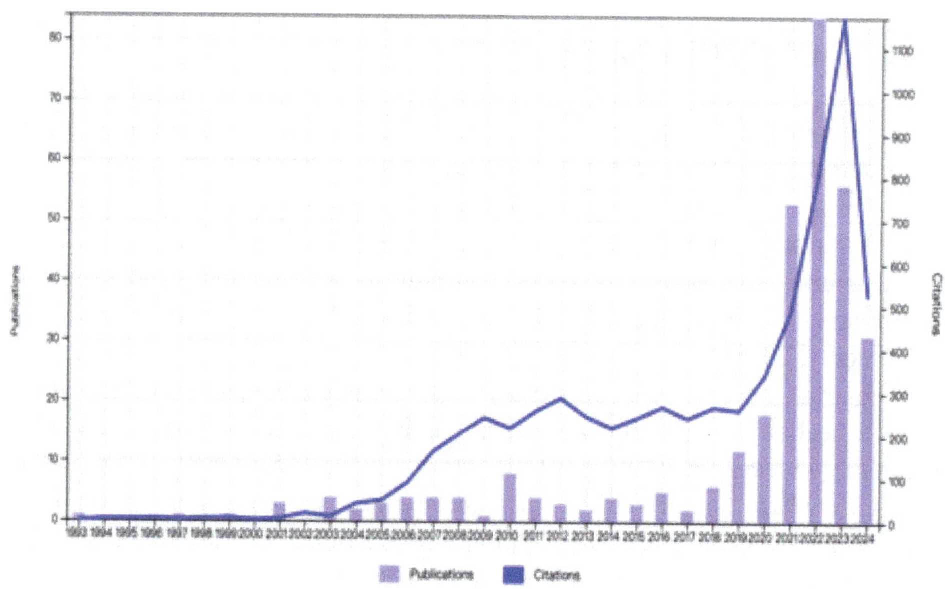

Figure 2. Co-citation analysis of AI usage in K-12 education

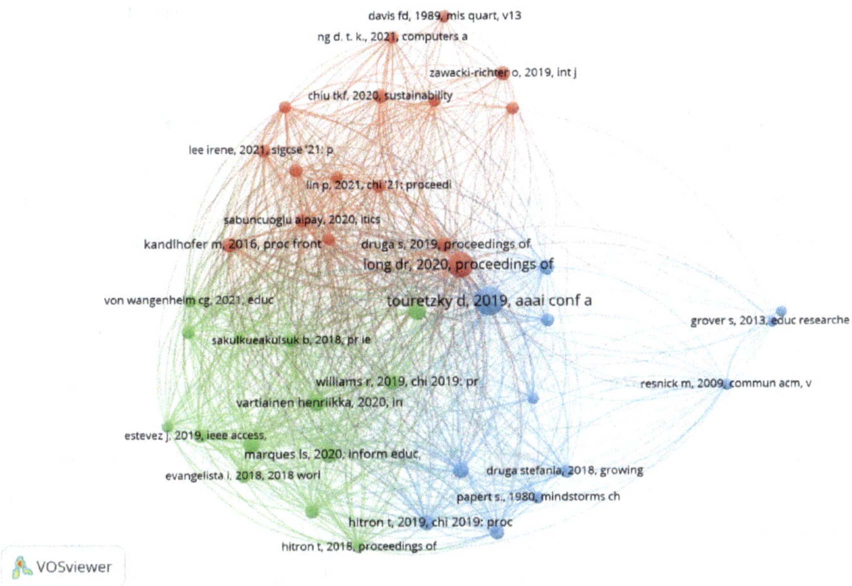

Figure 3. Co-word analysis of AI usage in K-12 education

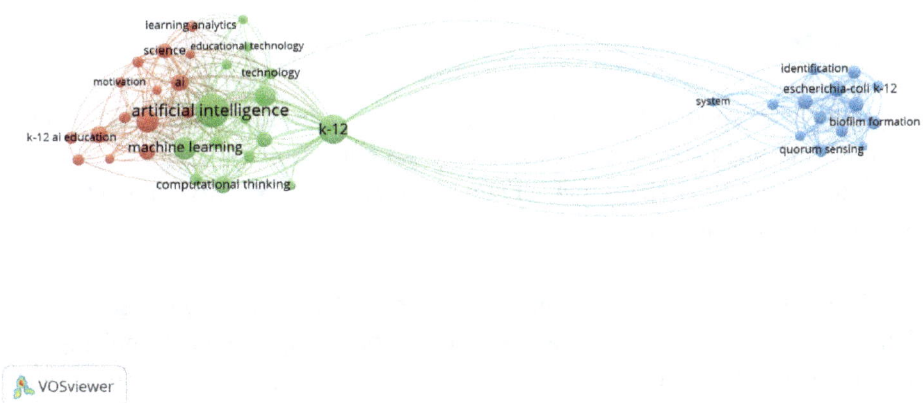

(4) Case Study: Qibin District, Hebi City

The Qibin District provides a concrete example of successful AI implementation in K-12 education, highlighting several key trends:

a. Focus on Personalized Learning and Innovation: The AI programs in Qibin District emphasize not only the technology itself but also its application in promoting personalized learning and fostering students' innovative abilities. This shift reflects a broader trend in education towards personalized and competency-based learning models.
b. Continuous Update of Course Content and Methods: As AI technology evolves, the educational content and teaching methods are continuously updated. This includes the use of AI for personalized teaching and intelligent assessments, which are becoming standard practices in many schools.
c. Investment in Infrastructure: The district has seen substantial investments in updating hardware and software systems, providing a robust foundation for AI education. This trend is mirrored globally, with schools increasingly recognizing the need for modern technological infrastructure to support AI tools.
d. Teacher Training and Capacity Building: Recognizing the pivotal role of teachers in AI education, Qibin District has prioritized professional development, regularly training teachers to enhance their competencies in using AI technologies. This approach is crucial for the successful integration of AI into educational practices.
e. Active Student Participation: Students in Qibin District actively participate in AI-related projects and competitions, which is closely linked to educational reforms that emphasize experiential learning and practical application of knowledge. This trend encourages students to engage deeply with AI technologies, fostering skills that are critical for the future workforce.

(5) Interview focus

The interviews mainly focus on the views of educators, students and parents, presenting a multi-dimensional perspective of AI education.

The interview results show that AI education has had a positive impact on students, teachers and parents:

a. Student: AI tools provide students with a personalized learning experience that helps them learn at their own pace and style. For example, educational apps can provide students with targeted exercises and review materials based on their academic performance and progress. In addition, AI tools can provide real-time feedback to help students understand their learning in a timely manner and make adjustments accordingly.

b. Educators: AI tools can help teachers better understand students' learning and adjust teaching strategies according to their learning needs. For example, teachers can use AI tools to analyze students' learning data and design personalized lesson plans based on their learning styles and interests. In addition, AI tools can help teachers reduce their workload, giving them more time to focus on the individual needs of students.
c. Parents: AI education can help parents better understand their children's learning and provide them with more effective learning support. For example, parents can use AI tools to track their children's progress and provide them with personalized learning resources based on their learning needs. In addition, AI education can also help parents better communicate with their children and encourage them to actively participate in their children's learning process.

While AI education has many positive implications, it also faces some challenges:

a. Reliability and stability of AI tools remains a challenge. For example, software glitches and compatibility issues can affect the availability of AI tools, disrupting the learning process; The instability of the network leads to the inability to generate content, which also affects the learning efficiency.
b. AI systems typically require access to a large number of users' data to function effectively, raising data privacy and security concerns. For example, measures need to be taken to ensure the security and confidentiality of user data.
c. Not all students have equal access to AI tools and reliable Internet connections, which could exacerbate existing educational inequalities.
d. Teachers need to receive AI-related training and support to effectively integrate AI tools into teaching practice. For example, some older teachers are not proficient in the use of electronic equipment, and their teaching will be affected if they are not well trained.

The results of the interview show that the future trend of AI education is positive and optimistic:

a. In the future, AI will become part of classroom activities, supporting everything from lesson planning to student assessment and personalized learning.
b. AI will drive the development of more advanced adaptive learning systems to provide students with a more personalized learning experience.
c. AI-driven analytics will play a greater role in guiding instructional strategies and improving educational outcomes.

d. AI will increasingly support teacher training and career development, helping teachers master new technologies and teaching methods.

(6) Broader Trends and Perspectives

Based on the interviews conducted with educators, students, and parents, several broader trends in AI deployment in K-12 education emerge:

a. Positive Impact on Learning and Teaching: AI tools provide personalized learning experiences that help students learn at their own pace and style. For educators, AI offers insights into student learning data, allowing for more tailored teaching strategies. Parents also benefit by gaining better insights into their children's learning progress, facilitating more effective support at home.
b. Challenges and Barriers: Despite the positive impact, several challenges remain. These include the reliability and stability of AI tools, data privacy and security concerns, unequal access to technology, and the need for comprehensive teacher training.
c. Future Prospects: The future of AI in education appears promising, with expectations of more advanced adaptive learning systems, greater use of AI-driven analytics in instructional strategies, and increased support for teacher training and career development. These trends suggest that AI will continue to play a significant role in shaping the educational landscape.

4. AI AND CURRICULUM INTEGRATION

(1) AI-Enhanced Curricula

The integration of AI into K-12 curricula is a growing trend aimed at enhancing the educational experience by leveraging technology to provide more personalized, efficient, and effective learning. AI-enhanced curricula include components such as AI literacy, coding, computational thinking, and digital literacy. These elements are essential for preparing students for future workforce demands where AI and related technologies will play a significant role (Chiu & Chai, 2020).

One of the key aspects of AI-enhanced curricula is the focus on AI literacy, which involves teaching students the basics of AI, including how it works, its applications, and its ethical implications. Studies have shown that early exposure to AI concepts helps students develop a better understanding and critical thinking skills about the technology (Chai et al., 2021). For example, initiatives like the AI4K12 framework provide guidelines for incorporating AI literacy into K-12 education, emphasizing concepts such as machine learning, robotics, and ethical AI (Touretzky et al., 2019).

Coding and Computational Thinking are other critical components of AI-enhanced curricula. These skills are foundational for understanding and working with AI technologies. Computational thinking involves problem-solving using computer science principles and is increasingly being recognized as a vital skill for students. Integrating coding and computational thinking into the curriculum helps students develop logical thinking and problem-solving skills, which are essential for AI-related tasks (Grover & Pea, 2013).

(2) Personalized Learning and Differentiated Instruction

AI's ability to provide personalized learning experiences is one of its most significant contributions to education. Personalized learning refers to tailoring educational content and experiences to meet the individual needs, strengths, and interests of each student. AI technologies, such as adaptive learning platforms, use data analytics and machine learning algorithms to adjust the difficulty level and type of content delivered to students in real-time, ensuring that each student receives an education that is best suited to their learning pace and style (Druga et al., 2019).

For instance, adaptive learning systems can track student progress, identify areas where they are struggling, and provide additional resources or alternative explanations to help them understand the material better. This approach not only improves learning outcomes but also increases student engagement by providing a more interactive and responsive learning environment (Vartiainen et al., 2021).

Differentiated instruction is another educational strategy enhanced by AI. Differentiated instruction involves providing different students with different avenues to learning, often in the same classroom, to accommodate their varied needs. AI can assist teachers in implementing differentiated instruction by offering insights into student performance, suggesting tailored teaching strategies, and even automating some aspects of instruction (Marques et al., 2020). For example, AI-driven platforms can group students based on their learning styles and progress, allowing teachers to design targeted activities that cater to each group's needs.

(3) Case Studies and Practical Applications

Several schools and educational systems have successfully integrated AI into their curricula, providing valuable case studies and practical examples of how AI can enhance education.

Qibin District, Hebi City, China: The Qibin District's approach to AI education serves as an excellent model. The district has implemented various AI-related courses, including programming and robotics, emphasizing the cultivation of students' innovative abilities. They have also established AI laboratories equipped with the latest technology, enabling students to engage in hands-on learning experiences (Case Study Analysis, 2024). This integration has led to increased student interest and improved educational outcomes, demonstrating the effectiveness of AI-enhanced curricula.

Middle School AI Literacy Programs: Programs designed to teach AI literacy in middle schools have also shown promising results. For instance, the use of AI tools such as Teachable Machine allows students to create their own machine learning models, providing a practical understanding of AI concepts (Carney et al., 2020). These programs not only teach technical skills but also encourage students to think critically about the ethical implications of AI.

(4) The Role of Teachers in AI Integration

Teachers play a crucial role in the successful integration of AI into the curriculum. Effective AI education requires teachers to be well-versed in both the technology and its pedagogical applications. Professional development and ongoing support are essential to help teachers understand how to use AI tools effectively and incorporate them into their teaching strategies (Lin & Van Brummelen, 2021).

Training programs for teachers often include workshops, online courses, and collaborative projects that focus on AI literacy, coding, and computational thinking. These programs aim to build teachers' confidence and competence in using AI tools, enabling them to create more engaging and effective learning experiences for their students (Chiu, 2021).

(5) Ethical Considerations and Curriculum Design

Integrating AI into the curriculum also involves addressing ethical considerations. Teaching students about the ethical implications of AI, such as data privacy, algorithmic bias, and the societal impact of automation, is critical. This holistic approach ensures that students not only learn about AI technology but also understand its broader implications and develop a responsible mindset towards its use (Payne, 2019).

Curriculum design for AI education should also be inclusive and equitable, ensuring that all students have access to AI learning opportunities regardless of their background. This includes providing resources and support for students with disabilities and those from underrepresented groups in technology (Williams et al., 2019).

5. IMPACT OF AI ON TEACHING AND LEARNING

(1) Effectiveness of AI in Enhancing Learning Outcomes

The integration of AI in education has shown significant potential in enhancing learning outcomes. AI tools such as adaptive learning platforms and intelligent tutoring systems provide personalized learning experiences that help students understand complex concepts and retain information more effectively. Research indicates that AI-driven personalized learning can lead to improved academic performance and greater student engagement (Luckin et al., 2016).

Adaptive learning platforms use AI algorithms to tailor educational content to the individual needs of each student. By analyzing data on student performance and learning behaviors, these platforms can adjust the difficulty level and type of content delivered, ensuring that each student receives instruction that is best suited to their learning pace and style. This personalized approach not only helps students grasp difficult concepts but also fosters a more engaging and interactive learning environment (Chiu & Chai, 2020).

Intelligent tutoring systems (ITS) mimic the one-on-one interaction between a student and a tutor. These systems provide immediate feedback and targeted instruction, helping students to identify and address their learning gaps. Studies have shown that ITS can significantly improve student learning outcomes, particularly in subjects such as mathematics and science, where individualized attention is crucial for understanding complex topics (Druga et al., 2019).

(2) Transforming Teacher Roles and Pedagogical Strategies

AI is transforming the role of teachers by automating routine administrative tasks and providing data-driven insights that inform instructional strategies. With AI handling tasks such as grading, attendance tracking, and performance analysis, teachers have more time to focus on instruction and student support (Holstein et al., 2019).

One of the significant impacts of AI on teaching is the shift towards data-driven instruction. AI tools provide teachers with detailed analytics on student performance, allowing them to identify areas where students are struggling and adjust their teaching strategies accordingly. This data-driven approach enables teachers to provide more targeted and effective instruction, which can lead to better student outcomes (Chiu et al., 2021).

Moreover, AI supports differentiated instruction by offering insights into the diverse learning needs of students. Teachers can use AI tools to create personalized learning plans that cater to the strengths and weaknesses of each student. This approach not only helps students who are struggling but also challenges those who are excelling, ensuring that all students receive a tailored educational experience (Grover & Pea, 2013).

AI also enhances collaborative learning by facilitating communication and collaboration among students. AI-powered platforms can group students based on their learning styles and progress, enabling them to work together on projects and assignments. This collaborative approach fosters a sense of community and encourages peer-to-peer learning, which is beneficial for developing critical thinking and problem-solving skills (Williams et al., 2019).

(3) Improving Student Engagement and Motivation

AI technologies can significantly enhance student engagement and motivation by making learning more interactive and enjoyable. Gamification, virtual reality (VR), and augmented reality (AR) are examples of AI-driven tools that create immersive learning experiences. These tools make learning more engaging by incorporating game-like elements and interactive simulations that capture students' interest and motivate them to participate actively in their education (Chai et al., 2021).

For example, VR and AR technologies can bring abstract concepts to life by providing visual and interactive representations. Students can explore historical sites, conduct virtual science experiments, or interact with 3D models of complex systems, making learning more tangible and exciting. These immersive experiences not only enhance understanding but also increase student motivation and enthusiasm for learning (Vartiainen et al., 2021).

Gamification involves integrating game elements such as points, badges, and leaderboards into educational activities. This approach leverages students' natural desire for competition and achievement, making learning more fun and engaging. Studies have shown that gamified learning experiences can improve student motivation, participation, and retention of information (Grover & Pea, 2013).

(4) Supporting Special Education and Inclusivity

AI has the potential to transform special education by providing personalized support for students with disabilities. AI-powered tools can adapt learning materials to meet the specific needs of students with various disabilities, offering a more inclusive educational environment. For example, speech recognition and natural language processing technologies can assist students with language impairments, while AI-driven text-to-speech and screen readers can support visually impaired students (Hitron et al., 2018).

AI can also facilitate the early identification of learning disabilities and provide targeted interventions. By analyzing student data, AI tools can detect patterns that may indicate learning challenges, enabling educators to intervene early and provide the necessary support. This proactive approach can help students overcome their difficulties and succeed academically (Druga et al., 2019).

(5) Ethical Considerations and Challenges

While AI offers numerous benefits, its implementation in education also raises ethical considerations and challenges. Issues such as data privacy, algorithmic bias, and the digital divide must be carefully addressed to ensure that AI tools are used responsibly and equitably.

Data privacy is a significant concern, as AI systems often require access to large amounts of student data to function effectively. It is essential to ensure that this data is collected, stored, and used in compliance with privacy regulations and that students' personal information is protected (Luckin et al., 2016).

Algorithmic bias is another challenge, as AI systems can sometimes exhibit biases that reflect the data they were trained on. This bias can lead to unfair outcomes, particularly for marginalized or underrepresented groups. It is crucial to continuously monitor and address any biases in AI algorithms to ensure that all students receive fair and equitable treatment (Grover & Pea, 2013).

The digital divide is also a significant issue, as not all students have equal access to AI technologies and reliable internet connections. Efforts must be made to bridge this gap and ensure that all students can benefit from AI-enhanced education, regardless of their socio-economic background (Williams et al., 2019).

6. CHALLENGES AND BARRIERS

(1) Ethical Concerns and Data Privacy Issues

One of the most significant challenges in the deployment of AI in K-12 education is ensuring the ethical use of AI technologies and protecting student data privacy. AI systems often require access to vast amounts of data to function effectively. This data includes sensitive information such as student performance, behavior, and personal details. Ensuring that this data is collected, stored, and used in compliance with privacy regulations is paramount. Any breach of data privacy can have severe consequences, including loss of trust and potential harm to students (Luckin et al., 2016).

To address these concerns, schools and educational institutions must implement robust data protection measures. This includes encrypting data, implementing strict access controls, and ensuring compliance with regulations such as the General Data Protection Regulation (GDPR) in Europe and the Family Educational Rights and

Privacy Act (FERPA) in the United States. Additionally, educating students and parents about data privacy and obtaining informed consent before collecting and using data is essential (Holstein et al., 2019).

(2) Algorithmic Bias and Fairness

Algorithmic bias is another critical issue in the deployment of AI in education. AI systems are trained on data sets that may contain inherent biases, which can lead to biased outcomes. For example, an AI system trained on historical data that reflects existing educational inequalities may inadvertently perpetuate these inequalities. This can result in unfair treatment of students from marginalized or underrepresented groups (Grover & Pea, 2013).

Addressing algorithmic bias requires a multifaceted approach. Developers must ensure that AI systems are trained on diverse and representative data sets. Regular audits of AI systems can help identify and mitigate biases. Moreover, involving educators, students, and other stakeholders in the development and evaluation of AI systems can provide valuable insights and help create more equitable AI tools (Holstein et al., 2019).

(3) Equity and Access

The digital divide is a significant barrier to the widespread adoption of AI in K-12 education. Not all students have equal access to AI technologies and reliable internet connections. Students from low-income families or rural areas may lack the necessary devices and connectivity to benefit from AI-enhanced learning. This disparity can exacerbate existing educational inequalities and leave some students behind (Williams et al., 2019).

To bridge the digital divide, educational institutions and policymakers must invest in infrastructure and resources to ensure that all students have access to the necessary technology. This includes providing devices such as laptops and tablets, as well as ensuring reliable internet connectivity. Additionally, offering training and support for students and families who may be less familiar with technology can help ensure that everyone can benefit from AI-enhanced education (Chai et al., 2021).

(4) Teacher Preparedness and Professional Development

Effective integration of AI in education requires teachers to be well-prepared and confident in using AI tools. However, many teachers lack the necessary training and experience to effectively incorporate AI into their teaching practices. This can be a significant barrier to the successful deployment of AI in K-12 education (Chiu, 2021).

Professional development programs focusing on AI literacy and its applications in education are essential. These programs should provide teachers with the knowledge and skills needed to use AI tools effectively and to understand their implications for teaching and learning. Workshops, online courses, and collaborative projects can all be valuable components of professional development. Additionally, ongoing support and resources are necessary to help teachers stay updated on the latest developments in AI technology (Lin & Van Brummelen, 2021).

(5) Reliability and Stability of AI Tools

The reliability and stability of AI tools are crucial for their successful implementation in education. Software glitches, compatibility issues, and network instability can disrupt the learning process and undermine trust in AI technologies. Ensuring that AI tools are reliable, stable, and user-friendly is essential for their widespread adoption.

Educational institutions should work closely with technology providers to ensure that AI tools are rigorously tested and continuously improved. Additionally, providing technical support and training for educators can help mitigate potential issues and ensure that AI tools are used effectively in the classroom (Hitron et al., 2018).

(6) Ethical Use and Implications of AI in Education

Ethical considerations extend beyond data privacy and algorithmic bias. The use of AI in education raises questions about the broader implications for society and the future of work. It is essential to teach students not only how to use AI tools but also to understand their ethical implications. This includes discussing topics such as the impact of automation on jobs, the ethical use of AI, and the importance of diversity and inclusion in AI development (Payne, 2019).

Incorporating these discussions into the curriculum can help students develop a more comprehensive understanding of AI and its implications. Additionally, fostering a culture of ethical awareness and responsibility among educators and students is crucial for the responsible use of AI in education (Vartiainen et al., 2021).

7. FUTURE PERSPECTIVES

(1) Innovations and Developments on the Horizon

The future of AI in K-12 education is filled with promising innovations and developments. As AI technologies continue to evolve, they are expected to bring even more transformative changes to the educational landscape. Here are some key trends and innovations that are likely to shape the future of AI in K-12 education:

(2) AI-Driven Immersive Learning Environments

One of the most exciting developments is the integration of AI with immersive technologies such as virtual reality (VR) and augmented reality (AR). These technologies have the potential to create highly engaging and interactive learning experiences. For instance, AI can be used to create virtual tutors that guide students through VR simulations, providing real-time feedback and personalized instruction. This can make learning more engaging and help students understand complex concepts by experiencing them in a virtual environment (Chai et al., 2021).

(3) Enhanced Adaptive Learning Systems

Adaptive learning systems are expected to become even more sophisticated, leveraging advanced AI algorithms to provide highly personalized learning experiences. These systems will be able to analyze vast amounts of data from various sources, including student performance, learning preferences, and behavioral patterns, to tailor educational content and activities to the individual needs of each student. This level of personalization can significantly improve learning outcomes and ensure that each student receives the support they need to succeed (Druga et al., 2019).

(4) AI-Driven Learning Analytics

Learning analytics powered by AI will play a crucial role in guiding instructional strategies and improving educational outcomes. By analyzing data from various educational activities, AI can provide educators with valuable insights into student performance, engagement, and progress. These insights can help teachers identify at-risk students, tailor their teaching strategies, and provide targeted interventions to support student learning. AI-driven learning analytics can also help schools and districts make data-informed decisions to enhance their educational programs and policies (Holstein et al., 2019).

(5) Human-AI Collaboration in Education

The future of AI in education will likely involve greater collaboration between humans and AI systems. AI can augment the capabilities of educators by automating routine tasks, providing data-driven insights, and supporting personalized instruction. This collaboration can free up teachers' time, allowing them to focus on more critical aspects of teaching, such as fostering creativity, critical thinking, and social-emotional skills. By working together, humans and AI can create a more effective and holistic educational experience for students (Luckin et al., 2016).

(6) Policy Frameworks for AI in Education

As AI becomes more integrated into K-12 education, it is essential to develop comprehensive policy frameworks to ensure its ethical and equitable use. These frameworks should address key issues such as data privacy, algorithmic bias, and access to technology. Policymakers, educators, and other stakeholders must work together to create guidelines and standards that promote the responsible use of AI in education.

(7) Data Privacy and Security

Protecting student data privacy and security is paramount. Policy frameworks should establish clear guidelines for the collection, storage, and use of student data. This includes ensuring that data is used transparently and only for educational purposes, as well as implementing robust security measures to prevent unauthorized access and breaches (Chiu, 2021).

(8) Addressing Algorithmic Bias

To ensure fairness and equity, policy frameworks must address the issue of algorithmic bias in AI systems. This involves regularly auditing AI algorithms to identify and mitigate biases and ensuring that AI systems are trained on diverse and representative data sets. Additionally, involving a diverse group of stakeholders in the development and evaluation of AI systems can help create more inclusive and equitable educational tools (Holstein et al., 2019).

(9) Promoting Access to Technology

Bridging the digital divide is essential for ensuring that all students can benefit from AI-enhanced education. Policy frameworks should focus on providing equal access to technology and internet connectivity for all students, regardless of their socio-economic background. This includes investing in infrastructure, providing devices and internet access, and offering training and support for students and families who may be less familiar with technology (Williams et al., 2019).

(10) Professional Development and Teacher Training

As AI continues to transform education, ongoing professional development and training for teachers will be crucial. Educators need to be equipped with the knowledge and skills to effectively integrate AI tools into their teaching practices. Professional development programs should focus on AI literacy, ethical considerations, and the pedagogical applications of AI. Additionally, providing ongoing support and resources can help teachers stay updated on the latest developments in AI technology and best practices for its use in education (Lin & Van Brummelen, 2021).

(11) Fostering a Culture of Innovation and Ethical Awareness

Creating a culture of innovation and ethical awareness is essential for the successful integration of AI in education. This involves encouraging educators, students, and other stakeholders to embrace AI technologies and explore their potential benefits while remaining mindful of ethical considerations. By fostering a culture of innovation, schools can create an environment that supports continuous improvement and adaptation to new technologies (Payne, 2019).

Educational institutions should also emphasize the importance of ethical awareness and responsibility in the use of AI. This includes teaching students about the ethical implications of AI, such as data privacy, algorithmic bias, and the societal impact of automation. By promoting ethical awareness, schools can help students develop a responsible mindset towards AI and prepare them to use these technologies in a way that benefits society as a whole (Vartiainen et al., 2021).

8. CONCLUSION

The integration of Artificial Intelligence (AI) in K-12 education marks a transformative era in the educational landscape. AI technologies, with their vast potential, promise to revolutionize the way students learn, teachers instruct, and educational institutions operate. The advancements in AI offer personalized, adaptive, and engaging learning experiences, fostering a more inclusive and effective educational environment. However, realizing the full potential of AI in education requires a balanced approach that addresses various challenges and ethical considerations.

(1) The Transformative Power of AI in Education

AI has shown significant promise in enhancing learning outcomes through personalized learning experiences. Adaptive learning platforms and intelligent tutoring systems provide tailored educational content, ensuring that each student learns at their own pace and style. These AI tools have been instrumental in improving student engagement, motivation, and academic performance. Moreover, AI-driven learning analytics offer valuable insights into student progress, enabling educators to make data-informed decisions and provide targeted interventions. This level of personalization and data-driven instruction is transforming traditional educational practices and paving the way for more effective teaching and learning methodologies.

(2) Addressing Challenges and Ethical Considerations

While the benefits of AI in education are substantial, several challenges and ethical considerations must be addressed to ensure its responsible and equitable implementation. Data privacy and security are paramount concerns, given the vast amounts of sensitive information that AI systems require to function effectively. Schools and educational institutions must implement robust data protection measures and comply with relevant regulations to safeguard student information.

Algorithmic bias is another critical issue, as biased AI systems can perpetuate existing inequalities and lead to unfair treatment of students. Ensuring that AI systems are trained on diverse and representative data sets and regularly auditing these systems for biases is crucial. Additionally, the digital divide remains a significant barrier, with many students lacking access to the necessary technology and internet connectivity. Bridging this gap requires substantial investments in infrastructure and resources to provide equal access to AI-enhanced education for all students.

(3) The Role of Educators and Professional Development

The successful integration of AI in education heavily relies on the preparedness and competence of educators. Teachers must be equipped with the knowledge and skills to effectively incorporate AI tools into their teaching practices. Ongoing professional development and training programs focusing on AI literacy, ethical considerations, and pedagogical applications are essential. These programs should provide educators with the confidence and capabilities to harness the potential of AI, ultimately enhancing their instructional strategies and improving student outcomes.

(4) Fostering a Culture of Innovation and Ethical Awareness

Creating a culture of innovation and ethical awareness is vital for the sustainable integration of AI in education. Schools and educational institutions should encourage experimentation with AI technologies while fostering a responsible approach to their use. Teaching students about the ethical implications of AI, including data privacy, algorithmic bias, and the societal impact of automation, is crucial. By promoting ethical awareness, educators can prepare students to use AI technologies responsibly and contribute positively to society.

(5) Future Perspectives and Policy Frameworks

Looking ahead, the future of AI in K-12 education is filled with promising innovations. AI-driven immersive learning environments, enhanced adaptive learning systems, and AI-powered analytics are poised to further revolutionize the educational landscape. However, achieving this potential requires comprehensive policy frameworks that address data privacy, algorithmic bias, and access to technology. Policymakers, educators, and other stakeholders must collaborate to develop guidelines and standards that promote the ethical and equitable use of AI in education.

(6) Final Thoughts

AI has the potential to fundamentally transform K-12 education by providing personalized learning experiences, supporting teachers, and fostering student engagement. However, realizing this potential necessitates addressing significant challenges related to data privacy, algorithmic bias, and the digital divide. By prioritizing ethical considerations, investing in professional development, and fostering a culture of innovation, educators and policymakers can harness the power of AI to create a more effective, equitable, and inclusive educational environment. The journey towards integrating AI in education is complex, but with careful planning and collaboration, it holds the promise of a brighter and more informed future for all students.

REFERENCES

Burns, S. M., Henriksen, D., & Mishra, P. (2020). AI and Education: Emerging Opportunities, Challenges, and Ethical Considerations. *AI Magazine*, *40*(3), 9–17.

Carney, M., Webster, B., Alvarado, I., Phillips, K., Howell, N., Griffith, J., . . . Chen, A. (2020,). Teachable machine: Approachable Web-based tool for exploring machine learning classification. In Extended abstracts of the 2020 CHI conference on human factors in computing systems (pp. 1-8).

Chai, C. S., Lin, P. Y., Jong, M. S. Y., Dai, Y., Chiu, T. K., & Qin, J. (2021). Perceptions of and behavioral intentions towards learning artificial intelligence in primary school students. *Journal of Educational Technology & Society*, *24*(3), 89–101.

Chiu, T. K. (2021). A holistic approach to the design of artificial intelligence (AI) education for K-12 schools. *TechTrends*, *65*(5), 796–807. DOI: 10.1007/s11528-021-00637-1

Chiu, T. K., & Chai, C. S. (2020). Sustainable curriculum planning for artificial intelligence education: A self-determination theory perspective. *Sustainability (Basel)*, *12*(14), 5568. DOI: 10.3390/su12145568

Druga, S., Vu, S. T., Likhith, E., & Qiu, T. (2019). Inclusive AI literacy for kids around the world. In *Proceedings of FabLearn 2019* (pp. 104-111). DOI: 10.1145/3311890.3311904

Gardner-McCune, C., & Touretzky, D. (2021). AI For All: Building AI Thinking In Students Through Distributed Learning. In *Proceedings of the ACM Conference on Computing Education Research*.

Grover, S., & Pea, R. (2013). Computational thinking in K–12: A review of the state of the field. *Educational Researcher*, *42*(1), 38–43. DOI: 10.3102/0013189X12463051

Hitron, T., Wald, I., Erel, H., & Zuckerman, O. (2018, June). Introducing children to machine learning concepts through hands-on experience. In *Proceedings of the 17th ACM conference on interaction design and children* (pp. 563-568). DOI: 10.1145/3202185.3210776

Holstein, K., McLaren, B. M., & Aleven, V. (2019). Student-Centered AI in Education: Bringing Context and Policy Considerations into Design and Implementation. *AI Magazine*, *40*(2), 54–63.

Lin, P., & Van Brummelen, J. (2021, May). Engaging teachers to co-design integrated AI curriculum for K-12 classrooms. In *Proceedings of the 2021 CHI conference on human factors in computing systems* (pp. 1-12). DOI: 10.1145/3411764.3445377

Luckin, R., Holmes, W., Griffiths, M., & Forcier, L. B. (2016). *Intelligence Unleashed: An Argument for AI in Education*. Pearson.

Marques, L. S., Gresse von Wangenheim, C., & Hauck, J. C. (2020). Teaching machine learning in school: A systematic mapping of the state of the art. *Informatics in Education, 19*(2), 283–321. DOI: 10.15388/infedu.2020.14

Payne, B. H. (2019). An ethics of artificial intelligence curriculum for middle school students. MIT Media Lab Personal Robots Group., Retrieved October 10, 2019, from.

Touretzky, D., Gardner-McCune, C., Breazeal, C., Martin, F., & Seehorn, D. (2019). A year in K–12 AI education. *AI Magazine, 40*(4), 88–90. DOI: 10.1609/aimag.v40i4.5289

Vartiainen, H., Toivonen, T., Jormanainen, I., Kahila, J., Tedre, M., & Valtonen, T. (2021). Machine learning for middle schoolers: Learning through data-driven design. *International Journal of Child-Computer Interaction, 29*, 100281. DOI: 10.1016/j.ijcci.2021.100281

Williams, R., Park, H. W., & Breazeal, C. (2019, May). A is for artificial intelligence: the impact of artificial intelligence activities on young children's perceptions of robots. In *Proceedings of the 2019 CHI conference on human factors in computing systems* (pp. 1-11). DOI: 10.1145/3290605.3300677

Zawacki-Richter, O., Marín, V. I., Bond, M., & Gouverneur, F. (2019). Systematic Review of Research on Artificial Intelligence Applications in Higher Education – Where Are the Educators? *International Journal of Educational Technology in Higher Education, 16*(1), 39. DOI: 10.1186/s41239-019-0171-0

Chapter 5

Designing a Teacher Training Program of AI Literacy for K-12 Educators

Ruhi Lal
Manav Rachna International Institute of Research and Studies, India

Aarzoo
http://orcid.org/0009-0006-7604-2583
Manav Rachna International Institute of Research and Studies, India

ABSTRACT

As AI grows more significant across businesses, educators must understand technology to educate kids for the future. This study will create a K-12 AI teacher training course that seamlessly blends AI literacy and ethics. The study discusses ethical education and the best AI literacy teaching methods and resources for teacher training. The best methods were found by qualitative literature review. A comprehensive AI literacy and ethical education method boosts educators' confidence and proficiency. Success requires AI initiatives, ethical exploration, and professional development. Interactive workshops, real-world AI applications, and collaborative learning are essential for education. The study reveals a well-planned AI teacher training course can prepare K-12 teachers to teach AI literacy and ethics. Teachers may include AI by using hands-on projects, emphasizing ethics, and promoting growth. This method prepares pupils for a tech-driven future by explaining AI and its morality.

DOI: 10.4018/979-8-3693-6346-1.ch005

INTRODUCTION

AI literacy has become essential for educators dealing with K-12 students in the ever-changing field of education (Kjær Bilstrup et al., 2020). Given the growing use of AI technologies across society, educators must comprehend their principles, uses, and potential effects (DiPaola, Payne, & Breazeal, 2020). This understanding is vital to providing students with future-ready skills and knowledge (Alexandre et al., 2021). However, AI literacy training for teachers is lacking (Aung et al., 2022). This limitation hinders educators' ability to integrate AI education into their lessons (Chiu, 2021). This gap underlines the need for a comprehensive and specialist teacher training approach to improve AI literacy among K-12 educators (Crompton, Jones, & Burke, 2022). A training plan like this gives educators the information, skills, and materials needed to seamlessly integrate AI literacy into many academic disciplines and grade levels (Dai et al., 2023). The programme educates educators about AI concepts, ethics, and applications (Henry, Hernalesteen, & Collard, 2021). It encourages critical thinking, problem-solving, and digital literacy in kids (Jaskie et al., 2021). This study also addresses societal issues like AI algorithm bias, privacy problems, and AI ethics (Kandlhofer & Steinbauer, 2021). Developing an AI literacy teacher training course is difficult without a universal curriculum and publicly available resources (Kim et al., 2023). Current AI education training programmes lack clarity, consistency, and depth (Lin & Brummelen, 2021). This lack of training leaves educators unprepared for AI education's many complexities (Russell, 2021). Thus, the proposed course will prioritise a well-organized curriculum, teaching tools, and practical activities that follow educational norms and methods (Suh & Ahn, 2022). The programme will also emphasise inquiry-based learning, collaborative problem-solving, and AI application in real-world situations (Van Brummelen et al., 2021a). By actively engaging educators through interactive seminars, online courses, and peer learning groups, the project intends to foster AI education professional development and innovation (Xia et al., 2022). This paper examines the rationale, aims, and methods of a K-12 teacher training initiative to improve AI literacy (Yau et al., 2022). We will define the program's core aspects and recommend its implementation and evaluation by synthesising scholarly works, educational frameworks, and field experts (Dai et al., 2023).

Research Objective

1. To find out implementation of an effective AI teacher training program for K-12 educators.
2. To integrate AI literacy and ethical education into the K–12 education curriculum.

Research Questions

RQ1.How can AI literacy be effectively integrated into K-12 teacher training programs?
RQ2. What key components of ethical education should be included in AI teacher training for K-12 educators?
RQ3. What teaching strategies and resources are most effective for teaching AI literacy for ethical education in K–12 classrooms?

Relevance of the Study

This study is of greatest significance in gaining insights into the relationship between AI literacy and AI-driven innovation in teachers training program in K-12 education. With the ever-changing educational landscape, AI plays an important role. It offers insights into effective strategies for integrating AI into educational programmes. In addition, it highlights the possible challenges and advantages of these methods, offering K12 educational institution valuable insights to navigate the competitive educational technology industry. The main objective of this study is to provide assistance and ensure the long-term viability of K-12 educational institution that utilise AI technology for teachers training and AI literacy.

Significance of the Study

This study holds immense value for K-12 educational institution as it provides valuable insights into the successful integration of brand promotion and AI-driven innovation. In a rapidly evolving era of educational technology, it is crucial to grasp the importance of utilising partnerships, social media marketing, and content development to enhance capabilities in digital innovation. Through an exploration of the integration of AI into educational programmes and an examination of the challenges and opportunities that arise, this study offers a valuable roadmap for institutions seeking to improve their products and services. In the end, these discoveries will assist institutions in attaining long-term sustainability and triumphing in the fiercely competitive educational technology industry.

The rationale of the Study

The rationale for this study arises from the desire to comprehend the intricate interplay between AI literacy and the development of teacher training programs in K12 education.

REVIEW OF LITERATURE

Artificial intelligence (AI) has recently become a major educational topic (Haque et al., 2023). Various methods can enhance education (Haque et al., 2022). Machine learning algorithms and data analysis, the driving forces behind AI technology, offer new opportunities to personalise learning, enhance education, and streamline administrative procedures. Personalized learning is a significant AI used in education. This strategy uses AI to customise learning experiences and content for each student. Personalize uses AI algorithms and data analysis to provide personalised training, adaptive feedback, and targeted resources (Wang, 2021). This method has considerable promise (Chen et al., 2022). Traditional education treats all pupils equally, regardless of their needs and learning styles (Yao et al., 2022). To customise learning routes, intelligent tutoring systems and adaptive learning platforms may analyse massive volumes of learner data, including performance, preferences, and progress (Prakash et al., 2023). These systems provide personalised training and feedback based on each student's speed, skills, and limitations (Miao et al., 2021). AI improves student engagement, motivation, and retention by personalising learning (Holmes & Tuomi, 2022). AI also influences grading and evaluation (Kumar et al., 2023). AI algorithms grade student assignments, quizzes, and examinations in automated grading systems (Zhai et al., 2021). This saves instructors time and ensures objective, consistent grading, reducing prejudice. AI-powered plagiarism detection technologies may also detect academic dishonesty, maintaining evaluation integrity (Schiff, 2022). AI has become a solid educational tool. Its use in personalised learning, assessment, administrative duties, and data analytics might transform education for students, educators, and administrators (Lee & Lee, 2021). Using AI in education can improve outcomes and prepare students for the future by creating efficient and exciting learning environments (Lim et al., 2023). The 1970s saw the first applications of AI in educational settings (Ronquillo et al., 2021). The goal of the research at the time was to determine whether one-on-one human tutoring, considered the most effective method of instruction but not available to most people, might be replaced by computers (Nemorin, 2021). Initially, efforts to automatically adjust or customise the learning for each learner employed rule-based AI algorithms (Miao, Holmes, Huang, & Zhang, 2021). Since its inception, the utilisation of AI in education has progressed in various ways, starting with AI tools that aid in learning and assessment for students and expanding to include AI tools that support teaching for teachers and AI tools that assist in managing educational institutions (Zhai et al., 2021). The relationship between AI and education extends beyond using AI in classrooms for learning purposes (Schiff, 2022). It also encompasses teaching AI methodologies and equipping individuals to thrive in the era of AI, promoting collaboration between humans and AI (Lee & Lee, 2021). Integrating AI in education brings attention to pedagogy, organisational structures, access, ethics, equity, and sustainability (Lim et al., 2023). To automate a process, a comprehensive understanding of it is essential (Chiu, 2021). Moreover, to fully achieve the potential of AI in supporting education for sustainable development, it is necessary to identify and utilise all the potential advantages of these technologies, while also recognising and reducing the associated dangers (Su & Yang, 2023). Therefore, it is necessary to consistently evaluate and perhaps overhaul the structure of education to align it with the primary objective of achieving SDG 4. The utilisation of AI technology is progressively becoming more prevalent in the facilitation of education management and delivery (Ouyang & Jiao, 2021). Instead of immediately assisting with teaching or learning, these system-facing apps are specifically designed to automate various areas of school administration, utilising Education Management Information Systems as a foundation.

Artificial intelligence (AI) in K-12 education is expanding quickly, leading to ethical problems (Adams, Pente, Lemermeyer, & Rockwell, 2023). This literature review explores the concepts of transparency, fairness, confidentiality, accountability, and security in AI ethics (Akgun & Greenhow, 2022). The paper analyses the use of these principles in the field of education, namely in the K-12 system. Transparency in artificial intelligence (AI) pertains to the clarity and openness with which AI systems interact with individuals and arrive at choices (Eguchi, Okada, & Muto, 2021). K-12 education transparency entails providing unambiguous and comprehensive information on using artificial intelligence (AI) techniques in education (Yau et al., 2023). Learning analytics and personalised learning platforms are artificial intelligence (AI) tools that enhance the educational experience for educators, learners, and guardians (Tedre et al., 2021). Transparency facilitates stakeholders' comprehension of the functioning of AI technology, fostering a well-informed and cooperative educational setting (Zhang et al., 2023). Transparent AI systems in schools may enhance stakeholder confidence and facilitate informed consent. Implementing new educational technologies is of utmost importance (Nguyen et al., 2023). Equity in artificial intelligence (AI) entails impartial treatment of all users, devoid of biases that may unfairly penalise any group. Recognises systems with inadequate construction can perpetuate or introduce biases (Williams et al., 2023). This can result in inequitable treatment of pupils from specific socioeconomic or ethnic backgrounds in K-12 education (Celik, 2023). Detecting and alleviating biases to guarantee equity in the AI algorithms employed for student evaluations and suggestions is crucial (Ng, Leung, Chu, & Qiao, 2021). Privacy, mainly regarding children, is paramount (Casal-Otero et al., 2023). Extensive data on students' performance, behaviour, and personal information is collected in educational AI systems (Sanusi et al., 2023). Safeguarding this data is essential for protecting students from misuse or security breaches (Su, Zhong, & Ng, 2022). Robust and comprehensive privacy standards guarantee that data is gathered and utilised in compliance with legislative mandates such as the Children's Online Privacy Protection Act (Wang & Cheng, 2021). Establishing clear accountability for the activities and effects of AI systems is crucial. It entails attributing responsibility for the behaviour and outcomes of AI systems to particular individuals or organisations (Kim, Lee, & Cho, 2022). Accountability enhances transparency and surveillance in the process of developing and using AI. Educators and administrators must be able to articulate and rationalise their choices of action (Yang, 2022). It has been shown that AI systems lacking accountability can significantly restrict the options available to children and their parents when there are malfunctions or negative results (Adams et al., 2021). Ensuring the safety of AI systems is essential to preventing any physical or emotional harm to students (Su, Zhong, & Ng, 2022). Before implementation in education, AI-driven technology should undergo comprehensive testing (Yau et al., 2023). Recommend implementing a system of monitoring and analysis to address any problems promptly (Lim et al., 2023).

RESEARCH METHODOLOGY

A wide range of research approaches will be utilised to accomplish this investigation's goals. A qualitative approach would start with a depth review of reports, curriculum documents of the K12 schools and conducting in-depth interviews with K-12 educational institutions, driven by artificial intelligence for grades K–12. These interviews were conducted to gain an understanding of the AI integration in their teaching and teachers training programs as well as their potential for contributing to teaching innovation. Case studies were generated and utilised to do this. The case study strategy involves a systematic, step-by-step analysis of cases (Shaika et al.,2021) involving K-12 education and AI integration. To develop results as well as responses to the issues that were given by the study, thematic analysis was performed to construct information (Kumar & Lal, 2023). To gain a better understanding of the present trends in artificial intelligence integration, digital innovation, and K–12 teachers training program development, the purpose of this study is to analyze these emerging trends.

Methodological Framework

The present study employed an interpretive, multiple case study approach to design and evaluate an artificial intelligence (AI) teacher training programme targeted towards K-12 educators. The interpretive approach facilitated a thorough comprehension of the viewpoints and experiences of the participants, while the utilisation of the multiple case study method enabled a comprehensive exploration of different educational settings and contexts (Rahman et al., 2022).

Research Design

1. Case Selection
   - The selection process will involve choosing schools that have different levels of technological integration and demographic diversity. This will help to ensure that a wide range of K-12 educational environments are represented in the study.
   - The study selected five schools from urban, suburban, and rural areas to capture a range of educational contexts and finally two cases were developed from them.
2. Participants
   - Teachers: K-12 educators from various subjects and grade levels who were willing to participate in AI training.
   - Administrators: School principals and officials provided valuable insights into institutional support and policy considerations.
   - Students: Researchers selected groups of students to receive feedback on the integration of AI literacy in their curriculum.

Data Collection Methods

1. Interviews
   - The researcher conducted semi-structured interviews with teachers, administrators, and students to collect qualitative data on their experiences, challenges, and perceptions (Sarkar & Lal, 2023) related to AI literacy and ethical education.
   - Researchers explored the effectiveness of the training programme, exchanged best practices, and identified potential areas for improvement.
   - Researchers evaluated students' understanding and engagement with AI concepts post-implementation.
2. Observations
   - Conducted classroom observations during AI literacy lessons to evaluate teaching methods, measure student engagement, and analyse interaction dynamics.
3. Document Analysis

   Analysis of curriculum documents, lesson plans, and teaching materials employed in the AI training programme.

Steps in Case Study Development

1. Initial Literature Review
    - The researcher undertook a comprehensive examination of the current body of literature (Lal, 2023) about AI literacy, ethical education, and teacher training programmes to discern fundamental principles and exemplary methodologies.
2. Development of Training Program
    - The design of the AI teacher training programme was based on identified best practices and took into account ethical considerations.
    - The components of this programme consisted of various educational activities designed to enhance the participants' understanding and skills in the field of artificial intelligence. These activities will encompass interactive workshops, online modules, hands-on AI projects, and collaborative learning sessions.
3. Pilot Testing
    - The proposed approach involves the implementation of the training programme in a limited number of schools, specifically one or two, to enhance the content and delivery methods through the incorporation of feedback and observations.
4. Full Implementation
    - The revised training programme was implemented across all selected case study sites.
    - It was crucial to closely observe and provide assistance to educators during the entire implementation process.
5. Data Collection
    - The data collection process involves gathering information through various methods such as interviews, observations, and document analysis, as mentioned previously.
6. Data Analysis
    - Thematic analysis was employed to discern and categorise recurring patterns and themes within the qualitative data (Singh et al., 2021).
7. Cross-Case Analysis
    - Examined the results obtained from various educational institutions to ascertain shared obstacles, effective approaches, and distinctive contextual elements (Lal, 2023) .
8. Reporting and Dissemination
    - The synthesised findings were compiled into a comprehensive report that provides a detailed analysis of the effectiveness of the training pro-

gramme (Lal & Sharma, 2021). Additionally, the report includes recommendations for broader implementation of the programme.

- The findings of the study were disseminated to relevant stakeholders through various means such as presentations, workshops, and academic publications (Singh et al., 2022).

The report generated was employed as an interpretive approach and multiple case studies were developed. This approach allowed for a comprehensive exploration of the topic at hand, namely the integration of AI literacy and ethical education into K-12 teacher training programmes. The findings of this study offer a detailed and nuanced understanding of the effective strategies and practices that can be employed in this context. The methods described in this study provide a comprehensive analysis of the process of developing, implementing, and evaluating the training programme. This research offers significant findings that can be of great value to educators, policy-makers, and researchers who are interested in equipping students with the necessary skills for a future that is heavily influenced by technology (Rahman et al., 2024) .

Case Story 1

Camp K12, an innovative online school with a global reach, is dedicated to transforming K-12 education by incorporating AI literacy and ethical education into its curriculum. Established in 2020, Camp K12, Gurgoan, Haryana utilises engaging and interactive sessions to educate students on coding and STEAM subjects. With a keen understanding of the importance of teacher training, they crafted a thorough AI training programme for educators (Williams, 2024). This programme covers everything from AI principles to ethical considerations and effective teaching strategies. Through close collaboration with AI experts and educators, as well as a strong focus on continuous professional development and community building, Camp K12 is dedicated to empowering teachers with the essential skills needed to effectively prepare students for an AI-driven future.

Case Story 2

Pacific world, a Future Ready K-12 School, in Greater Noida, India created AI teacher training for this unique endeavour. Teaching is this company's speciality. Problem-solving and school/district student equality are their strengths. The consulting team carefully designed and taught the course for real-world relevance. Interactive seminars, live AI demonstrations, and collaborative learning spaces were offered by the school. Review updated AI literacy training approaches and resources, teachers quickly integrated AI into lessons. The researchers addressed algorithmic injustice and privacy. Teacher training on critical thinking, problem-solving, and digital literacy prepared students for a tech-driven future (Moustaghfir, & Brigui, 2024). This well-run study showed unique pedagogical tactics can improve K-12 AI instruction with professional leadership and fairness.

Table 1. Challenges and strategies

S.No.	Case Story	Challenges Faced	Strategies Implemented
1.	Camp K12, founded in 2020, is transforming K-12 education by integrating AI literacy and ethical education into its curriculum. With engaging coding and STEAM sessions, as well as a comprehensive AI training programme for educators, Camp K12 works closely with AI experts to empower teachers and equip students for a future driven by AI.	Integrating AI literacy and ethical education into the curriculum	Created engaging interactive sessions, designed a comprehensive AI training programme for educators, and worked closely with AI experts to ensure ongoing professional development and foster a sense of community.
2.	Pacific World, Future Ready Schools, AI teacher training programme emphasises ethics, problem-solving, and equity in K-12 teaching. Teachers learned how to easily integrate AI into their teachings by attending interesting seminars and seeing live AI demonstrations. They addressed algorithmic inequality and privacy to prepare pupils for a tech-driven world.	Addressing algorithmic injustice and privacy concerns in AI training for teachers to ensure real-world relevance.	Developed a thorough course that includes engaging seminars, live AI demonstrations, collaborative learning spaces, and an evaluation of different AI literacy training methods. Highlighted the importance of ethics and critical thinking. I conducted focus groups, semi-structured interviews, and classroom observations to evaluate the situation.

Source: (Stake,2013) Author's Compilation

To ensure accuracy and consistency throughout cleaning and preprocessing, prioritised data organisation. To increase data analysis superfluous and irrelevant entries were removed. By carefully selecting variables, analysis parameters were set.

Table 2. Framework of case study consideration

Consideration Type	Case Story 1: Camp K12, Gurgaon.	Case Story 2: Pacific World, Greater Noida.
Philosophical Consideration	Revolutionising education by incorporating AI literacy and ethical education into the K-12 curriculum.	Highlighting the importance of fostering problem-solving skills and ensuring equal opportunities for students in AI literacy education from kindergarten to twelfth grade.
Research Logic Consideration	Employs interactive sessions and engages in partnership with AI experts to develop a comprehensive AI training programme for educators.	Utilises practical applications by offering meticulously crafted courses, engaging workshops, and live demonstrations of artificial intelligence.
Ethical Consideration	Emphasises ethical values in artificial intelligence, ongoing professional growth, and fostering a sense of community among teachers.	Seeks to rectify unfairness and bias in algorithms, safeguard privacy, and advocate for equal opportunities and fairness in AI education.

Source: (Stake,2013) Author's Compilation

Data Analysis & Interpretation

The research methodology combines a qualitative approach to provide a thorough understanding. The qualitative approach involves conducting thorough reviews of reports and policy documents, as well as conducting interviews with K-12 educational institutions that are utilising AI. Case studies are carefully crafted to showcase AI integration in teacher training programs and opportunities. Thematic analysis is used to organise information and generate answers to the research questions. The study utilises an interpretive, multiple-case study approaches to develop and evaluate an AI teacher training programme. This methodology promotes a clear understanding of participant perspectives and allows for the exploration of various educational contexts.

The researcher carefully selected schools with different levels of technological integration and diverse demographics to ensure a well-rounded representation. Participants consist of K-12 educators, administrators, and students, offering comprehensive feedback. Various methods can be used to collect data, such as semi-structured interviews, focus groups, classroom observations, and document analysis. Pre- and post-training surveys are used to assess the impact of the training on teacher confidence, knowledge, and attitudes towards AI literacy and ethics.

The methodology consists of conducting an initial literature review, creating an AI training programme using best practices, conducting pilot testing, fully implementing the programme, and collecting data through various qualitative methods. Thematic and cross-case analysis help identify patterns, effective approaches, and contextual elements in a way that is cohesive and logical. The findings are organised into a comprehensive report and shared with stakeholders through presentations, workshops, and publications.

Table 3. Findings and uniqueness of results

S.No.	Finding/Result	Description
1.	Holistic Integration	Highlighting the significance of incorporating AI literacy and ethical education into K-12 curricula to adequately equip students for a future heavily influenced by AI.
2.	Ethical Emphasis	Highlighting the importance of ethical considerations in AI education, addressing issues of algorithmic injustice, and privacy concerns, and promoting equal opportunities.
3.	Comprehensive Training	Our AI training programmes for educators are carefully designed to provide a cohesive and logically structured learning experience. They include interactive workshops, live demonstrations, and collaborative learning spaces.
4.	Diverse Representation	Including schools with different levels of technological integration and diverse demographics to ensure findings that are applicable across various educational contexts.
5.	Effective Professional Development	Effective integration of AI literacy into teaching practices requires continuous professional development and community building among teachers.

Source: (Stake,2013) Author's Compilation

The study's methodology is thorough, and it places a strong emphasis on ethical considerations. This creates a solid foundation for future AI literacy initiatives in K-12 education. The qualitative approach along with the diverse representation of educational contexts, highlights the significance of holistic and equitable AI education.

CONCLUSION

The research emphasises the importance of integrating comprehensive AI literacy and ethical education into K-12 curricula, ensuring that students are well-prepared for the future driven by AI. After conducting a thorough analysis of relevant literature and case studies, the study uncovered several crucial elements that contribute to the success of AI teacher training programmes. These factors encompass the incorporation of AI principles and ethical considerations into the curriculum, the significance of ongoing professional development for educators, and the utilisation of interactive, real-world applications to captivate students. Case studies from Camp K12 and Pacific World, Future Ready Schools showcased the effective execution of AI literacy programmes that prioritised ethical factors, including algorithmic justice and privacy. These programmes also emphasised the importance of having a variety of perspectives in educational settings and the need for educators to continuously foster a sense of community. The results indicate that an organised AI teacher training programme, which includes practical projects, ethical discussions, and collaborative learning settings, can greatly improve teachers' confidence and skills in AI education. By effectively integrating AI literacy into their teaching practices, educators can prepare students for future challenges in a technology-driven world. The study promotes a comprehensive approach to AI literacy that integrates ethical education and practical training. This approach aims to equip educators with the necessary tools to cultivate critical thinking, problem-solving, and digital literacy in their students. This approach not only tackles current gaps in teacher training but also lays the foundation for a fair and all-encompassing AI education framework

REFERENCES

Adams, C., Pente, P., Lemermeyer, G., & Rockwell, G. (2021, June). Artificial intelligence ethics guidelines for K-12 education: A review of the global landscape. In *International Conference on Artificial Intelligence in Education* (pp. 24-28). Cham: Springer International Publishing. DOI: 10.1007/978-3-030-78270-2_4

Adams, C., Pente, P., Lemermeyer, G., & Rockwell, G. (2023). Ethical principles for artificial intelligence in K-12 education. *Computers and Education: Artificial Intelligence*, *4*, 100131. DOI: 10.1016/j.caeai.2023.100131

Akgun, S., & Greenhow, C. (2022). Artificial intelligence in education: Addressing ethical challenges in K-12 settings. *AI and Ethics*, *2*(3), 431–440. DOI: 10.1007/s43681-021-00096-7 PMID: 34790956

Alexandre, F., Becker, J., Comte, M. H., Lagarrigue, A., Liblau, R., Romero, M., & Viéville, T. (2021). Why, What and How to help each citizen understand artificialintelligence? *Kunstliche Intelligenz*, *35*(2), 191–199. DOI: 10.1007/s13218-021-00725-7 PMID: 33994668

Aung, Z. H., Sanium, S., Songsaksuppachok, C., Kusakunniran, W., Precharattana, M., Chuechote, S., & Ritthipravat, P. (2022). Designing a novel teaching platform for AI: A case study in a Thai school context. *Journal of Computer Assisted Learning*, *38*(6), 1714–1729. DOI: 10.1111/jcal.12706

Casal-Otero, L., Catala, A., Fernández-Morante, C., Taboada, M., Cebreiro, B., & Barro, S. (2023). AI literacy in K-12: A systematic literature review. *International Journal of STEM Education*, *10*(1), 29. DOI: 10.1186/s40594-023-00418-7

Celik, I. (2023). Towards Intelligent-TPACK: An empirical study on teachers' professional knowledge to ethically integrate artificial intelligence (AI)-based tools into education. *Computers in Human Behavior*, *138*, 107468. DOI: 10.1016/j.chb.2022.107468

Chen, X., Zou, D., Xie, H., Cheng, G., & Liu, C. (2022). Two decades of artificial intelligence in education. *Journal of Educational Technology & Society*, *25*, 28–47.

Chiu, T. K. (2021). A holistic approach to the design of artificial intelligence (AI) education for K-12 schools. *TechTrends*, *65*(5), 796–807. DOI: 10.1007/s11528-021-00637-1

Chiu, T. K. F. (2021). A holistic approach to the design of artificial intelligence (AI) education for K-12 schools. *TechTrends*, *65*(5), 796–807. DOI: 10.1007/s11528-021-00637-1

Crompton, H., Jones, M. V., & Burke, D. (2022). Affordances and challenges of artificial intelligence in K-12 education: A systematic review. *Journal of Research on Technology in Education*. Advance online publication. DOI: 10.1080/15391523.2022.2121344

Dai, Y., Liu, A., Qin, J., Guo, Y., Jong, M. S. Y., Chai, C. S., & Lin, Z. (2023). Collaborative construction of artificial intelligence curriculum in primary schools. *Journal of Engineering Education*, *112*(1), 23–42. DOI: 10.1002/jee.20503

DiPaola, D., Payne, B. H., & Breazeal, C. (2020). Decoding Design Agendas: An Ethical Design Activity for Middle School Students. In *Proceedings of the Interaction Design and Children Conference* (IDC '20) (pp. 1-10). Association for Computing Machinery. DOI: 10.1145/3392063.3394396

Eguchi, A., Okada, H., & Muto, Y. (2021). Contextualizing AI education for K-12 students to enhance their learning of AI literacy through culturally responsive approaches. *Kunstliche Intelligenz*, *35*(2), 153–161. DOI: 10.1007/s13218-021-00737-3 PMID: 34376922

Haque, S., Zeba, S., Haque, M. A., Kumar, K., & Basha, M. P. A. (2023). An IoT model for securing examinations from malpractices. *Materials Today: Proceedings*, *81*, 371–376. DOI: 10.1016/j.matpr.2021.03.413

Haque MdA. Sonal D, Haque, S., Rahman, M., & Kumar, K. (2022). Learning management system empowered by machine learning. *AIP Conference Proceedings*, *2381*, 020085. DOI: 10.1063/5.0074278

Henry, J., Hernalesteen, A., & Collard, A.-S. (2021). Teaching artificial intelligence to K-12 through a role-playing game questioning the intelligence concept. *Kunstliche Intelligenz*, *35*(2), 171–179. DOI: 10.1007/s13218-021-00733-7

Holmes, W., & Tuomi, I. (2022). State of the art and practice in AI in education. *European Journal of Education*, *57*(4), 542–570. DOI: 10.1111/ejed.12533

Jaskie, K., Larson, J., Johnson, M., Turner, K., O'Donnell, M., Christen, J. B., & Spanias, A. (2021). Research experiences for teachers in machine learning. In *IEEE Frontiers in Education Conference (FIE)* (pp. 1–5). Lincoln, NE, USA. DOI: 10.1109/FIE49875.2021.9637132

Kandlhofer, M., & Steinbauer, G. (2021). AI K-12 education service. *Kunstliche Intelligenz*, *35*(2), 125–126. DOI: 10.1007/s13218-021-00715-9

Kim, J., Lee, H., & Cho, Y. H. (2022). Learning design to support student-AI collaboration: Perspectives of leading teachers for AI in education. *Education and Information Technologies*, *27*(5), 6069–6104. DOI: 10.1007/s10639-021-10831-6

Kim, K., Kwon, K., Ottenbreit-Leftwich, A., Bae, H., & Glazewski, K. (2023). Exploring middle school students' common naive conceptions of Artificial Intelligence concepts, and the evolution of these ideas. *Education and Information Technologies*, *28*(8), 9827–9854. Advance online publication. DOI: 10.1007/s10639-023-11600-3

Kjær Bilstrup, K.-E., Kaspersen, M. H., & Petersen, M. G. (2020). Staging Reflections on Ethical Dilemmas in Machine Learning: A Card-Based Design Workshop for High School Students. In Proceedings of the 2020 ACM Designing Interactive Systems Conference (pp. 1211–1222).

Kumar, D., Haque, A., Mishra, K., Islam, F., Mishra, B. K., & Ahmad, S. (2023). Exploring the transformative role of artificial intelligence and metaverse in education: A comprehensive review. *Metaverse Basic and Applied Research*, *2*, 55–55. DOI: 10.56294/mr202355

Kumar, D., & Lal, R. (2023). Technological Advancements in the Media Industry and the Current Job Market in India. In Naim, A. (Ed.), *Accreditation Processes and Frameworks in Higher Education* (pp. 289–314). Nova Science Publishers.

Lal, R. (2023). New Measures of Teaching Learning and Evaluating with Changing Technology. In Naim, A. (Ed.), *Accreditation Processes and Frameworks in Higher Education* (pp. 267–287). Nova Science Publishers.

Lal, R., & Sharma, G. (2021). Social media influencers for online purchase behaviour: Mediation by brand consciousness. Journal of Content. *Community & Communication*, *13*(7), 83–94.

Lee, H. S., & Lee, J. (2021). Applying artificial intelligence in physical education and future perspectives. *Sustainability (Basel)*, *13*(1), 351. DOI: 10.3390/su13010351

Lim, W. M., Gunasekara, A., Pallant, J. L., Pallant, J. I., & Pechenkina, E. (2023). Generative AI and the future of education: Ragnarök or reformation? A paradoxical perspective from management educators. *International Journal of Management Education*, *21*(2), 100790. DOI: 10.1016/j.ijme.2023.100790

Lin, P., & Brummelen, J. (2021). Engaging teachers to co-design integrated AI curriculum for K-12 classrooms. In *CHI '21: Proceedings of the 2021 CHI Conference on Human Factors in Computing Systems* (pp. 1–12). DOI: 10.1145/3411764.3445377

Miao, F., Holmes, W., Huang, R., & Zhang, H. (2021). *AI and education: A guidance for policymakers*. UNESCO Publishing.

Moustaghfir, S., & Brigui, H. (2024). Navigating Critical Thinking in the Digital Era: An Informative Exploration. International Journal of Linguistics. *Literature and Translation*, *7*(1), 137–143.

Nemorin, S. (2021). Fair-AI. Project Update #6. Preliminary Findings. Retrieved February 4, 2021, from https://www.fair-ai.com/projectupdate-6

Ng, D. T. K., Leung, J. K. L., Chu, K. W. S., & Qiao, M. S. (2021). AI literacy: Definition, teaching, evaluation and ethical issues. *Proceedings of the Association for Information Science and Technology*, *58*(1), 504–509. DOI: 10.1002/pra2.487

Nguyen, A., Ngo, H. N., Hong, Y., Dang, B., & Nguyen, B. P. T. (2023). Ethical principles for artificial intelligence in education. *Education and Information Technologies*, *28*(4), 4221–4241. DOI: 10.1007/s10639-022-11316-w PMID: 36254344

Ouyang, F., & Jiao, P. (2021). Artificial intelligence in education: The three paradigms. *Computers and Education: Artificial Intelligence*, *2*, 100020. DOI: 10.1016/j.caeai.2021.100020

Prakash, A., Haque, A., Islam, F., & Sonal, D. (2023). Exploring the Potential of Metaverse for Higher Education: Opportunities, Challenges, and Implications. *Metaverse Basic and Applied Research*, *2*, 40. DOI: 10.56294/mr202340

Rahman, Z. T., Lal, R., & Ratna, R. (2022). An Analytical Study on the Significance of Folk and Fairytales on the Psychology of Young Children. *International Journal of Early Childhood Special Education*, *14*(5).

Rahman, Z. T., Lal, R., & Rena, R. (2024). Challenges of Communication with Gen-Z in the Era of Artificial Intelligence-Interceded Digital Economy. In *AI-Oriented Competency Framework for Talent Management in the Digital Economy* (pp. 76–94). CRC Press. DOI: 10.1201/9781003440901-5

Ronquillo, C. E., Peltonen, L. M., Pruinelli, L., Chu, C. H., Bakken, S., Beduschi, A., Cato, K., Hardiker, N., Junger, A., Michalowski, M., Nyrup, R., Rahimi, S., Reed, D. N., Salakoski, T., Salanterä, S., Walton, N., Weber, P., Wiegand, T., & Topaz, M. (2021). Artificial intelligence in nursing: Priorities and opportunities from an international invitational think-tank of the Nursing and Artificial Intelligence Leadership Collaborative. *Journal of Advanced Nursing*, *77*(9), 3707–3717. DOI: 10.1111/jan.14855 PMID: 34003504

Russell, S. (2021). The history and future of AI. *Oxford Review of Economic Policy*, *37*(3), 509–520. DOI: 10.1093/oxrep/grab013

Sanusi, I. T., Oyelere, S. S., Vartiainen, H., Suhonen, J., & Tukiainen, M. (2023). A systematic review of teaching and learning machine learning in K-12 education. *Education and Information Technologies*, *28*(5), 5967–5997. DOI: 10.1007/s10639-022-11416-7

Sarkar, N., & Lal, R. (2023). Changing Trends of Media Ownership: Marketing Through Community Engagement in Hindi Television News Channels. In Global Applications of the Internet of Things in Digital Marketing (pp. 290-309). IGI Global.

Schiff, D. (2022). Education for AI, not AI for education: The role of education and ethics in national AI policy strategies. *International Journal of Artificial Intelligence in Education*, *32*(3), 527–563. DOI: 10.1007/s40593-021-00270-2

Schiff, D. (2022). Education for AI, not AI for education: The role of education and ethics in national AI policy strategies. *International Journal of Artificial Intelligence in Education*, *32*(3), 527–563. DOI: 10.1007/s40593-021-00270-2

Shaika, S., Lal, R., & Jonjua, M. (2021). Sustainable Development Goal 3: Case Study of using Folk media as a Potent tool in India. *Journal of Contemporary Issues in Business and Government*, *27*(1), •••.

Singh, R. K., Prakash, R., & Lal, R. (2021). Adoption of CAB model for instrument development of effectiveness of crime-based reality-shows. *Journal of Content Community and Communication*, *14*(7), 230–239. DOI: 10.31620/JCCC.12.21/19

Singh, R. K., Prakash, R., Lal, R., & Nanda, V. (2022). Mediation Role of Crime-Show Impact Between Creating Awareness About Crime and Novelty in Crime. *Journal of Pharmaceutical Negative Results*, •••, 1255–1262.

Su, J., & Yang, W. (2023). Unlocking the power of ChatGPT: A framework for applying generative AI in education. *ECNU Review of Education*, *6*(3), 355–366. DOI: 10.1177/20965311231168423

Su, J., Zhong, Y., & Ng, D. T. K. (2022). A meta-review of literature on educational approaches for teaching AI at the K-12 levels in the Asia-Pacific region. *Computers and Education: Artificial Intelligence*, *3*, 100065. DOI: 10.1016/j.caeai.2022.100065

Suh, W., & Ahn, S. (2022). Development and validation of a scale measuring student attitudes toward artificial intelligence. *SAGE Open*, *12*(2), 1–12. DOI: 10.1177/21582440221100463

Tedre, M., Toivonen, T., Kahila, J., Vartiainen, H., Valtonen, T., Jormanainen, I., & Pears, A. (2021). Teaching machine learning in K–12 classroom: Pedagogical and technological trajectories for artificial intelligence education. *IEEE Access : Practical Innovations, Open Solutions*, *9*, 110558–110572. DOI: 10.1109/ACCESS.2021.3097962

Van Brummelen, J., Heng, T., & Tabunshchyk, V. (2021a). Teaching tech to talk: K-12 conversational artificial intelligence literacy curriculum and development tools. *Proceedings of the AAAI Conference on Artificial Intelligence*, *35*(17), 15655–15663. DOI: 10.1609/aaai.v35i17.17844

Wang, T., & Cheng, E. C. K. (2021). An investigation of barriers to Hong Kong K-12 schools incorporating Artificial Intelligence in education. *Computers and Education: Artificial Intelligence*, *2*, 100031. DOI: 10.1016/j.caeai.2021.100031

Wang, Y. (2021). When artificial intelligence meets educational leaders' data-informed decision-making: A cautionary tale. *Studies in Educational Evaluation*, *69*, 100872. DOI: 10.1016/j.stueduc.2020.100872

Williams, R. (2024). Impact. AI: Democratizing AI through K-12 Artificial Intelligence Education (Doctoral dissertation, Massachusetts Institute of Technology).

Williams, R., Ali, S., Devasia, N., DiPaola, D., Hong, J., Kaputsos, S. P., Jordan, B., & Breazeal, C. (2023). AI+ ethics curricula for middle school youth: Lessons learned from three project-based curricula. *International Journal of Artificial Intelligence in Education*, *33*(2), 325–383. DOI: 10.1007/s40593-022-00298-y PMID: 35935456

Xia, Q., Chiu, T. K., & Chai, C. S. (2022). The moderating effects of gender and need satisfaction on self-regulated learning through Artificial Intelligence (AI). *Education and Information Technologies*. Advance online publication. DOI: 10.1007/s10639-022-11547x

Yang, W. (2022). Artificial Intelligence education for young children: Why, what, and how in curriculum design and implementation. *Computers and Education: Artificial Intelligence*, *3*, 100061. DOI: 10.1016/j.caeai.2022.100061

Yao, X., Ma, N., Zhang, J., Wang, K., Yang, E., & Faccio, M. (2022). Enhancing wisdom manufacturing as industrial metaverse for industry and society 5.0. *Journal of Intelligent Manufacturing*, •••, 1–21.

Yau, K. W., Chai, C. S., Chiu, T. K., Meng, H., King, I., Wong, S. W. H., & Yam, Y. (2022). Co-designing artificial intelligence curriculum for secondary schools: A grounded theory of teachers' experience. In *2022 International Symposium on Educational Technology (ISET)* (pp. 58–62). DOI: 10.1109/ISET55194.2022.00020

Yau, K. W., Chai, C. S., Chiu, T. K., Meng, H., King, I., & Yam, Y. (2023). A phenomenographic approach on teacher conceptions of teaching Artificial Intelligence (AI) in K-12 schools. *Education and Information Technologies*, *28*(1), 1041–1064. DOI: 10.1007/s10639-022-11161-x

Zhai, X., Chu, X., Chai, C. S., Jong, M. S. Y., Istenic, A., Spector, M., Liu, J.-B., Yuan, J., & Li, Y. (2021). A Review of Artificial Intelligence (AI) in Education from 2010 to 2020. *Complexity*, *2021*(1), 1–18. DOI: 10.1155/2021/8812542

Zhang, H., Lee, I., Ali, S., DiPaola, D., Cheng, Y., & Breazeal, C. (2023). Integrating ethics and career futures with technical learning to promote AI literacy for middle school students: An exploratory study. *International Journal of Artificial Intelligence in Education*, *33*(2), 290–324. DOI: 10.1007/s40593-022-00293-3 PMID: 35573722

Chapter 6
Educator Training for Artificial Intelligence Use in AI-Based K-12 Education System

Sheneen Hossain
http://orcid.org/0009-0005-0542-1829
Anhui University of Technology, Bangladesh

ABSTRACT

Artificial intelligence is, in particular, one of the fastest-developing areas within the education sector, especially at the K–12 levels. From personalized learning experiences to efficient processes for various administrative tasks, AI has massive potential, which could hugely affect teaching and learning. However, before that, educators need proper training in AI technology. The integration of AI into education exceeds just the boundaries of technical tools; it requires a more detailed cognition of how the technology can improve performance, further equity, and personalize experiences in an environment of inclusivity. This chapter delves into some basics of training AI teachers, the capabilities expected of a teacher, and some real-world examples of AI in the classroom. We will look with equal interest at how quality educator preparation can help resolve the challenges brought about through AI integration for the success of both instructors and students in an educational setup supported by AI.

DOI: 10.4018/979-8-3693-6346-1.ch006

INTRODUCTION

In the past ten years, there have been many significant changes in Technology in computing. Data-driven machine learning techniques led into the domain of conventional programming and rule-based "good old artificial intelligence", which has been the leading factor of automation for the past 70 years. It is hence argued that automation through machine learning is just an extended, polished era of rule-based programming because new systems that are run by software automation do not just involve computer technology that has been invented recently. It has been seen that for many problem areas, it is much easier to collect large datasets for machine learning methods than it is to provide the rules for rule-based software. The computer environment has seen another significant innovation over the past ten years. Recent data has brought new data processing techniques based on learning as opposed to classical programming and "ready-made" artificial intelligence of the automation area for the past 70 years [Tedre, M., Toivonen, T., Kahila, J., Vartiainen, H., Valtonen, T., Jormanainen, I. and Pears, A., (2021)]. The primary reason that machine learning approaches can automate many tasks which rule-based programming approaches would struggle with is the very reason some proponents predict the emergence of a 'second machine age'. For many application spaces, it has been observed that obtaining large enough data sets for machine learning is much easier for many problems compared to crafting rules needed for rule-based software.

As AI becomes increasingly embedded into numerous professions, the advent of AI into K–12 education holds great promise for bettering learning experiences, personalizing instruction, and increasing student achievement. But for truly capitalizing on AI in the classroom, teachers will have to be prepared to oversee these resources, implement them judiciously, and make certain they serve ethically.

The Artificial Intelligence (AI) Global Assistance System has a primary aim – to provide educators with the knowledge and skills to be able to integrate AI effectively in their teaching and the learning process. This implies that teachers need to be ready for the elimination of factors like safety of data, prejudices and disparities and also understand the capabilities of AI i.e. intelligent tutors, auto correctors, and adaptive learning systems.

LITERATURE REVIEW

As indicated by Chiu, T.K., (2021), teachers are very often in great demand of professional advancement programs regarding the above technologies; very few of them have AI technical grounding, but it is worth mentioning AI practitioners. Teachers may not be able to properly use AI, leading to an underutilization of well-integrated systems that would help in improving the education quality of a learner, the operations of the education institutions and even the present learning content. Akgun, S. and Greenhow, C., (2022). asserts that much of the power of AI will not be achieved by any education.

Another group of researchers which is in the process of completing a machine learning and K–12 review discovered that classical systematic reviews do not fit well with the theme mainly due to:1) the defined under research and adherence to some established terminology, and 2), the many ways of defining and approaching ai education, thus making their criticisms largely irrelevant. Exploration texts, on the contrary, are particularly advantageous compared to structured texts when it comes to finding relevant data [Azzam, A. and Charles, T., (2024)]. Upon conducting this study, the author applied a scoping study, which seeks to provide a quick overview of a new subject, including core ideas and their relationships, significant findings and important areas of future research. Such an approach has already been used in the scoping of stand-alone reviews of the same kind, for instance. The latter is because the scoping review approach is not built around a specific set of keywords, but aims to cover a wide range of information and is hence especially effective for searching an area like teaching machine learning in school settings for children with diverse linguistic backgrounds. Unlike standard systematic reviews. Several limitations of the scoping review include reduced replicability as well inability to aggregate results statistically and assess the quality of the found papers (as opposed to meta-reviews). They do not attempt to provide meta-analytic overviews of the literature.

Effective programs for educating teachers need to embrace both AI-related as well as pedagogical fundamentals. Essentially, while the pedagogical skills are aimed at promoting the effective use of AI tools for the students and within given courses, technical skills are important to understand how AI's function is executed. Most recent studies make an inference that the most beneficial way of training is using practical activities, particularly on AI and the trainers are engaging with these technologies in the classroom thus simultaneously learning the basics of AI. Woodruff, K., Hutson, J. and Arnone, K., (2023). This experience is instrumental in minimizing the theory-practice gap.

Likewise, there is a need to address concerns such as Data privacy, ethics and prejudices in AI systems which requires that both educators and practitioners continue to be supported. This means that the training agenda must include, among other things, an aspect on how to end discrimination, a nudge for pupils to reason critically, and how to use AI in a principled way (Yue et al., 2022).

In conclusion, the successful implementation of AI technologies in teaching school children can only be achieved purely with a proper in-service training system provided by teachers. Teacher training to help them make use of AI technologies effectively must expand as the technology changes.

UNDERSTANDING AI IN K-12 EDUCATION

Teacher machine learning in their computer curriculum has become more inclusive and low-cost thanks to introductory technologies that introduce Machine learning (ML) as a basic premise. In addition, it may be noted that ML technologies and applications have become a very natural part of the context of user's daily life. However, with the advent of user interfaces that can train machine learning models and with the curriculum becoming more and more "data-driven," it is possible to envisage end-user programming being merged with data-driven applications. Quite an extensive number of studies dealing with imparting machine-learning concepts to learners at different educational levels have increased in the last few years. Some examples clearly show that there is a lot of active transformation in the curriculum for state educational institutions. The specifics of a few of the alterations are discussed here.

Artificial intelligence (AI) theory and practice have been part of computer science curricula since the year of its introduction which was 1956. For the better part of their education in AI theory, these learners have been practising the calculations for the design of models that learn and can make future predictions of many different patterns within the majority of learning institutions. Besides this, widening the AI training scope of AI in practice often creates the implementation and use of AI types, theories, and techniques more advanced than their theoretical description or the learning process about them to enhance their utilization.

However, the use of AI in education has its disadvantages such as the need to guarantee that the teachers comprehend how to apply AI technology effectively yet in a pedagogical manner in regards to controlling the learning process. The rapid changes in the capabilities of AI necessitate regular training for teachers. [Adams, C., Pente, P., Lemermeyer, G. and Rockwell, G., (2023)]

Traditional AI applications in K-12 education, such as 1) Intelligent Tutoring Systems, 2) AI Based Learning Processes Investigation Tools, and 3) AI Based School Administration Support Systems, have usually been predominant in the field. This includes intelligent tutoring systems, learning object management system, pedagogical agents, adaptive educational systems, etc. Research has aimed to automate the representation of the different components of the learning process such as the learner, teaching, subject, environment, and materials other than adapting the approach that occurs during the learning. However, as technology progresses, and more educational paradigms come into focus, there has been a developed attitude towards the use of this service when it comes to education.

In comparison to the context of the 21st century, AI and education have come a long way. The educational system has long used artificial intelligence (AI) tools in three main ways: supporting learning processes, investigating learning processes, and helping to improve the organization of the schools. Design of intelligent tutor systems, oversight and monitoring actions in educational contexts, interaction with students by animated humanoid agents, and development of individual systems of studying and numerous other similar research undertakings have all attempted to create models of the learning situation to eliminate human operators. There are conflicting opinions regarding the use of artificial intelligence and education within various contexts as each technology and educational paradigm advances over time.

Teacher machine learning in their computer curriculum has become more inclusive and low-cost thanks to introductory technologies that introduce Machine learning (ML) as a basic premise. In addition, it may be noted that ML technologies and applications have become a very natural part of the context of user's daily life. However, with the advent of user interfaces that can train machine learning models and with the curriculum becoming more and more "data-driven," it is possible to envisage end-user programming being merged with data-driven applications. Quite an extensive number of studies dealing with imparting machine-learning concepts to learners at different educational levels has increased in the last few years. Some examples clearly show that there is a lot of active transformation in a curriculum for state educational institutions. The specifics of a few of the alterations are discussed here. The empowerment of kids also comes when their questions are answered concerning how learning machines make decisions and act. For instance, some of the common machine learning applications include face recognition, voice recognition, and pattern recognition.

THE ROLE OF EDUCATORS IN AI-POWERED CLASSROOMS

The role of educators is going through a lot of change with the emergence of artificial intelligence or AI in the educational sector. AI in education has turned out to be a game changer, with the allure of making students more involved, allowing teachers to focus better, and avoiding doing manual work for attending to students amongst several others. While there is no doubt that the advent of biometric education technology will greatly benefit the education process, it is teachers' responsibility to lead, support and help ensure that the technology is used effectively and competently.

Facilitators of Learning

One of the main benefits of artificial intelligence in education would be the ability to tailor content for every student. This is why the likes of Khan Academy and DreamBox rely on AI technologies to fashion tutorials, assessments, and educational materials to meet the learning needs of students, – individual learning style and effectiveness, subjects in a skill that has achieved perfection, and those that have been ignored. For example, the adaptive math software created by DreamBox, which is tailored according to the needs of students so they can learn at their own pace and thrive in education, achieves this by resolving the perceived issue of performing unfavourable routines. [Unal, A. and Unal, Z., (2024).]

Regardless of the advancements in AI, the role of educators in making meaning of that information is still indispensable. It is only through a systematic examination of student data that areas of improvement can be determined and teaching approaches be changed. There are educators at Khan Academy who can access reports on the progress of students and provide more assistance or advanced help where needed. To make sure that use of AI in education does not suppress the essential role of humans in the process of imparting soft skills such as collaborative skills, understanding, and reasoning, it is incumbent on teachers to practice a balance.

Ethical Oversight and Digital Literacy

AI –enabled gadgets will process significant volumes of student's personal information. This poses scope for concern due to issues of bias and privacy. As an example, there is an expectation that the use of AI in assessment, such as Socrative will adhere to the data restriction laws like FERPA. Such utilization may capture the responses of students to the various questions. Educators also hold a responsibility of teaching learners the dangers associated with artificial intelligence that lacks ethics.

For example, at Harvard University, teachers are integrating AI ethics education in their classes intending to aid students in developing critical thought on the societal use of technology. The trained teachers discuss measures that would counterbalance the harms caused by bias. And about how human rights and the distribution of work are at risk with the advancement of AI technologies. In AI-empowered classrooms, teachers are a must in steering students across the various problems in a world which is embracing technology at an increasingly fast pace.

Promoting Human-AI Collaboration

The progress of technology must not hinder the ability of teachers to adapt positively to these changes in order to remain effective. IBM developed the Watson Education tool for enhancing teaching and for this reason, it is an example in the context of the given statement. Watson generates data, using which instructors realize gaps and tendencies in the learning process of students. In the process of analysis, the artificial intellect of Watson understands the challenges that students face and recommends useful teaching methods. It is used by teachers to target the lesson to particular groups, among which they can spend more time on those with more problems. In the effort to avoid escalation of issues, teachers can resort to the use of Watson's machines and single out students who are at risk of performing poorly.

AI can also aid teachers by reducing the time spent on performing remit such as marking exercise books and keeping attendance registers- all of which help in the effective operations of the establishments. For instance, we have software like GradeScope that uses Artificial Intelligence to help IT teachers have more energy applied to the quality of teaching and on students than to the marking of exams. With even less effort these days, effective teaching is possible as teachers can take up the role of encouraging questions, ideas, and thoughts to a segment of the students one wishes to teach.

Professional Development and Lifelong Learning

Incorporating AI in the classroom forces educators like teachers to constantly up their game. Professional Development in this context has been provided by the Google for Education initiative for instance, by introducing courses that aid the educators to know and effectively implement AI or other digital resources in their learning spaces to good effect. In countries such as Singapore, substantial investments have been made by the governments to ensure that the educators too, are up-to-date with handling the changes that come with the integration of IT in schools including AI. [Martin, F., Zhuang, M. and Schaefer, D., (2023)]

By examining their teaching strategies, AI-powered technologies can also aid in the professional development of instructors. Platforms such as TeachFX, for instance, employ artificial intelligence (AI) to evaluate class conversations and provide feedback on how well professors are promoting student participation. Teachers may improve their teaching methods and interact with students more successfully with the use of this kind of data.

CORE ELEMENTS OF AI TRAINING FOR EDUCATORS

The use of artificial intelligence technology in education is aimed at improving the learning processes for both students and teachers. For example, AI integrates learning gaps with content, reduces time for repeated actions, supports individual learning during a session, and provides feedback almost instantly. However, every use of AI depends on the education system and the teacher or instructor must be trained first because AI is not easy. Teachers without the correct guidance will find it hard to understand how to apply AI in their teaching, lose an opportunity to carry out evidence-based correction and use AI in ways that harm the learning of students. Educators are also required to a certain extent comprehend the nuances of artificial intelligence and the associated ethical and social issues such as algorithmic bias, equity, data protection, inter alia. AI training programs that have yielded desirable outcomes for teachers need to address three significant concerns: enhanced technical knowledge, a sense of embedding in pedagogy and ethical considerations.

Technical Literacy: The teacher stands for an integrated knowledge of what the basic concepts of AI are, how AI works, what data AI draws from and the risks attached to the use of AI. Lack of such knowledge results in the use of AI in schools without sufficient evidence for the efficiency of the system and teachers' knowledge of the methods that can be incorporated in their classes.

Figure 1. Ninth-grade students recording samples of musical instruments they wanted their ML app to recognize

Seamless Pedagogy: The integration of AI tools, without imposing upon other educators' skills acquisition, can be viewed as yet another challenge against its effectiveness. Educating and shaping the character development of a child or a teenager is a human interaction-exclusive process. Hence, educators must develop the critical aspect of engaging every student, through the provision of effective digital experiences to every student, while still working towards the best person topic.

Legal and Ethical Responsibility: The inclusion of AI in pedagogy implies certain obligations on the part of educators concerning the legality and ethics of such practice. As practically all data about learners acquired by AI tools can be termed 'protected data' and learners' mere presence on the internet makes them highly vulnerable to disclosure, the rules governing the right to protect personal data must be revisited.

REAL-LIFE CASE EXAMPLES OF AI EDUCATOR TRAINING PROGRAMS

Thanks to machine learning, it is easy to understand the working model of the classroom and the examples of what is running in the classroom, as new ones can on the horizon. One such example is the continuous use of media applications relating to computer lessons. Making attempts to integrate teaching computers through music, images and video clips has a long history. Moreover, the lectures will not be simply about general abstract understanding, there are concrete areas where machine learning is to be applied in the school. For instance, machine learning can be used in the enhancement of media-enabled applications that include videos, images, sensors, and audio within the confines of the elementary-level education. Bus also college data, which is easy to access and to get, it employs machine learning, as per the nature of each application. An advantage common to most developments and applications of machine learning: as mentioned above, it is far easier to amass all of the correct data necessary to achieve a certain prescribed status with the help of a machine learning scheme than it is to write fixed numbers of lines to obtain the same type of output from a computer. For this reason, many K–12 machine learning activities pointed at the media are designed to be accessible and adaptable for various media domains, such as speech recognition, picture detection and music generation that is supposed to encode feelings.

Figure 2. A 3-year-old learning to identify and describe his own emotions by teaching a computer to recognize them

The motivating power of the concept "Iluzia Poznaniya" or its English phrase "Low floors and high ceilings" is very prevalent for K-12 students' machine learning assignments. To promote the activities that make use of MT & Robotics), was accepted as the main motivational mechanism among young learners. One such example can be the project where the school children suggested inserting different types of machine learning in workshop assimilation using the visualization of the up and removing spaces between the lips. An app is usable for middle school students that identify the safe-to-eat mushrooms and indicate the dangerous ones, an app that recognizes the colors of all objects to aid the colour-blind, and another one that detects positions of cheerleaders for other forms of training are some of the projects that garnered great interest in one such workshop. Such activity can be seen in a translation of women by the author (remaining in the same English speaker) as presented in a particular frame. Such activity is also a nice illustration of applying AI ethics to use cases. (Yue et al., 2024)

Aiming at the importance of co-design and articulating children's education in terms of real-world tools that are particularly applicable such theories concern concept formulation, and deconstructing the pedagogical process in terms of initiatives which involve imagining concepts and external representations and then changing them, by which one reaches and even goes beyond the subject matter. As for the significance of education, the co-design is a two-edged sword in the sense that the learners are sharing not just their ideas with fellow children in which their thoughts may broaden beyond the perceived understandings but also ideas, rather it allows them to come up with a system of links between certain ideas and logical structures, showing activity in such phenomena as organizing and creating the proactive steps on change of the existing system, designing making learning models, and deploying, and quality assurance among other activities. Quite some institutions and organizations are establishing support training for teachers to embrace and grapple with AI in the classroom contrary.

For Microsoft, it launched the AI + Education Program to boost the understanding of Artificial Intelligence among instructors hence the development of the "AI School" – an online educational platform. It is a series of various courses starting from machine learning concepts to practical learning a myriad of AI tools related to lectures and even some evaluation systems intended to educate teachers concerning the positive prospects and the utilization of AI in the classroom. It is also adhered to by the AI Education program, which shows how AZ helps educate trainers on integrating AI-cantered solutions for education purposes, such as Microsoft Learning Tools that help adjust education for children with impairments.

The initiative to popularize Artificial Intelligence implementation in schools (AI4K-12) is an initiative that has been taken up by The Association for the Advancement of Artificial Intelligence (AAAI) to design an AI curriculum for K–12 students and support educators in the teaching of AI topics. One key feature of the program is that to help educators adopt AI principles in their subjects, this initiative provides several curricular resources, web applications, and teacher training courses. The curriculum is noteworthy for being designed under this project is termed AI + Ethics for High School Students; offering high school teachers' guidance on how to teach students AI and key ethical matters to deter AI unpacking.

It has been specifically designed to cater to the professional needs of K-12 teachers. The Company offers professional development in the field of artificial intelligence, such as the AI Skills Academy. It offers young professionals access their resources and workshops related to the basics of AI, its purposes, and ethical challenges. Due to the IBM project, teachers, for example, eliminate such questions as to whether the introduction of AI can serve as a means to develop personalization in teaching using such aids as IBM Watson Education. They acquire skills that assist them in the assessment of student achievements as well as changing and adapting. Learning materials.

The Chinese Opportunities on AI Training for Principals: China is a country that has launched a massive campaign to teach every k12 teacher about AI and its applications in "AI for Education". The courses are provided by the Ministry of Education and industrial partners, which help train teachers on implementing AI in their curriculum. The training is also designed to help K-12 teachers identify and use Artificial intelligence tools for personalised learning, data analysis, and other educational purposes. However, the most significant role of technology use in the classroom is affection-related aspects such as the ability to facilitate fast learners or as well, slow learners.

Some ML learning platforms advocate for moving away from the so-called 'coding to teachable machines' approach by not delving into teaching kids about different algorithms more than necessary explaining motives even further and even providing actual sample datasets that should be worked on during the training, testing and operational stages instead of thinking about algorithms. It is more vital to have the right amount of data for the work at hand than to ascertain how individual steps of a particular operation can be executed accurately and repeatably given that you are dealing with young people who are learning their first steps to machine learning, i.e., school children. Learners must understand the underpinnings of machine learning decision-making, particularly through models and representations rather than coded logic. Models that operate on a higher level can be developed when implementing an algorithm. However, in practice programs usually have both rule-based and data-driven computation so there is no reason to stop using traditional CT. Machine Learning is an additional tool and not a replacement.

Over the years, the "user interface" has changed a lot because of the development of computers with majority progression being from the machine towards the user and the user communities. For instance, while exploring the domain of machine learning (ML) by creating ML models, fresh capabilities have opened up for natural language and body convergence which have been madder advances in designing interfaces for more than 70 years. Just the other day, kids learnt how to build PoseNet-based machine learning models for detecting different cheerleading poses such as the V pose using a training kit, which educates how ML works.

STRATEGIES FOR IMPLEMENTING EDUCATOR TRAINING PROGRAMS

To the end of guarantee that teachers have the necessary competencies and knowledge, the organization of teacher training programs towards Artificial Intelligence (AI) use in the system of primary and secondary education requires significant preparation, coordination, and use of change models. Their significance, apart from the development of technical proficiency, is in helping teachers appreciate the role of AI in improving the process of teaching and fostering inclusive education. [Tedre, M., Toivonen, T., Kahila, J., Vartiainen, H., Valtonen, T., Jormanainen, I. and Pears, A., (2021)]. They highlight some best ways how AI-related training for all stakeholders in K-12 education could be maintained and implemented. Schools should make sure that their teachers are prepared to effectively integrate AI technologies that will improve educational achievements in children as well as help protect and alleviate ethical issues in such integration behavioural strain. Experiential learning, teamwork, mentoring and continuing professional training shall be considered as enablers of the development of the following aims too.

Compile a detailed needs assessment.

Checking out the prospective AI skills and tech savviness among the trainers first is one of the pivotal tasks before incorporating the AI-based training. The assessment can also extend to the interest of Teachers, School principals and other guests as a survey approach to AI usage.

Identify Educational Twists: Determine the knowledge gaps from any of the respondents with respect to given concepts, such as what is artificial intelligence and its historical evolution, how to use the concept, its ethical concerns and its application to lessons in the classroom.

Understand Teacher's Choice: Additional materials will be recommended for some trainers rather than conventional face-to-face. This will help tailor the course in a way that can satisfy every teacher's personal education philosophy.

Asses The Technological Infrastructure: First of all, a better understanding of the operable technologies for the learners must be corrected by a somewhat strict evaluation of such AI tools and technologies which are at hand in schools and are needed for the training.

A blend-like learning approach is recommended

The advocated blended learning method is adaptive in its performance and could be used in various spheres of AI training as it uses a combination of both online and on-ground training. Such an entrance enables an opportunity for educators to sit down for a conversation and team-building activities sure but it also addresses the issue of learning disabilities as well as presents people with an option to learn at their own pace.

Teaching Modules for Flexible-Duration Online Learning Programs: AI ethics, basic principles of AI, and different AI applications in real life all have theoretical modules developed for self-paced learning for instructors.

In-person and Otherwise Virtual Workshops: Educators are given direct access to AI tools through highly collaborative workshops which also allow them to test teaching methods that integrate AI and very much appreciate intervention and discussions from authorities as well as their peers.

Interactive Discussion Groupings and Community Forums: This provides an opportunity for teachers to engage in some online forums or communities and are meant to focus on sharing challenges, experiences, or queries on using AI in education.

An Opportunity for hands-on exposure

Practising what a person preaches concerning AI educational tools is critical for teachers in improving their technical aptitude. Practice is execution; teachers should incorporate the learning in their lectures whenever possible, otherwise, no training is provided.

Adopt Case Presentation as a Training Method: Provide ways of interactive instruction where students can apply theoretical knowledge about AI in the context of practical issues solving tasks related to data analytics on educational processes, student assessment and individualized instruction.

Simulation and Pilot Programs: Before using AI-powered platforms or virtual assistants in the classroom, provide teachers the opportunity to test them out in a controlled setting through simulation and pilot programs. Before a full-scale integration, pilot programs can assist teachers in identifying possible problems and building confidence when employing AI technologies.

Make lesson plans for AI: Engage educators in creating projects or lesson plans that use AI in meaningful ways, such as virtual tutors, adaptive learning systems, or AI-powered grading tools.

Include Persistent Guidance and Assistance

The economic sector is a continuously growing field. Consequently, teachers will need support as they navigate the introduction of AI in their lessons. It's invaluable to have a mentor who is able to provide assistance with new assignments.

Mentorship Programs: Let tech coaches or even AI trainers support instructors in raising their proficiencies of debugging, understanding how AI is, or dealing with developer questions effectively.

Technical Support and Help Desk Access: Include easy-to-access help desk and tech support options to aid teachers in handling problems when using AI products.

Collaborative Learning Communities: Create communities where teachers can work together, share materials with other participants, and learn from mistakes other teachers made when using AI tools.

Promote cooperation and learning among peers

The most effective way of inculcating skills and confidence in the use of Artificial Intelligence technology among instructors is through fostering a culture of collaborative learning. This is because peer mentoring promotes a supportive atmosphere among the professionals for growth and also helps educators learn from the best of their colleagues including how to avoid the common problems [Ojo, O., (2024)].

In-Person Training: Let those educators who are more confident in handling AI software perform some teaching or other activities across the same or other faculty members. In most cases, for the teachers, this system is more friendly and encouraging to work with.

Joint Projects in The Field of AI: Formulate projects for the entire institution or cross-cutting AI training programs where inbound faculty from different departments are to work and swap notes plus attempt new AI learning methods.

Transition Leadership: Prompt teachers to create new practices in which they apply AI, experiment with teaching methods and present their findings to their peers.

Emphasize Moral Concerns in Educational Practices

Erecting AI into the system of education is a subject of serious ethical consideration making it imperative for lecturers to understand how to rightly deploy AI in the classroom. Key moral issues like data integrity, the differentially of AI algorithms and how they can influence the mental state of students in the classroom are part of the training.

Ethical Perspectives in Artificial Intelligence: Include additional lessons that go over the ethical implications of AI in the education field, focusing on sub-matters such as the issue of AI bias, equity in the adaptive learning technology, and the use of related laws like the Family Educational Rights and Privacy Act (FERPA) and General Data Protection Regulation (GDPR).

Artificial Intelligence and Equality: Hone students to appreciate how applications such as Artificial Intelligence could facilitate the levelling of the educational playing field in terms of different learning modes available or specific accommodations for all categories of learners including those with low attendance or disabilities.

Safeguard data privacy policies: Make instructions available to teachers on ensuring the confidentiality of students through AI applications and ensuring compliance with the privacy laws that are in force within the school while making it safe to use these technologies respectfully with the teachers and students.

Assess Achievements to Improve Training in the Future

Providing framing of the effectiveness indicators of the training program and identifying areas of improvement are essential for the training program to be effective and meet educators' requirements.

Feedback and Assessments: These elements force continual improvement as they seek ways to make each training session engaging, interesting and relevant. Based on this feedback, the training is modified to make it more desirable for future sessions.

Certifications and Evaluations: There is a rationale behind giving teachers exactly such tasks that check their competencies in the field of AI. It is possible to motivate teachers to pass the training in full by presenting them with certificates or degrees after the handling.

Monitor Effective AI Implementation in the Classroom: Review how far educators are placing AI resources within the construct of their teaching practice. The educator's feedback, students' reactions, and actual class practice can be used as the basis for the assessment of the use of AI.

Create a School Environment which Promotes Innovation and Growth

Creating a school that promotes continuous growth, creativity, and new approaches is crucial to successfully introduce artificial intelligence in K-12 education. Those responsible people for the entire teaching process should strive to establish an atmosphere in which practitioners can try out new technology without the fear of being wrong.

Leadership Support: The Principals and Administrators standing before the educators at the school should take a stand and encourage AI into all types of curriculums of the school. In addition, they should also provide Teachers with the necessary time, resources and even the motivation to achieve professional development.

Promote Experimentation: Enthusiasm amongst School staff is very important and encourages the adoption of AI and demands updates in the form of feedback from the educators. It is possible that teachers are less likely to struggle with lots of technological changes when they are provided with a safe atmosphere for trying or losing new things.

Celebrate Achievements: Show gratitude, award-masters as well as other forms of credits given by many colleges and universities for professional development or anything that calls for such development following the use of AI by educators.

CHALLENGES TO AI TRAINING FOR TEACHERS IN AN AI-BASED K–12 EDUCATION SYSTEM

The tactics of AI integration in K–12 convey great promise, coupled with challenges on how to train the teachers to make good use of these tools. One of these bottlenecks is that there is a good number of teachers without digital literacy, particularly those working in rural or under-resourced areas. Lacking in basic technical and computing knowledge, how can teachers connect with AI platforms, let alone use them to promote classroom instruction?

Secondly, there is the fact that the practical, targeted training opportunities have nothing to offer. The majority of training programs are either too theoretical or are only poorly linked to real classroom situations. Hence, teachers tend to find it difficult to relate training experiences to real classroom teaching. Secondly, teachers are so busy, there may be hardly any time to explore new technology and determine how it could assist in the teaching-learning process. Hell, especially when the adoption might be a challenge on its own.

Another reason for resistance is doubts. Some educators may be worried; rather, they may feel that their job is being undermined, or they question whether AI is relevant to anything other than STEM subjects. There are other considerations as well-the ethical issues that concern student data privacy or the unfairness of AI decision-making algorithms. Therefore, the concerns of the teachers have been extended.

THE USE OF ARTIFICIAL INTELLIGENCE IN THE K–12 EDUCATION SYSTEM PRESENTS CHALLENGES FOR TEACHER TRAINING.

Artificial Intelligence (AI) has tremendous potential for improving educational results, tailoring training, and enriching learning experiences in K–12 educational systems. But there are also significant obstacles to overcome, especially in terms of preparing teachers to use AI-based resources in the classroom. Even if AI has the potential to revolutionize education, resources, support, and training for teachers must change. With the potential of AI in education in K-12 schools being actualized, some challenges still exist that necessitate solving. These particular difficulties need to be tackled, if the education system wants to ensure that teachers are ready for exploiting AI in a classroom setting. Facing AI concepts ignorance issues and being afraid of possible access breaches, leadership concern over change and change in AI learning models. Schools can establish a foundation for supporting the productive and ethical use of AI by teachers if they have applicable and efficient teacher development programs that are in existence and are consistently provided this will in turn work in favour of teachers and pupils. The issues are necessary to address to fully unlock the potential of AI systems to contribute to establishing more customized accessible and just educational environments. With real-world examples, these are some of the main obstacles that educator training programs in AI-based K–12 systems must overcome.

Lack of Primer about AI Terminology and Tools

The description of AI-oriented techniques is among the most intense hindrances to in-service pedagogical education in technology [Ojo, O., (2024)]. It can be expected that various new data on artificial intelligence will demonstrate the basics of AI elements as machine learning components and related computing facilities. For instance, the presence of this knowledge could largely determine how best each teacher can adopt AI into his or her learning activities.

Suppose a high school science teacher, for example, is offered an AI system-driven teaching aid that changes its rate and style to match any student's learning competencies. One possibility in such a case is that the instructor might not effectively exploit the device because they are not well conversant with how artificially intelligent mechanisms work operating under the incorrect assumption that it can do more than it should or disregard its advice. Therefore, integration of the technology for nefarious purposes, such as a poor understanding of the concept of AI, may pose an impediment.

Solution: As educators have to understand AI, the use of the technologies in their work requires that there should be a comprehensive consideration of such issues including the basic principles and vocabulary level in the moulding of the teaching instructions. The study should include training on the application of AI such as learning management systems, adaptive learning platforms and automated assessment tools and the differences between traditional instructions.

Resistance to Change and Aversion to Innovation

Most likely, many educators won't be eager to use the innovative AI techniques just because it is not the way they used to teach. The fear of losing one's employment, the outright addiction to technology regarding employment and dark ages, or the scary unknown are some of the reasons there is scepticism against AI. To lessen such resistance, some more influential people should be dealt with by stopping such customary practices and convictions.

A junior high school teacher may not opt to integrate a machine-driven grading system, particularly as this one grades the essays on its own for the belief that it may undoubtedly bar any such one-to-one interactions with the learners. Such teachers are concerned about the use of technology because they believe that artificial intelligence cannot solve the mission of even more or at least less routine and flat independent tasks than students' original papers.

Solution: It's proposed that curricular design for teacher education should stress the fact that AI supports rather than replaces teaching and does justice to its explicit and intrinsic levels of capabilities as well. The learning of AI potential is never a one–time exercise in a workshop or a seminar but there should be many other opportunities for teachers to learn how AI can help them to learn about the students' peculiar needs, support self-assessment of their performance and carry out self-directed one-to-one teaching of curriculum.

The absence of means of delivery and resource access

Effective AI integration in the classroom involves significant technological infrastructure such as good internet connectivity, hardware (computers - laptops, tablets, smartphones and other AI tools, and software. The fact that many educational institutions, especially those located in areas that are well below the poverty line or in places far from urban centres, will be technology deficient and may not be able to deliver programs based on AI may limit the effectiveness of AI programs and the goals of teacher training.

Simply put, technology might introduce possible challenges for learners and instructors, among other things. In this situation, the focus is on the districts without adequate resources. An example will attempt to shed some light on the matter. Sometimes, especially in under-resourced school districts, a situation might exist that technology exists but the teachers might not be in a position to use it effectively. This might match a situation where there is cognitive dissonance.

Solution: A school that is able to work with technology in the classroom in 2020 must, such as a modern computer lab and a trustworthy network connection among other infrastructure facilities among others. To add to that teacher training should be structured in such a way that this technology runs on devices such as smartphones or thin-client computers without these trainees getting a lack of ICT disparities.

Failure in Providing Supportive In-Service Education Opportunities to Teachers

Should the AI implementation in education continue at such a pace educators, to keep abreast with the ever-developing technology and new theories and methodologies, will need consistent training. In that case, it is noted that. Unfortunately, most of the time, direct training is delivered through on-time meetings/sessions, which in other words is never enough hence, teachers are unable to cope with the nuances that are after the implementation of the new technology or those that constrict teaching processes at the moment.

Take for example a school teacher who goes to a workshop aimed at enlightening teachers on how to personalize learning using AI, goes back to school and begins to use AI tutoring in his or her classroom. However, such strategies may fail to work due to unavailability of skilled field experts to tackle challenges such as lack of enhanced student engagement or systemic errors within the software. But they may not handle the subject properly if they never get professional development.

Solution: Ways on how teachers should be able to develop in a lifelong perspective, for example, such contact workshops in the same area, the concept of mentorship or even technical consultancy, must be embedded in training schemes. Another option could be to create some kind of online community or groups so that teachers can meet, discuss, resolve issues and learn of new ways to incorporate AI in a class full of students.

Data privacy and ethical issues

The heavy dependency on data collection in AI systems raises concerns about student privacy, data security, and the likelihood of bias in the AI models. These concerns put a lot of pressure on educationists, as these questions pertain to the use of AI in schools and the treatment of students.

For example, if AI tools are used to create individual study programs for students, the tool could collect a variety of information about the students including their characteristics, academic performance, activities, and even ethnic background and religion. This may be a concerning issue to any teacher in charge of such an educational process regarding who can access the stored information, how it is stored and how it might be applied beyond classroom walls.

Solution: Technological measures like AI enablement are not enough unless those who possess authority, for example, educators, appreciate the essence of privacy and learn the importance of abiding by the General Data Protection Regulation (GDPR) or the Family Educational Rights and Privacy Act (FERPA) etc, therefore the training programs should include the regulation of the social impact of AI. The social impact of AI should be trained from a different perspective, it goes beyond its application concerning human rights, especially from female teachers' perspective [Olari, V. and Romeike, R., (2024)].

Difficulties in Pedagogical Adaptation to AI Tools

With its ability to provide quick feedback, automate grading, and provide individualized learning experiences, AI has the potential to drastically change the way educators educate. However, a significant obstacle is modifying teaching strategies to fully utilize AI's capabilities. To successfully integrate AI, educators must not only learn how to use AI technologies but also how to adapt their teaching strategies.

For example, it may be challenging for a teacher who is used to teaching through lectures to encourage the use of an AI-based education system that expects students to go through tailored information at leisurely paces. A teacher is not likely to be successful in incorporating AI in the right manner until guidance is provided on how to start adopting the new learner centered strategies in place of traditional ones.

Solution: It is necessary to make teacher education programs including the revision of traditional teaching methods to incorporate the Classroom LMS. It is important to know which other ways AI can be made use of so teachers and students benefit fully. These can be hi-tech techniques or very simple strategies like changing existing course materials to suit the students we currently have. Additional information on policies or course designs for the integration of AI into teaching is also encouraged.

The Impact of AI Training Data Inequality and AI Tools Monotony.

The efficacy of AI systems is dependent on the nature of the data used in their training. These algorithms may be conducive to advancing existing distinctions or fail to cater to the requirements of certain student populations if formulated using unsuitable data or consequences are impossible to guarantee due to the lack of diversity aspects in the development of AI technologies. Educators may be challenged to ascertain the fairness and inclusiveness of the AI resources they wish to utilize.

An AI-based language learning tool might have learned most of its human languages from mostly native English speakers, in a way that leaves a gap for learners from other backgrounds to participate in the learning. Consequently, such students might have educational inequalities caused by this discrimination.

Solution: It is vital that all teachers are wary of the inbuilt stereotypes in the AI program, and its applications, as there is an appeal to interact with and consider the capabilities of such programs as an enhancement, it is possible to rely on in them as supplementary modern technologies for broadening the curriculum offer. The program includes education on how to recognise and eliminate biases in the use of AI tools. AI providers are required to attach further techniques that promote the development of their all-encompassing algorithms.

Future Directions in AI Integration in K–12 Education

As the use of artificial intelligence (AI) in the K–12 education sector continues to grow, it becomes relevant to talk about what the future research and policy directions under such expansion should look like. Whereas short-term applications of AI integration—personalized learning, automation of administrative tasks, and adaptive assessments—seem to be promising, long-term consequences of AI integration on teaching and learning processes are yet to be understood. Therefore, future studies must investigate these concerns through longitudinal research that tracks instructors trained with AI technologies on their students' outcomes over a considerable period.

One promising avenue could be the evaluation of the efficacy of teacher training programs centered on AI: how teacher confidence, teacher pedagogical orientation, and strategies change in response to the persistent use of AI tools. Of course, future research would need to investigate, in the long term, whether these AI-trained teachers have indeed improved academic achievement, critical thinking, and engagement of students, especially across learning contexts.

CONCLUSION

Educator training programs for AI usage in K–12 education are effective if they utilize a lot of theory and practical application, offer continuous support, and most importantly ensure that all the concerns about ethics are well addressed. Schools can adopt different measures to guarantee that teachers are adequately prepared to integrate AI into pedagogical practices to improve the quality of student learning as well as eliminate of ethical and equity issues, such as including the teachers, using the students and ongoing training at school level to promote AI for beneficial practices.

REFERENCES

Adams, C., Pente, P., Lemermeyer, G., & Rockwell, G. (2023). Ethical principles for artificial intelligence in K–12 education. *Computers and Education: Artificial Intelligence*, *4*, 100131. DOI: 10.1016/j.caeai.2023.100131

Akgun, S., & Greenhow, C. (2022). Artificial intelligence in education: Addressing ethical challenges in K–12 settings. *AI and Ethics*, *2*(3), 431–440. DOI: 10.1007/s43681-021-00096-7 PMID: 34790956

Azzam, A., & Charles, T. (2024). A review of artificial intelligence in K–12 education. *Open Journal of Applied Sciences*, *14*(8), 2088–2100. DOI: 10.4236/ojapps.2024.148137

Chiu, T. K. (2021). A holistic approach to the design of artificial intelligence (AI) education for K–12 schools. *TechTrends*, *65*(5), 796–807. DOI: 10.1007/s11528-021-00637-1

Martin, F., Zhuang, M., & Schaefer, D. (2023). Systematic review of research on artificial intelligence in K–12 education (2017–2022). *Computers and Education: Artificial Intelligence*, 100195.

Ojo, O. (2024). *Promoting artificial intelligence education in K–12 through pre-service teachers' development* (Master's thesis, Itä-Suomen yliopisto).

Olari, V., & Romeike, R. (2024). Data-related concepts for artificial intelligence education in K–12. *Computers and Education Open*, *7*, 100196. DOI: 10.1016/j.caeo.2024.100196

Tedre, M., Toivonen, T., Kahila, J., Vartiainen, H., Valtonen, T., Jormanainen, I., & Pears, A. (2021). Teaching machine learning in K–12 classroom: Pedagogical and technological trajectories for artificial intelligence education. *IEEE Access : Practical Innovations, Open Solutions*, *9*, 110558–110572. DOI: 10.1109/ACCESS.2021.3097962

Unal, A., & Unal, Z. (2024). Evaluating the integration of artificial intelligence (AI) in K–12 education. *Journal of Interactive Learning Research*, *35*(3), 353–387. DOI: 10.70725/546995xiatpy

Woodruff, K., Hutson, J., & Arnone, K. (2023). Perceptions and barriers to adopting artificial intelligence in K–12 education: A survey of educators in fifty states.

Yue, M., Jong, M. S. Y., & Dai, Y. (2022). Pedagogical design of K–12 artificial intelligence education: A systematic review. *Sustainability (Basel)*, *14*(23), 15620. DOI: 10.3390/su142315620

Yue, M., Jong, M. S. Y., & Ng, D. T. K. (2024). Understanding K–12 teachers' technological pedagogical content knowledge readiness and attitudes toward artificial intelligence education. *Education and Information Technologies*, *29*(15), 1–32. DOI: 10.1007/s10639-024-12621-2

Chapter 7
Educators' Perspectives on AI Integration in Education:
Perceptions, Experiences, and Strategies

Anna Wen Huey Ong
http://orcid.org/0009-0001-9367-3305
Open University Malaysia, Malaysia

Chee Seong Low
http://orcid.org/0000-0001-5632-3296
Tunku Abdul Rahman University of Management and Technology, Malaysia

Yong Wei Yap
http://orcid.org/0009-0009-8267-7878
Tunku Abdul Rahman University of Management and Technology, Malaysia

Juliazilah Junit
http://orcid.org/0009-0009-9099-3264
Tunku Abdul Rahman University of Management and Technology, Malaysia

P. Sharimila Bai Pandurenga Rao
Tunku Abdul Rahman University of Management and Technology, Malaysia

ABSTRACT

The Ministry of Education Malaysia aims to promote digital education in schools. However, a disparity between government initiatives and educators' competency has been identified. Past studies suggest that educators' perspectives play an

DOI: 10.4018/979-8-3693-6346-1.ch007

important role in integrating technology in education. This qualitative research explored educators' perceptions of Artificial Intelligence (AI) use in education and the necessary strategies for AI-integrated education. A total of 11 educators from diverse backgrounds participated in the study, sharing their perceptions and experiences regarding AI-integrated education. The interviews covered three primary areas: experiences with technology use in teaching and learning, perceptions toward AI-integrated education, and suggested strategies. Thematic analysis identified the main themes related to these areas. The current findings not only contribute to the literature by presenting Malaysian educators' perspectives but also provide insights into designing effective training programs to facilitate AI-integrated education in Malaysia.

INTRODUCTION

The Fourth Industrial Revolution (IR4.0) marks an era of cyber-physical systems integrating computational, network, and physical processes with mobile device technologies (Buguin et al., 2013). This revolution has ushered in a new educational paradigm, Education 4.0, which promotes intelligent and smart thinking in education. Education 4.0 emphasizes flexibility and accessibility in learning, allowing students to access learning materials remotely, and breaking away from traditional constraints on learning (Sharma, 2019).

Historically, Education 1.0 viewed educators as the primary source of knowledge, and students as passive recipients within the brick-and-mortar school environment. Although the knowledge was accessible through online sources such as e-books and websites, the students engaged with these materials passively. With the evolution of the internet into Web 2.0, users could interact and edit content, leading to educational paradigm shifts. In Education 2.0, students became more active in learning, acquiring new knowledge through online sources while engaging with the materials (Rudman & Bruwer, 2016). Student-centred learning was emphasized in Education 3.0, while educators' role has shifted from the primary source of information to guiding students' learning. The advent of Web 4.0, characterized by machine learning, the Internet of Things (IoT), and Big Data, further transformed education by enhancing efficiency and productivity across various fields (Coşkun et al., 2019). These technological advancements have led to the emergence of Education 4.0, marked by nine key trends (Fisk, 2017):

1. **Learning can occur anytime and anywhere:** Technology facilitates flexible learning opportunities, such as remote and self-paced learning. Students can access educational content from different locations at any time.

2. **Personalized learning:** Educational content is designed to adapt to each student's capabilities, improving engagement and comprehension.
3. **Students can determine their learning paths:** Students are granted the autonomy to choose their learning process with tools they feel are necessary and suitable, increasing intrinsic motivation to learn and explore.
4. **Project-based learning and working:** Students learn authentically by applying knowledge to diverse situations. They develop basic skills, such as organizational, collaborative, and time management, which are crucial for their academic and career paths.
5. **Increased opportunities for real-world experiences relevant to students' future careers:** Project-based and hands-on learning experiences equip students with practical skills relevant to their future careers, bridging the gap between knowledge and practical implications.
6. **Data interpretation:** Computers handle the manual aspects of numerical literacy, while new aspects of numeric literacy have emerged, such as applying theoretical knowledge to numbers and using human reasoning to infer logic and data trends.
7. **Different ways of assessing learning:** Traditional assessments, typically through examinations, have been criticized as insufficient and outdated. Therefore, diverse assessment methods are needed to assess students' learning throughout the process.
8. **Student ownership of their learning:** Students are given autonomy to track their learning progress and set personal goals. Educators and students collaborate to maintain a relevant and up-to-date curriculum.
9. **Educators serve as mentors and facilitators of students' learning:** As students gain greater independence in their learning process, educators serve as mentors and facilitate their learning.

Reflecting on these trends, it becomes clear that technology is now integral to the learning experience. Artificial Intelligence (AI) is at the forefront of these educational shifts, playing a crucial role in shaping modern education.

School personnel, including school administrators, educators, and administrative staff, leverage AI to streamline work processes and enhance efficiency. AI impacts students both directly and indirectly. Directly, AI enhances students' learning experiences by personalizing materials and tasks according to individual competencies and paces. Personalized learning has proven effective in boosting comprehension and motivation by adjusting pace and content to meet students' needs (Makhambetova et al., 2021). AI tools facilitate differentiated instructions by gathering feedback on students' skill levels, classifying students, building feedback loops, predicting performance, and providing real-time classroom insights (Khor & K, 2024). Indirectly,

AI aids educators and administrative staff in performing tasks more efficiently. AI tools streamline administrative processes, such as using chatbots for communication and analyzing student performance data to offer early intervention (Murphy, 2019). Additionally, AI enables automated grading, ensuring fair and accurate evaluation (Zhang & Aslan, 2021). These efficiencies allow educators to repurpose their time for more meaningful interactions with students, enhancing overall educational quality.

Despite AI's ability to streamline operations, the significant role of educators remains unchanged. AI's emergence has shifted the educational paradigm, granting students greater autonomy in learning while redefining educators' roles from knowledge deliverers to facilitators. Educators now guide, motivate, and evaluate the learning process, necessitating competencies in pedagogy, social interaction, personal development, and professional skills (Fitria, 2021). AI can enhance educational efficiency, but educators are essential in upholding humanistic values and providing emotional support (Fitria, 2023). Furthermore, AI technologies enable educators to adopt a student-centred approach to teaching, creating interactive and engaging learning experiences (Onesi-Ozigagun et al., 2024). Incorporating multimedia elements, simulations, and games encourages students to participate actively throughout the teaching and learning sessions. Additionally, interactive activities facilitate students' critical thinking and collaboration with peers.

The adoption of AI has changed educators' roles and work dynamics. Educators' intentions to utilize AI tools are influenced by their confidence and the perceived relevance of these tools (Ayanwale et al., 2022). Expanding educators' competencies in technology use and pedagogical adjustments is crucial, as traditional teaching methods may no longer be sufficient in this new paradigm. Competence in using AI-driven technologies facilitates their adaptation to digital transformation, enhancing both their teaching and administrative work (Huang, 2021).

Educators hold different perspectives on the integration of AI technologies in education. A study by Mandal and Mete (2023) revealed that most educators agreed that AI technologies could help improve their teaching by making it more interactive and promoting an interdisciplinary approach. However, many educators perceived themselves as having limited knowledge regarding AI, particularly its functions and operational methods. Despite this, they demonstrated a positive attitude toward integrating AI into education and welcomed new learning opportunities (Chounta et al., 2022).

Even though educators are aware of the potential usefulness of AI technologies, they are concerned about the time and effort required to develop these competencies and the possible trust issues that may arise from AI integration (Shirin, 2022). Additionally, some educators are concerned about the potential drawbacks of AI integration, including over-reliance on AI, reduced interaction between educators and students, and the potential loss of the school's socialization function (Kim et al., 2020). While AI may be helpful in personalizing learning, it cannot interact emotionally with students. These concerns are likely to inhibit educators' intention to use AI technologies in their teaching and administrative work. Therefore, exploring educators' perceptions of AI-integrated education is critical.

The integration of AI into education has transformed teaching and learning globally. Schools and higher education institutions are exploring technological advancements to enhance educational experiences. However, significant challenges persist, such as training and support for educators and ethical implications. Various AI tools are available for educational use, and exploring these tools can be challenging. Therefore, training on the use of AI technologies in education is essential to enhance their effectiveness (Onesi-Ozigagun et al., 2024). Adequate competency in the use of AI enables educators to guide students effectively. Additionally, educators can use AI tools to analyze students' needs and competencies, which helps in designing curricula. On top of the use of AI tools, equipping educators with adequate ethical knowledge is essential. Data privacy and security are common concerns over the use of AI. AI technologies rely heavily on vast amounts of student data to personalize learning and provide real-time feedback. Therefore, educators should be well-equipped with the sensitivity of data and refrain from the occurrence of misuse or unauthorized access to data (Huang, 2023). Nonetheless, AI integrations may create greater discrepancies between students from different socioeconomic statuses, as some students may struggle to obtain adequate devices to support their learning. Addressing these issues is vital to harness AI's capabilities responsibly and inclusively, ensuring all students benefit from these technological advancements.

The Ministry of Education Malaysia (MOE) has aspired to promote digital education in schools, as evidenced by various initiatives such as online learning platforms like Google Classroom and CikgooTube. Additionally, the ministry aims to incorporate AI into the school curriculum starting in 2027 (Harun & Sallehuddin, 2024). However, a survey by the MOE showed that digital competence among educators is concerning. Specifically, 57.9% of educators reported basic digital competence, followed by 39.9% with moderate competency, and 2.2% with advanced competency (Kementerian Pendidikan Malaysia, 2023). The gap between the government's initiatives and educators' competency needs to be addressed, as it may hinder the effectiveness of these initiatives and lower Malaysia's global competitiveness.

The Diffusion of Innovations Theory (Rogers, 1962) is best suited for exploring and analyzing the adoption and diffusion of AI technologies in education. It serves as a guide to understanding the progress and factors that affect the adoption of new technologies. Several factors were found to be impactful in influencing the adoption of new technology, such as readiness, motivation, and perceived consequences (Dearing & Cox, 2018). It highlights the significant role of educators' perceptions in influencing the adoption of AI technologies in education.

This study aims to explore educators' perceptions of the use of AI in education and the strategies needed for AI-integrated education to provide insights to facilitate the adoption of AI technologies in education. The findings may identify possible barriers and suggest suitable support and resources to promote educators' readiness for AI-integrated education. A thorough exploration and analysis may guide educators and policymakers in harnessing AI's capabilities responsibly and inclusively.

METHODS

Research Design

This study employed an exploratory descriptive qualitative research design aimed at exploring educators' perceptions of the use of AI in education and the strategies needed for AI-integrated education. This research design allows researchers to explore and describe the selected phenomenon - AI-integrated education (Hunter et al., 2019). Semi-structured interviews were conducted for data collection, guiding the interviewers during the sessions while providing the flexibility to ask additional questions for clarification based on participants' responses (Magaldi & Berler, 2020). Open-ended and probing questions were used to gain in-depth insights into educators' perceptions and experiences with AI in education.

Participants

Malaysia's national education system can be divided into preschool, primary, secondary, and post-secondary education (Ministry of Education Malaysia, 2024). In line with the focus of the present study, purposive sampling was employed to recruit educators who are teaching from kindergarten to secondary school levels. The participants were then recruited through a snowballing method where interested participants introduced their colleagues who fulfilled the criteria. Considering that experiences and challenges may be influenced by the level of education that educators teach, three to four participants were recruited from three categories (kindergarten, primary, and secondary schools). In total, 11 female educators (M_{age} = 34.64) took part in the study, the demographic information is summarised in Table 1.

Table 1. Summary of the participants' demographic information

ID	Age	Profession	Type of School	Years of Teaching Experience
1	34	Kindergarten Principal	Kindergarten (Private)	11
2	28	Director	Development Centre (Private)	8
3	25	Learning Facilitator	Care Centre (Private)	2
4	28	Learning Facilitator	Care Centre (Private)	3
5	40	Teacher	Primary School (Public)	17
6	43	Teacher	Primary School (Public)	18
7	46	Teacher and Head of Panel	Primary School (Public)	20
8	40	Contract Teacher	Secondary School (Public)	4
9	27	Teacher	Secondary School (International)	5
10	25	Teacher	Secondary School (Private)	3
11	45	Teacher	Secondary School (Private)	22

Data Collection Procedure

Semi-structured interviews were conducted through virtual platforms such as Google Meet, Zoom, and Microsoft Teams to explore educators' perceptions of using AI in education and the strategies needed for AI-integrated education. The interview sessions were conducted by five individual researchers who were briefed on the interview procedures and questions. A series of interview questions were designed to guide the interviews, validated by a relevant expert, and deemed appropriate to achieve the study's aims. Open-ended questions were employed to explore demographic information, experiences of technology use in teaching and learning, perceptions toward AI-integrated education, and support or resources needed. All interview sessions lasted from 30 to 45 minutes. Each interview was audio-recorded and transcribed verbatim. All participants were informed about the purpose of the study, the procedure, confidentiality, and data protection. The interviewers then obtained informed consent from all participants.

Data Analysis

The six phases of thematic analysis proposed by Braun and Clarke (2006) were adopted to analyze the interview data. Researchers transcribed all interview sessions verbatim and repeatedly read the data to note the initial ideas. Initial codes were generated with the assistance of NVivo, and potential themes were identified. Researchers reviewed the themes in relation to the entire data set to reduce possible biases. Definitions and names for each theme were then developed through ongoing analysis. Finally, compelling examples extracted from the data were included in the report to illustrate the findings.

Reflexivity

There is an overlap in the roles of the researchers who conducted the interviews and those who analyzed the data. This overlap and the researchers' motivation to understand educators' perceptions of using AI in education is acknowledged to enhance transparency. Reflexivity is employed to improve researchers' awareness and reduce possible biases arising from personal experiences as educators in higher education institutions. The researchers recognized their perceptions and challenges regarding the use of AI in education. Acknowledging these perspectives allowed the researchers to approach the topic from different viewpoints. In addition, all decisions throughout the research process were made with careful consideration and supported by rationale and reliable sources, thereby reducing possible biases and enhancing the credibility of the findings.

FINDINGS

All educators shared their experiences with technology use in teaching and learning, perceptions toward AI-integrated education, and suggested strategies to facilitate AI-integrated education. The major themes and subthemes were identified through their responses and are summarized in Table 2. The actual responses were quoted to provide a better understanding of their experiences and opinions. Most of them perceived themselves as having a moderate familiarity with AI, while a few rated themselves as either highly familiar or less familiar.

Table 2. Summary of major themes and subthemes

Area	Major Themes	Subthemes
Experiences with technology use in teaching and learning	Usage	Generating idea Basic operational functions Integration into teaching and learning
	Perceived effectiveness	Convenience and efficiency Facilitate teaching and learning
Perceptions toward AI-integrated education	Perceived benefits	Supplementary tool Ease educator's workload Enhanced student learning experience Enhanced communication
	Perceived challenges	Limited usefulness in teaching children with special needs Students' integrity and behaviors Over-reliance on AI Lack of human interaction Hindering cognitive skills Changes in educators' role in education Limited funding Data privacy
	Perceived readiness	Prefer materials over AI Mixed readiness Need for training and exposure
Suggested strategies	Types of support	Training Infrastructure Financial resources Peer coaching system
	Training needed	Guidance on using specific AI tools and platforms Innovative teaching methods

Experiences with Technology Use in Teaching and Learning

Educators shared their experiences with technology use in terms of its usage and perceived effectiveness.

Usage

According to the educators, technology has been adopted and integrated into teaching and learning: "*I've been using technology for…if I have lessons, I mean within one week at least three times I will use technology in class.*". However, diverse exposure to technology use in teaching and learning was identified. The following verbatim quotes from educators illustrate this:

"Umm, I guess most of the time we don't rely on technology other than phones to maybe look things up. So, it's more reliant on books, physical things provided."

"Like when we had our online teaching, okay, I tried to adapt some of the technologies, but I'm not very good at it. I'm not hands-on with it, but I try to use it. When I need it, I use it."

"So, I don't use technology that much in government school. We don't have that type of technology or gadgets or any facilities or things like that in government schools."

Technologies have been adopted to perform basic operational functions, such as preparing and proofreading official documents: "*...in terms of grammar structures, and then how to use some sentences politely.*". Meanwhile, some educators shared their experiences using technology to generate ideas and gather information while performing job-related tasks.

Perceived Effectiveness

Educators expressed that the use of technology is convenient and efficient, cutting down the time spent on teaching-related tasks. "*Well, I find it pretty comfortable because adapting technology makes teaching for me much more convenient and if done right, it can be timesaving.*". In addition, they expressed the usefulness of technology in facilitating teaching and learning, such as enhancing student attention and engagement. However, educators must spend time exploring and experimenting with new tools before adopting them.

Perceptions Toward AI-integrated Education

Educators shared their perspectives on AI-integrated education, including perceived benefits, perceived challenges, and perceived readiness.

Perceived Benefits

They perceived AI technologies as supplementary tools that could ease their workload, particularly in gathering information, facilitating lesson planning, and performing administrative tasks. Notably, it enables educators to repurpose their time for other teaching-related tasks, such as preparing teaching aids and interacting with students. The significant role of educators should not be replaced by AI:

"...but I think it could be good in some ways, maybe to help the educators find a way to structure the learning sessions or something like that? But for the most part...because education is a very person-to-person thing."

"Okay. So, these times, all these times spent on instruction and lesson planning, can be saved and teachers can actually and finally focus on preparing better quality teaching aids, teaching tools and so on."

Apart from that, AI-integrated education enhances the student learning experience by improving their interest and engagement, and by providing personalized learning: "*It has the potential to personalize learning and then it is tailored to individual students' needs and also their learning process.*". At the same time, the integration of AI technologies potentially enhances interaction and communication between students and teachers. Although educators have a positive view of AI-integrated education, they emphasize the importance of combining different teaching methods and believe the choice should be based on the student's age group and capabilities.

Perceived Challenges

Educators expressed their concerns regarding the challenges potentially brought by AI-integrated education. Firstly, integrating AI technologies in education has limited usefulness in teaching students with special needs: "... *Because it's a very specialized setting where you have to deal with special children. So, I would think that computers won't be able to give.*".

On the other hand, educators raised concerns about over-reliance on AI technologies, as it could lead to various consequences, such as data privacy issues, inhibiting human interaction, and hindering cognitive skills like creativity and critical thinking. The following verbatim quotes from educators illustrate this:

"...But I am afraid that by integrating AI in most aspects of education, teachers as well as students, they might become, how to say, less creative."

"...but I think there are also negative impacts of AI where it can actually because recently, we also found out that it hinders the students critical thinking..."

"And in terms of social development or social interaction, there might also be wider gaps between all parties involved, the students and teachers, teacher-teacher interaction, teacher-student interaction, student-student interaction."

In addition, educators expressed their concerns about changes in student's behaviors and attitudes. They observed some changes in students' behavior, such as increased laziness and the perception that AI can complete everything on their behalf. Therefore, they believed in-class tasks are necessary to ensure authentic learning: "*...things that should be done outside of the classroom activity should be done inside of a classroom.*". Furthermore, AI-integrated education possibly changes the role of educators. Educators expressed various concerns over this matter, such as AI replacing educators and a lack of respect towards educators. "*Slight concern would be maybe the employers would try to incorporate this within the education system…try to replace human educators with AI.*"

Perceived Readiness

In general, most educators shared a moderate level of readiness toward AI-integrated education, while a few of them expressed a low level of readiness. Educators who are ready for the integration of AI expressed the need for training and exposure: "*…We need a lot more training. And a lot more exposure when it comes to AI*". Additionally, educators from different generations may have different levels of readiness, which could be due to their familiarity with technology, and some prefer traditional materials over technology. Most educators shared that they frequently use online and AI platforms like ChatGPT, YouTube, and Google, among others. Meanwhile, they are interested in exploring AI features on some online platforms like Canva and Quizzes.

Suggested Strategies

Two main themes emerged from educators' responses: types of support and specific training programs needed.

Type of Support

Educators commonly expressed the need for training, particularly on the use of specific AI tools that could benefit teaching and learning: "*…first and foremost a lot of training on basic technology. I think it's undeniable that a lot of teachers nowadays are pretty old.*"

In addition to training, educators shared that schools could initiate a peer coaching system, where those familiar with AI technology can guide those who are new to its integration: "*I think it will be best that if let's say in terms of an experienced teacher or like those teachers who are experienced in really using AI, probably they can give guidance to those teachers who are not familiar.*".

Besides, educators emphasized essential resources such as infrastructure and financial funding. They believed that physical resources like devices and access to online platforms could facilitate AI-integrated education: "*I think the schools need to be well equipped with good facilities so that every class must have a touchscreen board.*". At the same time, they emphasized the importance of having an expert to provide technical support to facilitate the integration process: "*…I would say technical support. Providing ongoing technical assistance for educators using AI* *technology in the classroom.*". Meanwhile, they acknowledged that these resources may be costly, emphasizing the importance of financial funding.

Specific Training Programmes

Educators need to learn the fundamental AI technologies and ways to integrate them into education. The following verbatim quotes from educators illustrate this:

"I think this general or training session to get familiar with the AI itself and what function it's supposed to serve within the field."

"...if they give us training and then they let us know what kind of tools that we can use, then it will be quite good that teachers can save time..."

Besides, educators expressed their interest in incorporating AI tools through innovative teaching methods, such as gamification: "*Specific training means how to use the AI, like games, language games.*".

DISCUSSION

Using a qualitative method, this research explored the emergence of AI changing educator's roles in education. Analysis of the interview responses identified three main areas: experiences of technology use in teaching and learning, perceptions toward AI-integrated education, and suggested strategies.

The first area disclosed experiences with technology use in teaching and learning. In line with the literature, educators agreed that AI has been very useful as they have adopted and integrated into teaching and learning. Undoubtedly, AI catalyzes generating ideas, enabling educators to brainstorm and create interactive content. However, basic operational functions like creating presentations or managing educational resources may require more time for focused pedagogical activities for educators (Shirin, 2022). Such issues could be due to lack of exposure, training, or poorly equipped facilities. With the advancement of technology, it is hoped that this matter will be resolved in the future. On the other hand, in terms of the perceived effectiveness of technology in education, it is emphasized with its convenience and efficiency where it assists in enabling communication or administrative tasks. It also facilitates learning experiences by providing access to a wealth of resources that enhance academic success. As Khor and Muthulakshmi (2024) stated, this is feasible as AI allows educators to gather feedback on students' skill levels or predict performance.

The second area explores educators' perceptions of the benefits, challenges, and readiness for integrating AI into education. Most educators widely agreed and recognized AI as a supplementary tool that brings significant benefits to them as well as students. Not only AI is perceived to enhance efficiency for educators by streamlining administrative work processes, but many educators also agree that AI tools enhance communication and promote personalized learning among students by adapting materials to students' competencies and learning pace, thereby improving their overall learning experience. This aligns with the literature that AI in education enables schools or educational institutions to tailor more personalized learning experiences (Fitria, 2021).

While educators recognized the significance of AI tools, they also acknowledged the challenges presented by AI tools. This includes the limited usefulness of AI tools in teaching children with special needs as AI tools may not be able to cater to the diverse needs of children that require special education in learning. Apart from that, educators also expressed concerns about the improper utilization of AI tools that impact students' integrity and behaviors citing the possibility of plagiarizing content generated by AI tools. Additionally, some educators also raised concerns about redefining educators' role in education which could raise questions about the relevance of educators in education. In line with the findings of Shirin (2022) where concerns were raised about the social aspects of learning as well as human-to-human interactions, the findings of this research also revealed that AI could contribute to the lack of human interaction between educators and students.

Moreover, some educators also viewed AI as a hindrance to the development of cognitive skills, including creativity and critical thinking among students despite acknowledging various benefits brought by AI. This emphasizes the need for further research into exploring whether AI fosters or hinders critical thinking as Onesi-Ozigagun et al. (2024) indicated that the automated tools, interactive lessons created by AI-powered tools as well as the real-time feedback by AI-powered tools could allow educators to concentrate more on learning facilitation and critical thinking skills development in students. Limited funding is also one of the challenges encountered by educators as the adoption of AI tools in education requires proper and adequate tools or devices and infrastructure. As AI technology relies on collecting data vastly in all of its subfields (Huang, 2023), some educators also identified data privacy as one of the challenges in adopting AI in education.

As for the levels of readiness in utilizing AI in education, educators generally exhibited varying levels of readiness with some feeling unprepared to integrate AI tools in education due to time constraints in learning AI tools, limited exposure to AI tools, and insufficient training. Some perceived themselves as moderately prepared to adopt AI tools as an educator, having a solid understanding of AI concepts and their application in education and some felt that they were adequately prepared to utilize AI tools for generating ideas in teaching. Limited resources and knowledge of AI hinder educators' readiness for AI-integrated education (Alnasib, 2023).

The third area examines educators' perceptions of the types of support and training needed to integrate AI into education. Based on the findings, educators highlighted four major types of support: training, infrastructure, financial resources, and a peer coaching system. This suggests that a comprehensive strategy is crucial for optimizing the integration of AI in educational settings. Firstly, specialized training programs provide educators with a fundamental understanding of AI, including its strengths, weaknesses, and ethical implications in educational contexts. Luckin et al. (2022) supported this idea by suggesting that a basic understanding of AI enables educators to incorporate AI technologies into their teaching more effectively. Secondly, it is also important to make technological resources accessible to educational institutions, educators, and students to leverage AI's capabilities and enhance learning experiences and outcomes. Druga et al. (2022) argued that closing the gap in access to these resources is vital for the effective use of AI in educational settings, which should include the deployment of the latest AI tools and the formation of an infrastructure that supports these technologies. In addition, Babina et al. (2023) observed that organizations investing in AI tools tend to have a higher proportion of younger, more educated, and more specialized employees. As a result, these organizations often have a flatter hierarchy and increased opportunities at the junior level. However, the use of AI can be challenging for educators who are not tech-savvy. As such, peer coaching or mentorship has emerged as an effective method to maximize the power of learning and achieve desirable outcomes. According to Hurst (2021), regular and collaborative interactions between colleagues can significantly enhance problem-solving and interpersonal skills, as well as foster a supportive environment conducive to professional growth and continuous learning.

To effectively integrate AI into education, educators pointed out that guidance in using AI tools and providing certification in AI training is necessary. This not only increases the competency of the user but also promotes innovative teaching methodologies. Sakulkueakulsuk et al. (2018) revealed that the application of AI in education enhances students' abilities to think futuristically and across disciplines. Moreover, AI training and certification aimed at increasing educators' competency will also help facilitate innovative teaching, which in turn helps students to learn more effectively. For example, Goel and Joyner (2017) illustrated the benefits of AI-enabled tools like intelligent tutors, which provide automated evaluations and feedback and have helped students understand and harness the capabilities of AI in their future professional and academic pursuits.

Overall, the findings extend the knowledge of educators' perspectives on AI-integrated education and provide valuable insights for designing strategies to facilitate AI-integrated education in Malaysia. Notably, several concerns may limit the generalization of the findings. Firstly, only female educators participated in this study, potentially ignoring opinions from male educators. As studies revealed that male educators tend to have a higher level of readiness compared to females, their perspectives could enrich the findings. Secondly, this study did not manage to recruit any educators from East Malaysia. Differences in resources for schools between West Malaysia and East Malaysia could contribute to the findings. Hence, it would be interesting to extend this study by involving male educators and those residing in East Malaysia.

This study explores the use of AI in K-12 education from the perspective of educators. Most educators view AI as beneficial for streamlining tasks, personalizing learning, and enhancing administrative efficiency. However, they also note significant challenges, including a lack of training on how to effectively use the technology. Thus, it is essential to invest in technology and support systems, such as peer coaching and tailored training programs, which cater to different levels of familiarity and expertise with AI technologies. Moreover, establishing clear guidelines is crucial to ensure that AI enhances rather than detracts from the educational process.

REFERENCES

Alnasib, B. N. M. (2023). Factors affecting faculty members' readiness to integrate artificial intelligence into their teaching practices: A study from the Saudi higher education context. *International Journal of Learning. Teaching and Educational Research, 22*(8), 465–491. DOI: 10.26803/ijlter.22.8.24

Ayanwale, M. A., Sanusi, I. T., Adelana, O. P., Aruleba, K. D., & Oyelere, S. S. (2022). Teachers' readiness and intention to teach artificial intelligence in schools. *Computers and Education: Artificial Intelligence, 3*, 100099. DOI: 10.1016/j.caeai.2022.100099

Babina, T., Fedyk, A., He, A. X., & Hodson, J. (2023). *Firm investments in artificial intelligence technologies and changes in workforce composition*. National Bureau of Economic Research. DOI: 10.3386/w31325

Braun, V., & Clarke, V. (2006). Using thematic analysis in psychology. *Qualitative Research in Psychology, 3*(2), 77–101. DOI: 10.1191/1478088706qp063oa

Buguin, J., Dobbs, R., Bisson, P., & Marrs, A. (2013). *Disruptive technologies: Advances that will transform life, business, and the global economy*. McKinsey Global Institute.

Chounta, I. A., Bardone, E., Raudsep, A., & Pedaste, M. (2022). Exploring teachers' perceptions of artificial intelligence as a tool to support their practice in Estonian K-12 education. *International Journal of Artificial Intelligence in Education, 32*(3), 725–755. DOI: 10.1007/s40593-021-00243-5

Coşkun, S., Kayıkcı, Y., & Gençay, E. (2019). Adapting engineering education to Industry 4.0 vision. *Technologies, 7*(1), 10. DOI: 10.3390/technologies7010010

Dearing, J. W., & Cox, J. G. (2018). Diffusion of innovations theory, principles, and practice. *Health Affairs, 37*(2), 183–190. DOI: 10.1377/hlthaff.2017.1104 PMID: 29401011

Druga, S., Otero, N., & Ko, A. J. (2022). The landscape of teaching resources for ai education. *Proceedings of the 27th ACM Conference on Innovation and Technology in Computer Science Education, 1*, 96-102. DOI: 10.1145/3502718.3524782

Fisk, P. (2017). *Education 4.0 … the future of learning will be dramatically different, in school and throughout life*. Retrieved from http://www.thegeniusworks.com/2017/01/future-education-young-everyone-taught-together

Fitria, T. N. (2021). Artificial intelligence (AI) in education: Using AI tools for teaching and learning process. *Prosiding Seminar Nasional & Call for Paper STIE AAS, 4*(1), 134-147. https://prosiding.stie-aas.ac.id/index.php/prosenas/article/view/106

Fitria, T. N. (2023). The use of Artificial Intelligence in Education (AIED): Can AI replace the teacher's role? *EPIGRAM, 20*(2), 165–187. DOI: 10.32722/epi.v20i2.5711

Goel, A. K., & Joyner, D. A. (2017). Using AI to teach AI: Lessons from an online AI class. *AI Magazine, 38*(2), 48–59. DOI: 10.1609/aimag.v38i2.2732

Harun, H. N., & Sallehuddin, Q. (2024, March 25). AI basics to be integrated into primary school curriculum by 2027. *New Straits Times.* https://www.nst.com.my/news/nation/2024/03/1030434/ai-basics-be-integrated-primary-school-curriculum-2027

Huang, L. (2023). Ethics of artificial intelligence in education: Student privacy and data protection. *Science Insights Education Frontiers, 16*(2), 2577–2587. DOI: 10.15354/sief.23.re202

Huang, X. (2021). Aims for cultivating students' key competencies based on artificial intelligence education in China. *Education and Information Technologies, 26*(5), 5127–5147. DOI: 10.1007/s10639-021-10530-2

Hunter, D., McCallum, J., & Howes, D. (2019). Defining Exploratory-Descriptive Qualitative (EDQ) research and considering its application to healthcare. *Journal of Nursing and Health Care, 4*(1). http://eprints.gla.ac.uk/180272

Hurst, A. (2021). *Developing future-ready skills with peer coaching. The Future of Workplace Learning*. MIT Sloan Management Review., https://f.hubspotusercontent10.net/hubfs/3046411/MITSMR-Future-of-Workplace-Learning-Executive-Guide-2021.pdf#page=7

Kementerian Pendidikan Malaysia. (2023). *Dasar pendidikan digital.* Kementerian Pendidikan Malaysia. https://www.moe.gov.my/storage/files/shares/Dasar/Dasar%20Pendidikan%20Digital/Dasar%20Pendidikan%20Digital.pdf?_t=1709571105

Khor, E. T., & Muthulakshmi, K. (2024). A systematic review of the role of learning analytics in supporting personalized learning. *Education Sciences, 14*(1), 51. DOI: 10.3390/educsci14010051

Kim, H., Park, J., Hong, S., Park, Y., Kim, E., Cho, J., & Kim, Y. (2020). Teachers' perceptions of AI in school education. *Journal of Educational Technology, 36*(3), 905–930. DOI: 10.17232/KSET.36.3.905

Luckin, R., Cukurova, M., Kent, C., & Du Boulay, B. (2022). Empowering educators to be AI-ready. *Computers and Education: Artificial Intelligence*, *3*, 100076. DOI: 10.1016/j.caeai.2022.100076

Magaldi, D., & Berler, M. (2020). Semi-structured interviews. In Zeigler-Hill, V., & Shackelford, T. K. (Eds.), *Encyclopedia of personality and individual differences*. Springer., DOI: 10.1007/978-3-319-24612-3_857

Makhambetova, A., Zhiyenbayeva, N., & Ergesheva, E. (2021). Personalized learning strategy as a tool to improve academic performance and motivation of students. [IJWLTT]. *International Journal of Web-Based Learning and Teaching Technologies*, *16*(6), 1–17. DOI: 10.4018/IJWLTT.286743

Mandal, R., & Mete, J. (2023). Teachers' and students' perception towards integration of Artificial Intelligence in school curriculum: A survey. *International Journal of Multidisciplinary Educational Research*, *12*(5), 95–103. http://ijmer.in.doi./2023/12.07.93

Ministry of Education Malaysia. (2024, February). *Education system*. Kementerian Pendidikan. https://www.moe.gov.my/en/dasarmenu/sistem-pendidikan

Murphy, R. F. (2019). Artificial intelligence applications to support K-12 teachers and teaching: A review of promising applications, opportunities, and challenges. *Rand Corporation*, *10*, 1–21.

Onesi-Ozigagun, O., Ololade, Y. J., Eyo-Udo, N. L., & Ogundipe, D. O. (2024). Revolutionizing education through AI: A comprehensive review of enhancing learning experiences. *International Journal of Applied Research in Social Sciences*, *6*(4), 589–607. DOI: 10.51594/ijarss.v6i4.1011

Rogers, E. M. (1962). *Diffusion of innovations* (1st ed.). Free Press.

Rudman, R., & Bruwer, R. (2016). Defining Web 3.0: Opportunities and challenges. *The Electronic Library*, *34*(1), 132–154. DOI: 10.1108/EL-08-2014-0140

Sakulkueakulsuk, B., Witoon, S., Ngarmkajornwiwat, P., Pataranutaporn, P., Surareungchai, W., Pataranutaporn, P., & Subsoontorn, P. (2018, December). Kids making AI: Integrating machine learning, gamification, and social context in STEM education. *2018 IEEE international conference on teaching, assessment, and learning for engineering (TALE)* (pp. 1005-1010). IEEE.

Sharma, P. (2019). Digital revolution of education 4.0. [IJEAT]. *International Journal of Engineering and Advanced Technology*, *9*(2), 3558–3564. DOI: 10.35940/ijeat.A1293.129219

Shirin, A. (2022). Artificial Intelligence technology on teaching-learning: Exploring Bangladeshi teachers' perceptions. *Embedded Self Organizing Systems*, *9*(4), 3–9. DOI: 10.14464/ess.v9i4.553

Zhang, K., & Aslan, A. B. (2021). AI technologies for education: Recent research & future directions. *Computers and Education: Artificial Intelligence*, *2*, 100025. DOI: 10.1016/j.caeai.2021.100025

Chapter 8

Ethical Considerations in the Integration of Artificial Intelligence Within K-12 Education:

Opportunities, Challenges, and Implications in Indian Context

Nandini Deb
http://orcid.org/0000-0002-7466-9677
Manav Rachna International Institute of Research and Studies, India

Ruhi Lal
Manav Rachna International Institute of Research and Studies, India

Deep Moni Gogoi
http://orcid.org/0000-0002-0941-9540
Manav Rachna International Institute of Research and Studies, India

ABSTRACT

This chapter addresses AI's potential, difficulties, and effects on learning utilization in research and implementation. AI's rapid expansion offers individualized learning, adaptive training, and AI-driven assessments, but it also raises ethical issues, especially in India. Data privacy, biased algorithms, the digital divide, and education equity are matters of concern in K–12 education. The study explores Indian primary, secondary, and high school AI integration, its potential, obstacles, and socio-cultural effects. Methods emphasize ethics, education, and assessment. How educators and schools can employ AI responsibly has been examined. AI affects Indian education's

DOI: 10.4018/979-8-3693-6346-1.ch008

ethics, learning, and culture. The study assesses AI-powered education's efficacy, and inclusion. Teachers, politicians, scholars, and technologists must work on data privacy and algorithmic bias. Student growth depends on ethical AI use, pedagogical congruence, and fair access to high-quality education.

INTRODUCTION

The advent of Artificial Intelligence (AI) in the educational sector represents a significant leap forward, holding the potential to fundamentally transform the ways in which teaching and learning are conducted. As AI technologies evolve and become increasingly sophisticated, their integration into educational systems has emerged as a critical area of exploration, particularly within the context of elementary, middle, and high school education. This chapter delves into the multifaceted landscape of AI in education, offering a thorough analysis of its potential, challenges, and impact on enhancing learning outcomes. By synthesizing findings from previous research, theoretical frameworks, and practical applications, this study aims to provide a comprehensive understanding of AI's role in contemporary education. AI has ushered in a new era of personalized and adaptive learning, where educational content can be tailored to meet the unique needs and learning paces of individual students. This customised approach is facilitated through various AI-driven tools, such as intelligent tutoring systems, adaptive learning platforms, and AI-powered assessment methods. These technologies not only enhance the learning experience by providing immediate feedback and customized content but also support teachers in identifying and addressing learning gaps more effectively. For instance, AI can analyze students' performance data to recommend specific resources or interventions, thereby promoting a more efficient and targeted educational approach. (Luckin, Holmes, Griffiths, & Forcier, 2016). Artificial Intelligence has the potential to democratize education by making high-quality learning resources accessible to a broader audience. In regions where educational resources are scarce, AI-driven platforms can offer valuable support, bridging gaps in educational provision and ensuring that all students can succeed. This democratization is particularly significant in countries like India, where disparities in educational quality and access are prevalent. (Mitra, 2018)

By enhancing curriculums and pedagogy, Artificial Intelligence can revolutionize the K-12 education in India. At the onset the future of K-12 education will eventually witness inclusive environment of teaching learning and also empowered educators who shall have access to infrastructure support. Interactive learning experiences give real time exposure to students which enhance comprehension and make it possible for an enthusiastic atmosphere of learning. This further augments the teachers' capability in creating an environment that furthers the cause of development and learning amongst students. With it's immense contribution to various field including transportation, healthcare and finance, Artificial Intelligence is bringing about ground-breaking solutions to personalised, adaptive and compelling learning experiences in the education field. Despite the promising potential of AI in education, its integration is fraught with ethical concerns and challenges that must be carefully navigated. One of the most pressing issues is the digital divide, which refers to the gap between those who have access to digital technologies and those who do not. In the context of India, where socio-economic disparities are pronounced, ensuring equitable access to AI-driven educational tools is a formidable challenge. Addressing this digital divide is crucial to prevent exacerbating existing inequalities in the educational system. (Kumar & Kumari, 2020). In the Indian educational landscape, the integration of AI presents unique opportunities and challenges. The country's diverse socio-cultural fabric necessitates a careful consideration of how AI technologies are implemented to ensure they are culturally sensitive and inclusive. Additionally, the scalability of AI solutions is a critical factor, given the vast and varied educational needs across different regions of India. Educational equity is a core concern in India, where there are significant disparities in access to quality education. AI has the potential to level the playing field by providing personalized learning experiences and resources that can cater to students from diverse backgrounds. However, achieving this requires concerted efforts to overcome infrastructural challenges, such as internet connectivity and the availability of digital devices in rural and underserved areas. (Chaudhary & Kaur, 2019). To harness the full potential of AI in education while addressing ethical and practical challenges, this study proposes a comprehensive model for integrating AI into primary, secondary, and high school learning environments. This model emphasizes ethical considerations, alignment with pedagogical principles, and continuous evaluation to ensure the effectiveness and equity of AI interventions. The model advocates for a collaborative approach involving educators, policymakers, technologists, and researchers. Educators play a crucial role in implementing AI-driven teaching methods that align with educational goals and promote holistic student development. Policymakers must establish robust frameworks and regulations to safeguard data privacy and encourage equitable access to AI technologies. Technologists are tasked with developing AI systems that are transparent, unbiased, and responsive to the needs of diverse learners. Researchers contribute by providing empirical evidence on the impact of AI in education and identifying best practices for its implementation. (Holmes, Bialik, & Fadel, 2021)

STATEMENT OF THE PROBLEM

The amalgamation of Artificial Intelligence in K-12 education holds significant potential to transform traditional educational practices, offering benefits such as personalized learning, adaptive instruction, and enhanced student engagement via empowering educators with infrastructural support. However, the rapid deployment of AI-driven technologies in educational settings also introduces a host of challenges and ethical dilemmas, particularly in the context of India. The Indian education system, with its vast and diverse student population, varying levels of resource availability, and unique socio-cultural dynamics, presents a complex environment for the implementation of AI in K-12 education.

Despite the promising opportunities AI offers, there are several critical issues that need to be addressed to ensure its effective and equitable integration into the Indian educational landscape. The digital divide remains a significant barrier to the equitable adoption of AI technologies in education. Socioeconomic disparities result in uneven access to digital devices and internet connectivity, limiting the reach of AI-driven educational tools to all students, particularly those in rural and underserved areas. The use of AI in education involves the collection and analysis of vast amounts of student data, raising concerns about data privacy and security. Ensuring the protection of sensitive student information and preventing data breaches are paramount to fostering trust in AI systems among educators, students, and parents.

AI algorithms are susceptible to biases that can perpetuate and even exacerbate existing inequalities. In the context of education, biased algorithms can lead to unfair treatment of students based on gender, socioeconomic status, or other demographic factors, thereby undermining the principles of fairness and inclusivity. The ethical implications of AI in education encompass issues such as transparency, accountability, and the potential for AI to replace human teachers. Ensuring that AI technologies are used responsibly and in ways that complement rather than replace human educators is crucial for maintaining the integrity of the educational experience. The successful integration of AI in K-12 education requires educators to possess the necessary skills and knowledge to utilize AI tools effectively. Professional development and training programs are essential to prepare teachers to leverage AI technologies to enhance their teaching practices and support student learning. AI has the potential to either bridge or widen educational inequalities. Ensuring that AI-driven educational innovations promote equity and inclusivity, providing all students with equal opportunities to benefit from advanced technologies, is a significant challenge that needs to be addressed.

Thus, it is essential to address these queries that align with the addressal of digital divide in a country where the lion's share of the population stays in the rural region with limited accessibility to internet and other resources required for education. Another area of inquiry is data privacy which is of paramount importance as children are vulnerable and preventing privacy breeches shall be the only bridge to help bring in AI integration in education. Checks on inclusivity and algorithms also need to be verified as the AI algorithm tends to be biased and may prolong existing inconsistencies.

Given these challenges, there is a critical need for comprehensive research to understand the potential, challenges, and ethical implications of integrating AI in K-12 education in India. This research aims to explore these issues in depth, providing insights into effective strategies and best practices for the responsible deployment of AI technologies in educational settings. By addressing the digital divide, ensuring data privacy, mitigating algorithmic bias, promoting ethical use, preparing teachers, and fostering educational equity, the study seeks to contribute to the development of a robust framework for integrating AI in K-12 education that aligns with the unique socio-cultural context of India.

RESEARCH OBJECTIVES

1. Examine the ethical considerations associated with the integration of AI in Indian K-12 education.
2. Examine the effect of socio-cultural factors on utilization of AI tools on various student populations in India.
3. Find out the elements necessary for ethical AI integration in Indian K-12 education that is in line with teaching methods and continuous assessment.

RESEARCH QUESTIONS

RQ1 What are the primary ethical considerations when implementing AI in K-12 education in India?
RQ2 Is there any impact of socio-cultural factors on the utilization of AI in K-12 schools in India?
RQ3 What elements are necessary to ensures ethical AI integration in Indian K-12 education, while aligning with educational principles and promoting ongoing evaluation?

REVIEW OF LITERATURE

AI raises numerous ethical issues related to education which includes access to materials and resources, personalized student recommendations, the teaching learning process, the concentration of personal data, liability, effects on employment, data privacy, and data ownership used in algorithms. Therefore, regulating AI will necessitate public dialogue on ethics, accountability, transparency, and security. (Pedro, 2019)

The integration of AI into education has significantly impacted the educational system. With the introduction of the National Education Policy (2020), these AI systems can be trained to provide more intelligent responses, addressing complex issues such as motivation, emotions, principles, ethics, and human nature. Advances in personal computers and computational systems have made AI increasingly pervasive. The presence of AI is now evident across various sectors with great impact on healthcare, finance and other sectors. Additionally, the ability to integrate computer-based technologies with different equipment and machines has greatly contributed to the widespread use of AI. However, the ethical dilemma into bringing in regulations in the AI process need to be given further thought. (Zafari, Bazargani, Sadeghi-Niaraki, & Choi, 2022)

AI platforms and services which are designed to improve educational outcomes and also handle administrative tasks are increasingly common, appearing in more classrooms and offices. Discussions about the disruptions and ethical issues caused by AI are taking place in many areas. However, the rapid development of this technology risks outpacing the academic discourse on its benefits and drawbacks in education. To ensure that AI benefits both learners and educators while addressing ethical concerns, the field must first identify and clarify these concerns. While it is expected that AI will empower educators, it is yet to be thought about how the ethical concerns about privacy and data safety are to be dealt with. (Ramien, 2019)

Artificial intelligence (AI) is quickly being integrated into K-12 education due to its growing social and pedagogical significance. This incorporation is expected to impact learners' lives and learning styles significantly, teachers' instructional methods, and the entire school management system. Thus, it is important to further look into the issues where AI and human interaction intersect as this is bound to create ethical perceptions never thought of earlier. New research avenues must delve deep into this area for furthering the study. (Karan & Angadi, 2024)

There needs to be more research on a standardized evaluation framework for AI teaching and learning in K-12 education. Mainstream collaborative programming tools used in undergraduate education may be too complex for K-12 AI instruction. Students' prior programming and understanding as well as their experience may significantly influence AI teaching and learning outcomes in K-12. Interactive AI resources and AI-driven games are more adaptable and suitable for various age groups. Various studies have also found that minimal gender differences exist in learning outcomes, perceptions, or participatory behaviours among young children. (Rizvi, Waite, & Sentance, 2023)

As Artificial Intelligence (AI) transforms the educational landscape, further exploration of the ethical dimensions of AI-based resources highlights the need for a meticulous and thoughtful approach. Several key reflections emerge alongside the aforesaid point, emphasizing the overarching principles that should guide educators, policymakers, and stakeholders in this evolving field. The multifaceted implications for learning in an AI-enhanced educational environment are undeniable. While AI offers personalized learning experiences, increased student engagement, and cognitive benefits, the nuanced challenges require careful consideration. Educators must be vigilant against algorithmic biases and strive to balance technological innovation with the preservation of essential human-centric skills. (Sharma & Kumar, 2024)

THE SIGNIFICANCE OF THE RESEARCH AND RATIONALE

Artificial Intelligence (AI) has the potential to completely transform K-12 education by revolutionizing teaching and learning methods. It can provide personalized learning experiences and greatly improve educational outcomes. Nevertheless, the swift integration of AI technologies also raises notable ethical considerations, especially in a country as diverse and socio-economically varied as India. This research holds great importance as it strives to tackle ethical concerns, guaranteeing responsible and fair integration of AI in Indian K-12 education. The study emphasizes the specific socio-cultural challenges and opportunities in the Indian context, offering valuable insights that can inform policy and practice in similar educational environments.

SCOPE AND UTILITY

The study centers on the education system in India, specifically primary, secondary, and high school levels. It involves analysing ethical considerations, socio-cultural impacts, and developing a comprehensive model for integrating AI in K-12 education. The research incorporates various methodologies such as case studies, literature review, and empirical evidence to substantiate its findings and recommendations. For Educators, it offers valuable insights on the ethical use of AI in classrooms, assisting teachers in seamlessly incorporating AI tools while upholding ethical standards. It provides valuable insights for policymakers regarding the essential regulatory frameworks and policies required to ensure fair and ethical integration of AI in education. For Technologists it emphasizes on the significance of creating AI systems that are impartial, transparent, and culturally aware, specifically designed for educational purposes. Researchers will contribute to the expanding field of literature on AI in education, providing a solid basis for future studies on the ethical implications of AI technologies. This research aims to promote a balanced and inclusive approach to AI integration in K-12 education by addressing the ethical, socio-cultural, and practical aspects. It seeks to benefit all stakeholders involved in the educational process.

RESEARCH METHODOLOGY

Research Design

This study utilizes a qualitative research design, incorporating a combination of secondary data review and semi-structured interviews to collect extensive data on the ethical considerations of AI integration in K-12 education in India. The approach to research ensures a comprehensive exploration of the objectives, resulting in a deep and broad understanding.

Data Collection Method

To compile and analyse current information on AI in education, including ethical considerations, within the specific context of the Indian educational system, the researchers relied on a variety of reputable sources such as academic journals, policy documents, reports from educational organizations, and previous research studies. After thoroughly searching and analysing pertinent literature from reputable databases such as JSTOR, Google Scholar, Web of Science and Scopus, the researchers found that the areas of expertise lie in conducting thorough and well-structured research through interview . With strong background in exploring topics such as the integration of AI in education, ethical considerations surrounding its implementation, the specific context of K-12 education in India, and the socio-cultural impacts that AI can have. The researchers are skilled at gathering relevant information and presenting it in a logical and cohesive manner. To gain a comprehensive understanding of the practical implications and ethical challenges associated with the integration of AI in educational settings. Important components consist of providing a comprehensive understanding of the research study's context and background, overview of AI tools and their practical applications, thorough ethical considerations have been taken into account. They are examining the effects on students and educators—insights gained and effective strategies.

Semi-Structured Interviews

Participants - Educators, policymakers, technology developers, and researchers.

Method - Create an interview guide with open-ended questions that are specifically tailored to each group of participants. It was founfd important to include questions that delve into various aspects of AI integration, such as personal experiences, ethical considerations, and recommendations for implementing best practices.

Sampling - Carefully selecting participants with relevant experience and knowledge, the researchers strived to achieve a diverse representation in terms of geography, school type (public vs. private), and socio-economic context.

Conducting Interviews - Interviews were conducted through online platforms Zoom and few in-person, based on participant availability and convenience. The duration of each interview was around 45-60 minutes.

Recording and Transcription: Interviews were be recorded and transcribed word-for-word for analysis, with the consent of the participants.

Selection of Samples

There were forty sample size for the interview from four different set of respondents.

Educators - Teachers and administrators from a wide range of K-12 schools across India, ensuring representation from urban, semi-urban, and rural areas were 10 in number

Policymakers- Government officials and representatives from educational bodies involved in formulating policies regarding AI and education were 10 in number

Technology Developers- Skilled individuals engaged in the creation of AI-driven educational tools and platforms were 10 in number

Researchers - Individuals who possess a deep understanding and extensive knowledge in the fields of education and AI, with a track record of published work or ongoing research projects that are directly relevant to the study's focus were 10 in number

The researcher conducted a thorough analysis of the interview data, starting with the necessary steps to clean and validate the semi-structured interview data. They ensured the accuracy of the transcription by carefully cross-referencing it with the audio recordings. They utilized transcription software such as Otter.ai for the initial transcription and then made manual corrections as needed. Ensuring participant confidentiality was of utmost importance, so personal identifiers were replaced with pseudonyms. Consistent referencing was ensured by using distinct codes (Lal, 2023), such as E1 for Educator 1 and P1 for Policymaker 1. The transcripts were meticulously formatted to ensure a consistent and professional appearance. The font, spacing, margins, and timestamps were all carefully considered to make referencing and reading the transcripts as effortless as possible.

The data was organized into smaller, meaningful segments through a process called data chunking. Relevant sections of the transcript were identified based on specific themes or questions, such as ethical considerations, practical challenges, or opportunities. Organic divisions were identified by carefully observing the natural pauses and shifts in the conversation. The labeling of each chunk was done accurately, providing clear descriptions of their content, such as "Privacy Concerns" or "Bias in AI." A coding system was developed to ensure consistent labeling throughout all transcripts. After conducting thorough research, the data was carefully organized by grouping similar chunks together to identify patterns and themes.

Initial Coding - The research methodology follows a systematic approach that includes various steps such as axial coding, selective coding, theme development, memoing, and refining the analysis .The researchers performed open coding on each chunk to identify initial codes based on the content (Kumar and Lal, 2023) . One important aspect was to identify and categorize the main concepts and ideas shared by the participants. The researchers utilized qualitative data analysis software such as NVivo to streamline the coding process and maintain a structured approach to organization. Grouping of Codes, data clustering organizing codes into broader categories or clusters, such as privacy, bias, and accessibility, through axial coding was done.

When conducting axial coding, it is important to document thoughts and observations about each cluster, paying attention to any recurring patterns or connections that may arise. Through careful examination of the relationships between clusters, data memoing involves the use of selective coding to identify core themes (Rahman et al., 2024) . When it comes to theme development, the main objective is to emphasize the connection between these themes and the research questions. An effective approach to coding involves iterative analysis, where similar themes are combined and excessively broad ones are divided.

It is important to record reflective observations while analyzing the data. This helps to document thoughts, insights, and analytical concepts. It is important to write memos while coding in order to document your initial impressions and emerging patterns. It is also important to write reflective memos right after each interview to capture immediate thoughts and observations and categorize these memos by themes or categories in order to maintain a structured record of analytical thinking. This will ensure that they are seamlessly incorporated into the final analysis, providing strong support and enhancing data interpretation.

Refining involves an ongoing process of analyzing and distilling insights through reflection and iteration. Thorough evaluation is conducted to improve comprehension and maintain a consistent analysis, while also seeking input from peers to ensure a robust and trustworthy analysis. The themes are carefully refined and adjusted through ongoing analysis and feedback. They may be merged, split, or redefined to establish clear and distinct conceptual themes that are supported by evidence from the data.

At the last step, researchers involved interpreting the clustered and coded data to draw meaningful conclusions and insights, which are crucial for the overall analysis process.

THEMATIC ANALYSIS

The researcher conducted a comprehensive analysis of the themes, examining their relevance to the research questions and assessing how the data aligned with or challenged existing knowledge. The evidence was collected by gathering pertinent quotes and examples from the data to effectively illustrate each theme and enhance the analysis. Throughout the content analysis, a thorough examination was carried out to identify the most common ethical considerations and challenges. This involved analyzing the frequency of themes and codes to ensure a comprehensive understanding. Analyzed findings from different participant groups, including educators and policymakers, to uncover different viewpoints and common themes through comparative analysis. The researcher employed various visual aids, such as tables, charts, and word clouds, to present the data analysis in a clear and effective manner. At last, a meticulously organized narrative was crafted, seamlessly weaving together the various themes and insights to provide a comprehensive grasp of the ethical considerations associated with the implementation of AI in K-12 education.

DATA ANALYSIS AND INTERPRETATION

The tables are presented to showcase the coding categories for the interview data collected during the study on ethical considerations in integrating AI in K-12 education in India

Table 1. Open coding

Sl No	Interview Excerpt	Open Code
1	"AI can significantly personalize learning experiences."	Personalization
2	"There are concerns about data privacy when using AI tools."	Data Privacy
3	"AI algorithms may have inherent biases."	Algorithmic Bias
4	"Teachers need proper training to use AI effectively."	Teacher Training

continued on following page

Table 1. Continued

Sl No	Interview Excerpt	Open Code
5	"AI can help in identifying students' learning difficulties early."	Early Identification
6	"The cost of implementing AI in schools is a major barrier."	Implementation Cost
7	"We must ensure AI use is ethical and transparent."	Ethical Use
8	"AI can support administrative tasks, reducing teacher workload."	Administrative Support
9	"There are socio-cultural barriers to AI adoption in rural areas."	Socio-cultural Barriers
10	"Continuous evaluation of AI tools is necessary."	Continuous Evaluation

Source Author's Compilation

Here is a table that presents the initial open codes obtained from the interview excerpts. The codes used in this research represent important points raised by participants, covering a range of key issues including personalization, data privacy, algorithmic bias, teacher training, early identification, implementation cost, ethical use, administrative support, socio-cultural barriers, and continuous evaluation. These points were carefully analyzed and organized to provide a comprehensive and cohesive understanding of the topic. These codes serve as the building blocks for further analysis.

Table 2. Axial coding

Sl. No	Axial Code	Open Codes	Description
1	Personalization and Support	Personalization, Early Identification, Administrative Support	How AI enhances learning personalization, early identification of issues, and administrative efficiency.
2	Ethical Concerns	Data Privacy, Algorithmic Bias, Ethical Use	Ethical challenges associated with AI, including privacy, bias, and ethical transparency.
3	Training and Implementation	Teacher Training, Implementation Cost	Issues related to the training required for teachers and the costs involved in implementing AI.
4	Socio-cultural Factors	Socio-cultural Barriers	Socio-cultural barriers affecting AI adoption, particularly in rural areas.
5	Continuous Improvement	Continuous Evaluation	The necessity for ongoing evaluation and improvement of AI tools.

Source: author's Compilation

Through the process of axial coding, related open codes are organized into broader categories, allowing for the discovery of deeper connections. Here are the axial codes- Exploring the Benefits of AI in Personalized Learning and Administrative Efficiency. Ethical Concerns -Addressing challenges related to data privacy, algorithmic bias, and ethical transparency. The code training and Implementation focused on exploring the importance of teacher training and the financial considerations of AI implementation. Exploring Socio-cultural Factors- Challenges of AI Adoption in rural areas. Continuous improvement means the importance of consistently assessing AI tools.

Table 3. Selective coding

Sl, No	Selective Code	Axial Codes	Core Theme
1	Enhancing Learning and Support	Personalization and Support	AI's role in personalizing education and supporting administrative tasks.
2	Addressing Ethical Challenges	Ethical Concerns	Ethical considerations, including privacy, bias, and transparency, in AI usage.
3	Overcoming Implementation Barriers	Training and Implementation, Socio-cultural Factors	Challenges and barriers in training, cost, and socio-cultural acceptance of AI in education.
4	Ensuring Continuous Improvement	Continuous Improvement	Importance of ongoing evaluation and refinement of AI tools to ensure effectiveness and ethical compliance.

Source Author's Compilation

Summary of Data Analysis Tables

Organized Coding – Core Themes

The process of selective coding involves synthesizing axial codes into core themes that capture the main findings of the study.

Improving Learning and Support- The Role of AI in Customizing Education and Assisting Teachers. Exploring Ethical Challenges -Examining the crucial ethical concerns surrounding the integration of AI, such as privacy and bias. AI has the potential to greatly enhance education by personalizing the learning experience, identifying students' needs at an early stage, and assisting with administrative tasks to alleviate the workload on teachers

Addressing Implementation Barriers- Exploring Challenges in Training, Cost, and Socio-Cultural Acceptance of AI.

Emphasizing the Need for Ongoing Improvement- The Significance of Regular Evaluation and Enhancement of AI Tools.

Addressing Ethical Challenges- It is crucial to acknowledge the ethical concerns surrounding AI, including data privacy and algorithmic bias, in order to ensure its safe and effective use.Successfully integrating AI into education involves addressing various challenges, including teacher training, implementation costs, and socio-cultural acceptance, particularly in rural areas.

Consistently Striving for Improvement: Regular evaluation and enhancement of AI tools are essential for upholding their effectiveness and ethical standards.

To successfully implement AI in K-12 education, it is crucial to overcome significant barriers. These include providing comprehensive teacher training and managing the high costs associated with AI tools. Furthermore, the adoption of AI faces challenges due to socio-cultural barriers, especially in rural areas. It is crucial to have strategies in place to overcome these barriers in order to achieve successful integration. Thorough and meticulous analysis of AI tools is essential for ensuring their ongoing effectiveness and adherence to ethical standards. Thorough evaluations can assist in identifying and addressing any potential problems, guaranteeing that AI continues to be a valuable asset in the field of education.

FINDINGS & RESULTS

Insights from a thorough analysis of the study by exploring the relationship between teacher autonomy and AI integration it was observed that numerous educators have raised concerns regarding the potential threat of AI undermining their autonomy. They believed that although AI tools can offer valuable assistance, they should not substitute the human judgment and creativity that teachers contribute to the classroom. This finding highlights the significance of developing AI systems that work alongside human educators, allowing teachers to maintain their independence and ensuring that AI is used as a tool to improve human decision-making.

Regarding the role of AI in addressing learning disabilities, interviewees emphasized the potential of AI in identifying and supporting students with learning disabilities. AI tools have the ability to provide personalized learning experiences and adjust to individual needs more efficiently compared to traditional methods. There is a notable potential for AI to make a significant impact in special education by offering personalized assistance and resources to students with varying learning requirements.

For examining the effect of socio-cultural factors on utilization of AI tools on various student populations in India researchers explored the cultural sensitivity in AI tools. Many participants highlighted the importance of AI tools being culturally sensitive and adaptable to various regional contexts within India. It was highlighted that AI systems developed in Western contexts may not be completely applicable or effective in Indian classrooms. This finding emphasizes the significance of creating

AI tools that are culturally relevant and responsive to the specific socio-cultural dynamics of Indian education.

Developing an Ethical AI Curriculum, educators proposed the inclusion of ethics education in the AI curriculum for students. This would involve teaching them about important topics such as data privacy, algorithmic bias, and the responsible use of AI technologies. This innovative approach fosters digital literacy and ethical awareness among students, equipping them to responsibly navigate and shape the future landscape of AI.

For exploring the relationship between parental involvement and perception of AI in education the level of parental understanding and acceptance of AI tools were analysed. How readily their children adopt and effectively utilize these technologies by implementing awareness programs and showcasing the advantages and reliability of AI tools, parents can be effectively engaged, leading to a more seamless integration and increased acceptance of AI in the field of education.

DISCUSSION

The incorporation of AI in K-12 education offers immense potential for transformation, yet also poses notable hurdles. The study highlights the importance of thoughtful implementation of AI in education to ensure that it enhances personalized learning, supports teachers, and addresses learning disabilities, while still preserving teacher autonomy and cultural relevance. Ensuring ethical considerations, such as data privacy and algorithmic bias, are of utmost importance. It is crucial to recognize the importance of AI tools being culturally sensitive and adaptable to regional contexts in India. This insight highlights the inadequacy of one-size-fits-all solutions. In addition, incorporating ethics education into the AI curriculum can empower students to responsibly utilize AI. The successful adoption of AI technologies is heavily influenced by parental involvement and perception.

CONCLUSION

The study suggests that for the successful integration of AI in K-12 education in India, a comprehensive approach is necessary. This approach should prioritize ethical considerations, cultural sensitivity, and continuous improvement. AI tools should work alongside teachers to enhance their role, rather than replacing them. It is important for these tools to be customized to address the specific socio-cultural dynamics present in Indian classrooms. Building trust in AI systems requires a strong focus on data privacy and the mitigation of algorithmic bias. In addition, involving parents and incorporating ethics education into the curriculum are crucial measures for cultivating a responsible and inclusive educational environment driven by AI.

FUTURE SCOPE OF THE STUDY

Advancement in the field of AI has opened up new possibilities for the development of culturally adaptable tools. These tools have the potential to revolutionize various aspects of our lives by seamlessly integrating with different cultural contexts. By focusing on this area of research, we can pave the way for a future where AI tools are not only intelligent but also sensitive to the diverse needs and preferences of individuals from different cultures.

Future research should prioritize the development of AI tools that can effectively adapt and respond to the diverse cultural and regional contexts within India. Working closely with educators and cultural experts is essential for developing AI systems that are applicable and efficient in diverse educational environments.

Conducting longitudinal studies to evaluate the long-term effects of integrating AI into education can offer valuable insights into the effectiveness and sustainability of AI-driven educational interventions. These studies will focus on assessing student outcomes, teacher efficacy, and overall educational equity.

Exploring AI applications in special education can reveal new methods to assist students with learning disabilities. These methods can provide personalized and adaptive learning experiences tailored to their individual needs.

Emphasizing ethics education in the AI curriculum for students can foster a more profound comprehension of the ethical ramifications of AI and equip the next generation to responsibly utilize and advance AI technologies.

Creating effective strategies to engage and educate parents about AI in education can improve their understanding and acceptance of AI tools, resulting in greater adoption of these technologies in K-12 education.

By considering these future directions, academic researchers and educators can further investigate the potential of AI in revolutionizing education, while prioritizing ethical, cultural, and practical considerations.

REFERENCES

Chaudhary, R., & Kaur, J. (2019). Bridging the Educational Divide with AI in Rural India. *International Journal of Educational Development*, •••, 301–310.

Holmes, W., Bialik, M., & Fadel, C. (2021). Artificial Intelligence in Education: Promises and Implications for Teaching and Learning. *OECD Education Working Papers*, 188.

Karan, B., & Angadi, G. (2024). Potential Risks of Artificial Intelligence Integration into School Education: A Systematic Review. *Bulletin of Science, Technology & Society; Sage Publications*.

Kumar, D., & Lal, R. (2023). Technological Advancements in the Media Industry and the Current Job Market in India. In Naim, A. (Ed.), *Accreditation Processes and Frameworks in Higher Education* (pp. 289–314). Nova Science Publishers.

Kumar, R., & Kumari, S. (2020). Digital Divide and AI in Indian Education. *Asian Journal of Educational Research*, 55-67.

Lal, R. (2023). New Measures of Teaching Learning and Evaluating with Changing Technology. In Naim, A. (Ed.), *Accreditation Processes and Frameworks in Higher Education* (pp. 267–287). Nova Science Publishers.

Luckin, R., Holmes, M., Griffiths, B., & Forcier, L. (2016).. . *Intelligence*.

Mitra, S. (2018). The Future of Learning: AI in Indian Classrooms. *Indian Journal of Educational Technology*, 97 - 109.

Pedro, F. (2019). Artificial intelligence in education: challenges and opportunities for sustainable development.

Rahman, Z. T., Lal, R., & Rena, R. (2024). Challenges of Communication with Gen-Z in the Era of Artificial Intelligence-Interceded Digital Economy. In *AI-Oriented Competency Framework for Talent Management in the Digital Economy* (pp. 76–94). CRC Press. DOI: 10.1201/9781003440901-5

Ramien, D. (2019). *Augmenting Education: Ethical Considerations for Incorporating Artificial Intelligence in Education*. Instructional Design Capstones Collection.

Rizvi, S., Waite, J., & Sentance, S. (2023). Artificial Intelligence teaching and learning in K-12 from 2019 to 2022: A systematic literature review. *Computers and Education: Artificial Intelligence*.

Sharma, S., & Kumar, N. (2024). Navigating the ethical landscape of AI Based resources in Education: Implications for Learning, Proper Usage and Course Design Enhancement. *The Online Journal of Distance Education and e-Learning : TOJDEL.*

Zafari, M., Bazargani, J. S., Sadeghi-Niaraki, A., & Choi, S. M. (2022). [Education: A Systematic Literature Review. *IEEE Access*]. *Artificial Intelligence and Applications (Commerce, Calif.)*, •••, K-12.

Chapter 9
FinTech Education With Artificial Intelligence

Arif Ahsan
http://orcid.org/0009-0007-2101-0602
Universiti Malaysia Perlis, Malaysia

Dayang Hasliza Muhd Yusuf
http://orcid.org/0000-0002-7309-1172
Universiti Malaysia Perlis, Malaysia

Juraini Zainol Abidin
http://orcid.org/0000-0002-7814-7702
Universiti Malaysia Perlis, Malaysia

ABSTRACT

The integration of Artificial Intelligence (AI) into FinTech education is transforming financial services and academic programs, bridging the gap between traditional learning and industrial expectations. This chapter focuses on how AI-driven FinTech education improves financial literacy, financial management, and FinTech adoption. It explores fundamental concerns about AI's role in FinTech education, its implementation, and its impact on learners and institutions, with a focus on educators, students, and industry professionals. The findings emphasise the possibilities of AI-powered FinTech solutions to customise learning, give market insights, and optimise financial decision-making to increase student engagement. The topic emphasises the importance of a multidisciplinary curriculum, regulatory constraints, and ethical concerns associated with AI integration in education. Finally, FinTech education boosted by AI is critical for equipping graduates with skills and encouraging financial inclusion.

DOI: 10.4018/979-8-3693-6346-1.ch009

INTRODUCTION: FINTECH MEETS AI IN EDUCATION

FinTech use technology to deliver financial services (Kou & Lu, 2025) . According to Thottoli et al., (2024) FinTech promotes innovation by incorporating modern technologies such as blockchain, AI, and big data analytics. It is a term that combines the words "financial" or "finance" with "technology" (Saha et al., 2025; Abilawa et al., 2023) . It is a sector that provides a variety of financial services using software (Ojiaku et al., 2024). It uses sophisticated technology such as blockchain, data analytics, and financial transactions to improve organizational efficiency (Jafri et al., 2024). In Figure 1, we can find the evolution of FinTech that initially starts with transmission of financial information, and at present, we are witnessing the rise of Artificial Intelligence (AI) (Jafri et al., 2024). The evolution of FinTech and AI is shown in the Figure 1:

Figure 1. Four major stages of FinTech development

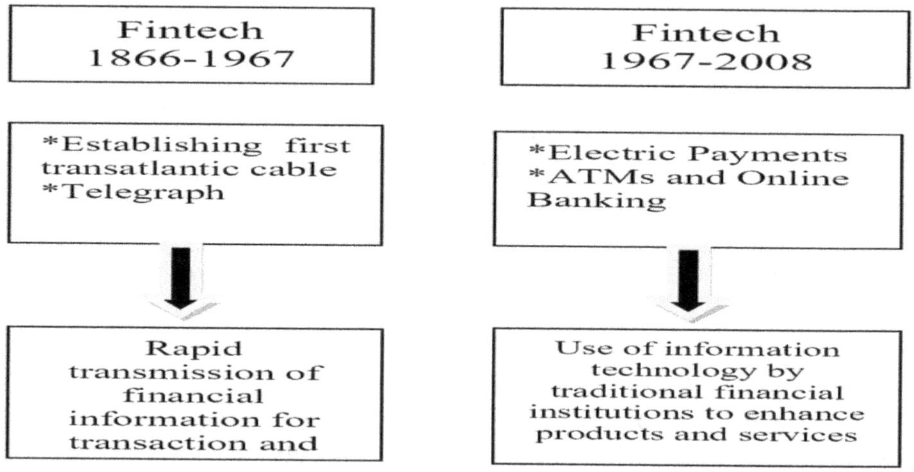

(Jafri et al., 2024; Tigges et al., 2024, Thakor, 2020)

In Figure 1, it clearly depicts that the evolution of FinTech has brought a classic change from traditional finance to AI/ML based finance. More specifically, since 2015 AI is in the stage of adopting alternative data that has the capacity to innovate various ideas and thought for the new entrants of a market. FinTech has various features that contributes in various financial services. The use of online mobile technology makes financial services efficient and accessible to others (Amnas et al., 2023). Furthermore, it offers more cost-effective solutions than traditional institutions, reducing both transaction time and financial costs (Shaikh et al., 2023; Rahman et al., 2021). This includes financial innovations, business structures, and technology-based products or services (Zhang & Cui, 2024) that reduces credit supply frictions and increases credit availability for businesses.

Globally, the success of any form of business is largely dependent on technical developments (Nalluri & Chen, 2024) which can be used in a variety of business applications such as mobile banking payments and crowdfunding (Liu et al., 2024). The reasons for continued success of "FinTech" is the revolutionary capabilities of FinTech in business operations (Akartuna et al., 2022). It has created the opportunity to shaking up traditional business operations, providing a chance for both newcomers and established companies to expand which can significantly improve the risk evaluation of financial transactions. Also, the integration of technology into a business model that improves an organization's financial services (Cao & Zhai, 2022) which could improve the performance of businesses globally. It has also found that the performance of FinTech is being accelerated while it is combined with AI (Cao et al., 2021) and technology (Tang, et al., 2024). There have been many practises of AI and Finance over decades has been done as a typical solution of AI (Mousa, 2022). In practical, the connection between AI and FinTech has been accelerated since the beginning of 21st century more specifically after Covid-19 pandemic (Yadav et al., 2022). The incorporation of AI in finance is considered as a major transformative advancement technology which ultimately introduces financial technology-FinTech (Cao, 2020). As AI-integrated FinTech transforms monetary systems, educational institutions must promptly equip students to leverage emerging technologies and contemplate their implications.

Why FinTech Education Needs AI: Drivers and Demand in Academia

The integration of AI in many industries such as marketing, finance, education, and manufacturing provides up several professional options for students with interdisciplinary backgrounds (Abulibdeh et al., 2024). AI helps to transform the fiction into reality through reestablishing every sector such as education, socio-economic, technological and political. Also, FinTech innovations, such as AI-powered learning platforms can help improve financial education. These tools increase financial literacy by making instruction more accessible and entertaining to consumers. According to Chikri & Kassou, (2024) AI tools are a prime example of how solutions are provided in the field of finance. The traditional education system has the limitation of struggling to adjust with the diversified learning systems and changing preferences of industries (Thimmanna et al., 2023) where AI reduces gap for traditional education system and technology-based education system (Tahiru, 2021). Besides, there has been a significant impact on changing the financial ecosystem (Cao & Zhai, 2022) not only in the business sectors but also in academia. Traditional curricula have been largely concerned with increasing students' financial awareness and providing academic understanding. However, with the changing business world, FinTech is a new field of study that has evolved and gained preferences in academia (Rajpal & Manglani, 2023) and businesses as well. According to Anan et al. (2023) since last decade the total valuation of FinTech organizations are valued at $550 billion. Additionally, there were more than 272 FinTech unicorns worth $936 billion, marking a sevenfold increase to $1 billion. So, the financial growth of FinTech make many universities realize the demand of FinTech preparedness for their students. This awareness makes the universities to offer FinTech related education and training (Wibowo et al., 2024). One of the major reasons of this preferences in academia is its contribution in the businesses that realize the need of FinTech graduates. According to Kwangmuang et al., (2025) universities must collaborate with industry leaders to determine the critical competencies and abilities required in the FinTech sector. Based on this, the authorities devised learning activities and evaluations that fit with industry demands, effectively preparing learners for their future employment. Also, as per Siddiqui & Rivera, (2023) the priorities of FinTech have increased among the job seekers. In the google trends search it is found that now a days there are more search on "FinTech" than "accounting" and "finance" which indicates the exponential increase of FinTech workforce. So, this is the gap where the academia can meet the demand of potential graduates as well as FinTech industry. Moreover, Siddiqui & Rivera, (2023) give importance of interdisciplinary higher education curriculum rather than monodisciplinary. Higher education curriculum has introduced a blended combination of finance, IT and other discipline. This comprehensive approach will assist experts in this sector to understand and appreciate the relationships between diverse disciplines (Ivanitskaya et al., 2002). Besides, this blended learning would help to develop holistic approach view for the learners which is very crucial to make innovative ideas and comprehensive connections. Also, young graduates will be more competitive to meet the challenges of latest perspective. Furthermore, AI and Finance into higher education represents a transformative change in educational outcomes (Abulibdeh et al., 2025). Moreover, the incorporation of IT would accelerate new grads who can improve their critical thinking and metacognitive skills while also learning about how diverse areas intersect (Weber et al., 2024). This combination of inter discipline will help to increase the adoption of FinTech although Kou & Lu, (2025) mentioned of low adoption of FinTech. The probable reason of less adoption is the gap between academic curriculum and industry professionals. So, the academicians have to play the role to mitigate this gap which would make the balance between demand and supply of skills and knowledge (Mahalingam, 2024). According to Kwangmuang et al., (2025) the implementation of FinTech education via an AI curriculum has dramatically improved learners' adaptability, creativity, and technical competency. Industry leaders, instructional designers, and online learning specialists must work together and iteratively to construct the 'AI & FinTech' curriculum for youngsters aged 15 to 24 aiming to prepare young students for future employment in AI and FinTech by providing a complete guideline with regular updates. Plus, (2025) asserts that the integration of AI and FinTech has transitioned from a future trend to an essential requirement. 75% of financial organisations now require AI and machine learning competencies inside their core teams. This alteration has generated a demand for specialists proficient in both finance and technology. In response, educational institutions are modifying their curricula to incorporate AI-driven technology for personalised learning, predictive analytics, and real-time financial simulations (Plus, 2025). Kwangmuang et al., (2025) highlights the importance of collaboration between corporations along with educational institutions for developing AI-enhanced FinTech programs. It is asserted that learner-centred design, experiential learning, and frequent curriculum updates are essential for preparing students for the rapidly evolving finance sector. This collaboration between the business sector and academics underscores the necessity of making finance education more flexible to technological advancements and aligned with student demands.

AI's Impact on the FinTech Sector: Setting the Context

We can leverage the capabilities of AI and the benefits of FinTech to make more informed decisions in finance planning. AI can personalized financial planning through the assessment of market trends, geopolitical factors, and economic conditions. This thorough analysis enables accurate predictions about market opportunities and risks. Insights from AI-driven financial planning systems empower learners to make informed decisions and capitalize on market opportunities. Additionally, using AI ensures that students can pursue their academic goals with confidence, free from the anxiety of market fluctuations. So, the incorporation of AI into FinTech education has been found popularity among the educators (Delello et al., 2025). Considering that a major transformation has been found around the FinTech ecosystem through increasing interest of using alternative data over the previous decades. This growing interest is mainly for the developing collaboration (Berg et al., 2022). Although 'Artificial Intelligence' and 'Machine Learning' are frequently used interchangeably in academic literature, it is important to recognize that Machine Learning is a part of AI. Machine Learning is a method to understand AI (Tigges et al., 2024). So, in this chapter we mainly focused on the combination between FinTech education and AI where both can contribute to integrate modern financial systems.

More specifically, AI accelerates the FinTech services. it has enhanced methodologies highlight limitations of traditional financial mechanisms (Wagdi and Tarek, 2022) through ensuring equitable use of financial services (Leal, 2024). So, AI technologies enable extended FinTech automation that can handle complicated services (Paudel, 2024). So, the adoption of AI helps professionals to solve problems and take strategic decisions (Baity, 2023). This usage of AI in financial activities in the organization also contributes to a country's economy by reducing financial poverty. This create opportunities for FinTech solutions for under privileged communities (Chen & Yuan, 2021). Moreover, AI stands out as a formidable tool in the FinTech landscape, surpassing other technologies in its impact. AI focused financial planning change the direction for conventional methods of financial analysis. Furthermore, it has the ability to examine large datasets that can influence strategic judgments (Yandong, 2024). This data-driven strategy has resulted in faster and more accurate judgments, which are critical in the rapidly expanding financial business. Moreover, it has the capacity to assess probable risk. Such as AI has the competence to detect fraudulent manipulation and inconsistency among financial transactions.

The combination of AI and FinTech has brought major impact and ease the way of work (Patel, 2024). The incorporation of AI into FinTech has positive impact in implementing various financial services and decisions in the financial sector. Implementing AI-based multilayered neural networks in FinTech offers significant advantages, including enhanced decision-making, improved risk management, and better fraud detection (Lee et al., 2022). AI can identify various financial risk bias reduction in credit scores, and continuous financial market monitoring (Giudici, 2018a) as per expected benefits. Furthermore, AI also provides suggestions (Table 1) for improvements in FinTech based services considering the stakeholders. The following Table 1, shows some contribution of AI in FinTech for different stakeholders:

Table 1. Stakeholder concern on AI/ML data in FinTech (Giudici, 2018b)

Stakeholder group	Perceived Benefits	Perceived risks	Suggested improvements
Entrepreneurs	Innovative ideas, business models, enhanced effectiveness, and exploring untapped market opportunities	Intense competition, potential for early acquisition, significant upfront costs, and resistance from banking institutions	Developing innovative business models and engaging in targeted, strategic lobbying efforts
Policymakers	Enhanced regulatory frameworks, deeper market insights, inclusive financial practices, boosted market competition, and economic expansion	Concerns about privacy, regulatory hurdles, unclear traceability and accountability, opaque systems, and biases in algorithms	More defined AI usage guidelines for financial projects.
ML Engineers	Cutting-edge advancements, emerging growth in employment, and the pursuit of next-generation AI	Misapplication of technology, excessive dependence on AI, challenges in human-machine interaction, and concerns about replaceability	Enhanced literacy on AI management, employment security measures, opportunities for re-skilling and executive training
Academic Researchers	Progress in knowledge, emerging research opportunities, and a detail knowledge of FinTech and AI	Ethics, Privacy infringements, and the absence of proper accountability.	Increased multidisciplinary research and enhanced collaboration with stakeholders.

From the above information, it is clearly understood that AI has the capability of contributing in not only in the education industry but also for the entrepreneurs, policy makers, ML Engineers and Academic Researchers. Although AI has risk of security breach but considering its immense benefits such as developing business models, analysing the market trends, enhancing the employability and creating opportunities for intense academic research. Overall, AI can provide invaluable support in various areas such as financial advisory for education, risk management, credit risk assessment, expense tracking, budgeting, and financial analysis. As artificial intelligence transforms the operations and strategies of FinTech, the integration of these tools in educational institutions becomes increasingly essential. This theme will now be examined through curriculum design, pedagogical approaches, and innovative use of technology in the classroom.

FINTECH EDUCATION WITH AI: PRINCIPLES, PEDAGOGY, AND POSSIBILITIES

Financial education is considered as one of the major ways of increasing financial inclusion (Adam, 2024). Furthermore, high financial knowledge is expected by many countries (Lusardi & Messy, 2023) considering technology-based study in finance (Levantesi & Zacchia, 2021). AI-powered educational technologies are proven to be game changers, transforming not only the classroom but also many other industries, including finance. By 2028, AI will drive 70% of education, research, and content development. This demonstrates how deeply AI will be integrated into everyday operations (Agrawal, 2025). So, it brings significant changes in university education for subjects that adopts them into their curriculum (Levantesi & Zacchia, 2021) because there are many companies and countries that find better performances (Adam, 2024). AI is set to significantly enhance education finance planning for students globally. AI-driven solutions assist educational institutions in addressing disparities in student performance and retention, thereby fostering diversity and equity in education (Huong, 2024). So, the education institutions now can easily understand the behavioural pattern of a student. Based on which, they can suggest their students and take corrective actions. AI algorithms accelerate literature reviews, data analysis, and hypothesis development, driving scientific advancements and discoveries. Moreover, AI algorithms have become integral to the finance industry, enhancing various aspects such as customer service, risk management, fraud detection, and investment decisions. In FinTech, AI encompasses numerous algorithms that are employed to optimize and streamline financial operations (Baity, 2023). This increased research speed enhances the influence of academic institutions in tackling societal issues and expanding the boundaries of knowledge (Liu et al., 2023). Further uses of AI are found in many developed countries like USA. According to Techflow, (2022) the incorporation of AI in FinTech education is getting more focus in the United States education system, where it can develop learning outcome and academic performance. Organizations are also benefited with the use of AI. That is why, many of the organizations are turning to AI to gain a competitive advantage. Financial institutions are using AI prediction models to examine historical data, reduce risk, estimate cash flow, improve credit rating, and detect fraud (Baity, 2023). So, the incorporation of finance into FinTech education is considered positive (Adam, 2024) for higher education as the FinTech education has helped to transform the traditional finance to digital finance. It is highly required to use technology-based finance education with the help of financial literacy. According to Croitoru et al., (2025) higher education institutions are leveraging digital technology and collaborating with the business and financial institutions.

Role of Financial Literacy and AI Tools in FinTech Pedagogy

FinTech is a vital support tool for literacy in finance. In this context, advances in FinTech open up new avenues for improving financial literacy by providing more inclusive and accessible teaching resources. So, FinTech training programs must cover important issues like budgeting, savings, and credit management in order to educate users with financial literacy (Croitoru et al., 2025). So, technology based financial education with sufficient financial literacy is highly required. For example, the success story of Squirrel AI could be one of the good examples of how AI helps to transform the education system in terms student question accuracy (Haoyang & Towne, 2025). So, to fulfil this technology requirement, education institutions have to incorporate technology-based curriculum into their studies. Furthermore, interdisciplinary curriculum should be developed by reflecting the need of the industry. So that, the students can perform into various industry after graduation. This would also help to increase the employability of the students and increase the reputation of the institutions. As we know, technology has been used in finance education from the first generation of computers and subsequent updates. There are many uses of technology which has the capability of increase learning outcomes, personalize the learning experiences and improve teaching efficiency(Placide, 2024). Moreover, it provides customized feedback and recommendations for classroom education. Therefore, it's use in finance is increasing day by day (Placide, 2024).

Curriculum Gaps, Challenges, and Strategies for Educational Reform

Realizing the demand of FinTech based finance education in financial market, the offered FinTech course aims to familiarize students with both the theory and practice of FinTech. Additionally, it seeks to train and develop understanding of disruption within AI across different areas, such as money, markets, marketplaces, and infrastructure. This would enable students to address gaps in the financial services sector while also helping them build more robust economic institutions (Charaia & Lashkhi, 2023). In general, the finance courses should focus on student-oriented learning style which would be a combination of problem solving, discussion, seminars, essays/reports, lectures, debates, panels and brainstorming. Additionally, the inclusion of AI centric FinTech practices such as financial forecasting through analysing financial data which offers a plethora of FinTech solutions tailored for education, enhancing financial management significantly. AI tools can elevate financial literacy and guide through best practices for budgeting and loan management which tools assist students in budgeting and expense tracking, enabling effective financial management. So, the incorporation of AI and FinTech is important for finance students. As learners often take out loans to finance their education, AI tools can help them devise strategies to pay off debts, improve credit scores, and consolidate loans. This approach offers a chance for business school curricula to boost interdisciplinarity, industry relevance, information sharing, and social impact. Many of the universities and colleges offer minimum FinTech education in undergraduate or postgraduate level although students had interest (Milner et al.,2023). Barrett, (2018) conducted research on the alumni of U.S universities where they found that many US business schools offer minimum FinTech courses, and those that do frequently fail to teach the subject well. Many colleges avoid FinTech because they believe it just refers to app development. It is also found that most FinTech programs at US universities focus on regulation, security, and their impact on the market. This broad approach tends to overlook detailed discussions of specific technologies using AI, leaving students to gain this knowledge through practical experience or additional elective courses (Earls, 2019) considered as unprepared challenge in the field of FinTech and AI. Moreover, the growing demand of FinTech indicates the need of finance educational program to merge with AI skilled professionals (Vishwanath, 2023). That is why, integrating FinTech and AI into curricula equips students with the necessary knowledge and abilities to flourish in rapidly evolving sectors.

ETHICS, REGULATION AND RISK: A THEMATIC CLUSTER IN AI-DRIVEN FINTECH

Due to the convergence of ethical, regulatory, and risk-related concerns in AI-driven FinTech, an integrated analytical approach is necessary. Ikumapayi, (2025) asserts that the implementation of AI in financial services enhances operational efficiency while simultaneously exposing the system to dangers, including algorithmic bias, data misuse, regulatory arbitrage, and cyber threats. Regulatory bodies are introducing new regulations that emphasise transparency, accountability, and cross-border compliance (KPMG, 2024). The universal implementation of AI in commerce has engendered significant ethical dilemmas, including algorithmic bias, breaches of data privacy, and deficiencies in accountability. The risks are particularly pronounced in the financial services sector, where ambiguous decision-making frameworks can exacerbate inequality and diminish public trust (Milner et al.,2023). According to Snyder, (2025) the World Economic Forum cautions that the unregulated use of AI might lead to failures proliferating throughout interconnected financial institutions. This underscores the significance of implementing robust monitoring and ethical safeguards. Consequently, FinTech education must evolve to enable students to harness the advantages of AI while critically evaluating its societal and systemic implications.

According to Dahlin, (2025) asserts. that confidence in AI cannot be solely engineered through technical measures like explainability; instead, it should be regarded as a socio-technical construct shaped by user perception and institutional context. Radanliev, (2025) similarly emphasises the imperative of incorporating transparency and equity across the AI lifespan, especially in vital industries like finance, where algorithmic obscurity can exacerbate bias and erode public confidence. These insights underscore the imperative for FinTech education to transcend mere technical proficiency, equipping learners to critically evaluate social, and financial implications. So, AI technologies are increasingly prevalent in financial institutions, the regulations governing them remain weak and poorly defined. This regulatory loophole raises significant concerns, including algorithmic bias, data misuse, and systemic vulnerabilities. KPMG, (2024) asserts that this year signifies a "regulatory shift," with varying AI supervision regulations across countries, complicating compliance for banks and other financial organizations in their operations. Kapron, (2025) asserts that the utilization of AI in FinTech is increasing; yet, regulatory bodies are struggling to achieve equilibrium between consumer protection and fostering innovation, particularly with credit scoring and automated investment guidance. These issues underscore the necessity for future FinTech workers to possess not only technological proficiency but also critical thinking skills regarding regulatory ethics, adaptive compliance strategies, and the societal and economic implications of unregulated AI utilization.

PRACTICAL APPLICATIONS IN LEARNING ENVIRONMENTS

Innovative techniques in artificial intelligence are significantly transforming the FinTech landscape. Deep learning models, particularly transformer-based architectures, are increasingly favoured for forecasting financial trends, assessing credit risk, and asset management due to their capability to process complex, high-dimensional data (Reis et al., 2025). Reinforcement learning (RL) methodologies, such as Deep Q-Networks and Proximal Policy Optimisation, are increasingly employed in dynamic portfolio optimisation. These methodologies offer adaptive solutions that outperform conventional models during market instability (Garud, 2024). Individuals are concerned about trust and accountability due to the complexity of these notions. In response, explainable AI (XAI) solutions are gaining prominence due to their aim of enhancing transparency in financial decision-making. (Yeo et al., 2025) organised a detail investigation on XAI approaches tailored for the financial sector, emphasising their importance in maintaining ethics. These modifications indicate that FinTech education must also evolve. Students must acquire the skills for understanding ethical and legal dimensions of AI-driven finance. So, AI makes life easier for inquiries on different financial services for providing guidance on customer service, academic queries, financial decision making and financial forecasting (Jamro et al., 2024).

Customer service

AI in FinTech has found in customer service and personalization. This is possible using chatbots and customer driven support system. This helped the FinTech organization to enhance their operational efficiency. Furthermore, AI has further contribution to detect fraud and ensure security in FinTech. By detecting patterns that suggest fraudulent activity, advanced algorithms to protect transactions (Josyula, 2023). Financial inclusion is enhancing the use of formal financial services for disadvantaged communities. These communities predominantly consist of low-income individuals, vulnerable groups, those with limited credit history. Moreover, AI can understand the psychological trend of the customer while a customer seeks for financial advice. For this reason, most of the organization uses AI now a days to chat with their potential customer. Once the AI understand the psychological trend of the customer, it starts giving accurate suggestions. So, the contribution of AI into customer service department has brought a significant change with improved performance.

Students finance planning

FinTech solutions for student finance planning encompass financial management tools that help to manage expenses. With the rising costs of higher education becoming a significant concern for students everywhere, effective financial planning is more critical than ever. Navigating through the myriads of available financial solutions can be daunting, but AI and FinTech innovations promise to simplify the process, making education finance planning more accessible and efficient for students (Miller, 2024). AI is set to revolutionize education finance planning, offering a high level of personalization to learners around the globe. Digital lending systems offer students the convenience of applying for loans with minimal documentation. Additionally, FinTech companies are exploring personalized financing solutions for students, reviewing financial data from various sources to eliminate traditional loan approval hurdles. The integration of AI and FinTech empowers students to make more informed and smarter financial decisions (Miller, 2024). Students can now utilize AI for more straightforward credit risk assessment, expense tracking, budgeting, and financial analysis. This methods equip students to understand better lectures (Thimmanna et al., 2023).

Financial decision making, prediction and market trend analysis

AI can provide in-depth sentiment analysis on news, psychological biases, and social media to gauge how the market operates. AI can assist in financial analysis and planning by offering valuable insights into market dynamics, potential risks, and investor sentiment. Accurate financial planning leads to better strategies that safeguard against market volatility.

Financial institutions can use AI to anticipate market volatility and consumer behaviour, allowing them to build proactive strategies (Zhou and Wang, 2022). This prediction capacity is critical for being competitive in the ever-changing financial market. AI in FinTech is a rapidly evolving field that requires constant research to fully realize its promise with various features. Now a days, most of the financial predictions are conducted with the support from AI. The incorporation of AI and finance enhances the opportunity for better and accurate predictions that ultimately provides more accurate results than before. AI is increasingly driving financial innovation, particularly in areas of corporate finance to understand the risk and return. Also, recurrent neural networks, particularly LSTMs, outperform traditional intelligence like random prediction (Chaudhary, 2025). Similarly, Wang, (2025) find that ensemble models, that includes decision trees, neural networks and excel at forecasting equity return probabilities and generating steady investment returns.

CHALLENGES IN IMPLEMENTING AI IN FINTECH EDUCATION

Integrating AI into FinTech for financial services necessitates the collection and analysis of substantial personal information, which has prompted significant privacy concerns among experts. Data privacy and securing authorization from the individuals whose data is being used are critical ethical concerns. Also, there are some ethical problems to consider. For example, AI deals with provided data. If the data is biased, so will the results. This is unethical behaviours of FinTech (Lozi et al., 2022). Additionally, individuals' awareness and consent to data usage is need to be considered, while using alternative data. Prior researchers also found privacy issues of suing FinTech based AI (Gülen, 2023). Main issues raise concerns for data protection and data security of the users so that it cannot be shared with others. For example, in Chinese classroom data privacy raises ethical issue, while using AI. According to Tigges et al., (2024) there is a protection line between using AI and privacy (Table 2) of using FinTech. The following Table 2, shows various privacy concerns and various strategies to mitigate those concerns:

Table 2. Different privacy concerns (Tigges et al., 2024)

Concern	Description	Mitigation strategy	Impact assessment
Data privacy	The potential exposure of vulnerable information	Secure space solutions, and adherence to GDPR regulations	Decreased likelihood of data breaches
Consent	Unauthorized Utilization of Personal Information	Establish transparent protocols for obtaining user consent and provide clear opt-out options	Adherence to Regulatory Standards
Transparency	Challenges in Comprehending AI Policy development	Acceptance of reasonable AI framework	Trustworthiness
Data accuracy	Inaccurate and Deceptive data	Quality development by removing biased data	Improved flexibility
Bias and discrimination	Risk of biasness	Biased auditing	Additional reasonable counting

In Table 2, we can find the importance of various privacy concerns about AI such as data privacy, consent of the users, transparency, accuracy and avoidance of discrimination. Furthermore, we also understood that taking proper mitigation strategy to avoid security or privacy concern is more important rather than only understanding the concerns. According to the 2024 guidelines from NIST, integrating AI into FinTech involves several risks. These include concerns related to privacy, security, interaction between AI and human, maintaining integrity, addressing issues of toxicity, bias, and homogenization. Additionally, there are challenges in value chain and component integration that need to be considered. At present, the performance of AI and FinTech is unclear in terms of user's perspective.

To overcome various challenges or AI's effect on FinTech, strong regulations need to be developed that can hinder unexpected interference in financial activities. The regulators who develop rules and regulations for technology based financial services, need to more careful. Until regulatory frameworks are established, individuals have free rein. Implementing regulatory sandboxes could be a viable solution, enabling controlled and regulated testing environments. These concerns are especially notable given the considerable influence these technologies can have on individuals' financial well-being, as well as the functionality and stability of financial markets. However, AI can lead to major losses, if the system is not authentic (N. Wang & Wang, 2022). The performance of risk management techniques is directly influenced by the quality and biases of the data fed into AI systems (Adepetun et al., 2022). Addressing these challenges beyond mere technicalities; it encompasses issues of equity, trust, and institutional accountability. Having examined the readiness and regulation of AI-powered FinTech education across several global locations, we will now analyse their responses to the demand for it.

GLOBAL PERSPECTIVE ON AI IN FINTECH EDUCATION

Countries worldwide are employing various strategies to integrate AI into FinTech education as the global educational landscape evolves rapidly. The pace and concentration of AI adoption vary based on economic, cultural, and technological conditions. National platforms supported by policy and localized pilot initiatives exist. According to Techflow, (2022) the US education system prepares their students for expanded and dispersed workforce to tackle various technology-based challenges.

United States and China: Personalized Learning and Innovation in FinTech Use

In the United States, it is expected that by 2034 the market size would be US$112.30 billion with 36.02% of growth. Moreover, North America is found to have the largest market worldwide (Zoting, 2024). Therefore, higher education service provides need to realize the changing trend of education into technology-based education to prepare their graduates for the future. So, from now they must develop interdisciplinary curriculum that will incorporate the knowledge of technology among various disciplines. The use of intelligent teaching systems helps to improve the learning experiences. As a result, impressive improvements are shown among students. They can solve problems more efficiently through adaptive learning platforms such as Virtual reality (VR) and augmented reality (AR). Also, in China, the education system follows advance testing with the integration of AI and FinTech. This helps Chinese education system to develop their learning outcomes. Such as Squirrel AI helps students to be more financially literate and develop skills for AI based digital economy.

Future Directions: Generative AI, Reg Tech, and Embedded Learning Models

The emergence of generative AI represents a significant technological transformation currently confronting the FinTech sector. As these tools transform financial services and risk analysis, their inclusion in educational institutions becomes essential and imperative. Generative adversarial networks (GANs), is rapidly transforming the financial services sector. These models enable enhancements in algorithmic trading, detection of fraud, and provision of highly tailored financial services. Gurram, (2025) discusses how generative AI architectures, such as GANs and Transformer models, enhance the precision of risk management, consumer profiling, and regulatory compliance. He also raises new issues regarding bias mitigation and data protection. Mo & Ouyang, (2025) discuss the transformative impact of GenAI on financial economics, particularly its influence on company decision-making, asset pricing, and family finance. Recent research Mohammed & Aysan, (2024) indicates that AI-driven RegTech solutions facilitate regulatory reporting, money laundering activities, and customer identification. Incorporating RegTech into FinTech education enables students to explore the interrelations of financial regulation, ethics, and AI automation. This prepares them to create systems that are both innovative and ethically sound. These alterations indicate that FinTech education must evolve accordingly. Courses should incorporate GenAI technology and instruct students on ethics and risks of using AI based finance.

CONCLUSION

The integration of FinTech with higher education is rapidly transforming how future generations utilize technology, make critical decisions, and engage with financial systems. FinTech, utilizing AI, possesses the capacity to foster financially literate cultures, enhance the resilience of national economies, and prepare students to navigate an increasingly complex world.

Effective AI-driven FinTech education necessitates a collaborative synergy between educators and developers. In this novel paradigm, educators assume the role of learning architects. They employ AI to develop dynamic, tailored learning experiences while remaining significant mentors and advisors. According to Patterson, (2023) 71% educators and 65% of students recognize the significance of AI in enhancing performance in academic and professional settings. This illustrates the significance of preparing for this transition. To capitalize on this potential, schools must invest in AI infrastructure and provide training for educators. Individuals are actively developing innovative methods to implement adaptive learning platforms and generative AI in educational settings, hence transforming the resources utilized by educators. The shift towards personalization is particularly crucial in financial education: AI-driven solutions assist students in planning, budgeting, and making informed financial choices based on data. They facilitate the resolution of substantial finance obstacles via FinTech innovation. However, this transformation necessitates a renewed emphasis on financial education. To engage effectively in FinTech, one must possess the ability to interpret AI-enhanced financial data. Financial education is crucial; nonetheless, it is frequently deprioritized due to institutional inertia, cultural stigmas, or ambiguous rules. To address these issues, educational institutions, governmental bodies, and civil society must collaborate to include financial literacy as a fundamental component of economic equity and individual empowerment.

The future of FinTech education relies not on selecting between technology and educators, but on using their respective capabilities collaboratively. AI enables data analysis and customization, whereas human educators facilitate judgment, comprehension, and empathy towards others. They may collaborate to create learning environments that are more inclusive, beneficial, and future-ready. As this domain evolves, forthcoming study ought to enhance interdisciplinary links and explore innovative, inclusive methodologies to advance AI-integrated FinTech education.

REFERENCES

Abilawa, A., Rahmawati, A., & Surwanti, A. (2023). Enhancing insight into FinTech adoption through VOSViewer: A bibliometric exploration. *Multidisciplinary Reviews*, *7*(1), 2024006. DOI: 10.31893/multirev.2024006

Abulibdeh, A., Baya Chatti, C., Alkhereibi, A., & El Menshawy, S. (2025). A Scoping Review of the Strategic Integration of Artificial Intelligence in Higher Education: Transforming University Excellence Themes and Strategic Planning in the Digital Era. *European Journal of Education*, *60*(1), e12908. Advance online publication. DOI: 10.1111/ejed.12908

Abulibdeh, A., Zaidan, E., & Abulibdeh, R. (2024). Navigating the confluence of artificial intelligence and education for sustainable development in the era of industry 4.0: Challenges, opportunities, and ethical dimensions. *Journal of Cleaner Production*, *437*, 140527. DOI: 10.1016/j.jclepro.2023.140527

Adam, C. (2024). Segmenting female students' perceptions about FinTech using Explainable AI. *Frontiers in Artificial Intelligence*, *7*, 1504963. Advance online publication. DOI: 10.3389/frai.2024.1504963 PMID: 39726890

Adepetun, A., Odutola, O., & Dopemu, E. M. (2022). Exploring The Impact of Machine Learning on Financial Decision-Making in The Nigerian Banking Sector. *International Journal of Scientific and Management Research*, *05*(12), 212–221. DOI: 10.37502/IJSMR.2022.51215

Agrawal, N. (2025, January 10). *AI in Education: Offering a transformative Potential.* Hans India. https://www.thehansindia.com/hans/young-hans/impact-of-ai-on-personalised-learning-in-k-12-education-936345

Akartuna, E. A., Johnson, S. D., & Thornton, A. (2022). Preventing the money laundering and terrorist financing risks of emerging technologies: An international policy Delphi study. *Technological Forecasting and Social Change*, *179*, 121632. DOI: 10.1016/j.techfore.2022.121632

Amnas, M. B., Selvam, M., Raja, M., Santhoshkumar, S., & Parayitam, S. (2023). Understanding the Determinants of FinTech Adoption: Integrating UTAUT2 with Trust Theoretic Model. *Journal of Risk and Financial Management*, *16*(12), 505. DOI: 10.3390/jrfm16120505

Anan, L., Isaza, D. C., Figuieredo, F., & Flototto, M. (2023). *FinTech: A new paradigm of growth.* https://tinyurl.com/s6jmwhn6

Baity, A. H. H. (2023). The Artificial Intelligence Revolution in Digital Finance in Saudi Arabia: A Comprehensive Review and Proposed Framework. *Sustainability (Basel), 15*(18), 13725. DOI: 10.3390/su151813725

Barrett, H. (2018, January 23). Business schools have a problem with FinTech. *Financial Times.*

Berg, T., Fuster, A., & Puri, M. (2022). FinTech Lending. *Annual Review of Financial Economics, 14*(1), 187–207. DOI: 10.1146/annurev-financial-101521-112042

Cao, L. (2020). AI in Finance: A Review. SSRN *Electronic Journal.* DOI: 10.2139/ssrn.3647625

Cao, L., Yang, Q., & Yu, P. S. (2021). Data science and AI in FinTech: An overview. *International Journal of Data Science and Analytics, 12*(2), 81–99. DOI: 10.1007/s41060-021-00278-w

Cao, Y., & Zhai, J. (2022). A survey of AI in finance. *Journal of Chinese Economic and Business Studies, 20*(2), 125–137. DOI: 10.1080/14765284.2022.2077632

Charaia, V., & Lashkhi, M. (2023). Innovative FinTech technologies at educational institutions. *Georgian Journal of European Studies,* 119–124. https://gjes.tsu.ge/index.php/gjes/issue/view/6

Chaudhary, R. (2025). *Advanced Stock Market Prediction Using Long Short-Term Memory Networks: A Comprehensive Deep Learning Framework.* https://doi.org//arXiv.2505.05325DOI: 10.48550

Chen, W., & Yuan, X. (2021). Financial inclusion in China: An overview. *Frontiers of Business Research in China, 15*(1), 4. DOI: 10.1186/s11782-021-00098-6

Chikri, H., & Kassou, M. (2024). Financial revolution: Innovation powered by FinTech and Artificial Intelligence. *Journal of Theoretical and Applied Information Technology, 15*(9). www.jatit.org

Croitoru, I. M., Dragan (SPIRIDON), P.-P., Ignat, N. D., & Jumanca, R. (. (2025). Exploring Financial Literacy in Higher Education with the Help of FinTech: A Bibliometric Analysis of Linkages to Access, Behavior, and Well-Being Through Digital Innovation. *FinTech, 4*(1), 4. DOI: 10.3390/fintech4010004

Dahlin, E. (2025). Trust in AI. *AI & Society, 40*(8), 6089–6095. Advance online publication. DOI: 10.1007/s00146-025-02429-0 PMID: 40225305

Delello, J. A., Sung, W., Mokhtari, K., Hebert, J., Bronson, A., & De Giuseppe, T. (2025). AI in the Classroom: Insights from Educators on Usage, Challenges, and Mental Health. *Education Sciences, 15*(2), 113. DOI: 10.3390/educsci15020113

Earls, E. M. (2019). *Preparing Students for a Future in FinTech.* https://eric.ed.gov/?q=Preparing+Students+for+a+Future+in+FinTech

Garud, S. (2024). Reinforcement Learning for Dynamic Portfolio Optimization in FinTech. *Journal of Information Systems Engineering & Management, 2025*(45s), 10. https://www.jisem-journal.com/

Giudici, P. (2018a). Financial data science. *Statistics & Probability Letters, 136*, 160–164. DOI: 10.1016/j.spl.2018.02.024

Giudici, P. (2018b). FinTech Risk Management: A Research Challenge for Artificial Intelligence in Finance. *Frontiers in Artificial Intelligence, 1*, 1. Advance online publication. DOI: 10.3389/frai.2018.00001 PMID: 33733089

Gülen, K. (2023, February 3). *Introduction to artificial intelligence in education.* Data Economy. https://octaedro.com/libro/introduction-to-artificial-intelligence-in-education/

Gurram, A. (2025). Demystifying Generative AI for Financial Services. *European Journal of Computer Science and Information Technology, 13*(16), 73–86. DOI: 10.37745/ejcsit.2013/vol13n167386

Haoyang, D. L., & Towne, J. (2025, January 9). *AI in education: Real-world success stories.* World Economic Forum. https://tinyurl.com/2s4xkphn

Huong, X. V. (2024). The implications of artificial intelligence for educational systems: Challenges, opportunities, and transformative potential. *The American Journal of Social Science and Education Innovations, 06*(03), 101–111. DOI: 10.37547/tajssei/Volume06Issue03-17

Ikumapayi, J. O. (2025). The Convergence of FinTech Innovations, AI, And Risk Management: Transforming Traditional Banking, Accounting, And Financial Services. *International Research Journal of Modernization in Engineering Technology and Science, 7*(2). Advance online publication. DOI: 10.56726/IRJMETS67253

Ivanitskaya, L., Clark, D., Montgomery, G., & Primeau, R. (2002). Interdisciplinary learning: Process and outcomes. Innovative Higher Education. *Innovative Higher Education, 27*(2), 95–111. DOI: 10.1023/A:1021105309984

Jafri, J. A., Mohd Amin, S. I., Abdul Rahman, A., & Mohd Nor, S. (2024). A systematic literature review of the role of trust and security on FinTech adoption in banking. *Heliyon, 10*(1), e22980. DOI: 10.1016/j.heliyon.2023.e22980 PMID: 38163181

Jamro, M. Y., Jamro, F. A., & Print, O. (2024). *AI Matters: Chatbot Integration in Holistic STEM Education.* https://researchprofiles.herts.ac.uk/en/publications/ai-matters-chatbot-integration-in-holistic-stem-education

Josyula, H. P. (2023). *Fraud Detection in FinTech Leveraging Machine Learning and Behavioral Analytics*. DOI: 10.21203/rs.3.rs-3548343/v1

Kapron, Z. (2025, March 5). *AI In FinTech: Regulations, Opportunities, Ethical Imperatives*. Forbes. https://www.forbes.com/sites/zennonkapron/2025/03/05/ai-in-FinTech-regulations-opportunities-ethical-imperatives/

Kou, G., & Lu, Y. (2025). FinTech: A literature review of emerging financial technologies and applications. *Financial Innovation, 11*(1), 1. DOI: 10.1186/s40854-024-00668-6

KPMG. (2024). *Ten Key Regulatory Challenges of 2025*. https://kpmg.com/us/en/articles/2024/ten-key-regulatory-challenges-of-2025.html

Kwangmuang, P., Somabut, A., Duangngern, P., Changpetch, S., Dhithjaroen, C., Techapornpong, O., Sarakan, P., Chaijaroen, S., & Samat, C. (2025a). Designing an AI-enhanced blockchain and FinTech curriculum for youth: A case study of educational and industrial collaboration. *Education and Information Technologies, 30*(10), 13961–13997. Advance online publication. DOI: 10.1007/s10639-025-13384-0

Kwangmuang, P., Somabut, A., Duangngern, P., Changpetch, S., Dhithjaroen, C., Techapornpong, O., Sarakan, P., Chaijaroen, S., & Samat, C. (2025b). Designing an AI-enhanced blockchain and FinTech curriculum for youth: A case study of educational and industrial collaboration. *Education and Information Technologies, 30*(10), 13961–13997. Advance online publication. DOI: 10.1007/s10639-025-13384-0

Leal, A. A. (2024). *Algorithms, Creditworthiness, and Lending Decisions*, 321–353. DOI: 10.1007/978-3-031-47946-5_17

Lee, D. K. C., Lim, J., Phoon, K. F., & Wang, Y. (2022). *Applications and Trends in FinTech I* (Vol. 04). WORLD SCIENTIFIC., DOI: 10.1142/12578

Levantesi, S., & Zacchia, G. (2021). Machine Learning and Financial Literacy: An Exploration of Factors Influencing Financial Knowledge in Italy. *Journal of Risk and Financial Management, 14*(3), 120. DOI: 10.3390/jrfm14030120

Liu, C., Chen, Y., & Mo, F. (2023). Transforming organic chemistry research paradigms: Moving from manual efforts to the intersection of automation and artificial intelligence. *National Science Open, 20230037*, 20230037. Advance online publication. DOI: 10.1360/nso/20230037

Liu, X., Wang, C., Zhao, S., Ding, J., & Jia, Y. (2024). Role of FinTech adoption in the impact of sustainable policy intervention on enterprise transformation in resource-based cities: Evidence from China. *Resources Policy*, *88*, 104443. DOI: 10.1016/j.resourpol.2023.104443

Lozi, A. E., Alfityani, A., & Alsmadi, A. A., Al_Hazimeh, A. M., & Al-Gasawneh, J. A. (. (2022). The role of big data in financial sector: A review paper. *International Journal of Data and Network Science*, *6*(4), 1319–1330. DOI: 10.5267/j.ijdns.2022.6.003

Lusardi, A., & Messy, F.-A. (2023). The importance of financial literacy and its impact on financial wellbeing. *Journal of Financial Literacy and Wellbeing*, *1*(1), 1–11. DOI: 10.1017/flw.2023.8

Mahalingam, T. (2024). Bridging the gap between academia and industry: A case study of collaborative curriculum development. *International Journal of Business Performance Management*, *25*(4), 589–603. DOI: 10.1504/IJBPM.2024.139482

Miller, D. (2024, October 24). *AI and FinTech: Revolutionizing Education Finance*. Future Skills. https://futureskillsacademy.com/blog/ai-and-FinTech-in-education-finance-planning/?form=MG0AV3

Milner, A. E., Thomas, M., Kobbe, E., Fowler, B., Cardon, P., & Marshall, B. (2023). FinTech curricula: A survey of is, accounting, and finance department chairs. *Issues in Information Systems*. Advance online publication. DOI: 10.48009/2_iis_2023_119

Mo, H., & Ouyang, S. (2025). *(Generative) AI in Financial Economics* *. https://papers.ssrn.com/sol3/papers.cfm?abstract_id=5287110

Mohammed, M. M., & Aysan, A. F. (2024). *Ascent of Regtech: A Bibliometric Analysis of Regulatory Technology*. Eurasian Studies in Business and Economics., DOI: 10.1007/978-3-031-55813-9_9

Mousa, A. (2022). Detecting Financial Fraud Using Data Mining Techniques: A Decade Review from 2004 to 2015. *Journal of Data Science : JDS*, *14*(3), 553–570. DOI: 10.6339/JDS.201607_14(3).0010

Nalluri, V., & Chen, L.-S. (2024). Modelling the FinTech adoption barriers in the context of emerging economies—An integrated Fuzzy hybrid approach. *Technological Forecasting and Social Change*, *199*, 123049. DOI: 10.1016/j.techfore.2023.123049

Ojiaku, O. C., Ezenwafor, E. C., & Osarenkhoe, A. (2024). Integrating TTF and UTAUT models to illuminate factors that influence consumers' intentions to adopt financial technologies in an emerging country context. *International Journal of Technology Marketing*, *18*(1), 113–135. DOI: 10.1504/IJTMKT.2024.135674

Patel, M. (2024, September 24). *AI in FinTech: How Artificial Intelligence Will Change the Financial Industry*. Linearloop. https://www.linearloop.io/blog/ai-in-FinTech-how-artificial-intelligence-will-change-financial-industry?form=MG0AV3

Patterson, C. (2023, March 1). *ChatGPT Used by Teachers More Than Students*. Walton Family Foundation. https://www.waltonfamilyfoundation.org/chatgpt-used-by-teachers-more-than-students-new-survey-from-walton-family-foundation-finds?utm_source=chatgpt.com

Paudel, R. (2024). The Impact of Automation and Artificial Intelligence (AI) on Leadership and the Workforce. *Indonesian Journal of Banking and Financial Technology*, *2*(2), 109–124. DOI: 10.55927/fintech.v2i2.8904

Placide, E. (2024). *The Integration of Artificial Intelligence in Education*. University College of the Cayman Islands.

Plus, b. (2025, April 25). *AI education for FinTech in 2025: A comprehensive guide*. Byteplus. https://www.byteplus.com/en/topic/394296?title=ai-education-for-FinTech-in-2025-a-comprehensive-guide

Radanliev, P. (2025). AI Ethics: Integrating Transparency, Fairness, and Privacy in AI Development. *Applied Artificial Intelligence*, *39*(1), 2463722. Advance online publication. DOI: 10.1080/08839514.2025.2463722

Rahman, B., Ahmed, O., & Shakil, S. (2021). FinTech in Bangladesh: Ecosystem, Opportunities and Challenges. *International Journal of Business and Technopreneurship*, *l*(11). https://www.researchgate.net/publication/350849277

Rajpal, S., & Manglani, A. (2023)... *The Impact of FinTech on Accounting Education.*, *7*(5). Advance online publication. DOI: 10.55041/IJSREM22599

Reis, P., Serra, A. P., & Gama, J. (2025). The Role of Deep Learning in Financial Asset Management: A Systematic Review. *Cornell University*. https://arxiv.org/abs/2503.01591

Saha, B., Ahsan, A., Hasliza Muhd Yusuf, D., Aminul Islam, M., Huda, N., & Suryani, I. (2025). Exploring the Drivers of FinTech Adoption in SMEs: A Study from Bangladesh. *International Journal of Business and Technology Management*, *7*(1), 59–71. https://tinyurl.com/peh4bdx9

Shaikh, A. A., Glavee-Geo, R., Karjaluoto, H., & Hinson, R. E. (2023). Mobile money as a driver of digital financial inclusion. *Technological Forecasting and Social Change*, *186*, 122158. DOI: 10.1016/j.techfore.2022.122158

Siddiqui, Z., & Rivera, C. A. (2023). Embedding FinTech-specific content in higher education. *Risk Governance and Control: Financial Markets and Institutions, 13*(4), 18–29. DOI: 10.22495/rgcv13i4p2

Snyder, J. (2025, January 19). *Beyond The Illusion - The Real Threat Of AI: WEF Global Risks Report 2025*. Forbes. https://www.forbes.com/sites/jasonsnyder/2025/01/19/beyond-the-illusionthe-real-threat-of-ai-wef-global-risks-report-2025/

Tahiru, F. (2021). AI in education: A systematic literature review. In *Journal of Cases on Information Technology,* 23 (1),1–20. IGI Global. DOI: 10.4018/JCIT.2021010101

Techflow. (2022, January 11). *AI in Education: Global Success Stories Unveiled.* https://teachflow.ai/ai-in-education-global-success-stories-unveiled/?form=MG0AV3

Thakor, A. V. (2020). FinTech and banking: What do we know? *Journal of Financial Intermediation, 41*, 100833. DOI: 10.1016/j.jfi.2019.100833

Thimmanna, Sharma, A. V. N. S., Naik, M. S., Radhakrishnan, S., & Sharma, A. (2023). Personalized Learning Paths: Adapting Education with AI-Driven Curriculum. *European Economic Letters*. DOI: 10.52783/eel.v14i1.993

Thottoli, M. M., Islam, M., Ahsan, A., Yusof, M. F., Hassan, M. S., & Chowdhury, R. S. (2024). Exploring mediating and moderating factors of FinTech adoption for innovations in SMEs. *Cogent Economics & Finance, 12*(1), 2387443. Advance online publication. DOI: 10.1080/23322039.2024.2387443

Tigges, M., Mestwerdt, S., Tschirner, S., & Mauer, R. (2024). Who gets the money? A qualitative analysis of FinTech lending and credit scoring through the adoption of AI and alternative data. *Technological Forecasting and Social Change, 205*, 123491. DOI: 10.1016/j.techfore.2024.123491

Vishwanath, M. (2023). The intelligent solution: automation, the skills shortage and cyber-security. *International Conference on Artificial Intelligence*. https://doi.org/DOI: 10.31219/osf.io/8t9sa

Wang, N., & Wang, K. (2022). Internet Financial Risk Management in the Context of Big Data and Artificial Intelligence. *Mathematical Problems in Engineering, 2022*, 1–6. DOI: 10.1155/2022/6219489

Wang, Z. (2025). A time-series stock price prediction and asset portfolio optimization model based on long- and short-term memory networks. *Journal of Combinatorial Mathematics and Combinatorial Computing, 124*, 243–258. DOI: 10.61091/jcmcc124-17

Weber, P., Carl, K. V., & Hinz, O. (2024). Applications of Explainable Artificial Intelligence in Finance—A systematic review of Finance, Information Systems, and Computer Science literature. *Management Review Quarterly*, *74*(2), 867–907. DOI: 10.1007/s11301-023-00320-0

Yadav, H., Kar, A. K., & Kashiramka, S. (2022). *Artificial Intelligence Adoption for FinTech Industries - An Exploratory Study About the Disruptions.* Antecedents and Consequences., DOI: 10.1007/978-3-031-15342-6_1

Yandong, Q. (2024). *A case study of the technology acceptance model of FinTech companies using AI in FinTech innovations.* Siam University. https://tinyurl.com/nh5ehzp9

Yeo, W. J., Van Der Heever, W., Mao, R., Cambria, E., Satapathy, R., & Mengaldo, G. (2025). A comprehensive review on financial explainable AI. *Artificial Intelligence Review*, *58*(6), 189. DOI: 10.1007/s10462-024-11077-7

Zhang, Y., & Cui, X. (2024). FinTech, business regulations, and urbanization: Shaping the landscape of natural resource rent in G10 countries. *Resources Policy*, *89*, 104551. DOI: 10.1016/j.resourpol.2023.104551

Zoting, S. (2024, August 9). *AI in Education Market.* Precedence Research. https://www.precedenceresearch.com/ai-in-education-market

ADDITIONAL READING

Boukherouaa, E. B., Shabsigh, M. G., AlAjmi, K., Deodoro, J., Farias, A., Iskender, E. S., Mirestean, M. A., & Ravikumar, R. (2021). Powering the digital economy: Opportunities and risks of artificial intelligence in finance. IMF. https://www.elibrary.imf.org/view/journals/087/2021/024/087.2021.issue-024-en.xml

Doshi, R., Dadhich, M., Poddar, S., & Hiran, K. (2024). *Integrating generative AI in education to achieve sustainable development goals.* IGI Global., DOI: 10.4018/979-8-3693-2440-0

Gopal, S., & Pitts, J. (2024). *The FinTech Revolution.* Springer Nature Switzerland., DOI: 10.1007/978-3-031-74418-1

Gupta, A., Dwivedi, D. N., & Shah, J. (2023). *Artificial Intelligence Applications in Banking and Financial Services.* Springer Nature Singapore., DOI: 10.1007/978-981-99-2571-1

Hamdan, R. K., Hamdan, A., Alareeni, B., & Khoury, R. E. (2024). Information and communication technology in technical and vocational education and training for sustainable and equal opportunity: Business governance and digitalization of business education. Springer Nature. https://link.springer.com/book/10.1007/978-981-99-6909-8

Lamine, W., Jack, S., Fayolle, A., & Audretsch, D. (2024). De Gruyter handbook of digital entrepreneurship. Walter de Gruyter GmbH & Co KG. https://www.degruyterbrill.com/document/doi/10.1515/9783110764222/html

Narayan, M. Pooja Shukla, Dileep Kumar, M., Mani, N. (2025). Generative AI in FinTech: Revolutionizing Fraud Detection, Personalized Advising, and Predictive Analytics. In: Dutta, S., Rocha, Á., Agarwal, A.K., Tiwari, R.G., Bhattacharya, A. (eds) Generative AI in FinTech: Revolutionizing Finance Through Intelligent Algorithms. Information Systems Engineering and Management, 26. Springer, Cham. DOI: 10.1007/978-3-031-76957-3_7

KEY TERMS AND DEFINITIONS

AI Driven Decision Making: It highlights the extensive use of AI to analyse different data sets, identify the trends, and optimize financial strategy as per trend analysis. Furthermore, it accelerates the capacity of secure investment decision efficiently and effectively.

AI in Finance: It includes predictive analytics, and automated financial systems. Such as financial fraud, risk valuation, and client services. The advantage of using AI in Finance is to accelerate the efficiency and effectiveness of various financial services such as banking, investment, and financial planning.

AI Powered Financial Literacy: AI powered financial literacy is the implementation of AI in finance to improve the finance education. It offers various services such as individualized insights and automated financial planning. It helps to make better financial decision by enabling the capacity to forecast future expenditures.

Digital Transformation: Digital transformation in FinTech Education is the incorporation of updated technology like AI, blockchain and cloud computing among financial education. The transformation of traditional to digitalization into technology-based education improves the learning experiences, increase the access to financial knowledge and prepares students to fit with changed financial environment.

Financial Inclusion: Financial inclusion indicates the process ensuring barrier free participation in the formal financial system that allows people to engage more informed financial decisions by managing risks. The understanding of finance that helps to incorporate more financial activities that ultimately results to the increase of financial practices.

Financial Literacy: It is the determinator of thoughtful basic finance which mainly focuses on financial planning and management. It develops the ability of understand about various financial products and services such as evaluating critical financial products and services.

FinTech Education: FinTech education indicates financial training with academic and professional mindset that creates the opportunity to understand technology based financial activities such as block chain, artificial intelligence, and data analysis. This education has significant contribution among students and industry professionals. Furthermore, it erases the gap between traditional financial services and modern technology-based finance.

Interdisciplinary Curriculum Development: Interdisciplinary curriculum development is the scope of creating educational programs that combines various disciplines such as finance, technology and business. The concept of interdisciplinary curriculum development enhances the holistic understanding of FinTech, that creates the opportunity of diversified abilities to handle the challenges of technology based financial systems.

Chapter 10

Including AI in K-12 Education:
Key Concepts, Paradigms, and Optimal Approaches

Tahsin Raysha Mallik
http://orcid.org/0009-0002-3696-3928
BRAC University, Bangladesh

Zeun Tafsir Nova
BRAC University, Bangladesh

Humayra Anjum
BRAC University, Bangladesh

Maisha Binte Saroar
BRAC University, Bangladesh

ABSTRACT

This chapter focuses on the underlying concept paradigms, and best practices for integrating AI into elementary, middle, and high school curricula. This chapter aims to educate teachers, lawmakers, and stakeholders how AI might improve training, administrative efficiency, and critical thinking. As AI technologies grow, K-12 AI education must prepare kids for employment changes. AI advances are transforming science, economics, law, farming, food security, and health in industry and government. K-12 education will soon transform in the "Age of AI". AI will change employment, training, and procedures. AI will work with humans in several fields. Teaching artificial intelligence (AI) in grades K-12 is a significant issue in the world of teaching research, especially because schools and instructors are having

DOI: 10.4018/979-8-3693-6346-1.ch010

a hard time incorporating AI into their lessons. Research into the testing, training, development, and implementation of AI learning systems by humans is very lacking. This is especially true for elementary and secondary schools.

1. INTRODUCTION

Artificial Intelligence (AI) has turned into an intriguing issue of conversation and has fundamentally influenced various callings and organizations. In a brief period, man-made brainpower (artificial intelligence) has shown to be a unique advantage in training. The improvement of simulated intelligence has extraordinarily helped training, which is a crucial part of both society's development and self-awareness. How educators educate, how understudies learn, and how foundations work are changing because of computer-based intelligence's coordination into schooling systems. No big surprise, computer-based intelligence is changing training, shutting holes, and advancing a more comprehensive and useful learning climate by customizing opportunities for growth, robotizing regulatory errands, and giving constant criticism. Given the significance of AI, it is necessary to consider its effects on education. Given an examination of accessible writing, our goal is to explore the potential impacts of computer-based intelligence on schooling.

With the arrival of ChatGPT in November 2022, the utilization of artificial intelligence in the public eye went through an ocean change. The exceptional writing and comprehension abilities of ChatGPT surprised many, attracting a diverse audience and unprecedented attention (Mintz et al., 2023). It was the initial time the potential and quick nature of computer-based intelligence was completely valued by a group of people outside the AI field. It could be argued that the education sector benefited the most from ChatGPT. There is a great deal of debate around ChatGPT's capacity to give insightful coaching frameworks and, on the opposite side, be utilized as a device for scholarly untrustworthiness. Specialists at auxiliary and postsecondary instructive establishments have communicated worry about potential understudy abuse of ChatGPT and have requested its guidelines. The majority of Bangladeshi educational establishments do not officially prohibit the use of ChatGPT on student devices and networks. However, it does not appear to be able to prevent students from using AI. The best course of action is, in the end, incorporating AI into the educational system and making use of its potential to enhance student learning outcomes. In this review, we look at the likely benefits and dangers of man-made intelligence to supplement the conversation on the most effective way to utilize it.

2. PRIMARY AIM OF THE CHAPTER

This chapter primarily aims to demonstrate the fundamental ideas, paradigms, and best practices for incorporating integrated AI into schooling at all levels. l curricula. The ambition of this chapter is to educate teachers, lawmakers, and stakeholders on how AI may enhance training, increase administrative efficiency, and stimulate critical thinking. K-12 AI education must educate students for a changing job market as AI technologies evolve. Developing, implementing, and increasing AI literacy curricula is tough. This chapter defines AI literacy using a component-based approach, efforts for the advancement of artificial intelligence education at all grade levels, and analyzes AI in the classroom from kindergarten to twelfth grade, how it is implemented into language arts, STEM, and social science curricula, and how administrators and teachers can benefit from AI professional development.

AI innovations are fast-changing science, transportation, security, business, law, agriculture,and health in industry and government. AI will impact practically every aspect of society. Furthermore, these effects are developing and changing rapidly. The "Age of AI" will change K-12 education soon. Students today will join an employment economy transformed by AI. AI is going to transform jobs, training, and processes. AI and humans will share tasks in diverse jobs. The industry is going to emphasize "AI teaming" skills that allow people and AI to solve issues jointly, each using their strengths. Human-AI collaboration will reward employees who understand AI's potential, "AI job sharing," and what AI can do best.

Knowledge of artificial intelligence is using AI technologies, methodologies, and frameworks ethically and effectively in different sociocultural contexts. AI can help instructors gather crucial ideas, analyze creative paradigms, and apply optimal methods to create interactive, customized, and effective learning experiences for students. This chapter aims to help instructors integrate AI and prepare students for an AI-driven society. All students should take I education, and advanced AI courses should be offered for AI engineers and researchers. Not all students need to understand difficult AI concepts or mathematics for AI literacy. Students should understand AI capabilities, restrictions, applications, and ethics.

3. BACKGROUND

The application of artificial intelligence has raised a lot and shortly AI practitioners will be in higher demand. To tackle the public policy issues related to AI, all conscious citizens are recommended to grasp the basics of AI. Also, in the rapidly evolving and tech-oriented world, children are required to get enough knowledge to engage with AI. Moreover, children must be trained enough so that they can secure their future employability and maintain their career growth (Touretzky, 2017).

China, the UK, Thailand, and South Korea are making standardized protocols to integrate AI education at different levels by setting learning objectives. A guideline has been set for the teachers to teach AI from K-12 through the advancement of artificial intelligence and computer science teachers association which includes different topics such as machine learning, robotics, and AI. The association also suggested which grade students learn which topic (Kim et al., 2021). Moreover, the association has created an online learning material inventory for educators to discover AI content, videos, tutorial videos for software, and all other resources so that they can easily incorporate those materials into their lesson plans.

An organization named AI4K12 proposed a framework consisting of five major concepts. The framework includes natural interaction, representation, learning, perception, and social impact with proper examples, and definitions for each of the categories. For instance, perception refers to a process by which it will extract meaning from sensory inputs which include voice recognition, face recognition, scene, and number plate reading. Students who are in grades k to 2 can learn to identify the sensors placed with workstations, automated machines, and intelligent devices and they can also learn about the use of AI agents such as Siri or Alexa. Those learners who are in grades 3 to 5 should know how those sensors got inputted are translated to digital signals, they must also know how to create an application by using perception. Students who are in grades 6-8 must know the explanation of how the sensor barriers affect computer perception, and how all the algorithms are used in the perception system. Those who are in grades 9 to 12 must be able to describe the knowledge of how voice recognition is aligned with computer perception (Su & Zhong, 2022).

This outline conveys factors of different types of learning activities as well as helps learners to master relevant study tools for their better understanding of AI education.

4. LITERATURE REVIEW

Artificial Intelligence (AI)

The field of artificial intelligence (AI) has an extensive background and is rapidly expanding. This particularly focuses on intelligent agents that are man-made or machines that sense and adapt their environment and act to get their chances of success, (Shabbir & Anwer, 2018). AI started its lifespan as computers and computer-based technologies then climbed the ladder to intelligent education systems that are mainly web-based. It finally developed web-based chatbots and humanoid robots that could perform instructions independently or in collaboration with teachers by combining computer systems with other technologies, (Chen et al., 2020). According to Chen, integrated into robots, artificial intelligence (AI), computers, and related hardware allow the development of robots that enhance student learning, starting with the most important educational program—early childhood. Since attention is a vital component of learning, robots can draw and hold students' attention in the classroom. This in and of itself would be helpful to teachers, but having educational cobots in the classroom would also help them differentiate instruction so that students receive more specialized instruction, (Timms, 2016).

Teaching AI in the 21st century has grown in significance due to the widespread impact of AI-driven technologies beyond the IT sector on many areas of human existence and the recommendation of some scholars that children in grades K-12 study AI (e.g., Goel, 2017; Yang, 2019; Touretzky et al., 2019).

To help pupils become prepared for the future, it is essential to improve teachers' digital literacy. Consistent with previous research, teachers may enhance their AI education through professional development opportunities that incorporate thorough evaluations of performance, portfolio reviews, action research, and lessons (Darling-Hammond, 1999).

Wilson (2011) also performed research.

Learning Tools

Learning tools and their design should be accessible to all kinds of students. Distinctively, it should be Convenient for the specially-abled students. It is important to acknowledge and create multiple options for specially-abled students by knowing their strengths while designing learning materials. (Fleger et al., 2023).

Sanusi et al. (2021) evaluated a few gadgets for tutoring machine learning in k to 12. They even reviewed Software development tools and simulations which are free and easy to access for users with internet connections. Those who do not have stable internet connection are being missed out on using these sorts of resources (Williams, 2024). By considering age-appropriateness and learning capacity, course structure should be designed. Also, the AI curriculum needs to be upgraded while considering the learners who have disabilities. Technological integration might bring advantage to the blind students (Sanusi et al., 2021). There are lots of barriers that need to be addressed and solved by incorporating AI.

Ethical Concern

According to Akgun and Greenhow (2022), other ethical concerns with AI-enhanced classrooms go beyond issues of prejudice and privacy. We agree with this assessment. For instance, according to Hernandez-Orallo and Vold (2019, p. 509), AI may "enable, aid, enhance, or improve cognition" while acting as a cognitive extender. Still, this beneficial impact is diminished when the element is absent. Every researcher, even those who seek theory along posthuman lines, must embark on the essential ethical journey of being aware of and correcting the persistent injustices that are a result of colonialism's legacy and are woven into our institutions. According to Hakli (2018), AI-powered, superhuman-level thinking may achieve a more "humanized" experience.

Curricula Approaches

As said by Kelly (2009), a curriculum signifies the extent of the experiences of the student in the academic procedures, and which is aimed and led by instructors along with erudite within students in distinctive situations like as individuals, classrooms, groups, online, after-school. The research has proposed four main tactics for curriculum: product, praxis, process, and content, which is also mentioned by Kelly (2009); Grundy (1987); Glatthorn et al. (2018). These in particular are advantageous for analysis on curricula contrivance as well as for experts actualizing or amending curriculum.

Observing the curricula while practicing, turns out to be the primary goal, as well as mentoring is considered as unwavering execution and concerns on cohering of the apprehension in the learning procedures by bridging it to real-life approaches, as claimed by Glatthorn et al. (2018); Grundy (1987). As stated by Chiu (2021), directed by educators, learners will grasp with their peers to solve real-life problems by working out initiatives for gaining content erudition together with obtaining the outcomes. The cognition procedures and consequences are consistently examined.

Machine Learning

As stated by Naqvi, A., ML is imitative from logarithmic learning approaches along with uses of figures and algorithms to accomplish activities that are generally executed by human-beings. ML is hereabouts creating computers exploit or carry out without being inclined any step-by-step process as believed by Holmes, W., Bialik, M., Fadel, C. As described by Mohri, M., Rostamizadeh, A., Talwalkar, A., the functions of ML are the erudition model's disclosure to abundant measures of quality figures.

ML algorithms initially examine the figures to determine conceptions and to construct a model after which forecast subsequent time values throughout the models. That is to say, ML can be determined through three-pace procedures. As said by Holmes, W., Bialik, M., Fadel, C., Waller, M., Paul, W., in the first place, it evaluates and collects the facts, and after that, it erects a representation for various functions, and conclusively, it approaches the mechanisms and creates the coveted results efficaciously beyond human intervention. The extensively acknowledged AI applications including instructor or computerized face authentication approaches have been made achievable throughout the propositions of ML.

5. METHODOLOGY

The current status of artificial intelligence (AI) integration in K–12 education is thoroughly evaluated in this chapter. Considering the uniqueness of the subject in K–12 settings, secondary data analysis is the main method used in this study. The data sources will include journal articles, educational websites, and government reports.

A thorough research has been conducted using Google Scholar to sort the best research articles that have been published within the last five years. The keywords that have been used are, "AI in K-12 Education", "AI in K-12 Classrooms", "Current trends of AI in K-12 Education", "AI-driven teaching", and "Ethical considerations of AI in Education".

The websites of respectable academic institutions and groups that support AI integration in K-12 education have been researched for case studies and best practices.

Lastly, both national and international government reports, and policies regarding AI in education (e.g., OECD, UNESCO) have been studied to get insights about proposed policies and suggestions about AI in education.

6. DISCUSSION

Everything has two sides to its usage, the same as AI. AI integration in daily life changes everyone's life. As education plays the biggest role in building future generations, AI and its integration need to be placed carefully, especially in K-12 education.

6.1 Key Concepts

Using AI students can now learn topics like how the integration of algorithms with software makes machines work and present almost like human-generated results. Moreover, it knows how to answer difficult questions within a second with the help of one click.

- **Computer Vision (CV):** This AI concept enables computer interpretation and analysis of visual data. Intriguing learning exercises can be conducted to investigate applications such as object detection and picture recognition, (Sophokleous et al., 2021). This particular sector of artificial intelligence (AI) tutors' computers and systems to identify and interpret accurate information from digital images, videos, and other visual inputs. When it identifies errors or any other issues, it can then provide corrective actions or appropriate suggestions. This task is completed by the usage of neural networks and machine learning. Computer vision allows computers to see, observe, and comprehend, just as AI allows them to think. Except for human vision, computer vision replicates the mechanisms of human vision. One advantage of having human sight is that it has lifetimes of context to learn how to identify and differentiate things, calculate distances between them, detect motion, and recognize when an image is not accurate.

By assessing students' levels of involvement in both traditional and virtual classrooms, computer vision in education can help enhance learning results. Lectures are given in the contemporary educational system by considering the whole class. Nonetheless, every pupil possesses a distinct comprehension style and varying degrees of intelligence. As a result, some students may find a given lecture boring because they cannot comprehend the material or find the instructor's style unappealing. However, with a teacher-to-teacher-to-student ratio very low, these students can go unnoticed in a huge classroom. This may impact such pupils' grades. For teachers to take the necessary steps to increase their pupils' levels of interest in the school, computer vision can assist in identifying disengaged kids. Teachers can perform their duties more efficiently by using computer vision in the classroom, such as keeping an eye on students during exams.

- **Machine Learning (ML):** A small yet significant part of computer science and artificial intelligence called machine learning (ML) that utilizes data and algorithms so that AI can replicate human learning processes and progressively become more authentic. It is considered one of the most common and widely used concepts of AI. Where algorithms, devoid of explicit programming, learn from data to generate predictions or conclusions. Here students may come across programs like chatbots and recommendation systems, (Kuleto et al., 2021). Machine learning is used for personalized learning for each student.

The act of gathering, evaluating, and applying learner data to create profiles and examine student behavior is known as learning analytics. Using these profiles as a starting point, machine learning algorithms design unique educational plans for each student. Adaptive learning describes this procedure. Here, students can go at their own speed while they study. In the classroom, learning analytics can be a powerful tool for collecting data on students' attendance and test scores, as well as for tailoring comments to each student's individual needs. The use of chatbots and artificial intelligence (AI) to personalize the learning experience has been on the rise in the last five years (Applications of Machine Learning in Education, 2023). School administrators and classroom teachers can now modify "Snatch Bot" and like bots to meet the needs of their particular school. These bots can greatly benefit any school by tailoring information to each student's unique needs. They are in a position to guarantee that every student is actively participating in their education. In reality, some bots enable educators to create their very own assessments, including games, polls, quizzes, and even solutions to math and English problems. With the help of these bots, students can learn a wide range of topics, including nutrition, health, finance, and business. Teachers can use this data to adjust the tempo of their classes generally.

- **Natural Language Processing (NLP):** It is a principle in artificial intelligence that lets machines interpret and analyze human speech. Essential for the skill sets of the future, natural language processing (NLP) finds use in areas such as AI tutors, sentiment analysis, and machine translation (Yu, 2020). By combining statistical and machine learning models with computational linguistics, which focuses on modeling human language based on rules, NLP empowers computers and other digital devices to detect, comprehend, and produce text and speech. NLP is a subfield of AI and powers various devices and applications. It enables translation of text between languages, responds to spoken or typed commands, identifies and authenticates users based on voice, summarizes large amounts of text, determines the sentiment or intent of text or speech, and even generates text, graphics, or other content on demand.

Natural Language Processing is a well-known field in language learning worldwide. K-12 Education can benefit from NLP in several ways. It is successfully used in several languages as a productive means of enhancing the quality of educational systems. The majority of research studies indicate that English is the most widely recognized language, demonstrating its effectiveness in employing the natural language learning process in the educational process. NLP is a useful strategy for enhancing the educational system around the world as well. Although there are several ways to improve social and educational environments, natural language processing (NLP) is the most appropriate method since it produces NLP tools that advance education. The foundation of these tools is the use of numerous successful strategies to support higher education at the college and university levels. This necessitates creating regional language instructional materials and corpus resources. One application of NLP in the first role is the automated evaluation of student texts based on linguistic features like grammatical correctness or organizational structure. The second role, dialogue technologies are being utilized to economically and scalable provide the advantages of human one-on-one tutoring, especially in STEM fields. Examples of the third function include creating exam questions for teachers automatically, analyzing content from the web to tailor lessons to each student's interests, or (semi-) automating the creation of educational technology systems.

- **Virtual Mentoring:** Another AI tool that can be used in education. Through technology, virtual mentorship promotes professional development. Here mentors and mentees connect via email, chat, and video, this is not based on in-person interactions, (Klamma et al., 2020). It breaks through geographical constraints to provide flexibility and increase the available knowledge.

For students in grades K-12, there are several advantages to virtual mentoring programs. It eliminates geographical obstacles by pairing underprivileged students or those from rural areas with mentors who possess specialized expertise or technical abilities. All sorts of fascinating new opportunities present themselves to these children. Furthermore, by offering personalized feedback and virtual mentorship it surpasses traditional classroom teaching. Additionally, they provide support for particular academic requirements, such as learning efficient study techniques, establishing regular study habits, and finishing assignments. This strategy guarantees that students not only fully understand the topic but also develop self-assurance by utilizing a personalized teaching style. In addition, students are encouraged to think ahead and research other career options through virtual coaching. By sharing wisdom and insights gained from working in a variety of fields, mentors help young people make better decisions regarding their academic and professional futures. By starting early, they will have the chance to make well-informed decisions about what to study in school and other aspirations they may have for the future.

- **Voice Assistant:** There is a resemblance between this AI technology and virtual mentors. Simply put voice engagement and communication are the primary modes of interaction for Voice Assistant. Using cloud computing and artificial intelligence, voice assistants may converse with consumers in natural language (Terzopoulos & Satratzemi, 2019). Voice Assistant technology has also been included by a number of Edutech platforms to assist students in finding information and resources more quickly and effectively.

One of the most well-known and frequently utilized AI technologies across a variety of industries, including education, is the voice assistant. A few well-known voice assistants are Cortana from Microsoft, Siri from Apple, Google Assistant from Google, and others. With the Voice Assistant, students can look for resources, books, articles, and reference questions by only reading out loud or mentioning keywords. In addition, this particular tool will present the data that students select to look up based on the terms they enter. Like a personal assistant, a Voice Assistant may speak and explain the information you need in addition to providing it to you in the form of text and visuals. Voice assistants facilitate communication with a variety of educational resources without requiring interaction with the instructor. The learning platform can therefore be accessed at any time and from any location. In this manner, even in the absence of an instructor or tutor, the students can study on their own without fear of confusion because any information that is unclear can be provided solely by voice. Virtual mentors and voice assistants using artificial intelligence are comparable. Simply put, Voice Assistant uses the voice feature more as an intersection for engagement and conversation.

- **Smart Content:** Another artificial intelligence tool called "smart content" makes it easier and faster to distribute and locate programmable digital books and material content. Digital libraries in public, academic, and classroom settings are common places to find instances of this technology's implementation. AI can swiftly and methodically locate and classify the books we seek. Even book recommendations and other content pertinent to your search will be provided to us. A compilation of different learning resources, such as digital textbooks and adaptable user interfaces, is called smart content, for instance, Cram101 and Netext Learning.
- **Presentation Translator:** AI offers numerous chances for global knowledge exchange. With the aid of AI solutions, students can take a variety of classes and training courses. The greatest tutors' interactive learning resources are available on numerous platforms. Students with vision or hearing impairments, as well as multilingual students, can benefit from AI. For instance, an AI-Powered tool known for providing real time subtitle rendering is called

Presentation Translator. Students can listen or read in their mother tongues because of this speech recognition tool. This technology is comparable to Voice Assistant in that both rely on voice. Presentation Translator's usability specification is all it takes to explain or display the material from the original dialect into another language. So, there is no need for students to read. All they have to do is listen to various voice texts, articles, or digital books. And students can hear in their native tongue with AI Speech Recognition. It is easier and faster for them to read and comprehend books, periodicals, and articles written in any language.

Furthermore, while applying AI, some things need to be considered such as, how much ethical consideration is important while using artificial intelligence. (Holstein & Aleven, 2022).

6.2 *Case Studies on AI Implementation*

China's AI Education Pioneer

The first artificial intelligence textbook, backed by SenseTime, was included on the curriculum from kindergarten to high school in 2018 by the Ministry of Education to get a foundational understanding of deep learning, identification of images and texts, and voice recognition at 40 pilot schools. (Sensetime, 2018; Yu et al., 2021). The three most prevalent approaches to teaching artificial intelligence in K-12 classrooms were web classes, massive online open courses, and the flipped classroom model. Students were motivated to improve their AI expertise, abilities, attitudes, and behavioral intentions through the use of pedagogies grounded in constructivism, which included investigational and practical education (Kim et al., 2021; Oguz̆ Ünver & ArabacioGlu,̆ 2011).

China is racing to pursue AI education with a diverse range of emerging technologies, including biotechnology, drones, and artificial intelligence, thanks to its competitive edge in AI giants and massive data sets.

Comprehensive Curriculum Reform in Hong Kong

The Education Bureau updated its Technology Education curriculum guide for grades 1–6 in 2017. To build pupils to address societal requirements and technological advancement, the K-12 curriculum has been revised to incorporate technology education classes (Curriculum Development Council, 2017). These lessons aim to encourage computational thinking abilities in students. The Hong Kong Education

City, often known as EdCity, has also introduced the "Go AI Scheme" to further AI development.

The introduction of self-paced learning platforms in Hong Kong's educational system and improving the expertise of both instructors and students on artificial intelligence and 21st century abilities that are prepared for the future (EdCity, 2021).

Holistic Education in Japan

Starting in elementary school and continuing through high school, the Japanese government will implement a plan to help pupils become more data literate and proficient in information technology. What followed was a policy and study from the country's Department of Educational Affairs, Arts, athletics, Science, and Technology that highlighted the potential for students to use AI to create value for businesses. (Duan & Gong, 2019). Beginning in 2020, elementary schools in Japan were required by the national curriculum to include computer science classes. To facilitate the planning of the future, Japan's competitiveness depends on the K-12 kids who can comprehend and utilize AI-enhanced technologies (Kanemune et al., 2017).

in a world dominated by artificial intelligence. It also helps get the message out to children in grades K-12 about the importance of AI ethics. According to the five AI Big Ideas, schools should implement AI curricula that show students how AI works and provide them with opportunities to make things with AI (Eguchi et al., 2021).

Singapore: National AI Strategy

Aiming to enhance students' AI capabilities, the Singaporean government unveiled the "AI Singapore" initiative in 2018. To help students increase their AI knowledge and build the skills necessary to drive Singapore's AI initiatives, the project brought together academic institutes, AI companies, and startups to develop AI-powered educational tools. Presented with

Concurrent with the commencement of the AI research project were the "AI for Students" and "AI for Kids" initiatives.

This earlier trend seeks to provide a course of study for all students in secondary school through organized and unstructured learning opportunities (such as the Society Discussion Forum, Data Camp, and AI Makerspace). In a similar vein, AI for Kids is a program that teaches elementary school students about AI and how to utilize it responsibly in their daily lives (AI Singapore, 2018b).

UK Government's Active Investment in AI for Education

In 2021, the UK launched a 10-year National AI Strategy, and as a contribution the government committed financing for AI skills programs (e.g., developing AI Turing Fellowships and conversion MSc courses) and also funded research into AI in education via UK Research and Innovation (UKRI) grants. under this, education was highlighted in two respects: developing AI skills and leveraging AI to revolutionize education delivery (Etheredge, 2025). The government of UK or more specifically the Department for Education (DfE) completely pivoted it's focus on AI in school by granting £1 million to Education Services Australia (Etheredge, 2025). Which was considered their partnership with international AI experts. The reason behind this collaboration was to incorporate an AI product safety framework for education.

A UK based AI learning platform named Century Tech obtained multi-million-pound series which broaden the personalized lessons by integrating AI engine. Moreover, Kognity a platform which shows contents by integrating AI insights and Perlego a digital AI driven library upraised notable capital. In 2023, Century Tech's AI platform was accustomed in 1200 different schools over England (Etheredge, 2025). Their system provides flexible curriculum pathway for individual students as well as live data tracking for teachers.

In January 2025, the Education Secretary unveiled a "digital revolution" plan to invest in AI tools, minimizing teacher impose and boosting access. This proposal involves collaborating with tech companies like Google, Microsoft, and Adobe to improve the safety of AI tools in UK classrooms (Etheredge, 2025). This is an in-kind investment by business associated with the government. The UK prioritizes investment in AI for education to maintain its competitive edge and meet domestic issues, including teacher shortages.

Korea Promotes AI Literacy

To increase AI competitiveness by 2030, the Korean government launched the "National AI Strategy" in 2019 (Kim et al., 2021). In 2021, all students in high school were supposed to learn artificial intelligence, and by 2025, all kids in kindergarten, middle, and kindergarten would have had the same instruction. AI basics, usage, and ethics will be taught to elementary and middle school students. There has to be an emphasis on AI literacy in elementary AI education. The proposed AI curriculum aims to help elementary school children become more AI savvy by enhancing their knowledge, skills, and mindset. To start, understanding artificial intelligence entails being familiar with its many forms, issues, searches, reasoning, data, machine learning, and applications. Two other things about AI: the ability to system, computational thinking, and tool use. Thirdly, the attitude of AI includes the influence on society and the partnership. Also, Korean researchers from the Korea Foundation for Science and Creativity examined K-12 AI educational programs. Students with different levels of proficiency were given different learning subjects. The course covers a wide range of topics, including, but not limited to, programming languages (Python, Scratch, and App Inventor), rules and inference, machine learning, search techniques, and much more.

Finland, Brazil, Spain, and the US were the most common locations for AI research. National curricula in Singapore, Korea, China, and Japan have been updated in recent years to reflect the global trend in artificial intelligence education. Methods and strategies for artificial intelligence education can benefit from a review of Asian-Pacific studies. Past studies on topics like computational thinking and media literacy in K-12 computer science initiatives shows that AI is clearly making waves and contributing significantly to the field.

6.3 Considerable Paradigms

Influencing Creativity & Fostering Innovation: This paradigm falls under the theory; Paradigm of Behaviorism, which highlights the erection of thoroughly organized consequences of content leading to the learner's accomplishment (Skinner, 1965). AI has the potential to be a very effective tool for promoting innovation and creativity, (Brem et al., 2023). AI-powered resources can assist students in coming up with ideas, considering various options, and trying out novel ideas. According to Füller et al., (2022), this paradigm assists learners develop their analytical reasoning skills and innovative abilities so they can use AI to innovate, The AI methods in this Paradigm suggest the attributes of the learning mechanism (Skinner, 1965), which embodies prudently introducing subject understanding as well as necessitating unmistakable replies from students (Burton et al., 2004). The AI methods would not adjust their response to the students as distinct or as typical of a class of individuals. AI formed on numerical logical methods is generally used to portray erudition as a set of rules, ascertain individual patterns in learner's actions, or propose instinctive evaluation. Also, this paradigm says, AI leads all attributes of learning, granting learners with the applications they need to solve problems, engage in intellectual investigation, as well as meet cognitive goals. Moreover, as stated by du Boulay (2019), the learner is contrived down individual learning ways presuming by the AI system, where the method asserts the learning material, process, as well as aim, although few approaches collect the input of the learner to determine the learning update. The perspective of the may consequence in a stereotype about the acknowledgment and capabilities the AI approaches could foresee the apprentice to possess discussed by Kay (2001), as the goals, characteristics, and requirements of each learner are not taken into account.

AI Knowledge Development: This paradigm focuses on giving students the information and abilities to comprehend AI's potential and constraints rather than just utilizing AI technologies. The underlying algorithms, possible biases, and ethical issues related to AI research and application are taught to students.

Collaborating Human and AI: This paradigm highlights how crucial it is for instructors to continue playing a key role in the educational process. While AI is a useful tool that helps with data-driven insights, task automation, and personalized learning, instructors are still the ones who help kids with critical thinking, knowledge application, and social-emotional skill development, (Kim et al., 2022).

6.4 Teaching Strategies

There is growing interest in education research about setting up large language model (LLM) based teach-assisting models due to the amazing logical reasoning and problem-solving capabilities of LLMs.

Large language models like ChatGPT and Gemini AI are already being used in classrooms in ways that can help and hinder student development at the same time. They can support teachers in preparing for lectures and researching, enable them to teach new kinds of courses and make their load lighter (Mollick & Mollick, 2023). Furthermore, it is also employed by students as a method of cheating or copy-pasting while learning. However, what has largely been left out of discussions on AI use within classrooms is how it supports the expansion of teacher capacity to apply difficult but well-tested pedagogical methods that require significant amounts of work. By removing previous burdensome and everyday tasks these underlying algorithms allow teachers' attention to be focused on things like classroom instructions that do not have a substitute among current machine learning models. For Instance,

- **Question Generation:** Question Generation (QG) is establishing itself as one of the most well-liked study subjects in LLMs' application for education because of its extensive use in pedagogical practice (Xiao et al., 2023). Course instructors can implement textbook exercise passages and additional reading materials to fine-tune LLMs before using an easy-to-use controlled text generation approach to guide them in producing more coherent passages based on specific topic keywords. This allows instructors to leverage LLMs to generate reading comprehension questions. The suggested framework may provide multi-generation control modules, prompt assembly, and MCQs with a single right answer, well-crafted distractions, and easily comprehensible language. To generate high-quality varied questions, this can be useful for producing dynamic math word problems when the question's equation has underlying variance controls, (Zhou et al., 2023).

- **Integration of Automatic Grading:** This system of auto-grading refers to a process of allocating grades to students. This technological advancement has reformed the way of evaluating students' accomplishments more efficiently and consistently. In this method, educators have the option to implement AI for scoring the open-ended questions. Also, this process allows educators to create questions by facilitating the criteria for LLM. Moreover, LLM can be used to evaluate students' flawed areas by doing an analysis based on their results. Furthermore, by incorporating comprehensive contexts, precise rubrics, and examples based on real-life situations, LLMs can demonstrate exceptional performance in grading tasks. Additionally, providing timely grading along with personalized feedback can assist students in understanding and identifying areas for improvement. (Fagbohun et al., 2024).
- **Teaching material creation:** The idea of creating teaching material with LLM has huge potential to assist the course instructors. Before AI, teachers had to go through multiple books, course structures, and supplementary books just to address the outdated contents which was very time-consuming. But now, teachers can even invest a little time to create personalized teaching materials with the help of AI. However, various factors needs to be considered:
- **Contextualization:** It would be a great advantage for teachers to use local context by utilizing ChatGPT. This tool will help teachers to incorporate the local context for a certain learning environment. Also, implementing local context to make tailored questions will help students to learn things more easily.
- **Students' individual needs:** An educator can develop study materials by including each student's first language and their following culture. Also, an educator can select fonts, texts, and different design activities for relevant levels. Moreover, ChatGPT has features like creating variations for the same task which can also be applied to different types of formats for similar tasks. Furthermore, to learn English as a Foreign Language course, ChatGPT-4 can play a significant role. Incorporating the zero-shot prompt technique with GPT-4 will enhance the learning process. (Mikeladze, 2023).

6.5 Ethical Approaches

Beyond concerns regarding privacy and biases, Akgun and Greenhow (2022) state that there are other more ethical issues with AI-enhanced schools. There is merit to this assessment. Any situation involving children, including those in K-

12 education, may necessitate additional ethical and pedagogical requirements, as proposed in this chapter. There was a void in the literature until the four pillars of children's rights, pedagogical appropriateness, teacher well-being, and AI literacy were considered. This was because earlier evaluations of policy papers failed to take their wellbeing into account. In addition to the principles proposed by Jobin et al. (2019), these pillars are included. No thorough evaluation of the interplay between these four "new" principles and the more established AI ethical principles (such as Justice and Fairness, Transparency, etc.) has been incorporated into the development of AI ethical standards for AIEdK-12. Nonetheless, each of these ideas has received attention from academics. Given the existing bias in AI ethical principles that are influencing policy formulation, it is unable to address larger ethical problems and create solutions that prioritize human demands above ecological, non-human, and future concerns.

In brief, it is important to make sure that all individuals involved are fully informed before using AI in education. Additionally, every student deserves a fair chance to get a higher education. and AI systems must be designed and implemented with justice and fairness as top priorities. That way, we can be confident that AI algorithms don't have any inherent biases that may discriminate against or otherwise negatively impact certain student groups due to factors like gender, race, or socioeconomic status.

Again, strict privacy measures and security are necessary to protect students' sensitive data, and no negative impact must be felt on students' emotional, social, physical, cognitive, and developmental growth. Pedagogically acceptable AI applications should enhance learning without causing stress. Ethical AI integration ought to value teacher wellness as well as professional growth. Through professional development, educators will be able to help students realize that artificial intelligence (AI) should be user-friendly and safe and that it should work in collaboration with teachers rather than in instead of them.

Moreover, the utilization of trailing or observation approaches in K–12 programs, which gather comprehensive figures on the attitudes and tastes of educators as well as learners, provides further virtuous activities. Artificial Intelligence pursuing approaches adopt algorithms and ML models to forecast users' afterward inclination as well as actions on top of necessitating action surveillance. AI predictive techniques can use observation to forecast learners' learning outcomes, abilities, areas for improvement, and preferred methods of learning. For example, research shows that educators' direct usage of social media for professional objectives face several issues which include worries about privacy limits, accessibility and liability. While paying attention to and patrolling students' attitudes can be noticed as a part of an educator's part together with a handy learning method to intrude in hazardous situations, these actions may also be noticed as inspection approaches that pose isolation intimidation to learners. Learners' contribution while they are still in the learning period, may feel uneasy about having their online discussions and activities observed and recorded, which could slow their progress. Another source of concern is the fact that new technologies can make people less autonomous, which means they are less able to follow their interests and moral compass. For example, algorithm-driven predictive systems put students and teachers in a less autonomous position, and when algorithms are used to forecast people's actions based on what they know, questions about fairness and human autonomy arise. Predictive analysis may additionally reinforce existing biases and preconceptions about social

According to philosophers who have an anthropocentric view, technology is subservient to and inferior to people because of our inherent agency and autonomy. An excerpt from UNESCO's (2021) AI and Education: Guidance for Policy Makers brought to light the fact that ethical standards have their limits when they assume that humans and their technology are entirely separate entities.

Below, we take a quick look at posthumanism, an approach that considers the evolving hybrid entanglements between humans and AI, as well as the point at which the clear borders of humanist thought start to blend. People who engage with AI transform into hybrids of the two species, becoming enmeshed in a web of diverse relationships and interconnected systems. There will inevitably be a division of labor in AI-human hybrids. The idea of humans, as well as the boundaries of their rights and duties, will shift as AI becomes increasingly present in people's daily lives.

7. CHALLENGES

AI is a promising area, but there are a lot of technological roadblocks. When dealing with issues related to educational applications, the problems tend to be more complicated. Also, AI cannot create ideas or content on its own, rather It delivers the data which are generated based on human-developed algorithms. So, certainly, it has some limitations. (Zhai et al., 2021).

Technical Limitations: Machine learning algorithms need large datasets to train effectively, which can be challenging to obtain in educational settings. Additionally, AI systems may have difficulty with ambiguity, context dependency, and complex cognitive tasks that require human-like reasoning and creativity. Moreover, AI cannot immediately generate examples based on a specific situation due to the constraints of the algorithm it needs to follow. (Larysa Sytnyk & Oksana Podlinyayeva, 2024).

Dependency On AI: There is a risk of relying too much on technology at the expense of human interaction and autonomy. While AI can enhance learning experiences and provide personalized support, it should be complementary support for the students, rather than replacing the educators. So, it is necessary to keep a balance between technological-based learning and educator-focused learning. Only human-centered learning can help students to learn about meaningful engagement such as building social development skills. (Larysa Sytnyk & Oksana Podlinyayeva, 2024).

Many AI & ED tools raise ethical, pedagogical, and educational issues. Some of the challenges are discussed below:

Firstly, the belief that AI is smart can devalue human intelligence, especially educators, and lead to overreliance on AI systems, which might be harmful. This can impair critical thinking, creativity, problem-solving, and complex scenario understanding. A suggestion that AI can teach ignores the larger goals of education- 'socialization', 'individuation', and 'qualification'. Tech companies and governments routinely claim AI's intelligence, which is debatable. Similar claims to support AI deployment in areas like education can distract from AI's negative impacts, such as bias, discrimination, and disempowerment.

Another worry is promoting 'personalized learning' to solve educational issues like disengagement. Personalized learning using technology may have drawbacks. Social standing can drop. Neglecting teacher-student and peer relationships can damage trust, motivation, and involvement. Teachers may be overlooked in kids' social and emotional development. Reductive thinking can value skills, competencies, and test results over student growth and education's purpose. These methods may aim to organize learning rather than empower students to succeed.

Again, AI in education has been praised for saving teachers time and letting them focus on teaching. Despite a century-old allegation, it has never been confirmed. Technology may help teachers write prompts and modify GenAI results, but it is uncertain if it reduces their workload. It might increase unemployment. Many AI & ED systems dictate what students should learn, how, and when, discounting teachers and outsourcing their professional privacy. Teachers are treated as service providers, not professionals. IT will misinterpret their expertise and role. It may weaken teacher autonomy, motivation, confidence, prestige, and leadership. While automating grading and assessment is tempting, replacing teachers with AI & ED technology may lower the quality of classroom activities and young people's education.

Also, Commercial goods are often used in schools to integrate AI. AI tools continue to advance. AI may pose further issues. Defined testing, while marketable, may neglect student needs and impede intellectual curiosity and creativity. That might not prepare them for life. Commercial AI-enabled gadgets in schools raise privacy, tracking, and exploitation issues for vulnerable groups. Mishandling student and teacher data may breach privacy rights and erode educational system trust through constant monitoring and assessment.

Privacy and Security Concerns: Due to the rise in AI specifically in large language models (LLM) privacy and security have become a topic of great importance, mainly in the education sector where closer scrutiny is rightfully demanded. LLMs are excellent tools for understanding intricate verbal patterns and producing replies that make learning more fun and easier. These strong models do, however, carry some privacy and security hazards. Das et al. (2024), conducted a detailed survey addressing the privacy and security challenges of large language models where security attacks like prompt injection, jailbreaking attacks, backdoor attacks, and data poisoning attacks are explored. The survey also covers several varieties of privacy attacks, for instance, gradient leakage attacks, membership inference attacks, etc.

Also, one of the major security challenges of AI is unauthorized access and data breaches. Large volumes of sensitive data, such as financial information of the student's parents, the collection of academic records, and personal information about students, are gathered and stored by educational institutions, and any unauthorized access to that information breaks confidentiality. It is considered one of the major vulnerabilities of AI and LLM.

Societal Challenges: When software programmers create "solutions" for various societal problems, they often end up impacting a huge population. However, software engineers typically do not possess any social science training whatsoever; their education is solely focused on computer science (Burton et al. 2017). Because of this, software engineers may lack the necessary knowledge of politics, sociology, psychology, and ethics to comprehend the complex interplay between various factors in the contexts where their technology will be used, and how it will impact those areas (Goldsmith and Burton 2017). Rather, individuals are compelled to adhere to a "I-methodology" that extrapolates their own characteristics and life experiences to other people (Akrich 1995). According to Brey (2010), Hyysalo (2016), and Oudshoorn et al. (2016), this frequently results in specific areas of inattention, misunderstanding, or faulty reasoning. Finally, during the digital technology application phase, unintended and undesirable technological effects arise, necessitating further measures to reduce their impact. There is an immediate need for a comprehensive knowledge of human societies, relationships, and ethics among AI researchers due to the widespread use of AI applications. It should be mentioned that most software engineers and programmers have received only technical training, even though the technical communities are to be commended for promoting interdisciplinary research projects and drawing more attention to the significance of the intersection of computer and social sciences (Campolo et al. 2017).

Unattainability of Secured AI Apps: AI apps are being utilized more and more to protect against, identify, and thwart cyberattacks. "Watson for Cyber Security" by IBM and "For-tiguard Artificial Intelligence" by Fortinet are just two examples of relevant programmes. They can be utilized to enhance the effectiveness of procedures pertaining to security. The flip side is that AI can study "good" cyber defense AI's detection methods and find ways to get around them. Despite the ongoing arms race in information technology security, AI-based applications still have their fair share of flaws (Amodei et al. 2017). One example of a technical context in which these vulnerabilities might pose serious concerns is in driverless cars, where non-secure image recognition software is utilised (Sitawarin et al. 2018). Attacks against ML-based apps might take many forms. Data poisoning assaults, as described by Biggio et al. (2013) and Jagielski et al. (2018), include the intentional manipulation of training data sets with misleading data in order to undermine learning algorithms during their training phase. Secondly, in evasion assaults or adversarial inputs, the goal is to have ML applications misclassify data by feeding them fake inputs (Goodfellow et al. 2018; Szegedy et al. 2013). By inserting little bits of text into larger texts, for instance, one can fool text processing programmes (Jia and Liang 2017). A wholly inaccurate "understanding" of the texts is produced by this tiny alteration. Similar issues arise in image, audio, or face recognition systems; small changes to these files, which would largely be unnoticeable to humans, can lead to utterly inaccurate interpretations (Carlini and Wagner 2018; Eykholt et al. 2018; Goswami et al. 2018; Hendrycks and Dietterich 2018; Rosenfeld et al. 2018; Szegedy et al. 2013). The third step is to "game the system" by reconstructing existing ML approaches using model stealing techniques (Tramér et al. 2016).

8. CONCLUSION

AI and its implementation is adding a new era to the educational institution. However, while it comes to using AI, there are multiple factors that need to be addressed such as, ethical consideration, challenges, educational tools.

While the obstacles of AI in K-12 education are countless, they are not impossible to overcome. Probably the biggest hurdle is that it requires a significant investment in infrastructure, including good internet connectivity and current hardware, which can be tough to secure for cash-strapped schools. They also need regular professional development opportunities for how to use these AI tools well and what they can and cannot do.

Moreover, online resources and learning tools are essential stuff for students which allows the students to learn at their self-determined time also, the use of intelligent tutoring systems allows immediate feedback and personalized learning paths. Those platforms can help the students to find out their weakest subjects and provide them additional exercise to help learning.

Along with lots of benefits, it is also important to keep balance while AI serves us. Its main task is to facilitate not the replacement of anything. The teachers will always be there, as they provide motivation, emotional support. However, ethical guidelines and policies must be evolved along with the development of AI by ensuring the responsible use of it.

REFERENCES

Akgun, S., & Greenhow, C. (2022). Artificial intelligence in education: Addressing ethical challenges in K-12 settings. *AI and Ethics*, *2*(3), 431–440. DOI: 10.1007/s43681-021-00096-7 PMID: 34790956

Brem, A., Giones, F., & Werle, M. (2023, February). The AI Digital Revolution in Innovation: A Conceptual Framework of Artificial Intelligence Technologies for the Management of Innovation. *IEEE Transactions on Engineering Management*, *70*(2), 770–776. DOI: 10.1109/TEM.2021.3109983

Darling-Hammond, L. (1999). Target Time Toward Teachers. *Journal of Staff Development*, *20*(2), 31–36.

Das, B. C., Amini, M. H., & Wu, Y. (2024). Security and Privacy Challenges of Large Language Models: A Survey. *arXiv (Cornell University)*. https://doi.org//arxiv.2402.00888DOI: 10.48550

Etheredge, L. (2025). AI in Education: Global Trends and Country-by-Country Analysis (2018-2023). *TBD*. https://www.researchgate.net/publication/389043586_AI_in_Education_Global_Trends_and_Country-by-Country_Analysis_2018-2023

Fagbohun, O., Iduwe, N. P., Abdullahi, M., Ifaturoti, A., & Nwanna, O. M. (2024). Beyond Traditional Assessment: Exploring the Impact of Large Language Models on Grading Practices. Journal of Artificial Intelligence. *Machine Learning and Data Science*, *2*(1), 1–8. DOI: 10.51219/JAIMLD/oluwole-fagbohun/19

Fleger, C. B., Amanuel, Y., & Krugel, J. (2023, May). Learning tools using block-based programming for AI education. In *2023 IEEE Global Engineering Education Conference (EDUCON)* (pp. 1-5). IEEE.

Füller, J., Hutter, K., Wahl, J., Bilgram, V., & Tekic, Z. (2022, May). How AI revolutionizes innovation management – Perceptions and implementation preferences of AI-based innovators. *Technological Forecasting and Social Change*, *178*, 121598. DOI: 10.1016/j.techfore.2022.121598

Glatthorn, A. A., Boschee, F., Whitehead, B. M., & Boschee, B. F. (2018). *Curriculum leadership: Strategies for development and implementation*. SAGE publications.

Goel, A. (2017). AI Education for the World. *AI Magazine*, *38*(2), 3–4. DOI: 10.1609/aimag.v38i2.2740

Häkli, J. (2018). The subject of citizenship–Can there be a posthuman civil society? *Political Geography*, *67*, 166–175. DOI: 10.1016/j.polgeo.2017.08.006

Holmes, W., Bialik, M., & Fadel, C. (2019). *Artificial intelligence in education promises and implications for teaching and learning*. Center for Curriculum Redesign.

Holstein, K., & Aleven, V. (2022). Designing for human–AI complementarity in K-12 education. *AI Magazine, 43*(2), 239–248. DOI: 10.1002/aaai.12058

Kay, J. (2001). Learner control. *User Modeling and User-Adapted Interaction, 11*(1), 111–127. DOI: 10.1023/A:1011194803800

Kelly, A. (2009). The curriculum. *Theory into Practice.*

Kim, J., Lee, H., & Cho, Y. H. (2022, January 28). Learning design to support student-AI collaboration: Perspectives of leading teachers for AI in education. *Education and Information Technologies, 27*(5), 6069–6104. DOI: 10.1007/s10639-021-10831-6

Kim, S., Jang, Y., Kim, W., Choi, S., Jung, H., Kim, S., & Kim, H. (2021). Why and What to Teach: AI Curriculum for Elementary School. *Proceedings of the AAAI Conference on Artificial Intelligence, 35*(17), 15569–15576. DOI: 10.1609/aaai.v35i17.17833

. Klamma, R., Lange, P. de, Neumann, A. T., Hensen, B., Kravcik, M., Wang, X., & Kuzilek, J. (2020). Scaling Mentoring Support with Distributed Artificial Intelligence. Intelligent Tutoring Systems, 38–44. DOI: 10.1007/978-3-030-49663-0_6

Kuleto, V., Ilić, M., Dumangiu, M. A., Ranković, M., Martins, O., Păun, D., & Mihoreanu, L. (2021, September 18). Exploring Opportunities and Challenges of Artificial Intelligence and Machine Learning in Higher Education Institutions. *Sustainability (Basel), 13*(18), 10424. Advance online publication. DOI: 10.3390/su131810424

Mikeladze, T. (2023). Creating teaching materials with ChatGPT. In 13th International Research Conference on Education, Language and Literature. https://www.academia.edu/110954212/Creating_teaching_materials_with_ChatGPT

Mintz, J., Holmes, W., Liu, L., & Ortiz, M. P. (2023, November 28). *Artificial Intelligence and K-12 Education: Possibilities, Pedagogies and Risks*. https://www.tandfonline.com/doi/full/10.1080/07380569.2023.2279870

Mintz, J., Holmes, W., Liu, L., & Perez-Ortiz, M. (2023). Artificial Intelligence and K-12 Education: Possibilities, Pedagogies and Risks. *Computers in the Schools, 40*(4), 325–333. DOI: 10.1080/07380569.2023.2279870

Mohri, M., Rostamizadeh, A., & Talwalkar, A. (2018). *Foundations of machine learning*. MIT press.

Mollick, E. R., & Mollick, L. (2023). Using AI to Implement Effective Teaching Strategies in Classrooms: Five Strategies, Including Prompts. Social Science Research Network. DOI: 10.2139/ssrn.4391243

Naqvi, A. (2020). *Artificial intelligence for audit, forensic accounting, and valuation: a strategic perspective*. John Wiley & Sons.

Sanusi, I. T., Oyelere, S. S., Agbo, F. J., & Suhonen, J. (2021, October). Survey of resources for introducing machine learning in K-12 context. In 2021 IEEE frontiers in education conference (FIE) (pp. 1-9). IEEE.

Shabbir, J., & Anwer, T. (2018). Artificial Intelligence and its Role in Near Future. *arXiv (Cornell University)*. https://doi.org//arxiv.1804.01396DOI: 10.48550

Skinner, B. F. (1965). *Science and human behavior (No. 92904)*. Simon and Schuster.

Sophokleous, A., Christodoulou, P., Doitsidis, L., & Chatzichristofis, S. A. (2021, March 19). Computer Vision Meets Educational Robotics. *Electronics (Basel)*, *10*(6), 730. Advance online publication. DOI: 10.3390/electronics10060730

Su, J., & Zhong, Y. (2022). Artificial intelligence (AI) in early childhood education: Curriculum design and future directions. *Computers and Education: Artificial Intelligence*, *3*, 100072. DOI: 10.1016/j.caeai.2022.100072

Sytnyk, L., & Podlinyayeva, O. (2024). AI in education: Main possibilities and challenges. *InterConf*, *45*(201), 569–579. DOI: 10.51582/interconf.19-20.05.2024.058

Terzopoulos, G., & Satratzemi, M. (2019). Voice Assistants and Artificial Intelligence in Education. *Proceedings of the 9th Balkan Conference on Informatics*, 1–6. DOI: 10.1145/3351556.3351588

Timms, M. J. (2016). Letting Artificial Intelligence in Education Out of the Box: Educational Cobots and Smart Classrooms. *International Journal of Artificial Intelligence in Education*, *26*(2), 701–712. DOI: 10.1007/s40593-016-0095-y

Touretzky, D., Gardner-McCune, C., Breazeal, C., Martin, F., & Seehorn, D. (2019). A year in K–12 AI education. *AI Magazine*, *40*(4), 88–90. DOI: 10.1609/aimag.v40i4.5289

. Touretzky, D. S. (2017, October 1). Computational thinking and mental models: From kodu to calypso. IEEE Xplore. DOI: 10.1109/BLOCKS.2017.8120416

Williams, R. (2024, February 1). Impact.AI: Democratizing AI through K-12 Artificial Intelligence Education. Dspace.mit.edu. https://dspace.mit.edu/handle/1721.1/153676

Wilson, S. M. (2011, May). Effective STEM teacher preparation, induction, and professional development. In *NRC Workshop on Highly Successful STEM Schools or Programs. Available:* http://www7. nationalacademies. org/bose/Successful_STEM_Schools_Homepage. html *[May 2011]*.

Xiao, C., Xu, S. X., Zhang, K., Wang, Y., & Xia, L. (2023). Evaluating Reading Comprehension Exercises Generated by LLMs: A Showcase of ChatGPT in Education Applications. DOI: 10.18653/v1/2023.bea-1.52

Yang, X. (2019). Accelerated move for AI education in China. *ECNU Review of Education*, *2*(3), 347–352. DOI: 10.1177/2096531119878590

Yu, Z. (2020, October). Visualizing Artificial Intelligence Used in Education Over Two Decades. *Journal of Information Technology Research*, *13*(4), 32–46. DOI: 10.4018/JITR.2020100103

Zhai, X., Chu, X., Chai, C. S., Jong, M. S. Y., Istenic, A., Spector, M., Liu, J.-B., Yuan, J., & Li, Y. (2021). A Review of Artificial Intelligence (AI) in Education from 2010 to 2020. *Complexity*, *2021*(8812542), 1–18. DOI: 10.1155/2021/8812542

Zhou, Z., Ning, M., Wang, Q., Yao, J., Wang, W., Huang, X., & Huang, K. (2023). Learning by Analogy: Diverse Questions Generation in Math Word Problem. DOI: 10.18653/v1/2023.findings-acl.705

Chapter 11
Inclusive LLM-Driven Curriculum Design for K-12 Education Integrating Special Needs

Yusuf Mshelia
http://orcid.org/0000-0001-7799-8583
Data Aid, Nigeria

Hyelhara Umaru Mshelia
Adamawa State University, Nigeria

Joan Mshelia
Data Aid, Nigeria

ABSTRACT

This chapter explores the potential of Large Language Models (LLMs) like ChatGPT in creating inclusive and adaptive K-12 curricula that effectively integrate the needs of students with special needs. Using Generative AI technologies like LLMs, this chapter presents innovative strategies for designing and implementing curricula that cater to diverse learning needs with an inclusive approach for special needs that ensures equal opportunities for students' academic success. Case studies and examples are further discussed to help reader towards implementing AI supported curriculum integration in educational settings.

DOI: 10.4018/979-8-3693-6346-1.ch011

I. INTRODUCTION

K-12 education forms the foundation of a student's academic journey, shaping their cognitive, social, and emotional development. Across the globe, educational systems aim to provide comprehensive learning experiences that prepare students for higher education, careers, and responsible citizenship. Despite these noble goals, the current state of K-12 education is marked by significant challenges that hinder the effective delivery of quality education to all students (Darling-Hammond et al., 2020).

The prevailing educational frameworks, especially in low-resource settings confine learning to traditional systems with scarcity of tailored learning resources and an unintentional disregard for the diverse and specific needs of individual learners. This deficiency becomes particularly evident when considering learners with distinct requirements, such as those with autism, whose learning dynamics markedly differ from those of their neurotypical counterparts. Consequently, the existing educational paradigm is marked by deficiencies in resource availability, teacher competency in catering for diverse learner-set, personalized learner assessment, and the incorporation of adaptive tools to tailor educational content.

This complex challenge demands a paradigm shift towards recognizing and addressing the unique attributes and requirements of learners, thereby presenting a considerable hurdle for parents, educators, and policy administrators striving to deliver relevant, age-appropriate, and effective learning experiences. While localized learning materials fall short in accommodating the heterogeneous classroom landscape, crafting custom-made content for each student proves impractically labor-intensive. The constrained educational systems in terms of resources not only lack comprehensive educational content but also fail to provide requisite instructional tools, modern technologies, and the specialized skill sets necessary to bridge this educational gap.

Challenges in Traditional Curriculum Design

One of the most pressing challenges in traditional curriculum design is the inherent lack of flexibility. Standardized curricula often follow a one-size-fits-all approach, which fails to accommodate the diverse learning needs and paces of individual students. This rigidity can lead to disengagement, particularly among students who do not fit the traditional mold of learning styles and abilities (Tomlinson, 2014).

Moreover, traditional curricula tend to focus heavily on content delivery rather than fostering critical thinking, creativity, and problem-solving skills. This content-centric approach often overlooks the importance of developing soft skills and socioemotional competencies, which are crucial for students' overall growth and future success (Rotherham & Willingham, 2009).

In addition, the diverse classroom demographics present another layer of complexity. Educators are tasked with addressing the varied cultural, linguistic, and socio-economic backgrounds of their students. This diversity requires curricula that are not only inclusive but also culturally responsive (Gay, 2018), ensuring that all students feel represented and valued in their learning environment. However, many traditional curricula fall short in this regard, leading to disparities in educational outcomes.

Importance of Inclusivity in Education

Inclusivity in education goes beyond merely accommodating students with different learning needs; it encompasses creating a learning environment where every student feels valued, supported, and capable of achieving their full potential (Hehir et al., 2016). Inclusive education is particularly vital for students with special needs, who often face additional barriers to learning. These barriers can include inadequate access to specialized resources, insufficiently trained educators, and a lack of tailored instructional methods.

An inclusive curriculum recognizes and addresses these barriers, ensuring that all students, regardless of their abilities or backgrounds, have equal opportunities to succeed. This approach not only benefits students with special needs but also enriches the learning experience for all students by promoting empathy, understanding, and collaboration (Meyer et al., 2014).

Large Language Models (LLMs)

Large Language Models (LLMs) represent a significant advancement in artificial intelligence, with capabilities that have the potential to transform educational practices. These models, which include sophisticated AI systems like GPT-4, can process and generate human-like text based on vast amounts of data. LLMs are capable of understanding and responding to natural language inputs, making them powerful tools for personalized and adaptive learning (Brown et al., 2020).

The integration of LLMs into curriculum design offers a promising solution to the challenges faced by traditional educational systems. By leveraging the capabilities of LLMs, educators can create curricula that are more flexible, personalized, and inclusive. These models can assist in developing tailored learning pathways for individual students, providing real-time feedback, and continuously adapting instructional methods to meet the evolving needs of learners (Holmes et al., 2023).

In this chapter, we will explore how LLM-driven curriculum design can revolutionize K-12 education, particularly in the context of integrating special needs. We will examine the principles of inclusive curriculum design, the role of LLMs in personalization and differentiation, and practical strategies for implementation. Through this exploration, we aim to provide a roadmap for creating a more inclusive and effective educational system that harnesses the power of AI to support all students.

II. UNDERSTANDING SPECIAL NEEDS IN THE K-12 CONTEXT

This section will define and classify various special needs, including learning disabilities, physical disabilities, emotional and behavioral disorders, and autism spectrum disorders. It will discuss the educational challenges faced by students with special needs, such as access to appropriate resources, tailored instructional methods, and social and emotional support. Understanding these challenges is crucial for designing effective LLM-driven curricula.

Furthermore, the prevailing K-12 educational frameworks, especially in low-resource settings confine learning to traditional systems with scarcity of tailored learning resources and an unintentional disregard for the diverse and specific needs of individual learners. This deficiency becomes particularly evident when considering learners with distinct requirements, such as those with autism, whose learning dynamics markedly differ from those of their neurotypical counterparts. Consequently, the existing educational paradigm is marked by deficiencies in resource availability, teacher competency in catering for diverse learner-set, personalized learner assessment, and the incorporation of adaptive tools to tailor educational content.

This complex challenge demands a paradigm shift towards recognizing and addressing the unique attributes and requirements of learners, thereby presenting a considerable hurdle for parents, educators, and policy administrators striving to deliver relevant, age-appropriate, and effective learning experiences. While localized learning materials fall short in accommodating the heterogeneous classroom landscape, crafting custom-made content for each student proves impractically labor-intensive. The constrained educational systems in terms of resources not only lack comprehensive educational content but also fail to provide requisite instructional tools, modern technologies, and the specialized skill sets necessary to bridge this educational gap.

Definition and Classification of Special Needs

Special needs refer to a range of physical, emotional, behavioral, and learning disabilities that require specialized attention and educational strategies to ensure that affected students can achieve their full potential. These needs can be broadly classified into the following categories:

1. **Learning Disabilities:** Learning disabilities are neurological disorders that affect one or more of the basic processes involved in understanding or using language, whether spoken or written. This category includes dyslexia, dyscalculia, and dysgraphia. Students with learning disabilities often struggle with reading, writing, mathematics, and other academic areas (Hallahan et al., 2013).
2. **Physical Disabilities:** Physical disabilities involve impairments that may limit mobility, dexterity, or other physical functions. These can include conditions such as cerebral palsy, muscular dystrophy, and spinal cord injuries. Students with physical disabilities may require assistive technologies, modified classrooms, and specialized physical education programs to participate fully in school activities (Smith, 2010).
3. **Emotional and Behavioral Disorders:** Emotional and behavioral disorders encompass a range of mental health issues that can affect a student's ability to learn and interact socially (Kauffman, 1997). Examples include anxiety disorders, depression, bipolar disorder, and conduct disorders. These students may exhibit disruptive behaviors, have difficulty forming relationships, and require specialized support to manage their emotions and behaviors.
4. **Autism Spectrum Disorders (ASD):** Autism spectrum disorders are characterized by challenges with social skills, repetitive behaviors, speech, and nonverbal communication. The spectrum nature of autism means that it affects individuals differently and to varying degrees. Students with ASD may require tailored instructional strategies, social skills training, and sensory accommodations to succeed in an educational setting (Lord et al., 2018).

Educational Challenges Faced by Students with Special Needs

Students with special needs face numerous challenges that can impede their educational progress. These challenges often necessitate specific strategies and resources to ensure an equitable learning environment.

1. **Access to Appropriate Resources:** Ensuring that students with special needs have access to the necessary resources is critical. This includes specialized instructional materials, assistive technologies, and physical accommodations. Unfortunately, many schools lack the funding or infrastructure to provide these essential resources, leading to significant disparities in educational outcomes (Smith, 2010).

2. **Tailored Instructional Methods:** Traditional instructional methods often do not meet the unique needs of students with disabilities. Tailored instructional approaches, such as differentiated instruction and individualized education programs (IEPs), are essential for addressing the diverse learning styles and paces of these students(Tomlinson, 2014). However, the implementation of such methods requires significant training and support for educators.
3. **Social and Emotional Support:** Students with special needs frequently require additional social and emotional support to navigate the school environment successfully. This support can include counseling services, peer mentoring programs, and social skills training. A lack of adequate support can lead to feelings of isolation, increased stress, and behavioral issues, further hindering academic achievement (Kauffman, 1997).

Designing Effective LLM-Driven Curricula

Understanding the challenges faced by students with special needs is crucial for designing effective curricula powered by LLMs. LLMs have the potential to address these challenges in several ways:

1. **Personalization and Adaptation:** LLMs can analyze student data to personalize learning experiences, adapting content and instructional methods to meet individual needs. For example, they can provide customized reading materials at appropriate difficulty levels for students with dyslexia or offer alternative ways to demonstrate knowledge for students with physical disabilities (Holmes et al., 2023).
2. **Resource Provision:** LLMs can assist in identifying and generating resources tailored to specific disabilities. This includes creating accessible content formats, suggesting assistive technologies, and offering real-time feedback and support to both students and educators (Brown et al., 2020).
3. **Social and Emotional Support:** LLMs can be programmed to recognize and respond to the emotional states of students, providing timely interventions and support. This can include automated check-ins, stress-relief exercises, and connecting students with counselors or support groups when needed (Holmes et al., 2023).

III. THE ROLE OF LLMS IN CURRICULUM DESIGN

Large Language Models (LLMs) are a class of artificial intelligence (AI) models designed to understand and generate human-like text based on extensive training data. Their capabilities have significant implications for the field of education, particularly in the areas of natural language processing, personalized content creation, and adaptive learning systems:

1. **Natural Language Processing (NLP):** LLMs excel in natural language processing, which involves understanding and generating human language. This capability enables them to interpret complex queries, understand context, and provide accurate and coherent responses. In educational settings, NLP allows LLMs to facilitate better communication between students and digital learning platforms, enhance language learning, and support multilingual education by providing translations and language-specific assistance.
2. **Personalized Content Creation:** One of the most impactful capabilities of LLMs is their ability to create personalized educational content. LLMs can generate customized learning materials tailored to the individual needs, interests, and learning levels of students. This includes creating reading passages, practice problems, and instructional materials that align with each student's learning profile. Personalized content creation helps to engage students more effectively and supports differentiated instruction.
3. **Adaptive Learning Systems:** LLMs can underpin adaptive learning systems that dynamically adjust the difficulty and type of content based on real-time assessment of a student's performance. These systems provide immediate feedback, adjust instructional strategies, and offer additional resources or challenges as needed. Adaptive learning systems powered by LLMs can identify learning gaps and provide targeted interventions, thus enhancing the learning experience and improving educational outcomes.

Integration of LLMs into Curriculum Development

Integrating LLMs into curriculum development involves several key processes, from data collection and analysis to designing adaptive learning pathways and implementing continuous feedback and improvement mechanisms.

1. **Data Collection and Analysis:** Effective integration of LLMs begins with comprehensive data collection. This includes gathering information on student performance, learning behaviors, and engagement levels. LLMs can analyze this data to identify patterns and insights that inform curriculum design. For example, they can pinpoint common misconceptions or frequently encountered difficulties, allowing educators to address these areas proactively (Holmes et al., 2023).

2. **Designing Adaptive Learning Pathways:** Using insights gained from data analysis, LLMs can help design adaptive learning pathways tailored to individual students. These pathways provide personalized learning experiences by dynamically adjusting content, resources, and assessments. For instance, a student struggling with a particular math concept might receive additional practice problems, visual aids, or step-by-step tutorials generated by the LLM (Khan, 2012).
3. **Implementing Continuous Feedback and Improvement Mechanisms:** One of the significant advantages of LLMs is their ability to provide continuous feedback. As students interact with the curriculum, LLMs monitor their progress and offer immediate feedback on assignments, quizzes, and other learning activities. This real-time feedback helps students correct mistakes and reinforces learning. Additionally, LLMs can suggest modifications to the curriculum based on ongoing performance data, ensuring that the instructional approach remains effective and responsive to student needs.

IV. DESIGNING AN INCLUSIVE CURRICULUM WITH LLMS

Inclusive curriculum design aims to create educational environments that cater to the diverse needs of all students, including those with special needs. Key principles of inclusive curriculum design include Universal Design for Learning (UDL), differentiated instruction, and culturally responsive teaching.

Universal Design for Learning (UDL)

UDL is a framework that guides the development of flexible learning environments to accommodate individual learning differences. It is based on three primary principles (CAST, 2018; Meyer et al., 2014):

1. **Multiple Means of Representation:** Multiple means of representation involve providing diverse ways to present information to students, ensuring all learners can access and comprehend the material. This principle recognizes that students have varying sensory, perceptual, and cognitive needs. For example, educators might use text, audio, video, diagrams, and hands-on activities to explain concepts. This approach ensures that students with different learning preferences and abilities can grasp the content effectively
2. **Multiple Means of Action and Expression:** Multiple means of action and expression refer to offering various ways for students to demonstrate what they know and can do. This principle acknowledges that students have different

strengths and challenges in expressing their knowledge. For instance, while some students might excel in writing essays, others might be better at creating presentations, building models, or participating in discussions. By providing multiple options for assessment, educators can accommodate diverse abilities and learning styles

3. **Multiple Means of Engagement:** Multiple means of engagement involve using different strategies to motivate and involve students in learning. This principle focuses on the variability in students' interests, backgrounds, and emotional responses. Educators can offer choices in learning activities, relate content to real-world contexts, and use collaborative projects to keep students interested and invested in their learning. Engaging students through various methods helps sustain their motivation and promotes a deeper connection to the material

Differentiated Instruction

Differentiated instruction involves tailoring teaching methods and materials to accommodate the varying abilities, interests, and learning styles of students. This approach allows teachers to meet students where they are and help them progress at an appropriate pace(Tomlinson, 2014).

Culturally Responsive Teaching

Culturally responsive teaching emphasizes the importance of including students' cultural references in all aspects of learning. This approach seeks to make learning more relevant and effective by acknowledging and valuing students' diverse cultural backgrounds (Gay, 2018).

Enhancing UDL with LLMs

LLMs can significantly enhance the principles of UDL by providing personalized and adaptive learning experiences. Here's how LLMs can support each UDL principle:

1. **Multiple Means of Representation** LLMs can generate various formats of educational content, such as text, audio, and visual aids, to cater to different learning preferences. For example, an LLM can convert written text into audio for students who benefit from auditory learning or create visual summaries for those who are visual learners (Brown et al., 2020).
2. **Multiple Means of Action and Expression** LLMs can offer diverse methods for students to express their understanding. This could include written responses, oral presentations, or creative projects. By providing tools like speech-to-text

and text-to-speech, LLMs can accommodate students with physical or learning disabilities, allowing them to choose the mode of expression that best suits their abilities (Holmes et al., 2023).

3. **Multiple Means of Engagement** LLMs can personalize learning experiences based on students' interests and motivational factors. For instance, they can adapt reading materials to include topics that interest individual students or use gamification techniques to increase engagement. This tailored approach helps maintain student interest and motivation, which is crucial for effective learning (Holmes et al., 2023).

CASE STUDIES

Case Study for Personalized Reading Programs

In a pilot program, an LLM was used to create personalized reading assignments for students with diverse reading levels and interests. The AI analyzed students' reading histories and preferences to recommend books and articles that matched their skills and interests. This personalized approach led to significant improvements in reading engagement and comprehension among students.

Case 1: Hidayat's (2024)

Hidayat (2024) studied the use of AI-driven personalized reading plans in a middle school setting. The research focused on students with varying reading abilities, including those with dyslexia and other reading disabilities. The AI system used natural language processing (NLP) to analyze each student's reading level, interests, and progress. Based on this analysis, the system generated customized reading materials and activities that matched the students' individual needs.

Key Findings

1. **Improved Reading Skills:** Students showed significant improvement in their reading skills over a semester. The personalized plans helped them engage with texts that were neither too easy nor too difficult, promoting steady progress.
2. **Increased Engagement:** The alignment of reading materials with students' interests led to higher levels of engagement and motivation to read.
3. **Positive Feedback from Educators:** Teachers reported that the AI system reduced their workload in lesson planning and allowed them to focus more on direct instruction and support.

Case 2: Miles and Ari (2022)

Miles and Ari (2022) conducted a similar study in an elementary school environment, focusing on young readers, including English Language Learners (ELLs) and students with special educational needs. Their approach involved integrating personalized reading plans with traditional teaching methods, providing a hybrid learning experience.

Key Findings

The key findings from these studies shows:

1. **Enhanced Comprehension:** The personalized reading plans significantly improved reading comprehension scores. By adjusting the complexity of texts and providing contextual support, students could better understand and retain information.
2. **Language Development:** For ELL students, personalized reading plans facilitated language acquisition by presenting texts that incorporated both familiar and new vocabulary in meaningful contexts.
3. **Support for Special Needs:** Students with special educational needs benefited from the tailored approach, which accommodated their unique learning challenges and preferences.

Practical Implementation

Both studies highlight practical strategies for implementing personalized reading plans with the following steps:

1. **Initial Assessment:** Conduct thorough assessments of students' reading levels, interests, and specific needs.
2. **Dynamic Adjustments:** Continuously monitor student progress and adjust reading plans accordingly to maintain optimal challenge and support levels.
3. **Integration with Classroom Activities:** Combine personalized plans with collaborative and traditional classroom activities to create a balanced learning environment.
4. **Teacher Training:** Provide professional development for teachers to effectively integrate AI tools and personalized plans into their instruction.

Case 3: (McLaren et al., 2022)

McLaren et al. (2022) investigated the application of personalized reading plans in a large urban school district, focusing on elementary and middle school students. The study utilized AI technologies to tailor reading materials and instructional strategies based on each student's unique profile, including their reading level, learning pace, interests, and specific needs.

With AI Integration in analyzing student data, including previous reading performance, standardized test scores, and teacher assessments. This analysis informed the creation of individualized reading plans. The AI system curated a variety of reading materials, ranging from traditional texts to multimedia resources, aligned with students' interests and reading abilities from diverse texts and activities.

Key Findings

1. **Improved Reading Proficiency:** Students demonstrated significant improvements in reading proficiency over the academic year. The personalized approach ensured that students engaged with texts suited to their reading levels, promoting better comprehension and retention.
2. **Enhanced Engagement and Motivation:** Personalized reading plans led to higher levels of student engagement and motivation. By aligning reading materials with students' interests, the AI-driven system made reading more enjoyable and relevant, fostering a positive attitude toward learning.
3. **Support for Diverse Learners:** The study highlighted the effectiveness of personalized reading plans in supporting diverse learners, including English Language Learners (ELLs) and students with special educational needs. Tailored reading materials and adaptive support strategies helped address individual challenges and learning preferences.
4. **Positive Teacher Feedback:** Teachers reported that the AI system significantly reduced the burden of lesson planning and allowed them to focus more on interactive and individualized instruction. They appreciated the real-time insights into student progress, which enabled more targeted interventions.

Practical Implementation

Based on the findings of McLaren et al. (2022), several practical strategies for implementing personalized reading plans were identified:

1. **Initial and Ongoing Assessment:** Conduct thorough initial assessments and maintain continuous monitoring to adapt reading plans to evolving student needs.

2. **Diverse and Relevant Content:** Use AI to curate a wide range of reading materials that cater to different interests and reading levels, making learning more engaging.
3. **Teacher Training:** Provide professional development for teachers to effectively integrate AI tools and personalized reading plans into their instructional practices.
4. **Collaborative Learning:** Combine personalized plans with collaborative classroom activities to enhance social learning and peer support.

Case 4: (Cheng et al., 2022) - Culturally Responsive Teaching Aided by AI

Cheng et al. (2022) conducted a study in an elementary school environment, focusing on the role of teacher technology experiences and school technology interactivity in implementing personalized reading plans that support culturally responsive teaching (CRT). The study aimed to understand how AI-driven tools can aid in creating culturally relevant reading materials and the impact on student engagement and academic performance.

Key Findings

1. **Enhanced Cultural Relevance:** The personalized reading plans incorporated students' cultural backgrounds, languages, and interests. This cultural relevance significantly increased student engagement and motivation.
2. **Improved Reading Proficiency:** Students showed marked improvement in reading proficiency. Tailored reading materials aligned with their cultural contexts helped students better understand and relate to the content, enhancing comprehension and retention.
3. **Positive Teacher Experiences:** Teachers reported that their experiences with technology were overwhelmingly positive. The AI tools reduced their workload in creating culturally responsive materials and allowed them to focus more on interactive and personalized instruction.
4. **School-Wide Technology Interactivity:** The school's robust technology infrastructure facilitated effective use of AI tools across classrooms. The interactivity between various technological systems enabled smooth implementation and ongoing adaptation of personalized reading plans.

Practical Implementation

The practical strategies for implementing personalized reading plans that support CRT:

1. **Comprehensive Teacher Training:** Provide extensive training for teachers on using AI tools to create and implement personalized, culturally relevant reading plans.
2. **Robust Technology Infrastructure:** Develop and maintain a school-wide technology framework that supports the seamless integration of AI tools and interactive learning environments.
3. **Continuous Feedback Mechanisms:** Establish regular feedback loops involving both teachers and students to continuously improve the relevance and effectiveness of personalized reading plans.
4. **Collaboration and Support:** Foster a collaborative environment where teachers can share experiences, strategies, and resources related to technology and culturally responsive teaching.

V. INTEGRATING SPECIAL NEEDS INTO LLM-DRIVEN CURRICULA

The focus will be on personalization and differentiation, detailing how LLMs can tailor content to individual student profiles and adjust pace and complexity based on student needs. The section will discuss support tools and resources, including assistive technologies, speech-to-text and text-to-speech features, and visual and auditory aids. It will also cover monitoring and assessment strategies, such as real-time progress tracking and adaptive assessments.

Tailoring Content to Individual Student Profiles

LLM possess the ability to personalize educational content to meet the unique needs of each student. By analyzing individual learning profiles, LLMs can adjust the pace, complexity, and type of content provided, ensuring that each student receives an education that is tailored to their abilities and interests.

1. **Adjusting Pace and Complexity:** LLMs can monitor student performance in real time and dynamically adjust the difficulty level of instructional materials. For example, if a student demonstrates mastery of a concept, the LLM can introduce more challenging problems or advanced topics. Conversely, if a student struggles, the LLM can provide additional practice or simplify the content to reinforce foundational skills.
2. **Customizing Learning Paths:** By leveraging data from student interactions, LLMs can create individualized learning paths that align with each student's learning style and progress. This includes recommending specific activities, re-

sources, and assignments that match the student's current level of understanding and areas of interest.

Support Tools and Resources

To facilitate personalized and differentiated instruction, LLMs can integrate various support tools and resources that enhance accessibility and engagement for all students.

1. **Assistive Technologies:** Assistive technologies play a crucial role in supporting students with special needs. LLMs can incorporate these technologies to help students overcome barriers to learning. Examples include screen readers for visually impaired students, alternative input devices for those with physical disabilities, and communication aids for students with speech impairments.
2. **Speech-to-Text and Text-to-Speech Features:** LLMs can provide speech-to-text capabilities, allowing students to dictate their responses, which is particularly beneficial for those with writing difficulties or physical disabilities. Text-to-speech features enable students to listen to written content, aiding those with reading difficulties or visual impairments. These features enhance accessibility and ensure that all students can engage with the curriculum effectively.
3. **Visual and Auditory Aids:** Visual aids, such as diagrams, infographics, and videos, can help clarify complex concepts for visual learners. Auditory aids, including recorded lectures and podcasts, support auditory learners. LLMs can generate and recommend these types of aids based on individual student preferences, making learning more engaging and comprehensible.

Monitoring and Assessment Strategies

Effective personalization and differentiation require robust monitoring and assessment strategies. LLMs excel in providing real-time progress tracking and adaptive assessments to ensure that educational interventions are timely and appropriate.

1. **Real-Time Progress Tracking:** LLMs can continuously monitor student performance through their interactions with the learning platform. This includes tracking quiz results, assignment submissions, and participation in discussions. By analyzing this data, LLMs can provide educators with detailed insights into each student's progress, highlighting areas of strength and those needing improvement.

2. **Adaptive Assessments:** Adaptive assessments adjust their difficulty based on the student's responses, providing a more accurate measure of their knowledge and skills. LLMs can administer these assessments, instantly analyzing the results to adjust future content and instruction accordingly. This ensures that assessments are fair, relevant, and capable of identifying specific learning needs (Brown et al., 2020).

VI. IMPLEMENTATION STRATEGIES

Practical Strategies for Implementation

Implementing LLM-driven inclusive curricula involves several practical strategies, including effective prompting techniques, collaboration with special education experts, robust technical infrastructure, and comprehensive policy and administrative support.

After identifying special learning needs in the learners, here are three diverse examples of how these strategies can be applied:

Customized Learning Modules for Students with Dyslexia

i. Understanding the Specific Learning

1. **Ask Open-Ended Question Prompts:** Use open-ended questions to encourage students to express their thoughts and feelings about their learning experiences. This can help identify specific challenges they face.
   Prompt: "*Can you tell me about a time when you found a lesson particularly difficult? What made it hard for you?*"
   Prompt: "*How do you feel when you are reading or writing? Are there specific parts that you enjoy or find challenging?*"
2. **Reflection Prompts:** Encourage students to reflect on their learning processes and self-assess their skills and difficulties.
   Prompt: "*What do you think are your strengths in learning? Where do you think you need more help?*"
   Prompt: "*When you are working on a math problem, what steps do you find easiest, and which do you find most challenging?*"
3. **Task-Specific Prompts:** Ask students to describe their thought process while working on specific tasks to pinpoint where they struggle.
   Prompt: "*Can you walk me through how you approach a reading assignment? What do you do first, and what parts do you find confusing?*"

Prompt: "*When you solve a math problem, what strategies do you use? What happens when you get stuck?*"

4. **Hypothetical Scenario Prompts:** Present hypothetical scenarios to understand how students might handle different learning situations.
   Prompt: "*Imagine you have to write a story. How would you start? What kind of help would you need to complete it?*"
   Prompt: "*If you were given a science experiment to do on your own, what steps would you take, and where might you need assistance?*"
5. **Problem-Solving Prompts:** Ask students to identify problems and suggest solutions related to their learning difficulties.
   Prompt: "*What do you think could make learning this subject easier for you?*"
   Prompt: "*If you could change one thing about the way we do assignments, what would it be and why?*"
6. **Emotional Response Prompts:** Explore the emotional aspects of learning by asking students how they feel about different subjects or tasks.
   Prompt: "*How do you feel when you have to read aloud in class? What makes you feel that way?*"
   Prompt: "*What emotions do you experience when you get a difficult homework assignment?*"
7. **Preference and Interest Prompts:** Identify students' interests and preferences which can influence their engagement and success in learning.
   Prompt: "*What subjects do you enjoy the most and why?*"
   Prompt: "*Are there any topics or activities that you look forward to in school? What makes them interesting for you?*"
8. **Retrospective Prompts:** Ask students to look back on past experiences to identify consistent challenges or successful strategies.
   Prompt: "*Think about a time when you did really well on an assignment. What did you do differently?*"
   Prompt: "*Looking back on this school year, what were the hardest assignments for you, and why do you think they were difficult?*"

General Prompt for Condition Specific Special Need

Ask the LLM system to generate learning and teaching content for the specific context specific to the child's special need, age, strength, etc. This can be modified with the description of the student with special need. The data generated from the questions asked from the prompts above can also be integrated into the prompts below as input for describing the student learning strengths and weakness.

Prompt:

1. *"Develop a teaching/reading outline for teaching a 5-year-old boy, that exhibits autistic signs and is weak in speech"*
2. *"Develop a reading outline for a 5-year-old boy, that exhibits autistic [or specify condition] signs and is weak in speech"*
3. *"Develop the learning content for [specify the topic] a 5-year-old boy, that exhibits autistic signs and is weak in speech"*

Guides for Implementing the Techniques

1. **Active Listening:** Pay close attention to the student's responses and ask follow-up questions for clarification.
2. **Non-Judgmental Approach:** Create a safe and supportive environment where students feel comfortable sharing their difficulties without fear of judgment.
3. **Document Responses:** Keep a record of the student's responses to track patterns and inform individualized learning plans.
4. **Collaborative Problem-Solving:** Work together with the student to develop strategies and interventions that address their specific learning needs.
   - ii. **Generating reading materials tailored to the individual reading levels of students with dyslexia.** In addition to the specific preferences identified from the thread prompts above, prompt the LLM to generates lesson content/reources/material uniquely for the the characterized special need.
   - iii. Prompt LLM to provide simplified text alongside more complex versions distinguished by age, level of understanding or the specific learning need, allowing students to choose the level that suits them best.
   - iv. Integrate multisensory learning prompts, such as incorporating text-to-speech features where the LLM reads aloud the text while highlighting the words on the screen.

Practical Considerations: The teacher must ensure that content generated by the LLM is validated by special education experts to maintain accuracy and appropriateness. Also use LLMs to offer interactive feedback and suggestions for improvement based on student responses.

Technical Infrastructure and Support: Where assistive technologies are used, technical infrastructure and support should be provided in the classrooms with devices that support text-to-speech and other assistive technologies. Training for teachers on how to use LLM-generated materials and tools effectively should be prioritized.

Policy and Administrative Considerations: At management and administrative level, there should be policies in place that mandate the use of inclusive technologies and provide the necessary funding and resources. There should also be collaboration with special education departments to create guidelines for using AI tools in inclusive education.

Interactive Science Lessons for Students with Autism Spectrum Disorder (ASD)

Prompting Techniques:

1. Use LLMs to create interactive and visual-rich science lessons that cater to students with ASD.
2. Prompt the LLM to include visual aids, such as diagrams and videos, to explain scientific concepts.
3. Develop social stories and simulations to help students with ASD understand complex social interactions and scientific procedures.

Practical Considerations: First, work with autism specialists to ensure that content and interaction methods are suitable for students with ASD. Secondly, implement LLMs to provide step-by-step guidance and immediate feedback to help students stay on task and understand the material.

Technical Infrastructure and Support: Access to tablets or computers with high-resolution screens and video capabilities should be provided with a support team to assist with the technical aspects of deploying and maintaining LLM-driven tools.

VII. CHALLENGES AND CONSIDERATIONS

Ensuring Student Data Protection

The integration of AI in education necessitates the collection and analysis of vast amounts of student data, raising significant privacy concerns. Protecting this data is paramount to maintain trust and ensure the ethical use of AI technologies.

1. **Data Privacy Regulations and Compliance:** Educational institutions must comply with data privacy laws such as the Family Educational Rights and Privacy Act (FERPA) in the United States and the General Data Protection Regulation (GDPR) in Europe. These laws mandate strict guidelines for data collection, storage, and sharing to protect students' personal information (Mshelia et al., 2022).
2. **Anonymization and Encryption:** To safeguard student data, schools should implement data anonymization techniques, which remove personally identifiable information (PII) from datasets. Encryption should also be used to protect data both at rest and in transit, ensuring that unauthorized individuals cannot access sensitive information (Holmes et al., 2023).

3. **Transparent Data Practices:** Institutions should be transparent about their data practices, informing students and parents about what data is being collected, how it is used, and who has access to it. Consent should be obtained before collecting any data, and stakeholders should be given the option to opt out if they choose (Riedl, 2019).

Ethical Considerations in the Use of AI in Education

The use of AI in education presents several ethical challenges that should be addressed to ensure fair and responsible use of these technologies.

1. **Bias and Fairness** is a common problem with AI systems. AI systems can inadvertently perpetuate biases present in the training data, leading to unfair outcomes. It's crucial to ensure that AI models are trained on diverse and representative datasets and regularly audited for bias. Fairness metrics should be employed to assess and mitigate any discriminatory impacts.
2. **Accountability and Transparency** of AI systems should be prioritized also by educators. Schools and educators should be accountable for the decisions made by AI systems. This involves understanding how these systems work and ensuring that their use is transparent. Clear guidelines should be established for the ethical use of AI, including regular reviews and updates to address any emerging ethical concerns.
3. **Student Autonomy and Consent** should be integrated as a pre-requisite to initiating AI-driven activities. Students should have a say in how AI is used in their education. This includes obtaining informed consent and allowing students to opt out of AI-driven interventions if they prefer. Ensuring that students and parents are educated about the benefits and risks of AI in education is critical to maintaining autonomy and trust.

Strategies for Overcoming Resistance to Change

Adopting AI-driven technologies in education can encounter resistance from educators, parents, and other stakeholders. Strategies to address this resistance and foster acceptance include:

1. **Professional Development and Training:** Comprehensive training programs for teachers should be provided on how to effectively use AI tools can alleviate fears and increase confidence. Continuous professional development ensures educators are well-equipped to integrate AI into their teaching practices.

2. **Engaging Parents and Stakeholders:** Parents and stakeholders should be well informed about the benefits and uses of AI in education helps build trust. Regular updates, workshops, and open forums can address concerns and highlight the positive impacts of AI on student learning.
3. **Demonstrating Success Stories:** Share success stories and case studies where AI has positively impacted student outcomes can help mitigate skepticism and illustrate the potential benefits (Muhammad, 2022; Seo et al., 2024). Sharing case studies and real-world examples of successful AI implementations can illustrate the positive impact of these technologies. Highlighting improvements in student engagement, personalized learning, and educational outcomes can help build support among skeptical stakeholders.

Steps in Ensuring Equity and Access to Technology

To ensure that all students benefit from AI-driven education, particularly those from underserved communities, equitable access to technology is essential.

1. **Bridging the Digital Divide:** Schools should address the digital divide by providing devices and internet access to students who lack these resources. Partnerships with technology companies and community organizations can help supply the necessary hardware and connectivity.
2. **Equitable Resource Allocation:** Resources should be distributed equitably, ensuring that underserved schools receive the support they need to implement AI technologies. This includes funding for technology, training for teachers, and support for infrastructure development.
3. **Inclusive Curriculum Design:** AI-driven curriculum should be designed with input from diverse communities to ensure they meet the needs of all students. This includes considering cultural relevance, language diversity, and accessibility for students with disabilities.

VIII. FUTURE DIRECTIONS AND INNOVATIONS

Under-Explored AI Technology Used in Education

AI technology is transforming education by introducing advanced tools and methodologies that enhance teaching and learning experiences. Some notable advances include that has been under-used, yet holds great potentials are:

1. **Intelligent Tutoring Systems:** AI-powered tutoring systems offer personalized instruction and feedback, simulating one-on-one tutoring sessions. These systems can provide explanations, pose questions, and track student progress to offer tailored support (Nkambou et al., 2010).
2. **Automated Grading and Feedback:** AI algorithms can grade assignments, quizzes, and exams with high accuracy and consistency. These systems not only save time for educators but also provide instant feedback to students, facilitating timely learning improvements(Holmes et al., 2023).
3. **Natural Language Processing (NLP) Tools:** NLP tools enable the development of applications such as chatbots and virtual assistants that can interact with students in natural language. These tools can answer questions, provide resources, and support language learning (Brown et al., 2020).
4. **Virtual and Augmented Reality (VR/AR):** AI-driven VR and AR applications create immersive learning environments that enhance engagement and comprehension. These technologies can simulate real-world scenarios, making learning more interactive and experiential (McLaren et al., 2022).

Potential Future Applications in Education

1. **Emotion AI:** Emotion AI, also known as affective computing, can detect and respond to students' emotional states. By analyzing facial expressions, voice tones, and other cues, AI can adapt the learning environment to better support student well-being and engagement (D'Mello et al., 2012).
2. **Predictive Analytics:** Predictive analytics can forecast student performance and identify at-risk students early. By analyzing historical data and learning patterns, AI can provide insights that help educators intervene proactively to support student success (Siemens & Baker, 2012).
3. **Collaborative Learning Platforms:** AI can facilitate collaborative learning by forming student groups based on complementary skills and learning styles. These platforms can monitor group dynamics and provide feedback to enhance collaboration and peer learning (Holmes et al., 2023).
4. **Blockchain for Credentialing:** AI combined with blockchain technology can offer secure and verifiable credentialing systems. This can help in maintaining and validating educational records and certifications, ensuring academic integrity and portability of credentials (Grech & Camilleri, 2017; Grech et al., 2021).

Long-Term Impact of Inclusive LLM-Driven Curricula on Special Needs Education

LLM can drive impact in in curricula development for special needs in diverse ways:

LLM-driven inclusive curricula can significantly improve accessibility for students with special needs by providing personalized and adaptive learning experiences. AI tools can accommodate diverse learning styles and needs, ensuring that all students have equal opportunities to succeed.

Secondly, By automating routine tasks and providing data-driven insights, AI allows educators to focus more on individualized instruction and student support. This shift can lead to more effective teaching strategies and better outcomes for students with special needs.

Thirdly, AI enables the development of scalable solutions that can be implemented across various educational settings. This scalability ensures that high-quality special education resources are accessible to a larger number of students, including those in underserved areas.

LLM-driven curricula can support continuous learning and skill development beyond traditional K-12 education. By fostering adaptive learning habits and personalized learning pathways, AI can help students with special needs achieve long-term academic and career success (McLaren et al., 2022).

Preparing for Future Challenges and Opportunities

1. **Ethical AI Use:** Ongoing monitoring, transparency, and the involvement of diverse stakeholders is required in ensuring the ethical use of AI in education requires. Developing ethical guidelines and frameworks can help address potential biases and ensure fairness (Binns, 2018).
2. **Data Privacy and Security:** Protecting student data is ensuring student. Schools must implement robust data privacy measures and comply with legal regulations to safeguard sensitive information. This includes educating all stakeholders about data protection practices.
3. **Equity and Access:** To ensure that all students benefit from AI-driven education, schools must address the digital divide by providing necessary resources and support. Policies and initiatives aimed at promoting equitable access to technology are crucial (Smith, 2010).
4. **Ongoing Professional Development:** Continuous professional development for educators is essential to keep up with the evolving AI landscape. Providing training and resources helps educators effectively integrate AI tools into their teaching practices.

IX. CONCLUSION

In conclusion, this chapter has highlighted the transformative potential of LLM-driven curriculum design in creating inclusive educational environments that cater to the diverse needs of all students, including those with special needs like dyslexia, austism, etc. the use of AI aided technologies such as adaptive learning systems, personalized content creation, and real-time progress tracking, educators can provide tailored learning experiences that enhance accessibility and engagement. Understanding and addressing the educational challenges faced by students with special needs is crucial for effective curriculum development. The ethical use of AI, ensuring data privacy, and overcoming resistance to change are essential for successful implementation. As we move forward, it is imperative to embrace the opportunities presented by AI and commit to innovative, inclusive educational practices that empower every student to succeed. Educators, policymakers, and stakeholders should collaborate to adopt these technologies in order to ensure equity and access for all, particularly for underserved communities and students with special needs.

REFERENCES

Binns, R. (2018, January). Fairness in machine learning: Lessons from political philosophy. In Conference on fairness, accountability and transparency (pp. 149-159). PMLR.

Brown, T., Mann, B., Ryder, N., Subbiah, M., Kaplan, J. D., Dhariwal, P., & Amodei, D. (2020). Language models are few-shot learners. *Advances in Neural Information Processing Systems*, *33*, 1877–1901.

CAST. (2018). *The UDL Guidelines*. Retrieved 31/05/2024 from https://udlguidelines.cast.org/

Cheng, M. M., Chuang, H. H., & Smith, T. J. (2022). The role of teacher technology experiences and school technology interactivity in teachers' culturally responsive teaching. *Computers in the Schools*, *39*(2), 163–185.

D'Mello, S., & Graesser, A. (2012). Dynamics of affective states during complex learning. *Learning and Instruction*, *22*(2), 145–157.

Darling-Hammond, L., Flook, L., Cook-Harvey, C., Barron, B., & Osher, D. J. A. d. s. (2020). Implications for educational practice of the science of learning and development. *24*(2), 97-140.

Gay, G. (2018). *Culturally responsive teaching: Theory, research, and practice*. teachers college press.

Grech, A., & Camilleri, A. F. (2017). *Blockchain in education*. Publications Office of the European Union.

Grech, A., Sood, I., & Ariño, L. (2021). Blockchain, self-sovereign identity and digital credentials: Promise versus praxis in education. *Frontiers in Blockchain*, *4*, 616779.

Hallahan, D. E., Kauffman, J. M., & Pullen, P. C. (2013). *Exceptional Learners: An Introduction to Special Education: Pearson New International Edition*. Pearson Higher Ed.

Hehir, T., Grindal, T., Freeman, B., Lamoreau, R., Borquaye, Y., & Burke, S. (2016). *A summary of the evidence on inclusive education*. Abt Associates.

Hidayat, M. T. J. J. L. D. (2024)... *Effectiveness of AI-Based Personalised Reading Platforms in Enhancing Reading Comprehension.*, *11*(1), 115–125.

Holmes, W., Bialik, M., & Fadel, C. (2023). *Artificial intelligence in education*. Globethics Publications.

Kauffman, J. M. (1997). *Characteristics of emotional and behavioral disorders of children and youth*. ERIC.

Khan, S. (2012). *The one world schoolhouse: Education reimagined*. Twelve.

Lord, C., Elsabbagh, M., Baird, G., & Veenstra-Vanderweele, J. J. T. l. (2018). Autism spectrum disorder. *392*(10146), 508-520.

McLaren, B. M., Richey, J. E., Nguyen, H., Hou, X. J. C., & education. (2022). How instructional context can impact learning with educational technology: Lessons from a study with a digital learning game. *178*, 104366.

Meyer, A., Rose, D. H., & Gordon, D. J. (2014). Universal design for learning. *Theory into Practice*.

Miles, H., & Ari, F. J. T. (2022). Implementing Personalized Reading Plans with an E-Book Library to Support First-Grade Students'. *Reading Engagement and Comprehension.*, *66*(6), 914–922.

Mshelia, Y. U., Apeh, S. T., Ikerionwu, C., Blamah, N. V., Erike, A. I., & Elei, F. (2022). A Design-to-Test Technique for Inclusion Coefficients in AI-Driven Systems. 2022 IEEE Nigeria 4th International Conference on Disruptive Technologies for Sustainable Development (NIGERCON)

Muhammad, M. H. (2022). *Culturally Responsive Teaching with High School Teachers Walden University.*

Nkambou, R., Mizoguchi, R., & Bourdeau, J. (2010). *Advances in intelligent tutoring systems* (Vol. 308). Springer Science & Business Media. DOI: 10.1007/978-3-642-14363-2

Rotherham, A. J., & Willingham, D. J. E. l. (2009). 21st century. *67*(1), 16-21.

Seo, K., Yoo, M., Dodson, S., & Jin, S.-H. J. J. o. R. o. T. i. E. (2024). Augmented teachers: K–12 teachers' needs for artificial intelligence's complementary role in personalized learning. 1-18.

Siemens, G., & Baker, R. S. d. (2012). Learning analytics and educational data mining: towards communication and collaboration. Proceedings of the 2nd international conference on learning analytics and knowledge, Smith, D. D. J. (2010). Introduction to special education: Making a difference. DOI: 10.1145/2330601.2330661

Tomlinson, C. A. (2014). *The differentiated classroom: Responding to the needs of all learners*. Ascd.

Chapter 12

Is the AI-Enhanced K-12 Education Technique Compromising Academic Integrity?

Anika Zarin Chowdhury
http://orcid.org/0009-0005-4710-7141
BRAC University, Bangladesh

Saimah Kamal Promee
Stony Brook University, USA

Khadijatul Labannya
http://orcid.org/0009-0008-2117-7661
BRAC University, Bangladesh

Hasanat Fariha Noon
http://orcid.org/0009-0002-6165-5046
BRAC University, Bangladesh

Tanjila Azad
BRAC University, Bangladesh

ABSTRACT

Besides fulfilling its preceding objectives through AI-oriented tutoring techniques, multifarious chatbots have been introduced to assist students with their academic assignments. This qualitative review has been performed to answer whether the integration of artificial intelligence in education is a blessing or a curse for students' academic integrity, as not everyone is a wise user of innovation. The findings state

DOI: 10.4018/979-8-3693-6346-1.ch012

that AI education techniques have both optimistic and pessimistic impacts on students' academic integrity. Whether a student will adopt unfair means entirely depends on cognitive abilities and behavioral components. The future might be jeopardized if such practices persist, which creates doubts and prognostication about the ample scope of malpractices in the educational community. Thus, this chapter aims to make academicians and future researchers aware of the perception and consequences of academic integrity in the presence of AI learning modules.

1. INTRODUCTION

Artificial Intelligence is set to revolutionize our world in more ways than others. Since its inception, it has generated a large volume of interest among academic research and policymakers (Giczy et al., 2021). Artificial Intelligence can broaden the educational content and personalize it to an individual's learning objectives (Bu, 2022). Artificial Intelligence advancements will affect the social relationship and challenge its ethical concerns (Bu, 2022). Even though academic integrity stands to be a very big concern, AI is another big leap for us as students in the modern century. Integration of any new technology into our education, while very exciting, begs the question of academic integrity among students. Educators' efforts to include technology in the classroom can be traced back to the 1920s when Sidney Pressey, inventor of the teaching machine, wanted to push for personalized learning today (Watters, 2023). AI being a relatively new concept many organizations emphasize AI literacy among all staff (Ross, 2024). Since AI-relevant curricula for K-12 students are only now being developed, only a few teachers are prepared for this (Lee & Perret, 2022).

Protecting student's academic integrity is one of the main concerns when it comes to integrating AI into K-12 education techniques. In order for us to analyze whether or not a text is plagiarized we need to understand the relationship between the three states of plagiarization. The intention of the student, how other students behaved with plagiarism, and the solution to this act (Robles et al., 2020). With that in mind, one of the most effective ways of avoiding plagiarism among students is to educate them on what plagiarism truly is, thus helping them to be accountable for their own actions (Cotton et al., 2023). Since AI integration into our education system is a very new concept, there is a clear need for including AI education in policies like the Family Education Rights and Privacy Act (FERPA), Children's Internet Protection Act (CIPA), and the Children's Online Privacy Act (COPPA) as well as student privacy act (Ross, 2024).

Plagiarism, while it is of great concern, not learning how to use Artificial Intelligence, will be impairing our future generation of the vast knowledge and the global leap of technology. As we know the effect of AI is being directly reflected in the job market. Big corporations are harnessing AI to make smarter and personalized products using algorithms, resulting in greater customer satisfaction reports. They are investing in AI as a cheaper alternative to human workforces. AI is already replacing humans in various sectors. Since companies are not shying away from using AI tools to their advantage, not knowing how to integrate this new technology into our education is only putting us at a disadvantage. Leveraging the power of Artificial Intelligence is the only way to the future.

The world is gearing up for creating the opportunities using AI by educating their young students to learn the mechanisms of AI. China's State Council announced its goal of becoming a leader in Artificial Intelligence by including AI curriculum in Primary and Secondary education. They have already published books titled "Fundamentals of Artificial Intelligence". On the other hand, Korea has established six new AI schools to train highly skilled Korean Engineers (Eguchi et al., 2021). Artificial Intelligence is rapidly reducing the workforce and bringing in new ones. So when it comes to applying AI to education, there are three things to focus on. Firstly we have to prepare the student for the inevitable change in the job market, secondly we have to learn how AI functions; and, lastly, we need to train future intellectuals in different fields in the usage of AI (Wong et al., 2020). AI, being a technology with minimal research of its implications, has the potential of being harmful as well as dangerous to young students. The major concern right now is the inadequate amounts of funds for research and resources for the educators to learn about AI (Wong et al., 2020).

In fact, the widespread integration of any technology in the classroom remains an area that is met with a huge amount of resistance (Watters, 2023). While some scholars argue that avoiding chatbots in education will be a way of minimizing plagiarism, if these same emotions were shared at the advent of computers, our education would not have been as advanced. In order for development in this regard, there needs to be a curriculum appropriate for K-12 students integrated into the existing curricula and preparing teachers to offer AI tutorials (Lee & Perret, 2022). Banning the use of chatbots during certain exams and assignments can be a very effective means of making this an even playing field for the students. However, designing a course that helps students understand the advantages of using AI tools for their future can be immensely helpful. Regardless of how the education system currently is, the world will have Artificial Intelligence integration.

2. RESEARCH METHODOLOGY

2.1 Research Questions

RQ 1 Does the availability of chatbots influence students' intrinsic motivation for organic learning and understanding?

The innovation of chatbots signifies a personal virtual 24/7 assistant for students to initiate sustainable gains in their interest in enjoying their studies and paying concentration for a more elongated period. Besides building interest, the chatbot-based dialogue structure opens the door to revisit the formative feedback, establishes a mode of AI-Socialization, delivers independent education opportunities, and eases higher stress levels, which enhances student's intrinsic motivation for education (Yin et al., 2024). The attributes of chatbots are student-friendly because the experience of an engaging interaction lessens the disproportionate burden upon students' cognitive abilities and is more viable for theoretical understanding.

RQ 2 How can the long-term overreliance on AI for quality education impact students' academic and career development opportunities?

The use of Generative AI applications such as chatbots are influential tools that widen the diameter of learning and understanding; however, overreliance on these tools impedes the development of cognitive and interpersonal skills (Bozkurt & Sharma, 2023). Long-term possession of chatbots will jeopardize academic morals and the cultivation of corporate ethics. The pre-stored data do not hold human intelligence to evaluate the real problems using data from credible and regulated human sources. Rather, chatbots represent the answers to the queries in a statistical pattern, which does not eliminate the problem as expected (Giray et al., 2024). From writing assignments to corporate presentations, the overreliance will leave the students and future employees with poor skills, knowledge, and ability to unravel real-world problems, referencing reliable and valid sources.

RQ 3 Instead of compromising academic integrity, how can AI be used to enhance it?

Artificial Intelligence in Education (AIED) of K12 is supposed to be a revolutionary move to diminish the illiteracy rate, boost motivation to comprehend, vocabulary skill growth, education interpretation, and personalized and adaptive learning environments through the ease of access and customization (Gökçearslan et al., 2024). Besides having a plethora of potential to enhance the education module, it is also enhancing academic integrity through the creation of iThenticate, Turnitin, PlagAware, PlagScan, Unicheck, Urkund, and Viper to detect AI and plagiarized submissions of the students by checking it against millions of article databases (Foltýnek et al., 2020). It delivers similarity reports as well as grammatical errors that allow students to improve their writing and be aware of drawing a line between chatbots and integrity. Additionally, AI has introduced automated citation evaluation software by Large Language Models (LLM), which reduces hours of manual labor for reference to the original work (Zhang et al., 2024). Hence, AIED cannot wholly be remarked as a mode of compromising academic integrity.

RQ 4 How can the teachers of K-12 be empowered to detect plagiarism in Education 4.0?

As students are subject to numerous remote assignments, especially after the hit of COVID-19, the requirement to advance and update online proctoring and software to detect AI writing and plagiarism is an alarming need of the hour. The need led teachers to adopt anti-plagiarism tools to assess and grade students' assignments (Khalil & Er, 2023). These are the most used plagiarism detection software by academic institutions globally. Furthermore, the need for workshops or training and development for teachers of K-12 specializing in similarity detection methods, text-matching systems, and plagiarism policies, is vital to a teacher of Education 4.0 (Foltýnek et al., 2020). Committing plagiarism means a violation of academic integrity, and teachers need to have proper acknowledgment algorithms and rules and regulations to guide students in K-12 actively.

2.2 Article Selection and Study Procedure

To compose this book chapter, the authors opted for a Systematic Literature Review (SLR). In this method, to answer the research questions, pertinent publications and documents are explored, accumulated, synthesized, examined, and recapitulated (Mengist et al., 2020), as per the research criteria. Firstly, the authors searched the mentioned electronic databases using the keywords to gather relevant journal articles and research papers ranging from the year 2020 to 2024. Secondly, to address the relationship between artificial intelligence in education and academic integrity, they collected five articles from each year's publications, the results of which were obtained from primary data collection. This SLR contains a total of twenty-five articles that evaluate the purpose over the time of the integration.

2.3 Article Sources

Table 1. Sources of electronic database for systematic literature review

Sources	Online Access
ScienceDirect	https://www.sciencedirect.com/
Springer	https://www.springer.com/in
ResearchGate	https://www.researchgate.net/
BMC	https://www.biomedcentral.com/
Core	https://core.ac.uk/
IEEE Xplore	https://ieeexplore.ieee.org/Xplore/home.jsp
DOAJ	https://doaj.org/

2.4 Data Collection

Table 2. 25 articles, and a systematic literature review is conducted to evaluate whether AI-enhanced K-12 education techniques degrade a student's academic integrity

Sl no.	Authors & Year	Objectives	Methodology	Findings
1	Gustilo et al. (2024)	To identify to what extent the integration of ChatGPT, DWAs, MTs, and APTs in education triggers the current gap in academic integrity guidelines.	Conducted empirical study through snowball sampling among 100 educators and the Technology Acceptance Model (TAM) for the breakdown of the responses.	The use of GenAI contributed to maximizing academic productivity and enhanced computer self-efficacy for the learners but adequately expressed the need to implement modernized administrative and academic guidelines and comprehensive digital teacher empowerment, which could have reduced the percentage of degradation of academic integrity for essay-style assignments.
2	Lee et al. (2024)	To estimate the impact of generative AI chatbot technologies on high school students' academic integrity after its launch.	Conducted 20- to 40-minute surveys anonymously on students of three different types of high schools before and after the integration of GenAI to evaluate the differences in results for the cheating scale, multiple factors of academic integrity, and support from academicians to encourage deep learning offline.	Discovered a partial shift in behavioral patterns in minimal students used to extract resources from online sources before and after the launch and utilized chatbots and GenAI to edit papers.
3	Bouteraa et al. (2024)	To recognize the role of students' integrity in confining ChatGPT adoption behavior.	The Unified Theory of Acceptance and Use of Technology (UTAUT) and the Social Cognitive Theory (SCT) used to analyze the acquired 921 valid academic peer responses from ASEAN member states through a web-based survey to conduct cross-sectional research on aligning the ChatGPT usage model.	An esteemed tool for AI-based academic assistance for students with more elevated integrity in their assignments and studies, significant portions displayed greater self-efficacy towards ChatGPT adoption, whereas students of lower integrity opt for ChatGPT as a means of attaining an unsportsmanlike academic benefit.
4	Choi et al. (2024)	To detect the ethical awareness and attitude towards artificial intelligence being integrated into the education of the students.	Used the ADDIE model for the preparation of the pre-test and post-test questionnaire, and circulated among a group of 17 middle school students, before and after the integration of AI and ethical programs with the assistance of 10 domain experts for the quantitative research.	Students showed keen interest in chatbots being used as educational tools and shared concerns about data privacy being violated and stored in deep fakes with ethical dilemmas in place.
5	Gruenhagen et al. (2024)	To address the potential threats to academic integrity and the extent to which the students' different psychosocial factors are compromised.	Developed an online questionnaire using Qualtrics for a supplementary qualitative analysis and obtained 337 usable responses to assess the demographic and psychosocial factors of the students.	Students use GenAI and chatbots for academic assessment and are exposed to poor academic integrity and plagiarized content through idea generation.

continued on following page

Table 2. Continued

Sl no.	Authors & Year	Objectives	Methodology	Findings
6	Dakakni and Safa (2023)	To investigate the extent to which students were likely to resort to AI technologies for educational purposes, its reasons and their level of awareness about the correlation between ethics, education, and the usage of artificial intelligence.	Implemented descriptive, qualitative, and mixed research methods, firstly consisting of an online survey of 46 students, and then selected 6 teachers and 6 students for semi-structured focus group interviews.	Students use chatbots such as Bard, Quilbot, Grammarly, and ChatGPT for idea generation, and academic assistance in writing papers for the maintenance of good grades, breaching academic integrity, and cultivating the practice of the usage of plagiarized content.
7	Nashwan et al. (2023)	To figure out the driving tool for the adoption of GenAI in academics, which is threatening the position of academic integrity.	Retrieved 702 responses through online survey questionnaires from academicians and assessed the data using PLS-SEM, a variance-based modeling approach for quantitative research.	GenAI is treated as a time-saving tool to be used and integrated into academics at the cost of losing academic integrity and being influenced by peers to pursue it further.
8	Lai et al. (2023)	To scrutinize the association between intrinsic incentives and chatbots for designing an engaged learning environment.	Analyzed the reliability and validity of 473 students using analysis of moment structure (AMOS) and SmartPLS 3.0. (PLS) methods to conduct a quantitative cross-sectional survey-based study.	Students treat chatbots with higher interest for their lucrative features such as timeliness, user-friendliness, and customizability, letting students enjoy unexhausted interactive behavior to attend to their academic queries.
9	Algerafi et al. (2023)	To evaluate students' volition to embrace AI-based robots for academic pursuits.	Conducted pilot study with 60 students, evaluated data using Cronbach's alpha (CA), Composite Reliability (CR), and Average Variance Extracted (AVE) methods, and established a relationship between the responses, objectives, and TAM (Technology Acceptance Model) model.	Students are positively inclined to use AI-based robots for educational purposes, possessing no hints of fear or privacy hindrance issues, and are sufficiently equipped to operate the resources.
10	Fegade et al. (2023)	To explore the potential scope and challenges of the current application of GenAI in education.	Descriptive and quantitative methods were used to assess the data obtained from surveying 100 students and 100 teachers.	GenAI, such as ChatGPT, BERT, Claude, Meta, OpenAI, Google, Facebook, and Anthropic, allows academicians to experience transformative learning where significant attention and modification are required on the ethical components.
11	Novick et al. (2022)	To figure out to what extent the shift during the pandemic affected students' academic integrity and stress levels.	Surveyed 500 students and tested the data using three methods: the Chi-Square and Fisher's Exact Test, the Wilcoxon SignedRank Test, and the Mann-Whitney U tests.	Changes in question patterns acted as an accelerator to reduce online academic misconduct, and in-person learning was preferred over online learning.

continued on following page

Table 2. Continued

Sl no.	Authors & Year	Objectives	Methodology	Findings
12	Hossain (2022)	To measure the perception of students regarding academic integrity literacy.	Performed a survey on students using a Google Form that contained open-ended, close-ended, and 5-point Likert scale questions to determine the percentage of Academic Integrity Literacy awareness in high school and middle school through maintaining authenticity and authorship to refrain from plagiarism; conducted structured interviews with teachers, and the total sample size is 431.	Students barely obtained an in-depth understanding of Academic Integrity Literacy in K12, and this lack drove them to the habit of continued disregard for authenticity acknowledgment.
13	Sanusi et al. (2022)	To pinpoint the demanded competencies to implement an artificial intelligence literacy technique according to the academic institution's structural ability for K12.	Analyzed 605 K-12 student responses using WarpLS software to perform structural equation modeling research to prove the hypotheses.	The integration of artificial intelligence with academic study outlines has uplifted K12 students' cognitive and self-learning competence.
14	Hossain et al. (2022)	To investigate the contemporary situation of academic integrity guidelines and pedagogy in K-12 schools	Received a total of 559 responses from 81 countries by circulating Google Forms on social media platforms and, after filtering, used 222 responses for data analysis.	K-12 schools in developing countries have an unsatisfactory record on academic integrity education and its policy for a number of reasons, such as lack of support from the administrative authority, insufficient information literacy among teachers, and many more that are capping the possibilities for student flourishment.
15	Johansen et al. (2022)	To examine the issues of academic integrity of the K12 students that could be fixed using training.	Utilizing descriptive statistics and Spearman's correlation coefficient, 1654 participants from 51 institutions participated; data was collected through an online survey and analyzed.	Students have an insufficiency of knowledge and poor understanding, forming misconceptions regarding academic integrity and its aspects because of the teacher-delivered training has inferior influences on the students for undetermined reasons.
16	Alessio and Messinger (2021)	To evaluate how much academic integrity is impacted during the transition from offline to online.	150 students and 70 teachers participated in an online survey, the data of which was analyzed using Wilcoxon rank-sum tests.	The effectiveness of proctoring software is the sole way to tackle academic misconduct, as open-ended questions trigger misfortune, and teachers are concerned with data privacy.
17	Salvadore and Buck (2021)	To figure out the condition of novice writers when it comes to academic research and understand what plagiarism is.	18 students from diverse cultures connected the dots of the notion of information ownership through filtering, skimming, synthesizing, and incorporating references relevant to their research questions.	Students' core visions regarding plagiarism are changeable depending on how they craft the research methodology and expand or limit their boundaries.
18	Lai (2021)	To analyze how pleased students are with AI-assisted learning systems.	64 students and academicians participated in a descriptive form of survey.	Students found GenAI applications to be an AI-social tool that accelerates the joy of flexibility but degrades the notion of critical learning and in-person experience.

continued on following page

Table 2. Continued

Sl no.	Authors & Year	Objectives	Methodology	Findings
19	Stephens et al. (2021)	To examine the influences of the compulsory academic integrity course on students.	Accumulated data of 1,388 responses of the students performing the survey twice, in the years 2012 and 2017, for data analysis using methods such as confirmatory factor analysis (CFA), Cronbach's alphas, Pearson correlation coefficients feeding data in SPSS version 25 and its AMOS program.	Teaching academic integrity courses as part of their education promotes changes in their perception and academic behavior toward integrity.
20	Forgas et al. (2021)	To study the volume of requests made in the search engine data for academic dishonesty in the online exams.	From 2016 to 2020, data gathered from organic Internet search engines, such as Keyboard Magic Tool, Google search engine, and Google Trends, and the data fed to SPSS version 20.	The pandemic flattened the rate of cheating on the internet when taking online exams, and this trend puts students at risk of committing fraud in the future as well.
21	Birks et al. (2020)	To detect the rapid mutation of plagiarism software and downgrading of the academic integrity of the academicians.	Provided 60-minute interviews with 27 students and academicians from three different countries.	Although academic integrity policies and management vary among institutions, common issues include a lack of maturity, personal integrity, and the mass availability of paraphrasing tools to students.
22	Paullet and Morris (2020)	To understand how academic assignments are completed, it is necessary to study the gap between teacher and student that leads to academic dishonesty.	532 students and academicians partook in a survey for an exploratory study.	The pandemic led students to opt for external resources during exams and assignment completion, which they regarded as ethical; this was not the case; many used GenAI applications for brainstorming.
23	Jian et al. (2020)	To identify personal attitudes, consciousness, and circumstantial consequences of college students towards performing academic misconduct.	Utilizing a content-based exploratory approach to scrutinize 120 responses from college students through interviews.	Performance anxiety is liable for cheating in their academic practises.
24	Vučković et al. (2020)	To examine whether students are competent in acknowledging ethical wrongdoing, comprehending the potential reasons for their involvement, and the manner in which they resolve their conditions.	Used qualitative and quantitative data and 162 academicians partook to be the sample for the study.	Factors such as stringent deadlines, gaps in communication, flawed learning strategies, inferior understanding of AI literacy, an insufficiency of teachers' pedagogical dexterities, ghostwriting, etc., are leading students to cheat, plagiarize, and suffer severe punishment to attain better scores.
25	Perkins et al. (2020)	To address how to enhance the composition of academic essay benchmarks of students, forces, and methods to lessen ethical misconduct.	Documented 12,937 cases of academic misconduct and studied through Viva-voce to detect the established pattern of contract cheating and plagiarism.	Quality of work drew the line between organic submission and contract cheating, but the integration of English writing courses contributed to reducing the ethical misconduct among the students.

2.5 Results

Addressing the factors liable for the arousal of the question of whether the integration of Artificial Intelligence in Education breaches the academic integrity of the students:

1. **Classification of Students:** Students of K-12 believe exemplary grades bring success and that maintaining exemplary grades is a must. Those who are good students with excellent cognitive skills and analytical thinking abilities most of the time do not prefer chatbots for learning assistance. They rarely use chatbots to generate ideas and revisit them whenever needed initially. These types of students strive to mitigate the hunger for knowledge and further learning, which facilitates the use of chatbots by maintaining a balance between AI and academic integrity. However, the average, weak, and introverted students generally use chatbots frequently for good grades and lack the confidence to interact with teachers.
2. **Assignment Pattern:** In assignments, when students are required to compose an essay, they opt for using chatbots for cognitive offloading and time management. Some students only use AI tools for brainstorming, and some fully copy the feedback provided by the chatbots word-to-word without verifying the sources.
3. **Deficit AI-Literacy:** Many students, while submitting plagiarized content, are unaware of the depth of AI tools and innovations that are available to assess their papers and reveal the truth of their work. Furthermore, as manual referencing takes a lengthy time, there are available reference generator templates to mark the authenticity of the work more accurately and precisely with multiple options. Sadly, many students have improper knowledge regarding the usage.
4. **Academic Integrity Courses:** In many institutions, the addition of specialized classes allows students to comprehend proper author citation, the pros and cons of citation, upholding higher academic integrity, and acknowledgment of when to draw a line between the usage of chatbots and one's own abilities. This course changes the perception of wholly relying on chatbots for answers and how such misconduct, plagiarised content, and cheating will hamper their corporate life. Teaching students the GenAI policies during their K-12 period minimizes students' performance anxiety in their higher education.
5. **Obsolete Teaching Practices and Academic Policies:** As AI is constantly updating and upgrading, the academic policies and teaching practises executed before the pandemic are obsolete and cannot be used after the pandemic. During and after the hit of the pandemic, multiple researchers vigorously stated that the usage of chatbots by students has grown. Strict policies and modernized academic policies with a minimal acceptance rate of plagiarism need to be implemented.

Further, interaction with the teachers beyond the class duration is required so that all types of students are privileged to get their questions answered.

In overview, the behavioral factors defining whether to be dependent on chatbots or not, or to use them with good intention or not, depends on the students. This intention is not steady and cannot be measured at once because of the ability of someone to either flourish or decline.

3. DISCUSSION

3.1 Recognizing Education 4.0 as a Non-Threatening Tool for Academic Integrity

Education has also been a subject that has been shaped and influenced by technological developments, and Education 4.0, which incorporates the use of artificial intelligence (AI), is included. Integrating techniques supported by artificial intelligence into K-12 education raises concerns about academic integrity. Nevertheless, these issues can be resolved if Education 4.0 is acknowledged as education for sustainable development and is not a threat but a positive factor reflecting academic integrity. This section focuses on the following aspects: the importance of different AI tools like chatbots or other AI tools that facilitate the students in performing their work smoothly incorporating K-12 Education. In addition, how AI can be non-threatening to the students who perform their work with the assistance of the different AIs used and the distinct ways in which these technologies may be employed to undermine the clave and academic honesty.

3.1.1 The Importance of AI in K-12 Education

In this fast-paced world, there can be several problems associated with traditional education, one prominent one being overcrowded classes, implying low levels of attention to every learner. While chatting still has its drawbacks as a system of education, the constant development of artificial intelligence lets us consider AI-based chatbots as one of the solutions that can help avoid some of these problems. Furthermore, with recent technological advancements, many AI tools have been adopted in K-12 education to aid different learning processes.

Most organizations are embracing AI-powered chatbots by realizing their significance in today's world. The incorporation of chatbots and virtual assistants in learning environments can also have a positive effect on support services, access, and overall. This means that students from less privileged backgrounds would be more beneficial to the AI chatbot in boosting their interactions and launching effective learning. Furthermore, the use of AI in the areas of learning can see intelligent chatbots on students' work, identifying the shortcomings and ways to address them, as well as guiding students in their learning process and enhancing comprehension and mastery of content. (Labadze et al., 2023). As pointed out by Kasneci et al. (2023), interacting with ChatGPT compared to its previous versions can improve students' interest and motivation in the learning process, thus making it easier and more enjoyable. Besides that, it can help to improve writing skills by providing recommendations for syntactic and grammatical changes and contribute to the development of problem-solving skills giving the step-by-step approach (Labadze et al., 2023). Similarly, like ChatGPT, other chatbots like Microsoft Pilot and Google Bard assist students in their academics and help to enhance their creative thinking.

In addition, machine translators like Google Translate and digital writing assistants (DWAs) like Grammarly help students to be more confident with their work as they help to enhance the quality of the work as well as add mechanics and framework for their work. It is also seen that tools like Grammarly can aid students in learning grammar, and Google Translate assists them in translating any language whenever required (Gustilo et al., 2024).

3.1.2 The Non-Threatening Aspect of Education 4.0

The integrated implementation of 4.0 technologies into K-12 education is fine with integrity in as much as it presents a chance to enhance it. When ethical considerations are incorporated into artificial intelligence systems, learners are exposed to a subject matter and modeled ethical behavior. Since AI is expected to be a teacher for students, such tools are expected to improve student performance, facilitate the application and achievement of learning goals and outcomes, and offer personalized, effective, and fast learning using applications and mobile gadgets, especially in the language classroom where students can practice learning required skills as per learning objectives and course requirements (Dakakni & Safa, 2023).

Furthermore, providing students with academic integrity courses helps to mitigate the problem of less academic integrity to some extent as students get to understand how plagiarism or dishonesty might affect them in the long run (Stephens et al., 2021). AI assists in the education process of the students by taking the students' characteristics, processing them, identifying the areas where they excel or lack knowledge, and then teaching the lessons based on the student's potential and requirements. The AI learning systems enable students to study at their own pace, get feedback and help, and direction in learning without input from their teachers (Dakakni & Safa, 2023).

Moreover, it is possible to create an AI system for tracing such situations that may be associated with cheating. It can be useful in tracking some patterns of student submissions; for example, if a student is usually low performing but in a particular task they perform better than ever, which might indicate cheating with the help of AI. Thus, when students are learning these issues they will understand that academic integrity and ethical issues play an important part in them to excel in their future endeavors (Cándida et al., 2023).

3.2 Recognizing Education 4.0 as a Threatening Tool for Academic Integrity

Artificial Intelligence (Al) is a man-made predictor that enriches human dynamism economically, socially, and personally. Undoubtedly, artificial intelligence is increasingly compelling and more satisfying in analyzing large amounts of data, whereas humans are better performers with incomplete data sets. However, the actions of artificial intelligence (AI) can also be seen as a powerful tool as well as a threatening tool in academic integrity. It has gradually become more preventive and powerful in various fields, including technology, education, and the health sector.

A prominent challenge in contemporary education is the over-reliance on artificial intelligence (AI) technologies, such as ChatGPT, DWAs, MTs, and other similar tools, to manage tasks and generate ideas (Gustilo et al., 2024). In Gustilo's survey, he analyzes this phenomenon by reviewing the shortcomings of academic guidelines regarding integrity in the context of incorporating AI tools into educational settings. His research has shown that the lack of specific guidance has led to widespread misuse of this technology in executive and idea generation. Again, artificial intelligence-drives threats, such as sophisticated phishing attacks, may increase dramatically. For example, Gruenhagen et al. (2024) address artificial intelligence as a potential threat to academic integrity. His research has revealed various psychosocial factors that influence students' behavior, with those using GenAI and chatbots for academic assessment being more at risk of engaging in unethical practices, including plagiarism.

Similarly, Buteraa et al. (2024) examined the relationship between student integrity and the adoption of AI technology and concluded that students showing off higher integrity are more inclined to engage responsibly with AI. Conversely, those who exhibit low levels of integrity are more susceptible to exploiting AI for academic benefit. This correlation emphasizes the importance of promoting integrity as a means of reducing potential risks associated with the use of AI (Bouteraa et al., 2024). Multiple researchers say that generative AI (GenAI) and chatbots hold significant potential for enhancing educational outcomes, but they also present significant risks to academic integrity.

In particular, these technologies can lead to unethical practices such as plagiarism and other forms of academic dishonesty, especially when students misuse these tools or lack sufficient awareness of the ethical implications. Sanusi et al. (2022) examined the skills needed for AI literacy in K-12 education and found that AI integration enhances cognitive and self-learning capabilities, much like the benefits of deep learning and automation in AI-generated content. For example, automation has facilitated deep learning, self-employment, and specialization modes of AI by providing application solutions, at low cost with high-efficiency rates and AI-generated learning content for students (Giuggioli & Pellegrini, 2022). These AI-driven advances support specialized learning solutions, offer cost-effective methods, and increase efficiency in educational settings (Sanusi et al., 2022; Giugioli & Pellegrini, 2022).

Meanwhile, Stephens et al. (2021) compare students' and teachers' perceptions of academic integrity, revealing that students are less aware of the ethical implications of AI use than teachers, further emphasizing the cognitive benefits of AI integration as well as the need for ethical considerations (Stephens et al., 2021). Currently, Hossain focuses on the role of school administration in promoting copyright literacy and academic integrity within K12 education. Through a mixed-methods study of 569 responses in 81 countries, they emphasized the importance of collaboration between administrative authority and teachers in promoting the ethical use of digital resources (Hossain et al., 2022). Meanwhile, Choi et al. (2024) explored the ethical awareness of AI in the education of students. Their study found that while students are enthusiastic about using chatbots, they express concerns about data privacy and ethical dilemmas, highlighting the need for technological integration as well as ethical education (Choi et al., 2024).

Additionally, Stephens et al. (2021) examined the effects of an academic integrity course on students. Their research concluded that such courses significantly improve students' understanding and behavior regarding academic integrity, suggesting the need for widespread implementation. The issue of academic dishonesty during online exams, particularly exacerbated by the pandemic, was highlighted by Forgas et al. (2021), who studied the volume of Internet searches related to academic misconduct. Their findings call for ongoing vigilance and education to prevent future instances of dishonesty. The difficulties presented by the swift advancement of plagiarism detection software were examined by Burks et al. (2020). They found that while these tools are essential to combating plagiarism, they are often outpaced by student creativity in finding ways to bypass them, indicating the need for constant updates and innovation in these technologies.

Artificial Intelligence (AI) presents significant challenges in the context of Education 4.0, influenced by various factors across different environments. AI, as a fully realized concept, refers to advanced systems capable of processing extensive datasets and information derived from their environment, subsequently making liberated decisions based on this analysis. It is important to note that when AI executes a decision, the process is entirely handled by the system, rather than human intervention, thereby reducing the scope for human interaction. In contrast, human decision-making involves numerous emotional factors, such as sensitivity, humility, and emotional state, all of which can directly or indirectly influence outcomes. The introduction of AI into this framework often renders these emotional considerations irrelevant.

3.3 Promoting Academic Integrity and Ethical Use

3.3.1 Integrative Learning Models and AI Ethics Programs

Teachers can help students to enhance their critical thinking and problem-solving abilities using a variety of pedagogical strategies. These strategies focus on active learning models that promote engagement and reflection. The study introduces the Integrative Collaborative Problem-solving (ICoPS) model, designed to enhance students' critical thinking by combining Problem-Based Learning, the Jigsaw method, and the TPACK framework. The ICoPS model features six steps: tackling real-world problems, forming expert groups, sharing knowledge, deeper investigation, presenting solutions, and evaluating outcomes. It is practical for classroom use and boosts collaboration and communication. (Sujatmika et al., 2024).

A study developed an AI ethics education program for middle school students, focusing on AI literacy, critical thinking, and problem-solving within AI ethics. This program was validated by ten domain experts, and was tested on 17 students using a pre-test and post-test design. Results showed a significant improvement in students' ethical awareness and attitudes towards AI across all measured areas after completing the program. The paired-sample t-test analysis confirmed that the program effectively enhanced students' understanding of AI ethics and positively influenced their perceptions of AI technology. These findings highlight the importance of integrating AI ethics education into the curriculum, as it plays a crucial role in preparing young learners for a future where AI is increasingly influential (Choi et al., 2024).

3.3.2 Effective Approaches for Integrating AI in Education and Upholding Academic Integrity

Teachers need clear and practical training to understand the ethical challenges and learn how to spot and prevent dishonesty with AI. This training helps them deal with the new problems AI brings to the classroom, so they can keep students honest while still using technology to make learning better. Teachers must understand how artificial intelligence (AI) tools might support or contradict academic integrity. Many of them believe that AI encourages dishonesty, which can impede student's ability to gain new skills. In order to promote a critical understanding of AI's role in academic integrity, training should include talks on the ethical implications of its usage in education (Mohammadkarimi, 2023). Teachers should be trained to recognize artificial intelligence (AI)-generated work using technology and plagiarism detection techniques. This entails being aware of the tools' limits and learning how to recognize real student work(Cotton et al., 2023).

Teachers can supervise the use of AI while encouraging ethical writing practices by including the “CARE” framework, which stands for critical, authorial, rhetorical, and educational. The CARE framework promotes the ethical use of AI by emphasizing four main areas: Authorial Responsibility, which fosters pride and ownership in students' work to deter dishonest practices; Rhetorical Awareness, which teaches students to consider context, audience, and purpose in their writing; Critical Engagement, which involves students thoughtfully analyzing AI tools and their ethical implications; and Educational Focus, which establishes a supportive learning environment that prioritizes growth over punishment. When combined, these components lessen the need for monitoring and encourage the ethical and responsible application of AI in the classroom (Pflugfelder & Reeves, 2024). Teachers should also use restorative justice techniques that focus on building strong relationships and encouraging students to take responsibility for their academic honesty. Practical methods, like discussing AI in class and designing assignments that ethically integrate AI, can boost students' understanding and engagement (Pawlychka, 2023).

To tackle the challenges of AI in schools, it is important to create strong policies that support academic honesty. Schools need clear rules that explain how AI should be used ethically and what happens if it is misused. Working together, policymakers, educators, and students can build a culture of integrity that keeps up with new technologies. (Akkaş et al., 2024). Schools can use AI software to check student work for plagiarism or content generated by AI. These tools compare student submissions with a huge database of existing work to spot similarities and possible cheating. This helps teachers detect dishonesty and support them in maintaining academic integrity. AI can also monitor students during exams, tracking things like typing speed or how responses flow to catch unusual behavior that might suggest cheating. These AI systems can give teachers helpful insights into student work, making it easier to identify dishonest practices. AI can create personalized learning experiences that encourage original thinking and reduce the urge to cheat. AI can also guide schools in creating policies for using AI tools properly in academic work. By analyzing data on cheating trends, schools can develop training programs for students and teachers to emphasize the importance of honesty and using technology responsibly. However, it is important to ensure that these policies do not become too strict, as they might discourage students from using AI in positive ways, which could limit innovation in learning (Kumar et al., 2024).

4. CONCLUSION AND RECOMMENDATIONS

While AI facilitates increased student engagement, collaboration, asynchronous communication, and real-time feedback, it also raises several concerns in regard to academic integrity and plagiarism (Cotton et al., 2023). There is a major need for AI plagiarism detection software, as well as including a few manual techniques to identify the usage of AI. AI integration into our education system is a very new concept. As a result, there is a clear need for including AI education in policies like the Family Education Rights and Privacy Act (FERPA), the Children's Internet Protection Act (CIPA), and the Children's Online Privacy Act (COPPA) as well as student privacy act (Ross, 2024). Since there has been little research on the implications of AI, it is possible that it could negatively impact young kids. The main issue at hand is the lack of resources and funding for educators to learn about artificial intelligence (Wong et al., 2020).

While the future of AI is yet to be decided, extensive research is important to protect K-12 students' privacy while assuring academic integrity. Disregarding AI from the K-12 curriculum could prove to be ineffective since the integration of AI to our day to day livelihood is rapid as of recently. Without curating a curriculum that facilitates the knowledge regarding harnessing the power of AI will only leave the young generation in the dark and incapacitate them from growing in the new age of technology.

In conclusion, when artificial intelligence (AI) is included in K–12 education, it presents both opportunities and challenges concerning academic integrity. While AI tools, like chatbots, can enhance learning and assist students in managing their workload, they also pose significant risks to academic integrity, particularly among students who lack AI literacy or face pressure to achieve high grades. The varying degrees of AI dependence among students, influenced by cognitive skills, confidence, and academic support, highlight the need for tailored educational strategies. Specialized courses on academic integrity, including the ethical use of AI, can mitigate these risks by equipping students with the knowledge and skills to balance AI assistance with personal effort. Moreover, outdated teaching practices and academic policies must be revised to keep pace with the evolving AI landscape. Ensuring a consistent focus on ethical behavior, combined with updated educational frameworks, can help maintain academic integrity while leveraging AI's potential in education. By encouraging ethical learning and growth, this method creates a responsible, AI-integrated learning environment that prepares students for upcoming problems in both academics and their professional lives.

REFERENCES

Akkaş, Ö. M., Tosun, C., & Gökçearslan, Ş. (2024). Artificial intelligence (AI) and cheating. In Advances in educational technologies and instructional design book series (pp. 182–199). DOI: 10.4018/979-8-3693-1351-0.ch009

Alessio, H. M., & Messinger, J. D. (2021). Faculty and Student Perceptions of academic Integrity in Technology-Assisted Learning and Testing. *Frontiers in Education*, *6*, 629220. Advance online publication. DOI: 10.3389/feduc.2021.629220

Algerafi, M. M., Zhou, Y., Alfadda, H., & Wijaya, T. T. (2023). Understanding the factors influencing higher education students' intention to adopt Artificial Intelligence-Based robots. *IEEE Access : Practical Innovations, Open Solutions*, *11*, 99752–99764. DOI: 10.1109/ACCESS.2023.3314499

Birks, M., Mills, J., Allen, S., & Tee, S. (2020). Managing the mutations: Academic misconduct in Australia, New Zealand and the UK. *International Journal for Educational Integrity*, *16*(1), 6. Advance online publication. DOI: 10.1007/s40979-020-00055-5

Bouteraa, M., Bin-Nashwan, S. A., Al-Daihani, M., Dirie, K. A., Benlahcene, A., Sadallah, M., Zaki, H. O., Lada, S., Ansar, R., Fook, L. M., & Chekima, B. (2024). Understanding the diffusion of AI-generative (ChatGPT) in higher education: Does students' integrity matter? *Computers in Human Behavior Reports*, *14*, 100402. DOI: 10.1016/j.chbr.2024.100402

Bozkurt, A., & Sharma, R. C. (2023). Challenging the status quo and exploring the new boundaries in the age of algorithms: Reimagining the role of generative AI in distance education and online learning. Zenodo *(CERN European Organization for Nuclear Research)*. DOI: 10.5281/zenodo.7755273

Bu, Q. (2022). Ethical Risks in Integrating Artificial Intelligence into Education and Potential Countermeasures. *Science Insights*, *41*(1), 561–566. DOI: 10.15354/si.22.re067

Cándida, M., Chávez, R., Troya, A. L., Santos, R., Rosa, C., Cordero, Z., Marisol, L., Orellana, G., & Pongo, O. E. (2023). Impact of Artificial intelligence in Promoting Academic Integrity in Education: a Systematic review. *Researchgate, 2197–5523*. https://www.researchgate.net/publication/370894108_Impact_of_Artificial_Intelligence_in_Promoting_Academic_Integrity_in_Education_A_Systematic_review

Choi, J., Yang, E., & Goo, E. (2024). The Effects of an Ethics Education Program on Artificial Intelligence among Middle School Students: Analysis of Perception and Attitude Changes. *Applied Sciences (Basel, Switzerland)*, *14*(4), 1588. DOI: 10.3390/app14041588

Cotton, D. R. E., Cotton, P. A., & Shipway, J. R. (2023). Chatting and cheating: Ensuring academic integrity in the era of ChatGPT. *Innovations in Education and Teaching International*, •••, 1–12. DOI: 10.1080/14703297.2023.2190148

Dakakni, D., & Safa, N. (2023). Artificial intelligence in the L2 classroom: Implications and challenges on ethics and equity in higher education: A 21st century Pandora's box. *Computers and Education Artificial Intelligence*, *5*, 100179. DOI: 10.1016/j.caeai.2023.100179

Eguchi, A., Okada, H., & Muto, Y. (2021). Contextualizing AI education for K-12 students to enhance their learning of AI literacy through culturally responsive approaches. *KI - Künstliche Intelligenz, 35*(2), 153–161. DOI: 10.1007/s13218-021-00737-3

Fegade, A., Raut, R., Deshpande, A., Mittal, A., Kaul, N., & Khanna, V. (2023). Unleashing the power of generative artificial intelligence: exploring its boundless potential and overcoming challenges in academic environments. *2023 6th International Conference on Contemporary Computing and Informatics (IC3I)*. DOI: 10.1109/IC3I59117.2023.10397917

Foltýnek, T., Dlabolová, D., Anohina-Naumeca, A., Razı, S., Kravjar, J., Kamzola, L., Guerrero-Dib, J., Çelik, Ö., & Weber-Wulff, D. (2020). Testing of support tools for plagiarism detection. *International Journal of Educational Technology in Higher Education*, *17*(1), 46. Advance online publication. DOI: 10.1186/s41239-020-00192-4

Forgas, R., Lancaster, T., Calvo-Sastre, A., & Sureda-Negre, J. (2021). Exam cheating and academic integrity breaches during the COVID-19 pandemic: An analysis of internet search activity in Spain. *Heliyon*, *7*(10), e08233. DOI: 10.1016/j.heliyon.2021.e08233 PMID: 34722942

Giray, L., Jacob, J., & Gumalin, D. L. (2024). Strengths, weaknesses, opportunities, and threats of using ChatGPT in scientific research. *International Journal of Technology in Education*, *7*(1), 40–58. DOI: 10.46328/ijte.618

Giuggioli, G., & Pellegrini, M. M. (2022). Artificial intelligence as an enabler for entrepreneurs: A systematic literature review and an agenda for future research. *International Journal of Entrepreneurial Behaviour & Research*, *29*(4), 816–837. DOI: 10.1108/IJEBR-05-2021-0426

Gökçearslan, Ş., Tosun, C., & Erdemir, Z. G. (2024). Benefits, Challenges, and Methods of Artificial intelligence (AI) chatbots in Education: A Systematic Literature review. *International Journal of Technology in Education*, *7*(1), 19–39. DOI: 10.46328/ijte.600

Gruenhagen, J. H., Sinclair, P. M., Carroll, J.-A., Baker, P. R. A., Wilson, A., & Demant, D. (2024). *The rapid rise of generative AI and its implications for academic integrity: Students' perceptions and use of chatbots for assistance with assessments*. ScienceDirect., DOI: 10.1016/j.caeai.2024.100273

Gustilo, L., Ong, E., & Lapinid, M. R. (2024). Algorithmically-driven writing and academic integrity: Exploring educators' practices, perceptions, and policies in AI era. *International Journal for Educational Integrity*, *20*(1), 3. Advance online publication. DOI: 10.1007/s40979-024-00153-8

Hossain, Z. (2022). University freshmen recollect their academic integrity literacy experience during their K-12 years: Results of an empirical study. *International Journal for Educational Integrity*, *18*(1), 4. Advance online publication. DOI: 10.1007/s40979-021-00096-4

Hossain, Z., Çelik, Ö., & Hertel, C. (2022). Academic Integrity Policy and Instruction in K-12 schools in Australia, Canada, England and the United States. *IASL Annual Conference Proceedings*. DOI: 10.29173/iasl8548

Jian, H., Li, G., & Wang, W. (2020). Perceptions, contexts, attitudes, and academic dishonesty in Chinese senior college students: A qualitative content-based analysis. *Ethics & Behavior*, *30*(7), 543–555. DOI: 10.1080/10508422.2020.1711758

Johansen, M. W., Goddiksen, M. P., Centa, M., Clavien, C., Gefenas, E., Globokar, R., Hogan, L., Merit, M. T., Nielsen, S. S., Olsson, I. S., Poškutė, M., Quinn, U., Santos, J. B., Santos, R., Schöpfer, C., Strahovnik, V., Wall, P. J., Sandøe, P., & Lund, T. B. (2022). Lack of ethics or lack of knowledge? European upper secondary students' doubts and misconceptions about integrity issues. *International Journal for Educational Integrity*, *18*(1), 20. Advance online publication. DOI: 10.1007/s40979-022-00113-0

Kasneci, E., Sessler, K., Küchemann, S., Bannert, M., Dementieva, D., Fischer, F., Gasser, U., Groh, G., Günnemann, S., Hüllermeier, E., Krusche, S., Kutyniok, G., Michaeli, T., Nerdel, C., Pfeffer, J., Poquet, O., Sailer, M., Schmidt, A., Seidel, T., & Kasneci, G. (2023). ChatGPT for good? On opportunities and challenges of large language models for education. *Learning and Individual Differences*, *103*, 102274. DOI: 10.1016/j.lindif.2023.102274

Khalil, M., & Er, E. (2023). Will ChatGPT get you caught? Rethinking of plagiarism detection. In *Lecture notes in computer science* (pp. 475–487). DOI: 10.1007/978-3-031-34411-4_32

Kumar, R., Eaton, S. E., Mindzak, M., & Morrison, R. (2024). Academic integrity and artificial intelligence: An overview. In Springer international handbooks of education (pp. 1583–1596). DOI: 10.1007/978-3-031-54144-5_153

Labadze, L., Grigolia, M., & Machaidze, L. (2023). *Role of AI chatbots in Education: Systematic literature review*. Researchgate., DOI: 10.1186/s41239-023-00426-1

Lai, C.-L. (2021). Exploring University Students' Preferences for AI-Assisted Learning Environment on JSTOR. www.jstor.org. https://www.jstor.org/stable/48629241?searchText=chatbot%20and%20academic%20integrity

Lai, C. Y., Cheung, K. Y., & Chan, C. S. (2023). Exploring the role of intrinsic motivation in ChatGPT adoption to support active learning: An extension of the technology acceptance model. *Computers and Education Artificial Intelligence*, *5*, 100178. DOI: 10.1016/j.caeai.2023.100178

Lee, I., & Perret, B. (2022). Preparing High School Teachers to Integrate AI Methods into STEM Classrooms. *Proceedings of the AAAI Conference on Artificial Intelligence*, *36*(11), 12783–12791. DOI: 10.1609/aaai.v36i11.21557

Lee, V. R., Pope, D., Miles, S., & Zárate, R. C. (2024). Cheating in the age of generative AI: A high school survey study of cheating behaviors before and after the release of ChatGPT. *Computers and Education Artificial Intelligence*, *7*, 100253. DOI: 10.1016/j.caeai.2024.100253

Mengist, W., Soromessa, T., & Legese, G. (2020). Method for conducting systematic literature review and meta-analysis for environmental science research. *MethodsX*, *7*, 100777. DOI: 10.1016/j.mex.2019.100777 PMID: 31993339

Mohammadkarimi, E. (2023). Teachers' reflections on academic dishonesty in EFL students' writings in the era of artificial intelligence. *Journal of Applied Learning & Teaching*, *6*(2). Advance online publication. DOI: 10.37074/jalt.2023.6.2.10

Nashwan, S. A., Sadallah, M., & Bouteraa, M. (2023). Use of ChatGPT in academia: Academic integrity hangs in the balance. *Technology in Society*, *75*, 102370. DOI: 10.1016/j.techsoc.2023.102370

Novick, P. A., Lee, J., Wei, S., Mundorff, E. C., Santangelo, J. R., & Sonbuchner, T. M. (2022). Maximizing academic integrity while minimizing stress in the virtual classroom. *Journal of Microbiology & Biology Education*, *23*(1), e00292-21. Advance online publication. DOI: 10.1128/jmbe.00292-21 PMID: 35496711

Paullet, K., & Morris, R. (2020). STUDENT AND FACULTY PERCEPTIONS OF ACADEMIC DISHONESTY IN ONLINE CLASSES. *Issues in Information Systems*. Advance online publication. DOI: 10.48009/3_iis_2020_327-333

Pawlychka, C. (2023). AI as part of the pedagogy: A restorative justice approach. *Canadian Perspectives on Academic Integrity*, *6*(1). Advance online publication. DOI: 10.55016/ojs/cpai.v6i1.76903

Perkins, M., Gezgin, U. B., & Roe, J. (2020). Reducing plagiarism through academic misconduct education. *International Journal for Educational Integrity*, *16*(1), 3. Advance online publication. DOI: 10.1007/s40979-020-00052-8

Pflugfelder, E. H., & Reeves, J. (2024). Surveillance work in (and) teaching technical writing with AI. *Journal of Technical Writing and Communication*, *54*(4), 419–438. Advance online publication. DOI: 10.1177/00472816241260028

Robles, V. C., Rivas, M. R., & Campos, J. a. S. (2020). Study of the reasons for and measures to avoid plagiarism in young students of education. *Profesorado Revista De Currículum Y Formación Del Profesorado*, *24*(1), 50–74. DOI: 10.30827/profesorado.v24i1.8572

Ross, J. (2024). *Guidance for developing policies to govern the adoption and use of artificial intelligence in K-12 schools*. https://eric.ed.gov/?id=ED655341

Salvadore, S., & Buck, R. H. (2021). Moving from plagiarism police to integrity Coaches: Assisting novice students in understanding the relationship between research and ownership. *International Journal for Educational Integrity*, *17*(1), 20. Advance online publication. DOI: 10.1007/s40979-021-00085-7

Sanusi, I. T., Olaleye, S. A., Agbo, F. J., & Chiu, T. K. (2022). The role of learners' competencies in artificial intelligence education. *Computers and Education Artificial Intelligence*, *3*, 100098. DOI: 10.1016/j.caeai.2022.100098

Stephens, J. M., St John Watson, P. W., Alansari, M., Lee, G., & Turnbull, S. M. (2021). Can online academic integrity instruction affect university students' perceptions of and engagement in academic dishonesty? Results from a natural experiment in New Zealand. *Frontiers in Psychology*, *12*, 569133. Advance online publication. DOI: 10.3389/fpsyg.2021.569133 PMID: 33679506

Sujatmika, S., Masykuri, M., Prayitno, B. A., & Sutarno. (2024). Cultivating students' critical thinking: A comprehensive approach with the integrative collaborative problem-solving (ICoPS) conceptual model. KnE Social Sciences. DOI: 10.18502/kss.v9i19.16502

Vučković, D., Peković, S., Blečić, M., & Đoković, R. (2020). Attitudes towards cheating behavior during assessing students performance: Student and teacher perspectives. *International Journal for Educational Integrity*, *16*(1), 13. Advance online publication. DOI: 10.1007/s40979-020-00065-3

Watters, A. (2023). *Teaching machines: The History of Personalized Learning*. MIT Press.

Wong, G. K. W., Ma, X., Dillenbourg, P., & Huan, J. (2020). Broadening artificial intelligence education in K-12. *ACM Inroads*, *11*(1), 20–29. DOI: 10.1145/3381884

Yin, J., Goh, T., Yang, B., & Hu, Y. (2024). Using a chatbot to provide formative feedback: A longitudinal study of intrinsic motivation, cognitive load, and learning performance. *IEEE Transactions on Learning Technologies*, *17*, 1–13. DOI: 10.1109/TLT.2024.3364015

Zhang, W., Aliannejadi, M., Yuan, Y., Pei, J., Huang, J.-H., & Kanoulas, E. (2024). Towards Fine-Grained Citation Evaluation in Generated Text: A Comparative Analysis of Faithfulness Metrics. https://arxiv.org/pdf/2406.15264

Chapter 13
Transformation of the Traditional Classroom to Artificial Intelligence-Enabled 21st Century Classrooms in India:
A Comprehensive Review

Aashish Jain
Directorate of Education, GNCT of Delhi, India

Rohit Khokher
Vidya Prakshan Mandir (P) Ltd., India

ABSTRACT

This research aims to explore the integration of artificial intelligence (AI) technologies into traditional classroom settings, assess their impact on teaching and learning practices, and address concerns related to ethics, equity, and pedagogical effectiveness. Through conducting a comprehensive review of existing literature, case studies, and empirical data, this research seeks to provide insights into the transformative potential of AI-enabled classrooms. Additionally, it will propose recommendations for effective implementation and address ethical considerations to ensure equitable and effective AI integration in education. This study also aims to identify best practices and highlight successful models of AI adoption in various educational contexts, providing a roadmap for policymakers, educators, and tech-

DOI: 10.4018/979-8-3693-6346-1.ch013

nologists to navigate both the challenges and opportunities presented by AI in education. By understanding AI's multifaceted impact, the research hopes to contribute to developing an inclusive and forward-thinking educational ecosystem in India.

Introduction

The integration of Artificial Intelligence (AI) into various aspects of life has enabled transformative changes, revolutionizing industries, services, and daily activities (Li, 2020). Education is a fundamental part of society that must continually evolve to meet the changing needs of learners and demands of the modern world. In the field of education, the emergence of AI heralds a new era, promising enhanced learning experiences, personalized education, and innovative pedagogical approaches (Rane et al., 2023). In India, the traditional classroom setting has long formed the cornerstone of education, characterized by a teacher-centred approach and limited access to technology. However, with the rapid advancement of artificial intelligence (AI) technology, there has been a shift toward integrating AI into classrooms to improve teaching and learning experiences. Artificial Intelligence (AI) in education is transforming the traditional classroom by fostering personalized learning, enhancing administrative efficiency, and providing intelligent tutoring systems (Roy, 2020; Tang, 2024; Zohuri & Rahmani, 2024). AI-driven tools such as adaptive learning platforms and virtual assistants customize educational experiences to individual student needs, accommodating diverse learning paces and styles. Predictive analytics and data-driven insights enable educators to identify at-risk students and implement timely interventions. Additionally, AI facilitates the automation of administrative tasks such as grading and attendance, allowing teachers to focus more on instruction and student engagement (Papadopoulos & Hossain, 2023).

Artificial intelligence in education has evolved globally, marked by significant developments and growing adoption across various educational systems. Initially, AI applications in education focused on automating administrative tasks and providing basic tutoring systems. Over time, these applications have developed into sophisticated adaptive learning platforms that personalize education based on individual student data, learning styles, and progress. Intelligent tutoring systems now offer real-time feedback and support, enhancing student engagement and learning outcomes. Countries such as the United States, China, and the United Kingdom have been at the forefront of integrating AI into their educational practices, leveraging technology to create more efficient and effective learning environments (Bal & Gill, 2020; Bhutoria, 2022). AI's role has expanded to include predictive analytics for identifying at-risk students, natural language processing for developing language skills, and virtual reality for immersive learning experiences. The global trend of AI in education reflects a shift towards more personalized, data-driven, and interactive learning models, setting the stage for the widespread transformation of traditional classrooms into AI-enabled 21st-century learning environments.

The importance and relevance of artificial intelligence in education within the Indian context are profound, addressing critical challenges such as quality, accessibility, and inclusivity. Artificial intelligence-driven solutions have the potential to bridge educational disparities in rural and urban regions by providing personalized learning experiences and access to high-quality educational resources regardless of geographical constraints (Božić, 2023). In India, where the student-teacher ratio often exceeds the recommended norms, artificial intelligence can alleviate the burden on educators by automating routine tasks and offering intelligent tutoring systems to support student learning outside the classroom. Moreover, artificial intelligence can enhance the effectiveness of teaching by providing data-driven insights into student performance, enabling tailored interventions for diverse learning needs. The National Education Policy 2020 emphasizes the integration of technology in education, underscoring the government's commitment to leveraging artificial intelligence for educational transformation. As India progresses towards becoming a global knowledge hub, the deployment of artificial intelligence in education is crucial for preparing students with the necessary skills to thrive in the 21st century, fostering a more equitable and innovative educational ecosystem (Aithal & Aithal, 2020; Kumar, 2021; Muralidharan et al., 2022; National Education Policy, 2020).

The early adoption and development of artificial intelligence (AI) in education in India have seen significant progress and targeted initiatives aimed at transforming the traditional classroom model. Government-led programs like Digital India and Samagra Shiksha Abhiyan (SSA) have played a pivotal role in integrating technology into the education sector (Charania, 2022; Ghosh, 2024; Ahmad et al., 2023). Early developments include the introduction of AI-driven platforms such as Digital Infrastructure for Knowledge Sharing (DIKSHA) and Class Sathi by Tag Hive, which offer personalized learning experiences and interactive content tailored to the Indian curriculum (Diksha, n.d.; Müller & Malhotra, 2024; Sheetlani & Jadimath, 2022; Tag-hive, n.d.). The adoption of AI tools like K-Yan, an integrated knowledge device, has enabled digital learning in classrooms with limited infrastructure, particularly benefiting rural areas (Leading Online Learning Platform & EdTech for Schools. , 2026). Furthermore, collaborations between the government, educational institutions, and technology companies have fostered the development of AI-based educational applications and tools facilitating better engagement and learning outcomes. These early efforts reflect India's commitment to leveraging AI for educational improvement, aiming to bridge gaps in accessibility, enhance the quality of education, and prepare students for the demands of the 21st century (Kumar, 2021).

This research has a two-pronged mission. First, it aims to conduct a comprehensive review of the integration of artificial intelligence technologies into traditional classrooms, examining the various ways AI is being utilized to enhance teaching and learning processes. Second, it seeks to address important concerns and challenges associated with this transformation, such as ethical considerations, pedagogical alignment, and technological infrastructure requirements.

Current State of AI in Indian School Education

Artificial Intelligence (AI) is steadily transforming the landscape of school education in India by integrating innovative technologies to enhance teaching and learning processes. This transformation is being driven by advancements in technology, proactive government policies, and the increasing adoption of AI-powered educational tools. India has made significant progress in technology, with widespread access to smartphones, tablets, and internet connectivity facilitating digital learning. AI-powered tools such as adaptive learning platforms, intelligent tutoring systems, and personalized learning applications are becoming increasingly prevalent in schools. These technologies analyse students' learning patterns to provide customized learning experiences, ensuring that each student receives tailored instruction.

Government Initiatives and Policies

The Government of India has taken meaningful steps to advance artificial intelligence (AI) in education through initiatives such as the Digital India campaign, Samagra Shiksha Abhiyan, and the National Education Policy of 2020. The National Education Policy emphasizes integrating technology into education and underscores AI's role in enhancing teaching and learning processes, improving access to education, and fostering innovation. The Government of India has launched various AI-enabled initiatives aimed at enhancing primary and secondary school education, as shown in Figure 1.

Figure 1. AI-enabled initiatives in education in India

Some of the key initiatives are as follows:

- *National AI Portal* (*IndiaAI*): Launched by the Ministry of Electronics and Information Technology (MeitY) and NASSCOM, the portal serves as a central hub for AI-related news, learning materials, and resources. It includes educational content to help students and educators understand and implement AI technologies (The National AI Portal of India,).
- *Digital Infrastructure for Knowledge Sharing* (*DIKSHA*): A national platform for school education that provides teachers and students with access to a wide range of e-learning content, including AI-powered interactive resources and personalized learning tools (Roy, 2020).

- *PM eVIDYA*: Part of the Atma Nirbhar Bharat Abhiyan, this initiative aims to unify efforts related to digital, online, and on-air education to enable multi-mode access to education. It includes AI-driven educational content and tools to enhance learning outcomes (PM e-Vidya,).
- *Smart Classrooms under the Samagra Shiksha Abhiyan*: This initiative promotes the use of AI-driven smart classrooms equipped with interactive boards, digital content, and AI-based assessment tools to enhance the teaching and learning experience. K-Yan is one such innovative initiative that integrates technology into education. It stands for "*Knowledge Vehicle for Young Aspiring Minds*" and is essentially a portable, multimedia, and interactive device designed for classrooms. It combines a projector, computer, speakers, and interactive whiteboard functionalities into a single unit, making it a versatile tool for teaching and learning (Leading Online Learning Platform & EdTech for Schools. , 2026).
- *Study Webs of Active-Learning for Young Aspiring Minds* (*SWAYAM*): An integrated platform for online courses provided by the Ministry of Education, offering AI-enabled interactive learning experiences and assessments for self-paced learning (Swayam Central,).
- *Pradhan Mantri Gramin Digital Saksharta Abhiyan* (*PMGDISHA*): While primarily aimed at digital literacy for rural adults, this initiative indirectly benefits school education by fostering a tech-savvy environment in rural areas. Increased digital literacy among parents and communities supports the integration of AI and digital tools in local schools (Pradhan Mantri Gramin Digital Saksharta Abhiyan,).
- *National Digital Library of India* (*NDLI*): Managed by the Indian Institute of Technology (IIT) Kharagpur, NDLI offers a vast repository of educational resources, utilizing AI to recommend personalized content based on user preferences and learning history (National Digital Library of India, 2015).
- *AI for All Initiative*: Launched by the National Association of Software and Service Companies (NASSCOM) in collaboration with the Ministry of Electronics and Information Technology (MeitY), this initiative aims to raise AI awareness among students and teachers and integrate AI curriculum into the school education system (All, 2026).
- *E-Pathshala*: An initiative by the Ministry of Education, E-Pathshala provides digital content for students, teachers, and parents. It incorporates AI-driven features to personalize learning experiences and make education more accessible (ePathshala,).
- *Atal Innovation Mission* (*AIM*): Under AIM, the Atal Tinkering Labs have been set up in schools across India to foster innovation and creativity among

students. These labs encourage the use of AI and other emerging technologies to solve real-world problems and develop critical thinking skills (AvianWe,).

- *CBSE AI Curriculum*: The Central Board of Secondary Education (CBSE) has introduced AI as a subject in the school curriculum for classes 8 to 12. This includes AI curriculum development, teacher training, and the establishment of AI labs to provide practical experience to students. This initiative aims to build AI literacy and equip students with the skills needed to thrive in an AI-driven future (Artificial Intelligence, 2022).
- *Artificial Intelligence and Robotics Technology Park* (*ARTPARK*): Supported by the Indian Institute of Science (IISc) and funded by the Department of Science and Technology (DST), ARTPARK focuses on advancing AI and robotics research. It aims to develop AI-based educational tools and platforms to enhance learning in schools (AI, 2019).
- *AI for Youth Program by Intel*: Supported by the Ministry of Education, this program aims to empower young students with AI skills. It includes training sessions, workshops, and resources to help students understand AI concepts and apply them in real-world scenarios (Intel, 2020).

Role of Private Sectors and EdTech Companies

The COVID-19 pandemic outbreak in 2019 significantly shifted entrepreneurial focus towards challenges in K-12 education. With schools suddenly closing, ensuring continued effective teaching and learning processes became urgently important. This situation provided fertile ground for educational technology companies to expand operations and offer sustainable solutions to pressing issues. Initiatives by educational technology companies during the pandemic not only served as a lifeline for students but continue evolving and growing in significance. These initiatives are now instrumental in addressing needs of remote learners, students with special needs, and those with limited access to traditional resources. The educational technology sector's crisis response highlighted adaptability, innovation, and role as a catalyst for positive change in education (Aaradhi & Chakraborty, 2024; Khanna et al., 2023; Peruzzo et al., 2022; Sikandar, 2022). Ongoing impact of these initiatives extends beyond the pandemic by shaping a more inclusive and accessible learning environment for diverse students in various backgrounds and circumstances. Some of the AI-enabled EdTech platforms that are being used in Indian school education are as follows:

- *Google for Education*: Google offers a suite of educational tools and platforms such as Google Classroom, Google Workspace for Education, and

Google Meet. These platforms facilitate online learning, collaboration, communication, and productivity for both teachers and students (Rastogi, 2019).

- *Khan Academy*: Khan Academy is a free online platform offering a vast library of instructional videos, practice exercises, and personalized learning resources across subjects like math, science, humanities, and test preparation. It promotes self-paced learning and mastery-based progression (Khan Academy, n.d.; Vidergor & Amram, 2020).
- *Embibe*: Embibe is an AI-powered education platform that offers personalized learning, test preparation, and analytics for students. It uses AI algorithms to provide adaptive practice, performance analysis, and targeted recommendations to improve learning outcomes (Tayade, 2021).
- *Microsoft Education*: Microsoft provides various edtech solutions including Microsoft Teams for Education, OneNote Class Notebook, and Minecraft Education Edition. These platforms support remote learning, digital classroom management, content creation, and immersive learning experiences (Microsoft, 2024).
- *Meritnation*: Meritnation provides online study materials, interactive videos, practice tests, and homework help for school students from classes 1 to 12. They cover subjects like math, science, social science, and English, supporting learning across different boards and curricula (Meritnation, 2019).
- *Unacademy*: Unacademy started as a platform primarily focused on test preparation for competitive exams but has expanded its offerings to cover a wide range of subjects and topics for school education as well. They offer live classes, recorded lectures, study materials, and test series for school students preparing for exams like CBSE, ICSE, and state board exams. Unacademy collaborates with educators and experts to deliver high-quality content and personalized learning experiences to students (Unacademy, 2018).
- *Toppr*: Toppr is an AI-driven learning platform that provides adaptive practice, mock tests, and personalized feedback to students. It covers a wide range of subjects and exam preparation courses, helping students enhance their academic performance (Toppr Answr - Get Help With Homework, 2023).
- *Teachmint*: Teachmint is an online teaching platform that supports teachers and schools in conducting live classes, managing student attendance, and engaging with parents. It provides tools for interactive teaching, assessments, and communication, facilitating effective teaching-learning experiences (Teachmint,).
- *Amar Ujala MyClassCampus*: MyClassCampus by Amar Ujala is an AI-enabled school management system that integrates various educational tools and features. It supports communication, attendance tracking, online assess-

ments, and parent engagement, enhancing the overall school experience (Ltd,).

- *Robomate+:* Robomate+ is an AI-powered learning app that focuses on STEM education and skill development. It offers interactive lessons, simulations, and robotics modules to engage students and promote hands-on learning experiences (robomateplus_admin, 2016).
- *Cuemath*: Cuemath is an AI-based learning platform for math education. It provides personalized math lessons, practice exercises, and real-time feedback to students, helping them build conceptual understanding and problem-solving skills (Cuemath,).

Some edtech platforms that collaborate with public-private partnerships (PPPs) to offer their services in school education are as follows:

- *EkStep Foundation*: EkStep Foundation works in collaboration with the government and various stakeholders to create open digital infrastructure and educational content. It focuses on improving learning outcomes, teacher capacity building, and access to quality education in schools (EkStep Foundation, 2026).
- *Class Sathi by Tag Hive*: Class Saathi provides teachers with an easy-to-use classroom solution that enables them to assess student proficiency across all subjects effortlessly. This platform also grants administrators and parents access to crucial learning data, promoting transparency and accountability throughout the educational process. Featuring a vast database of over 5,00,000 questions tailored to CBSE, ICSE, and 20 State Boards for grades 1-10, and aligned with the National Education Policy, Class Saathi adopts a "Data First" approach. This ensures that every student's learning journey is supported comprehensively, even in areas with limited internet or electricity access (Tag-hive, n.d.).
- *Pratham Books' StoryWeaver*: StoryWeaver is an open-source platform by Pratham Books that collaborates with government initiatives to promote reading and literacy among children. It provides a vast collection of digital storybooks in multiple languages for free use in schools and communities (Storyweaver,).
- *Educomp Solutions*: Educomp Solutions partners with government bodies and schools to provide digital learning solutions, smart classroom technologies, and teacher training programs. It focuses on enhancing teaching effectiveness, student engagement, and academic performance (Educomp, 2026).
- *Aakash Educational Services Limited* (*AESL*): AESL collaborates with government education departments and schools to offer digital learning resourc-

es, test preparation courses, and skill development programs. It aims to support students in their academic journey and competitive exam preparations (AESL,).

- *Next Education India Pvt. Ltd.*: Next Education partners with schools and government initiatives to provide digital content, assessment tools, and teacher training programs. It focuses on integrating technology into classrooms, improving learning outcomes, and promoting personalized learning experiences (NextEducation, 2024).
- *Extramarks Education*: Extramarks collaborates with schools, government bodies, and NGOs to offer digital learning solutions, interactive content, and assessment tools. It emphasizes personalized learning, adaptive practice, and data-driven insights to enhance student learning experiences (Extramarks,).
- *NIIT Limited*: NIIT partners with government education initiatives to provide digital skills training, vocational courses, and employability programs for school students. It aims to bridge the digital divide, empower youth with relevant skills, and enhance employability prospects (NIIT - Leading Online Course Provider I PG & Certificate Course, 2022).

Key AI Technologies in Education

Within the field of education, the integration of artificial intelligence (AI) has become a transformative force, reshaping traditional classrooms into dynamic and adaptive learning environments. This transition signals a new era in which technology plays a pivotal role in advancing instructional methodologies and the student experience. Several core AI technologies are propelling this transformation, each providing distinctive capabilities and values, as shown in Figure 2.

Figure 2. AI technologies

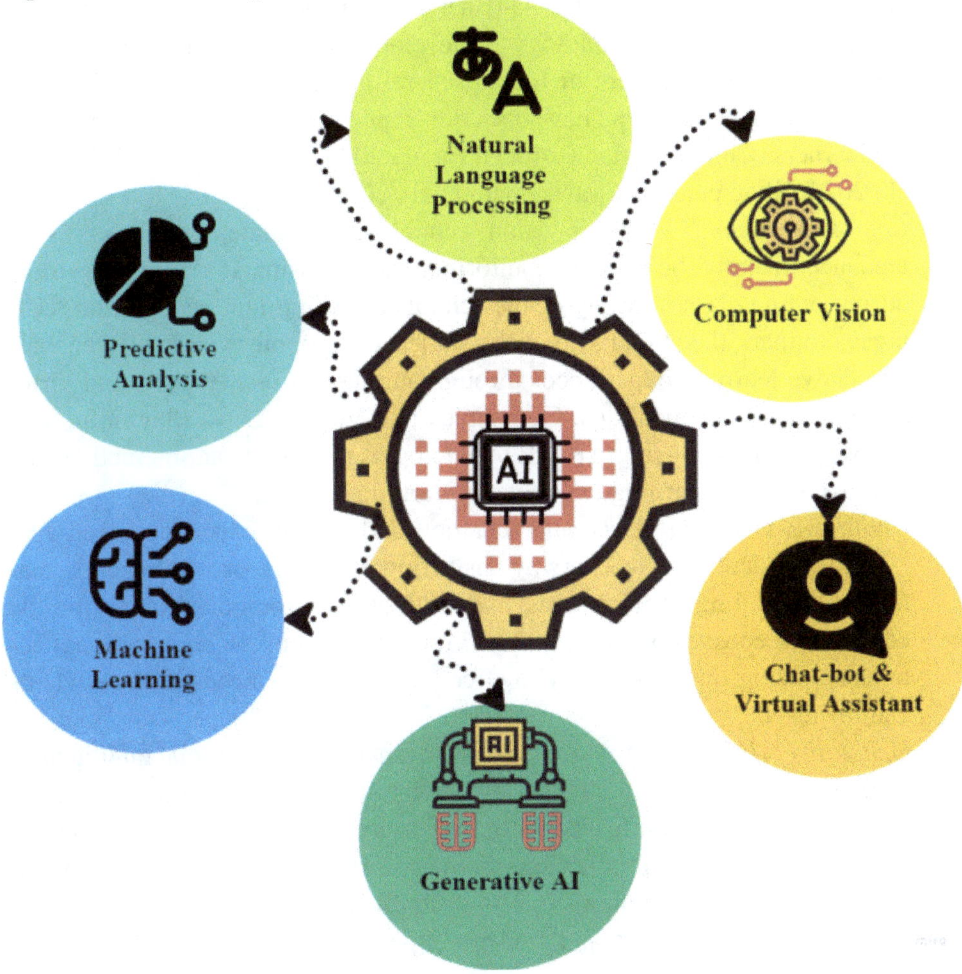

The key AI technologies are described as follows:

- *Machine Learning Algorithms and Predictive Analysis*: ML algorithms are at the core of many AI applications in education. They analyse large datasets to identify patterns, personalize learning experiences, and provide targeted recommendations for students and teachers. AI-driven predictive analytics forecasts student performance, identifies students who may need additional support and optimizes resource allocation to improve learning outcomes. The private EdTech platforms are using these technologies to recommend and suggest that students focus on the much-needed learning areas (Jaiswal & Arun, 2021).

- *Natural Language Processing (NLP)*: NLP enables AI systems to understand and generate human language. AI4Bharat, an innovative research Lab at IIT Madras, is using this technology to develop content in mother-tongue/ local languages for learners in India. Several applications such as Shoonya, Chitralekha, Anuvaad, etc. have been developed so far to cater to the needs of the learners (Chitale et al., 2024; Gala et al., 2023; Gala et al., 2024; Javed et al., 2024; Khan et al., 2024; Madhani et al., 2022).
- *Computer Vision*: Computer vision technology automates tasks such as attendance tracking, behaviour monitoring, and assessing student engagement during online classes. Many of the schools are using face recognition techniques to mark the attendance of the students. Computer vision also enables immersive learning experiences through augmented reality (AR) and virtual reality (VR) applications. Companies like Veative Labs, PlayShifu, and, TutAR in India are using AR/VR technologies to provide an interactive, and intuitive lifelong learning experience (Startuptalky, n.d.).
- *Chatbots and Virtual Assistants*: Chatbots and virtual assistants powered by AI assist students and teachers by answering questions, providing study materials, scheduling appointments, and facilitating communication within the educational ecosystem (Roy, 2020). Most of the above-mentioned applications are using this technology to effectively serve the needs of the students and the teachers.
- *Generative AI*: Generative AI, the latest advancement in artificial intelligence, empowers educators to craft innovative, intuitive, and engaging educational content for learners. It also facilitates swift responses to learner queries. Major platforms like Google Classroom and Microsoft Office are incorporating generative AI techniques into their applications, streamlining problem-solving for both teachers and students especially in rural areas (Bijithra & Devi, 2023).

Results and Discussions

The transition from traditional classrooms to artificial intelligence-enhanced environments in India has demonstrated promising outcomes across various dimensions of education. This analysis synthesizes the key conclusions from multiple research studies and pilot programs, emphasizing both the positive effects and the difficulties encountered during implementation. By assessing the incorporation of artificial intelligence technologies, one can gain a deeper understanding of how these innovations are reshaping education in India.

Key Findings

The adoption of artificial intelligence technologies in Indian educational settings has substantially advanced personalized instruction. AI allows for customized academic experiences that address the unique requirements of each learner. Below are some of the key findings from the researches explored (Bhatnagar, 2020; Dubey et al., 2022; Hemachandran et al., 2022; Jindal & Bansal, 2023; Kumar et al., 2022; Sandu & Gide, 2019; Singh & Malhotra, 2020; Sreedhar et al., 2023; Tandon & Tandon, 2020; Vij & Agarwal, 2024):

- *Enhanced Learning Experience*: The integration of AI in classrooms has significantly improved the learning experience for students. Personalized learning paths, adaptive assessments, and interactive content have made education more engaging and effective.
- *Increased Student Engagement*: AI tools have been effective in increasing student engagement by making learning interactive and fun. Gamified learning apps and AI-driven educational games have shown positive impacts on student motivation and participation.
- *Teacher Support and Efficiency*: AI tools like Class Saathi have empowered teachers by automating administrative tasks, providing real-time insights into student performance, and offering resources for differentiated instruction. This has allowed teachers to focus more on instructional quality and student engagement.
- *Professional Development for Teachers*: AI-enabled applications are being used for the professional development of teachers by providing personalized training programs, resources, and feedback. This continuous learning helps teachers stay updated with the latest educational trends and improve their teaching strategies.
- *Equity in Education*: AI has bridged educational inequalities by providing high-quality learning resources to all students, regardless of their socio-economic background. This democratization of education can contribute to a more equitable education system in India.
- *Accessibility and Inclusivity*: AI has played a crucial role in making education more accessible. Tools that offer offline capabilities and require minimal technological infrastructure have ensured that students in remote and underserved areas can benefit from AI-driven education.
- *Support for Special Education*: AI has proven beneficial for special education by providing personalized learning experiences for students with disabilities. AI tools can adapt to individual learning needs, offering customized support and enhancing learning outcomes for students requiring special education.

- *Data-Driven Decision-Making*: The adoption of a "Data First" approach has facilitated evidence-based decision-making in education. AI systems collect and analyse vast amounts of data, providing educators, administrators, and policymakers with actionable insights to improve curriculum design, teaching strategies, and resource allocation.
- *Early Identification of Learning Gaps*: AI systems can identify learning gaps early by continuously monitoring student performance and providing timely interventions. This proactive approach helps in addressing issues before they become significant barriers to learning.
- *Alignment with Educational Policies*: AI technologies in Indian classrooms are increasingly aligned with the National Education Policy (NEP) 2020, which emphasizes holistic, student-centric learning. The integration of AI supports the NEP's goals of fostering critical thinking, creativity, and lifelong learning.
- *Parental Involvement*: AI-driven platforms provide parents with real-time updates on their child's progress, encouraging greater parental involvement in the educational process. This transparency helps parents support their child's learning more effectively at home.
- *Scalability and Flexibility*: AI technologies offer scalable and flexible solutions that can be adapted to different educational contexts, from urban to rural settings, ensuring that AI benefits can be extended across diverse regions and populations.

Challenges in Implementation

Despite the promising advancements, the transformation to AI-enabled classrooms in India faces several significant challenges. Some of the major challenges addressed related to Indian education are (Bansal, 2023; Gupta & Ladiwal, 2021; Hooda & Chandan, 2023; Kalyanakrishnan et al., 2018; Patil & Kumar, 2023; Ramya & Manju, 2019):

- *Technological Barriers*: Despite the potential of AI, its implementation faces challenges such as inadequate infrastructure, limited internet access, and lack of technical expertise among educators.
- *Data Privacy and Security*: The use of AI in education raises concerns about data privacy and security. Ensuring that student data is protected and used ethically is paramount.
- *Resistance to Change*: There is often resistance from educators and administrators who are accustomed to traditional teaching methods. Professional development and continuous training are essential to facilitate the transition.

- *Cost and Funding*: Implementing AI solutions can be expensive, and many schools, especially in rural areas, may lack the necessary funding. Securing financial resources for initial setup and ongoing maintenance is a significant challenge.
- *Digital Divide*: The disparity in access to digital devices and the internet between urban and rural areas exacerbates educational inequalities. Ensuring that all students have access to AI tools is critical for widespread adoption.
- *Integration with Existing Systems*: Integrating AI tools with existing educational systems and curricula can be complex. Ensuring compatibility and seamless integration is necessary for effective implementation.
- *Teacher Training*: Comprehensive and ongoing training programs are required to help teachers integrate AI into their teaching practices effectively. Without proper training, the potential benefits of AI may not be fully realized.
- *Ethical Concerns*: The use of AI in education raises ethical issues, such as the potential for bias in AI algorithms and the need for transparency in AI decision-making processes. Addressing these ethical concerns is crucial for the responsible use of AI in education.
- Sustainability: The long-term sustainability of AI initiatives in education requires careful planning and continuous support. Ensuring that AI solutions remain relevant and effective over time is a key consideration.

Case Studies and Success Stories

Examining real-world implementations provides valuable insights into how AI can be effectively integrated into the education system. The following case studies highlight successful AI-driven initiatives across India, showcasing their impacts on learning outcomes, teacher support, and overall educational quality:

- *Class Saathi*: As highlighted, Class Saathi is a notable example of successful AI integration. It has shown that with the right tools, significant improvements in student performance and teacher efficiency can be achieved, even in resource-constrained environments (Tag-hive, n.d.).
- *AI in Government Schools*: Pilot projects in various states have demonstrated the potential of AI to enhance learning outcomes in government schools. These projects often involve collaborations between tech companies, educational NGOs, and government bodies. The first AI teacher, *IRIS*, developed as part of the Atal Tinkering Lab (ATL) project by NITI Aayog, has been deployed at KTC Higher Secondary School in Thiruvananthapuram. The AI teacher is equipped with a range of features designed to revolutionize tra-

ditional teaching methods (India's AI teacher Iris, a promise for intelligent workforce,).

- *ConveGenius*: ConveGenius is an edtech company that has deployed AI-powered learning solutions in several Indian states. Their chatbot-based learning platform has improved student engagement and personalized learning experiences, particularly in low-resource settings (Saluja, 2023).
- *Khan Academy India*: Utilizing AI-driven analytics, Khan Academy India has been able to offer personalized learning experiences to millions of students. Their partnership with the Ministry of Human Resource Development (MHRD) has further expanded their reach in government schools (Vidergor & Amram, 2020).
- *Dost Education*: Dost Education leverages AI to provide early childhood education to low-income families through mobile phones. Their voice-based AI system delivers short audio lessons to parents, helping them engage in their child's early learning process effectively (Beyond School Walls: Inspiration from Disruption,).
- *NITI Aayog's AI for All*: As part of the AI for All initiative, NITI Aayog has collaborated with several state governments to pilot AI-based educational tools in schools. These initiatives have shown positive results in improving student learning outcomes and teacher effectiveness (All, 2026).
- Microsoft's Project Sangam: Microsoft, through its Project Sangam, has used AI to provide training to teachers and students in India. The project focuses on enhancing digital literacy and vocational skills, bridging the gap between education and employability (Microsoft, 2024; Project Sangam: Enabling skilling at scale for a better tomorrow,).

Future Prospects and Trends

The integration of artificial intelligence within India's educational system shows great promise to enable further advancement and renewal moving forward. By confronting present obstacles and maximizing artificial intelligence's full capacities, the educational environment is poised for considerable enhancement. The following prospects highlight how AI can continue to revolutionize education in India:

- *Scalability*: For AI to transform education across India, scalable solutions that can be deployed in diverse educational contexts are needed. Public-private partnerships could play a crucial role in this regard, ensuring that AI-driven tools and resources reach even the most remote and underserved areas.
- *Innovative Pedagogies*: AI can enable new pedagogical approaches such as flipped classrooms, project-based learning, theme-based learning, peer learn-

ing, group learning, and competency-based education. These approaches can make learning more relevant and effective for students by fostering critical thinking, creativity, and problem-solving skills.

- *Integration with Emerging Technologies*: The integration of AI with other emerging technologies, such as augmented reality (AR), virtual reality (VR), and the Internet of Things (IoT), can create immersive and interactive learning experiences. These technologies can further enhance student engagement and understanding.
- *Global Collaboration*: Collaborating with international educational institutions and technology providers can help India adopt best practices and innovative solutions from around the world. Global collaboration can also facilitate the exchange of knowledge and resources, enhancing the overall quality of education.
- *Continuous Improvement*: The AI technologies themselves need to evolve continuously. Incorporating feedback from users (students, teachers, and administrators) can help in refining AI tools to better meet educational needs. Continuous improvement will ensure that AI solutions remain effective and aligned with educational goals.
- *Development of AI Literacy*: As AI becomes more integrated into education, there is a growing need for students and teachers to develop AI literacy. Understanding how AI works, its applications and its implications will be crucial for navigating an AI-driven world.
- *Focus on Lifelong Learning*: AI can support lifelong learning by providing personalized learning pathways and resources for individuals at all stages of their lives. This focus on continuous education can help individuals adapt to the changing job market and acquire new skills as needed.

Figure 3 below depicts the classroom environment expected to look like in future. The figure is self-generated through generative AI tool (Microsoft, 2024).

Figure 3. AI-enabled Indian classroom setting

CONCLUSION

The transformation of traditional classrooms to AI-enabled classrooms in India signifies a pivotal shift in the country's educational landscape. This transition is imperative to meet the evolving demands of the 21st century, characterized by rapid technological advancements and the need for a more personalized, inclusive, and effective education system. AI technologies have demonstrated significant potential in revolutionizing the learning experience by providing tailored educational content that aligns with each student's unique learning pace and style. Studies have shown that such personalized learning approaches can improve student performance by 30-40%, highlighting the efficacy of AI in addressing individual learning gaps more effectively than conventional methods. AI tools are also enhancing teacher efficiency by automating routine administrative tasks such as attendance tracking, grading, and lesson planning. This automation allows educators to allocate more time to instructional quality and student engagement. AI-driven analytics offer real-time insights into student performance, enabling teachers to swiftly identify areas where students are struggling and provide timely interventions. Research indicates that these tools can reduce the administrative burden on teachers by up to 20%, thereby empowering them to focus more on teaching and mentoring. One of the most significant benefits of AI in education is its ability to increase accessibility and inclusivity, particularly in remote and underserved areas. AI-enabled offline learning tools have reached over 3 million students in rural India, ensuring that lack of internet access does not impede learning. Initiatives like Dost Education, which delivers early childhood education through mobile phones, have impacted over 1 million parents and children, providing them with essential early learning resources. These efforts demonstrate how AI can bridge educational disparities and ensure that all students, regardless of their geographical or socioeconomic background, have access to quality education. The integration of AI in education is also in alignment with the goals of the National Education Policy (NEP) 2020, which emphasizes holistic, student-centric learning and the development of critical thinking, creativity, and lifelong learning skills. AI technologies support these objectives by offering personalized learning experiences, fostering critical thinking through interactive and engaging content, and facilitating continuous education beyond the traditional classroom setting. Looking ahead, the scalability of AI solutions is crucial for their widespread adoption across diverse educational contexts in India. Public-private partnerships and government initiatives will be instrumental in extending AI-driven tools and resources to the most remote and underserved regions. Pilot projects supported by NITI Aayog's AI for All initiative have already demonstrated the potential for scaling AI solutions nationwide. Furthermore, the integration of AI with other emerging technologies such as augmented reality (AR), virtual reality (VR), and the Internet of Things (IoT) promises to create immersive and interactive learning environments that enhance student engagement, skillsets, and comprehension. This is particularly important in a rapidly changing job market, where upskilling and reskilling are essential for maintaining competitiveness.

The transformation of Indian education through AI is not just a vision but an achievable reality. The benefits of AI in enhancing learning outcomes, supporting teachers, and promoting inclusivity are evident, and the successful implementation of AI in various educational initiatives across the country provides a strong foundation for future progress. By addressing the existing challenges and fostering a culture of innovation, India can harness the full potential of AI to create an inclusive, high-quality educational environment for all students. The future of education in India, empowered by AI, promises to be more personalized, engaging, and accessible, preparing students for the demands of the 21st century.

REFERENCES

Aaradhi, V., & Chakraborty, D. (2024). EdTech applications and their adoption in Indian education sector–a bibliometric analysis and systematic literature review. *Higher Education, Skills and Work-Based Learning*, *14*(2), 510–528. DOI: 10.1108/HESWBL-09-2022-0192

AESL. (n.d.). *Coaching Classes for NEET/ Medical, IIT JEE Main & Advanced and Olympiads - AESL* | Www.aakash.ac.in. https://www.aakash.ac.in/

AI. (2019). *ARTPARK @IISc - Leading AI & Robotics startup incubation*. ARTPARK @IISc - Leading AI & Robotics Startup Incubation. https://artpark.in/

Aithal, P. S., & Aithal, S. (2020). Implementation strategies of higher education part of national education policy 2020 of India towards achieving its objectives. *International Journal of Management, Technology, and Social Sciences*, *5*(2), 283–325. DOI: 10.47992/IJMTS.2581.6012.0119

All, A. F. (2026). *AI For All | Self learning online program*. Ai-For-All.in. https://ai-for-all.in/

Artificial Intelligence. (2022). Cbseacademic.nic.in. https://cbseacademic.nic.in/ai.html

AvianWe. (n.d.). *Atal Innovation Mission (AIM)*. Atal Innovation Mission (AIM). https://aim.gov.in/

Bal, R., & Gill, I. S. (2020). "Policy approaches to artificial intelligence based technologies in China, European Union and the United States". Duke Global Working Paper Series No. 26. DOI: 10.2139/ssrn.3699640

Bansal, U. (2023). Artificial intelligence in Indian education: Navigating challenges and embracing opportunities. *Journal Global Values*, *XIV*(S.Issue), 190–197. DOI: 10.31995/jgv.2023.v14iS3.024

Beyond School Walls: Inspiration from Disruption. (n.d.). https://resources.educationaboveall.org/sites/default/files/ngo/attachments/2020-08/04.%20Dost%20Education.pdf

Bhatnagar, H. (2020). Artificial intelligence- new horizon in Indian higher education. *Journal of Learning and Teaching in Digital Age*, *6*(1), 30–34.

Bhutoria, A. (2022). Personalized education and artificial intelligence in the United States, China, and India: A systematic review using a human-in-the-loop model. *Computers and Education: Artificial Intelligence*, *3*, 1–18. DOI: 10.1016/j.caeai.2022.100068

Bijithra, N. C., & Devi, R. S. (2023). "Behaviour inference in rural education using generative AI". In Proceedings of *International Conference on Computing Paradigms* (ICCP 2023), 164-170.

Božić, V. (2023). Artificial intelligence as the reason and the solution of digital divide. *Language Education & Technology*, *3*(2), 96–109.

Charania, A. (2022). *Integrated approach to Technology in Education in India: Implementation and impact*. Taylor & Francis. DOI: 10.4324/9781003300274

Chitale, P. A., Gala, J., & Dabre, R. (2024). "An empirical study of in-context learning in LLMs for machine translation". Retrieved from: https://arxiv.org/pdf/2401.12097

Diksha. (n.d.). https://diksha.gov.in/index.html

Dubey, G., Hasan, M., & Alam, A. (2022). Artificial intelligence (AI) and Indian education system: Promising applications, potential effectiveness and Challenges. *Towards Excellence*, *14*(2), 259–269. DOI: 10.37867/TE140223

Educomp. (2026). Educomp.com. https://www.educomp.com/

EkStep Foundation. (2026). *LinkedIn*. Linkedin.com. https://in.linkedin.com/company/ekstep-foundation

ePathshala. (n.d.). *Learning On The Go*. Epathshala.nic.in. https://epathshala.nic.in/

Extramarks. (n.d.). *CBSE, ICSE, NCERT Solution, JEE & NEET Preparation*. Www.extramarks.com. https://www.extramarks.com/

Gala, J., Chitale, P. A., Raghavan, A. K., Gumma, V., Doddapaneni, S., Kumar, A., Nawale, J., Sujatha, A., Pudupully, R., Raghavan, V., Kumar, P., Khapra, M. M., Dabre, R., & Kunchukuttan, A. (2023). "IndicTrans2: Towards high-quality and accessible machine translation models for all 22 scheduled Indian languages". Retrieved from: https://arxiv.org/pdf/2305.16307

Gala, J., Jayakumar, T., Husain, J. A., Kumar, A. M., Khan, M. S. U. R., Kanojia, D., Pudupully, R., Khapra, M. M., Dabre, R., Murthy, R., & Kunchukuttan, A. (2024). "Airavata: Introducing Hindi instruction-tuned LLM". Retrieved from: https://arxiv.org/pdf/2401.15006

Ghosh, S. S. (2024). "Transforming the Indian education landscape: The impact of personalized learning and adaptive technologies in continuing education". *Embracing Technological Advancements for Lifelong Learning*, edited by Mahmoud M. Kh. Hawamdeh and Faiz Abdelhafid, IGI Global, pp. 278-299. DOI: 10.4018/979-8-3693-1410-4.ch013

Gupta, A., & Ladiwal, O. (2021). Digital education in India: Future perspective and challenges. *SKIT Research Journal*, *11*(2), 87–92. DOI: 10.47904/IJSKIT.11.2.2021.87-92

Hemachandran, K., Verma, P., Pareek, P., Arora, N., Kumar, K. V. R., Ahanger, T. A., Pise, A. A., & Ratna, R. (2022). Artificial intelligence: A universal virtual tool to augment tutoring in higher education. *Computational Intelligence and Neuroscience*, *2022*, 1–8. DOI: 10.1155/2022/1410448 PMID: 35586099

Hooda, M., & Chandan, . (2023). Opportunities and challenges for artificial intelligence in Indian education. *Scholarly Research Journal for Humanity Science & English Language*, *11/57*, 124–135.

India's AI teacher Iris, a promise for intelligent workforce. (n.d.). INDIAai. https://indiaai.gov.in/article/india-s-ai-teacher-iris-a-promise-for-intelligent-workforce

Intel. (2020). *AI for Youth Program.* https://www.intel.com/content/www/us/en/corporate/artificial-intelligence/digital-readiness-ai-for-youth.html

Jaiswal, A., & Arun, C. J. (2021). "Potential of artificial intelligence for transformation of the education system in India". *International Journal of Education and Development using Information and Communication Technology* (*IJEDICT*), 17 (1), pp. 142-158.

Javed, T., Nawale, J. A., George, E. I., Joshi, S., Bhogale, K. S., Mehendale, D., Sethi, I. V., Ananthanarayanan, A., Faquih, H., Palit, P., Ravishankar, S., Sukumaran, S., Panchangnula, T., Murali, S., Gandhi, K. S., Ambujavali, R., Manickam, K. M., Vaijayanthi, C. V., Kaunganni, K. S. R., . . . Khapra, M. M. (2024). "IndicVoices: Towards building an inclusive multilingual speech dataset for Indian languages". Retrieved from: https://arxiv.org/pdf/2403.01926

Jindal, A., & Bansal, M. (2023). Knowledge and education about artificial intelligence among medical students from teaching institutions of India: A brief survey. *MedEdPublish*, *2020*, 1–9.

Kalyanakrishnan, S., Panicker, R. A., Natarajan, S., & Rao, S. (2018). "Opportunities and challenges for artificial intelligence in India". In 2018 *AAAI/ACM Conference on AI, Ethics, and Society* (*AIES '18*), February 2–3, 2018, New Orleans, LA, USA. ACM, New York, NY, USA, pp. 164-170. DOI: 10.1145/3278721.3278738

Khan Academy. (n.d.). https://www.khanacademy.org/

Khan, A. (2023). ICT and digital revolution: implications for teacher education. In Ahmad, J., & Masih, A. (Eds.), *Teaching and Teacher Education in India*. Springer., DOI: 10.1007/978-981-99-4985-4_17

Khan, M. S. U. R., Mehta, P., Sankar, A., Kumaravelan, U., Doddapaneni, S., Suriyaprasad, G., & Balan, G. V., Jain, S., Kunchukuttan, A., Kumar, P, Dabre, R., and Khapra, M. M. (2024). "IndicLLMSuite: A blueprint for creating pre-training and fine-tuning datasets for Indian languages". Retrieved from: https://arxiv.org/pdf/2403.06350

Khanna, P., Sehgal, R., Malviya, M., Khanna, A., & Dubey, A. M. (2023). "EdTech start-ups: A mode of transformation in teaching and learning". *Asia-Pacific Business Series| Indian SMEs and Start-Ups*, pp. 177-202.

Kumar, A. (2021). "New education policy (NEP) 2020: A roadmap for India 2.0". In W. B. James, C. Cobanoglu, & M. Cavusoglu (Eds.), *Advances in global education and research*, 4, pp. 1–8. USF M3 Publishing.

Kumar, K. S., Prabu, M. M., Kalaiyarasan, G., Selvan, A., Ramnath, R., & Kumar, N. S. (2022). Exploring artificial intelligence and robotics in Indian education: Potential for teacher substitution? *International Journal of Emerging Knowledge Studies*, *1*(1), 14–19. DOI: 10.70333/ijeks-01-12-003

Leading Online Learning Platform & EdTech for Schools. (2026). Schoolnetindia.com. https://www.schoolnetindia.com/offerings/digital-classrooms/k-yan.php

Li, R. (2020). *Artificial Intelligence Revolution: How AI will change our society, economy, and culture*. Skyhorse Publishing.

Ltd, H. I. P. (n.d.). *School ERP | Campus Management System | Education ERP*. MyClassCampus. https://myclasscampus.com/home

Madhani, Y., Parthan, S., Bedekar, P., Gokul, N. C., Khapra, R., Kunchukuttan, A., Kumar, P., & Khapra, M. M. (2022). "Aksharantar: Open Indic-language transliteration datasets and models for the next billion users". Retrieved from: https://arxiv.org/pdf/2205.03018

Malhotra, C. (2024). Digital India: Past, present and future. In Müller, M. H. P. (Ed.), *Indien im 21. Jahrhundert – Auf dem Weg zur postindustriellen Ökonomie*. Ökonomien und Gesellschaften im Wandel. Springer Gabler., DOI: 10.1007/978-3-658-43014-6_19

Meritnation. (2019). *Meritnation: The No.1 Education Site with Study Material & Live Classes for CBSE, ICSE, CPT, IITJEE, AIPMT & more*. Meritnation.com. https://www.meritnation.com/

Microsoft. (2024). *Technology Solutions for Schools | Microsoft Education*. Microsoft.com. https://www.microsoft.com/en-in/education

Microsoft. (2024). *Microsoft Designer - Stunning designs in a flash*. Designer. microsoft.com. https://designer.microsoft.com/

Muralidharan, K., Shanmugan, K., & Klochkov, Y. (2022). The new education policy 2020, digitalization and quality of life in India: Some reflections. *Education Sciences*, *12*(2), 75. DOI: 10.3390/educsci12020075

National Digital Library of India. (2015). Iitkgp.ac.in. https://ndl.iitkgp.ac.in/

National Education Policy. (2020). Policy Document released by Government of India, pp. 56-58. Retrieved from https://www.education.gov.in/sites/upload_files/mhrd/files/NEP_Final_English_0.pdf

NextEducation. (2024). *Next Education - India's Leading K-12 B2B EdTech Company*. Nexteducation.in. https://www.nexteducation.in/

NIIT - Leading Online Course Provider | PG & Certificate Course. (2022). In *niit.com*. https://www.niit.com/india/

Cuemath (n.d.). *Online Math and Coding Classes*. https://www.cuemath.com/

Papadopoulos, D., & Hossain, M. M. (2023). Education in the age of analytics: Maximizing student success through big data-driven personalized learning. *Emerging Trends in Machine Intelligence and Big Data*, *15*(9), 20–36.

Patil, S., & Kumar, P. (2023). "Case studies on artificial intelligence for sustainable education in 21st century". pp. 303-310. Retrieved from: https://www.researchgate.net/publication/378683480

Peruzzo, F., Ball, S. J., & Grimaldi, E. (2022). Peopling the crowded education state: Heterarchical spaces, EdTech markets and new modes of governing during the COVID-19 pandemic. *International Journal of Educational Research*, *114*, 1–14. DOI: 10.1016/j.ijer.2022.102006

PM e-Vidya. (n.d.). Pmevidya.education.gov.in. https://pmevidya.education.gov.in/

Pradhan Mantri Gramin Digital Saksharta Abhiyan. (n.d.). Www.pmgdisha.in. https://www.pmgdisha.in/

Project Sangam: Enabling skilling at scale for a better tomorrow. (n.d.). Microsoft Stories India. https://news.microsoft.com/en-in/features/project-sangam-skilling-anil-bhansali/

Ramya, P., & Manju, M. (2019). Artificial intelligence for sustainable education in India: Problems and prospects [*IJPTM*]. *International Journal of Production Technology and Management*, *10*(1), 135–143.

Rane, N., Choudhary, S., & Rane, J. (2023). "Education 4.0 and 5.0: Integrating artificial intelligence (AI) for personalized and adaptive learning". DOI: 10.2139/ssrn.4638365

Rastogi, H. (2019). Digitalization of education in India- an analysis. *International Journal of Research and Analytical Reviews*, *6*(1), 160–167.

robomateplus_admin. (2016). *Robomate Plus*. Robomate Plus. https://robomateplus.com/

Roy, M. (2020). AI intervention in education systems of India: An analysis. *Solid State Technology*, *63*(2s), 1395–1402.

Saluja, A. (2023). *Public-private partnerships in EdTech for transforming rural India: How start-ups are shaping the post-COVID landscape*. India's Technology-Led Development., Retrieved from https://www.worldscientific.com/doi/abs/10.1142/9789811271786_0006

Sandu, N., & Gide, E. (2019). "Adoption of AI-Chatbots to Enhance Student Learning Experience in Higher Education in India". *18th International Conference on Information Technology Based Higher Education and Training* (*ITHET*), Magdeburg, Germany, pp. 1-5. DOI: 10.1109/ITHET46829.2019.8937382

Sheetlani, J., & Jadimath, S. S. (2022). Effectiveness of digital India and artificial intelligence in Indian education system. *NeuroQuantology : An Interdisciplinary Journal of Neuroscience and Quantum Physics*, *20*(10), 5312–5318.

Sikandar, M. A. (2022). The rise of EdTech start-ups in India. *Recent Trends in Management & Social Sciences*, *2*, 24–32.

Singh, B., & Malhotra, M. (2020). The role of artificial intelligence in the Indian education sector. *OORJA*, *18*(1), 21–30. DOI: 10.55399/WGQO2090

Sreedhar, J., Kumar, M. V. P., Karthik, D. S., Ibrahim, M., Prakash, G. H., Ibrahim, S. K., & Sandeep, P. (2023). The future of AI in education: A review analysis [*IJSREM*]. *International Journal of Scientific Research in Engineering and Management*, *7*(11), 1–10.

Startuptalky. (n.d.). https://startuptalky.com/edtech-startups-using-ar-vr/

Storyweaver. (n.d.). *Digital Library of Stories for Kids | Stories* | Https://Storyweaver.org.in/. https://storyweaver.org.in/en/

Swayam Central. (n.d.). Swayam.gov.in. https://swayam.gov.in/

Tag-hive. (n.d.) .https://tag-hive.com/class-saathi/

Tandon, R., & Tandon, S. (2020). Education 4.0: A new paradigm in transforming the future of education in India [*IJISET*]. *International Journal of Innovative Science, Engineering & Technology*, *7*(2), 32–54.

Tang, Q. (2024). "A case study on the application of artificial intelligence in education industry". Proceedings of the 2023 3rd International Conference on Modern Educational Technology and Social Sciences (ICMETSS 2023). *Advances in Social Science, Education and Humanities Research*, *784*, 99–109. DOI: 10.2991/978-2-38476-128-9_12

Tayade, M. (2021). "Women entrepreneurs in education sector". *Role of Women in Nation Development* (Book of Conference Proceedings of NIT Jamshedpur 2020), 22, 184-191. DOI: 10.47531/MANTECH.2021.22

Teachmint. (n.d.). *Smart Learning Management System (LMS) & Integrated ERP Solution Compatible with Desktop & Mobile App*. https://www.teachmint.com/

The National AI Portal of India. (n.d.). INDIAai. https://indiaai.gov.in/

Toppr Answr - Get Help With Homework. (2023). Toppr Ask. https://www.toppr.com/ask/

Unacademy. (2018). *India's largest learning platform*. Unacademy. https://unacademy.com/

Vidergor, H. E., & Amram, P. B. (2020). Khan academy effectiveness: The case of math secondary students' perceptions. *Computers & Education*, *157*, 157. DOI: 10.1016/j.compedu.2020.103985

Vij, A., & Agarwal, P. (2024). Assessing the challenges and opportunities of artificial intelligence in Indian education [IJGSAR]. *International Journal for Global Academic & Scientific Research*, *3*(1), 36–44. DOI: 10.55938/ijgasr.v3i1.71

Zohuri, B., & Rahmani, F. M. (2024). Revolutionizing Education: The dynamic synergy of personalized learning and artificial intelligence. *International Journal of Advanced Engineering and Management Research*, *9*(1), 143–153. DOI: 10.51505/ijaemr.2024.9111

Compilation of References

Aaradhi, V., & Chakraborty, D. (2024). EdTech applications and their adoption in Indian education sector–a bibliometric analysis and systematic literature review. *Higher Education, Skills and Work-Based Learning*, *14*(2), 510–528. DOI: 10.1108/HESWBL-09-2022-0192

Abilawa, A., Rahmawati, A., & Surwanti, A. (2023). Enhancing insight into FinTech adoption through VOSViewer: A bibliometric exploration. *Multidisciplinary Reviews*, *7*(1), 2024006. DOI: 10.31893/multirev.2024006

Abulibdeh, A., Baya Chatti, C., Alkhereibi, A., & El Menshawy, S. (2025). A Scoping Review of the Strategic Integration of Artificial Intelligence in Higher Education: Transforming University Excellence Themes and Strategic Planning in the Digital Era. *European Journal of Education*, *60*(1), e12908. Advance online publication. DOI: 10.1111/ejed.12908

Abulibdeh, A., Zaidan, E., & Abulibdeh, R. (2024). Navigating the confluence of artificial intelligence and education for sustainable development in the era of industry 4.0: Challenges, opportunities, and ethical dimensions. *Journal of Cleaner Production*, *437*, 140527. DOI: 10.1016/j.jclepro.2023.140527

Adam, C. (2024). Segmenting female students' perceptions about FinTech using Explainable AI. *Frontiers in Artificial Intelligence*, *7*, 1504963. Advance online publication. DOI: 10.3389/frai.2024.1504963 PMID: 39726890

Adams, C., Pente, P., Lemermeyer, G., & Rockwell, G. (2021, June). Artificial intelligence ethics guidelines for K-12 education: A review of the global landscape. In *International Conference on Artificial Intelligence in Education* (pp. 24-28). Cham: Springer International Publishing. DOI: 10.1007/978-3-030-78270-2_4

Adams, C., Pente, P., Lemermeyer, G., & Rockwell, G. (2023). Ethical principles for artificial intelligence in K-12 education. *Computers and Education: Artificial Intelligence*, *4*, 100131. DOI: 10.1016/j.caeai.2023.100131

Adepetun, A., Odutola, O., & Dopemu, E. M. (2022). Exploring The Impact of Machine Learning on Financial Decision-Making in The Nigerian Banking Sector. *International Journal of Scientific and Management Research, 05*(12), 212–221. DOI: 10.37502/IJSMR.2022.51215

AESL. (n.d.). *Coaching Classes for NEET/ Medical, IIT JEE Main & Advanced and Olympiads - AESL* | Www.aakash.ac.in. https://www.aakash.ac.in/

Agrawal, N. (2025, January 10). *AI in Education: Offering a transformative Potential.* Hans India. https://www.thehansindia.com/hans/young-hans/impact-of-ai-on-personalised-learning-in-k-12-education-936345

Ahmad, K., Iqbal, W., El-Hassan, A., Qadir, J., Benhaddou, D., Ayyash, M., & Al-Fuqaha, A. (2024). Data-Driven Artificial Intelligence in Education: A Comprehensive review. *IEEE Transactions on Learning Technologies, 17*, 12–31. DOI: 10.1109/TLT.2023.3314610

AI. (2019). *ARTPARK @IISc - Leading AI & Robotics startup incubation.* ARTPARK @IISc - Leading AI & Robotics Startup Incubation. https://artpark.in/

Aithal, P. S., & Aithal, S. (2020). Implementation strategies of higher education part of national education policy 2020 of India towards achieving its objectives. *International Journal of Management, Technology, and Social Sciences, 5*(2), 283–325. DOI: 10.47992/IJMTS.2581.6012.0119

Akartuna, E. A., Johnson, S. D., & Thornton, A. (2022). Preventing the money laundering and terrorist financing risks of emerging technologies: An international policy Delphi study. *Technological Forecasting and Social Change, 179*, 121632. DOI: 10.1016/j.techfore.2022.121632

Akgun, S., & Greenhow, C. (2022). Artificial intelligence in education: Addressing ethical challenges in K-12 settings. *AI and Ethics, 2*(3), 431–440. DOI: 10.1007/s43681-021-00096-7 PMID: 34790956

Akkaş, Ö. M., Tosun, C., & Gökçearslan, Ş. (2024). Artificial intelligence (AI) and cheating. In Advances in educational technologies and instructional design book series (pp. 182–199). DOI: 10.4018/979-8-3693-1351-0.ch009

Alam, A. (2022). Employing adaptive learning and intelligent tutoring robots for virtual classrooms and smart campuses: Reforming Education in the age of Artificial Intelligence. In *Lecture notes in electrical engineering* (pp. 395–406). DOI: 10.1007/978-981-19-2980-9_32

Alam, A. (2023). Harnessing the power of AI to create intelligent tutoring systems for enhanced classroom experience and improved learning outcomes. In *Lecture notes on data engineering and communications technologies* (pp. 571–591). DOI: 10.1007/978-981-99-1767-9_42

Alessio, H. M., & Messinger, J. D. (2021). Faculty and Student Perceptions of academic Integrity in Technology-Assisted Learning and Testing. *Frontiers in Education, 6*, 629220. Advance online publication. DOI: 10.3389/feduc.2021.629220

Alexandre, F., Becker, J., Comte, M. H., Lagarrigue, A., Liblau, R., Romero, M., & Viéville, T. (2021). Why, What and How to help each citizen understand artificialintelligence? *Kunstliche Intelligenz, 35*(2), 191–199. DOI: 10.1007/s13218-021-00725-7 PMID: 33994668

Algerafi, M. M., Zhou, Y., Alfadda, H., & Wijaya, T. T. (2023). Understanding the factors influencing higher education students' intention to adopt Artificial Intelligence-Based robots. *IEEE Access : Practical Innovations, Open Solutions, 11*, 99752–99764. DOI: 10.1109/ACCESS.2023.3314499

All, A. F. (2026). *AI For All | Self learning online program.* Ai-For-All.in. https://ai-for-all.in/

Allen, C. T., Fournier, S., & Miller, F. (2018). Brands and their meaning makers. In *Handbook of consumer psychology* (pp. 773–814).

Alnasib, B. N. M. (2023). Factors affecting faculty members' readiness to integrate artificial intelligence into their teaching practices: A study from the Saudi higher education context. *International Journal of Learning. Teaching and Educational Research, 22*(8), 465–491. DOI: 10.26803/ijlter.22.8.24

Alrakhawi, H. A., Jamiat, N., & Abu-Naser, S. S. (2023). Intelligent Tutoring Systems In Education: A Systematic Review Of Usage, Tools, Effects And Evaluation. *Journal of Theoretical and Applied Information Technology, 101*(4), 1992–8645. https://www.researchgate.net/publication/369019319_INTELLIGENT_TUTORING_SYSTEMS_IN_EDUCATION_A_SYSTEMATIC_REVIEW_OF_USAGE_TOOLS_EFFECTS_AND_EVALUATION

Amnas, M. B., Selvam, M., Raja, M., Santhoshkumar, S., & Parayitam, S. (2023). Understanding the Determinants of FinTech Adoption: Integrating UTAUT2 with Trust Theoretic Model. *Journal of Risk and Financial Management, 16*(12), 505. DOI: 10.3390/jrfm16120505

Anan, L., Isaza, D. C., Figuieredo, F., & Flototto, M. (2023). *FinTech: A new paradigm of growth.* https://tinyurl.com/s6jmwhn6

Ananyi, S. O. (2023). COST-BENEFIT ANALYSIS OF ARTIFICIAL INTELLIGENCE INTEGRATION IN EDUCATION MANAGEMENT: LEADERSHIP PERSPECTIVES. Researchgate, ISSN: 2992-5614. https://www.researchgate.net/publication/375609860_COST-BENEFIT_ANALYSIS_OF_ARTIFICIAL_INTELLIGENCE_INTEGRATION_IN_EDUCATION_MANAGEMENT_LEADERSHIP_PERSPECTIVES

Artificial Intelligence. (2022). Cbseacademic.nic.in. https://cbseacademic.nic.in/ai.html

Aung, Z. H., Sanium, S., Songsaksuppachok, C., Kusakunniran, W., Precharattana, M., Chuechote, S., & Ritthipravat, P. (2022). Designing a novel teaching platform for AI: A case study in a Thai school context. *Journal of Computer Assisted Learning*, *38*(6), 1714–1729. DOI: 10.1111/jcal.12706

AvianWe. (n.d.). *Atal Innovation Mission (AIM)*. Atal Innovation Mission (AIM). https://aim.gov.in/

Ayanwale, M. A., Sanusi, I. T., Adelana, O. P., Aruleba, K. D., & Oyelere, S. S. (2022). Teachers' readiness and intention to teach artificial intelligence in schools. *Computers and Education: Artificial Intelligence*, *3*, 100099. DOI: 10.1016/j.caeai.2022.100099

Azzam, A., & Charles, T. (2024). A review of artificial intelligence in K–12 education. *Open Journal of Applied Sciences*, *14*(8), 2088–2100. DOI: 10.4236/ojapps.2024.148137

Babina, T., Fedyk, A., He, A. X., & Hodson, J. (2023). *Firm investments in artificial intelligence technologies and changes in workforce composition*. National Bureau of Economic Research. DOI: 10.3386/w31325

Baity, A. H. H. (2023). The Artificial Intelligence Revolution in Digital Finance in Saudi Arabia: A Comprehensive Review and Proposed Framework. *Sustainability (Basel)*, *15*(18), 13725. DOI: 10.3390/su151813725

Baker, T., Smith, L., & Anissa, N. (2019). *Educ-AI-tion rebooted? Exploring the future of artificial intelligence in schools and colleges*. Nesta Foundation.

Bal, N. G. (2024). Unlocking online language education: Opportunities, challenges, and recommendations. *Turkish Journal of Education*, 158–179. DOI: 10.19128/turje.1379149

Bal, R., & Gill, I. S. (2020). "Policy approaches to artificial intelligence based technologies in China, European Union and the United States". Duke Global Working Paper Series No. 26. DOI: 10.2139/ssrn.3699640

Balderas, D., Ponce, P., Lopez-Bernal, D., & Molina, A. (2021). Education 4.0: Teaching The Basis of Motor Imagery Classification Algorithms for Brain-Computer Interfaces. *Future Internet, 13*(8), 202. DOI: 10.3390/fi13080202

Baltodano, M. P. (2017). The power brokers of neoliberalism: Philanthrocapitalists and public education. *Policy Futures in Education, 15*(2), 141–156. DOI: 10.1177/1478210316652008

Bansal, U. (2023). Artificial intelligence in Indian education: Navigating challenges and embracing opportunities. *Journal Global Values, XIV*(S.Issue), 190–197. DOI: 10.31995/jgv.2023.v14iS3.024

Barrett, H. (2018, January 23). Business schools have a problem with FinTech. *Financial Times*.

Beke, E., & Tick, A. (2024). Applicability of education 4.0 in higher education: Engineering students' survey. *Journal of Technology and Science Education, 14*(2), 529. DOI: 10.3926/jotse.1845

Berg, T., Fuster, A., & Puri, M. (2022). FinTech Lending. *Annual Review of Financial Economics, 14*(1), 187–207. DOI: 10.1146/annurev-financial-101521-112042

Beyond School Walls: Inspiration from Disruption. (n.d.). https://resources.educationaboveall.org/sites/default/files/ngo/attachments/2020-08/04.%20Dost%20Education.pdf

Bhatnagar, H. (2020). Artificial intelligence- new horizon in Indian higher education. *Journal of Learning and Teaching in Digital Age, 6*(1), 30–34.

Bhutoria, A. (2022). Personalized education and artificial intelligence in the United States, China, and India: A systematic review using a human-in-the-loop model. *Computers and Education: Artificial Intelligence, 3*, 1–18. DOI: 10.1016/j.caeai.2022.100068

Bijithra, N. C., & Devi, R. S. (2023). "Behaviour inference in rural education using generative AI". In Proceedings of *International Conference on Computing Paradigms* (ICCP 2023), 164-170.

Binns, R. (2018, January). Fairness in machine learning: Lessons from political philosophy. In Conference on fairness, accountability and transparency (pp. 149-159). PMLR.

Birks, M., Mills, J., Allen, S., & Tee, S. (2020). Managing the mutations: Academic misconduct in Australia, New Zealand and the UK. *International Journal for Educational Integrity*, *16*(1), 6. Advance online publication. DOI: 10.1007/s40979-020-00055-5

Bouteraa, M., Bin-Nashwan, S. A., Al-Daihani, M., Dirie, K. A., Benlahcene, A., Sadallah, M., Zaki, H. O., Lada, S., Ansar, R., Fook, L. M., & Chekima, B. (2024). Understanding the diffusion of AI-generative (ChatGPT) in higher education: Does students' integrity matter? *Computers in Human Behavior Reports*, *14*, 100402. DOI: 10.1016/j.chbr.2024.100402

Božić, V. (2023). Artificial intelligence as the reason and the solution of digital divide. *Language Education & Technology*, *3*(2), 96–109.

Bozkurt, A., & Sharma, R. C. (2023). Challenging the status quo and exploring the new boundaries in the age of algorithms: Reimagining the role of generative AI in distance education and online learning. Zenodo *(CERN European Organization for Nuclear Research)*. DOI: 10.5281/zenodo.7755273

Braun, V., & Clarke, V. (2006). Using thematic analysis in psychology. *Qualitative Research in Psychology*, *3*(2), 77–101. DOI: 10.1191/1478088706qp063oa

Brem, A., Giones, F., & Werle, M. (2023, February). The AI Digital Revolution in Innovation: A Conceptual Framework of Artificial Intelligence Technologies for the Management of Innovation. *IEEE Transactions on Engineering Management*, *70*(2), 770–776. DOI: 10.1109/TEM.2021.3109983

Brown, T., Mann, B., Ryder, N., Subbiah, M., Kaplan, J. D., Dhariwal, P., & Amodei, D. (2020). Language models are few-shot learners. *Advances in Neural Information Processing Systems*, *33*, 1877–1901.

Buguin, J., Dobbs, R., Bisson, P., & Marrs, A. (2013). *Disruptive technologies: Advances that will transform life, business, and the global economy*. McKinsey Global Institute.

Bu, Q. (2022). Ethical Risks in Integrating Artificial Intelligence into Education and Potential Countermeasures. *Science Insights*, *41*(1), 561–566. DOI: 10.15354/si.22.re067

Burns, S. M., Henriksen, D., & Mishra, P. (2020). AI and Education: Emerging Opportunities, Challenges, and Ethical Considerations. *AI Magazine*, *40*(3), 9–17.

Burton, B., & Basiliere, P. (2016). *Architect digital platforms to deliver business value and outcomes* (Gartner Report No. G00318861). Gartner.

Cándida, M., Chávez, R., Troya, A. L., Santos, R., Rosa, C., Cordero, Z., Marisol, L., Orellana, G., & Pongo, O. E. (2023). Impact of Artificial intelligence in Promoting Academic Integrity in Education: a Systematic review. *Researchgate, 2197–5523.* https://www.researchgate.net/publication/370894108_Impact_of_Artificial_Intelligence_in_Promoting_Academic_Integrity_in_Education_A_Systematic_review

Cao, L. (2020). AI in Finance: A Review. SSRN *Electronic Journal.* DOI: 10.2139/ssrn.3647625

Cao, L., Yang, Q., & Yu, P. S. (2021). Data science and AI in FinTech: An overview. *International Journal of Data Science and Analytics*, *12*(2), 81–99. DOI: 10.1007/s41060-021-00278-w

Cao, Y., & Zhai, J. (2022). A survey of AI in finance. *Journal of Chinese Economic and Business Studies*, *20*(2), 125–137. DOI: 10.1080/14765284.2022.2077632

Carney, M., Webster, B., Alvarado, I., Phillips, K., Howell, N., Griffith, J., . . . Chen, A. (2020,). Teachable machine: Approachable Web-based tool for exploring machine learning classification. In Extended abstracts of the 2020 CHI conference on human factors in computing systems (pp. 1-8).

Casal-Otero, L., Catala, A., Fernández-Morante, C., Taboada, M., Cebreiro, B., & Barro, S. (2023). AI literacy in K-12: A systematic literature review. *International Journal of STEM Education*, *10*(1), 29. DOI: 10.1186/s40594-023-00418-7

CAST. (2018). *The UDL Guidelines.* Retrieved 31/05/2024 from https://udlguidelines.cast.org/

Cavanagh, S. (2013, April 22). Beta testing ed. products can get tricky for schools. *Education Week.* https://www.edweek.org/ew/articles/2013/04/24/29ii-betatest.h32.html

Celik, I. (2023). Towards Intelligent-TPACK: An empirical study on teachers' professional knowledge to ethically integrate artificial intelligence (AI)-based tools into education. *Computers in Human Behavior*, *138*, 107468. DOI: 10.1016/j.chb.2022.107468

Chai, C. S., Lin, P.-Y., Jong, M. S.-Y., Dai, Y., Chiu, T. K. F., & Qin, J. (2021). Perceptions of and behavioral intentions towards learning artificial intelligence in primary school students. *Journal of Educational Technology & Society*, *24*(3), 89–101. https://www.jstor.org/stable/27032858

Charaia, V., & Lashkhi, M. (2023). Innovative FinTech technologies at educational institutions. *Georgian Journal of European Studies*, 119–124. https://gjes.tsu.ge/index.php/gjes/issue/view/6

Charania, A. (2022). *Integrated approach to Technology in Education in India: Implementation and impact*. Taylor & Francis. DOI: 10.4324/9781003300274

Chassignol, M., Khoroshavin, A., Klimova, A., & Bilyatdinova, A. (2018). Artificial Intelligence trends in education: A narrative overview. *Procedia Computer Science*, *136*, 16–24. DOI: 10.1016/j.procs.2018.08.233

Chaudhary, R. (2025). *Advanced Stock Market Prediction Using Long Short-Term Memory Networks: A Comprehensive Deep Learning Framework*. https://doi.org// arXiv.2505.05325DOI: 10.48550

Chaudhary, R., & Kaur, J. (2019). Bridging the Educational Divide with AI in Rural India. *International Journal of Educational Development*, •••, 301–310.

Cheng, M. M., Chuang, H. H., & Smith, T. J. (2022). The role of teacher technology experiences and school technology interactivity in teachers' culturally responsive teaching. *Computers in the Schools*, *39*(2), 163–185.

Chen, W., & Yuan, X. (2021). Financial inclusion in China: An overview. *Frontiers of Business Research in China*, *15*(1), 4. DOI: 10.1186/s11782-021-00098-6

Chen, X., Zou, D., Xie, H., Cheng, G., & Liu, C. (2022). Two decades of artificial intelligence in education. *Journal of Educational Technology & Society*, *25*, 28–47.

Chikri, H., & Kassou, M. (2024). Financial revolution: Innovation powered by FinTech and Artificial Intelligence. *Journal of Theoretical and Applied Information Technology*, *15*(9). www.jatit.org

Chitale, P. A., Gala, J., & Dabre, R. (2024). "An empirical study of in-context learning in LLMs for machine translation". Retrieved from: https://arxiv.org/pdf/2401.12097

Chituc, C. (2021). A framework for Education 4.0 in digital education ecosystems. In *IFIP advances in information and communication technology* (pp. 702–709). DOI: 10.1007/978-3-030-85969-5_66

Chiu, T. K. F. (2021). A holistic approach to the design of artificial intelligence (AI) education for K-12 schools. *TechTrends*, *65*(5), 796–807. DOI: 10.1007/s11528-021-00637-1

Chiu, T. K., & Chai, C. S. (2020). Sustainable curriculum planning for artificial intelligence education: A self-determination theory perspective. *Sustainability (Basel)*, *12*(14), 5568. DOI: 10.3390/su12145568

Choi, J., Yang, E., & Goo, E. (2024). The Effects of an Ethics Education Program on Artificial Intelligence among Middle School Students: Analysis of Perception and Attitude Changes. *Applied Sciences (Basel, Switzerland)*, *14*(4), 1588. DOI: 10.3390/app14041588

Chokhani, R. (2017). Challenges and opportunities for Indian start-ups: Key points to note.

Chounta, I. A., Bardone, E., Raudsep, A., & Pedaste, M. (2022). Exploring teachers' perceptions of artificial intelligence as a tool to support their practice in Estonian K-12 education. *International Journal of Artificial Intelligence in Education*, *32*(3), 725–755. DOI: 10.1007/s40593-021-00243-5

Coşkun, S., Kayıkcı, Y., & Gençay, E. (2019). Adapting engineering education to Industry 4.0 vision. *Technologies*, *7*(1), 10. DOI: 10.3390/technologies7010010

Cotton, D. R. E., Cotton, P. A., & Shipway, J. R. (2023). Chatting and cheating: Ensuring academic integrity in the era of ChatGPT. *Innovations in Education and Teaching International*, •••, 1–12. DOI: 10.1080/14703297.2023.2190148

Croitoru, I. M., Dragan (SPIRIDON), P.-P., Ignat, N. D., & Jumanca, R. (. (2025). Exploring Financial Literacy in Higher Education with the Help of FinTech: A Bibliometric Analysis of Linkages to Access, Behavior, and Well-Being Through Digital Innovation. *FinTech*, *4*(1), 4. DOI: 10.3390/fintech4010004

Crompton, H., Jones, M. V., & Burke, D. (2022). Affordances and challenges of artificial intelligence in K-12 education: A systematic review. *Journal of Research on Technology in Education*. Advance online publication. DOI: 10.1080/15391523.2022.2121344

Cuemath (n.d.). *Online Math and Coding Classes*. https://www.cuemath.com/

D'Mello, S., & Graesser, A. (2012). Dynamics of affective states during complex learning. *Learning and Instruction*, *22*(2), 145–157.

Dahlin, E. (2025). Trust in AI. *AI & Society*, *40*(8), 6089–6095. Advance online publication. DOI: 10.1007/s00146-025-02429-0 PMID: 40225305

Dai, Y., Liu, A., Qin, J., Guo, Y., Jong, M. S. Y., Chai, C. S., & Lin, Z. (2023). Collaborative construction of artificial intelligence curriculum in primary schools. *Journal of Engineering Education*, *112*(1), 23–42. DOI: 10.1002/jee.20503

Dakakni, D., & Safa, N. (2023). Artificial intelligence in the L2 classroom: Implications and challenges on ethics and equity in higher education: A 21st century Pandora's box. *Computers and Education Artificial Intelligence, 5*, 100179. DOI: 10.1016/j.caeai.2023.100179

Danniels, E., & Pyle, A. (2023). Inclusive play-based learning: Approaches from enacting kindergarten teachers. *Early Childhood Education Journal, 51*(7), 1169–1179. DOI: 10.1007/s10643-022-01369-4 PMID: 35755935

Darling-Hammond, L., Flook, L., Cook-Harvey, C., Barron, B., & Osher, D. J. A. d. s. (2020). Implications for educational practice of the science of learning and development. *24*(2), 97-140.

Darling-Hammond, L. (1999). Target Time Toward Teachers. *Journal of Staff Development, 20*(2), 31–36.

Dearing, J. W., & Cox, J. G. (2018). Diffusion of innovations theory, principles, and practice. *Health Affairs, 37*(2), 183–190. DOI: 10.1377/hlthaff.2017.1104 PMID: 29401011

Delello, J. A., Sung, W., Mokhtari, K., Hebert, J., Bronson, A., & De Giuseppe, T. (2025). AI in the Classroom: Insights from Educators on Usage, Challenges, and Mental Health. *Education Sciences, 15*(2), 113. DOI: 10.3390/educsci15020113

Design and Children, Athens, Greece. DOI: 10.1145/3459990.3463394

Dhakshan, S., Balamurugan, G., Mohan, J. S. S., & Tyagi, A. K. (2024). Role of Emerging Technologies in Education 4.0: Challenges and future research directions. In *Role of Emerging Technologies in Education 4.0*. IGI Global., DOI: 10.4018/978-1-6684-9285-7.ch006

Diksha. (n.d.). https://diksha.gov.in/index.html

Dimitriadou, E., & Lanitis, A. (2023). A critical evaluation, challenges, and future perspectives of using artificial intelligence and emerging technologies in smart classrooms. *Smart Learning Environments, 10*(1), 12. Advance online publication. DOI: 10.1186/s40561-023-00231-3 PMID: 40478141

DiPaola, D., Payne, B. H., & Breazeal, C. (2020). Decoding Design Agendas: An Ethical Design Activity for Middle School Students. In *Proceedings of the Interaction Design and Children Conference* (IDC '20) (pp. 1-10). Association for Computing Machinery. DOI: 10.1145/3392063.3394396

Douse, M. (2024). Educational planning and artificial intelligence. *Educational Planning, 31*(2), ISSN-1537-873X. https://files.eric.ed.gov/fulltext/EJ1425308.pdf

Druga, S., Otero, N., & Ko, A. J. (2022). The landscape of teaching resources for ai education. *Proceedings of the 27th ACM Conference on Innovation and Technology in Computer Science Education, 1*, 96-102. DOI: 10.1145/3502718.3524782

Druga, S., Vu, S. T., Likhith, E., & Qiu, T. (2019). Inclusive AI literacy for kids around the world. In *Proceedings of FabLearn 2019* (pp. 104-111). DOI: 10.1145/3311890.3311904

Dubey, Mr. C. K. (2024). Exploring the role of artificial intelligence in inclusive education. Researchgate. https://www.researchgate.net/publication/378907681_Exploring_the_Role_of_Artificial_Intelligence_in_Inclusive_Education

Dubey, G., Hasan, M., & Alam, A. (2022). Artificial intelligence (AI) and Indian education system: Promising applications, potential effectiveness and Challenges. *Towards Excellence, 14*(2), 259–269. DOI: 10.37867/TE140223

Earls, E. M. (2019). *Preparing Students for a Future in FinTech.* https://eric.ed.gov/?q=Preparing+Students+for+a+Future+in+FinTech

Educomp. (2026). Educomp.com. https://www.educomp.com/

Eguchi, A., Okada, H., & Muto, Y. (2021). Contextualizing AI education for K-12 students to enhance their learning of AI literacy through culturally responsive approaches. *Kunstliche Intelligenz, 35*(2), 153–161. DOI: 10.1007/s13218-021-00737-3 PMID: 34376922

EkStep Foundation. (2026). *LinkedIn.* Linkedin.com. https://in.linkedin.com/company/ekstep-foundation

ePathshala. (n.d.). *Learning On The Go.* Epathshala.nic.in. https://epathshala.nic.in/

Etheredge, L. (2025). AI in Education: Global Trends and Country-by-Country Analysis (2018-2023). *TBD.* https://www.researchgate.net/publication/389043586_AI_in_Education_Global_Trends_and_Country-by-Country_Analysis_2018-2023

Evans, P. C., & Gawer, A. (2016). *The rise of the platform enterprise: A global survey.* Center for Global Enterprise.

Extramarks. (n.d.). *CBSE, ICSE, NCERT Solution, JEE & NEET Preparation.* Www.extramarks.com. https://www.extramarks.com/

Fagbohun, O., Iduwe, N. P., Abdullahi, M., Ifaturoti, A., & Nwanna, O. M. (2024). Beyond Traditional Assessment: Exploring the Impact of Large Language Models on Grading Practices. Journal of Artificial Intelligence. *Machine Learning and Data Science, 2*(1), 1–8. DOI: 10.51219/JAIMLD/oluwole-fagbohun/19

Fegade, A., Raut, R., Deshpande, A., Mittal, A., Kaul, N., & Khanna, V. (2023). Unleashing the power of generative artificial intelligence: exploring its boundless potential and overcoming challenges in academic environments. *2023 6th International Conference on Contemporary Computing and Informatics (IC3I)*. DOI: 10.1109/IC3I59117.2023.10397917

Feldmann, N., Kohler, M., Kimbrough, S. O., & Fromm, H. (2013). Service innovation analytics: Towards an approach for validating frameworks for service innovation capabilities via text mining. In Falcão e Cunha, J., Snene, M., & Nóvoa, H. (Eds.), *Exploring services science (IESS 2013)*. Springer. DOI: 10.1007/978-3-642-36356-6_6

Fernández-Martínez, C., Hernán-Losada, I., & Fernández, A. (2021). Early introduction of AI in Spanish middle schools. A motivational study. *KI. Künstliche Intelligenz/ KI - Künstliche Intelligenz, 35*(2), 163–170. DOI: 10.1007/s13218-021-00735-5

Fisk, P. (2017). *Education 4.0 … the future of learning will be dramatically different, in school and throughout life*. Retrieved from http://www.thegeniusworks.com/2017/01/future-education-young-everyone-taught-together

Fitria, T. N. (2021). Artificial intelligence (AI) in education: Using AI tools for teaching and learning process. *Prosiding Seminar Nasional & Call for Paper STIE AAS, 4*(1), 134-147. https://prosiding.stie-aas.ac.id/index.php/prosenas/article/view/106

Fitria, T. N. (2023). The use of Artificial Intelligence in Education (AIED): Can AI replace the teacher's role? *EPIGRAM, 20*(2), 165–187. DOI: 10.32722/epi.v20i2.5711

Fleger, C. B., Amanuel, Y., & Krugel, J. (2023, May). Learning tools using block-based programming for AI education. In *2023 IEEE Global Engineering Education Conference (EDUCON)* (pp. 1-5). IEEE.

Foltýnek, T., Dlabolová, D., Anohina-Naumeca, A., Razı, S., Kravjar, J., Kamzola, L., Guerrero-Dib, J., Çelik, Ö., & Weber-Wulff, D. (2020). Testing of support tools for plagiarism detection. *International Journal of Educational Technology in Higher Education, 17*(1), 46. Advance online publication. DOI: 10.1186/s41239-020-00192-4

Forgas, R., Lancaster, T., Calvo-Sastre, A., & Sureda-Negre, J. (2021). Exam cheating and academic integrity breaches during the COVID-19 pandemic: An analysis of internet search activity in Spain. *Heliyon, 7*(10), e08233. DOI: 10.1016/j.heliyon.2021.e08233 PMID: 34722942

Füller, J., Hutter, K., Wahl, J., Bilgram, V., & Tekic, Z. (2022, May). How AI revolutionizes innovation management – Perceptions and implementation preferences of AI-based innovators. *Technological Forecasting and Social Change*, *178*, 121598. DOI: 10.1016/j.techfore.2022.121598

Gala, J., Chitale, P. A., Raghavan, A. K., Gumma, V., Doddapaneni, S., Kumar, A., Nawale, J., Sujatha, A., Pudupully, R., Raghavan, V., Kumar, P., Khapra, M. M., Dabre, R., & Kunchukuttan, A. (2023). "IndicTrans2: Towards high-quality and accessible machine translation models for all 22 scheduled Indian languages". Retrieved from: https://arxiv.org/pdf/2305.16307

Gala, J., Jayakumar, T., Husain, J. A., Kumar, A. M., Khan, M. S. U. R., Kanojia, D., Pudupully, R., Khapra, M. M., Dabre, R., Murthy, R., & Kunchukuttan, A. (2024). "Airavata: Introducing Hindi instruction-tuned LLM". Retrieved from: https://arxiv.org/pdf/2401.15006

Gardner-McCune, C., & Touretzky, D. (2021). AI For All: Building AI Thinking In Students Through Distributed Learning. In *Proceedings of the ACM Conference on Computing Education Research.*

Garud, S. (2024). Reinforcement Learning for Dynamic Portfolio Optimization in FinTech. *Journal of Information Systems Engineering & Management*, *2025*(45s), 10. https://www.jisem-journal.com/

Gay, G. (2018). *Culturally responsive teaching: Theory, research, and practice.* teachers college press.

Ghosh, S. S. (2024). "Transforming the Indian education landscape: The impact of personalized learning and adaptive technologies in continuing education". *Embracing Technological Advancements for Lifelong Learning*, edited by Mahmoud M. Kh. Hawamdeh and Faiz Abdelhafid, IGI Global, pp. 278-299. DOI: 10.4018/979-8-3693-1410-4.ch013

Giray, L., Jacob, J., & Gumalin, D. L. (2024). Strengths, weaknesses, opportunities, and threats of using ChatGPT in scientific research. *International Journal of Technology in Education*, *7*(1), 40–58. DOI: 10.46328/ijte.618

Giudici, P. (2018a). Financial data science. *Statistics & Probability Letters*, *136*, 160–164. DOI: 10.1016/j.spl.2018.02.024

Giudici, P. (2018b). FinTech Risk Management: A Research Challenge for Artificial Intelligence in Finance. *Frontiers in Artificial Intelligence*, *1*, 1. Advance online publication. DOI: 10.3389/frai.2018.00001 PMID: 33733089

Giuggioli, G., & Pellegrini, M. M. (2022). Artificial intelligence as an enabler for entrepreneurs: A systematic literature review and an agenda for future research. *International Journal of Entrepreneurial Behaviour & Research*, *29*(4), 816–837. DOI: 10.1108/IJEBR-05-2021-0426

Glatthorn, A. A., Boschee, F., Whitehead, B. M., & Boschee, B. F. (2018). *Curriculum leadership: Strategies for development and implementation*. SAGE publications.

Goel, A. (2017). AI Education for the World. *AI Magazine*, *38*(2), 3–4. DOI: 10.1609/aimag.v38i2.2740

Goel, A. K., & Joyner, D. A. (2017). Using AI to teach AI: Lessons from an online AI class. *AI Magazine*, *38*(2), 48–59. DOI: 10.1609/aimag.v38i2.2732

Gökçearslan, Ş., Tosun, C., & Erdemir, Z. G. (2024). Benefits, Challenges, and Methods of Artificial intelligence (AI) chatbots in Education: A Systematic Literature review. *International Journal of Technology in Education*, *7*(1), 19–39. DOI: 10.46328/ijte.600

González-Calatayud, V., Prendes-Espinosa, P., & Roig-Vila, R. (2021). Artificial Intelligence for Student Assessment: A Systematic review. *Applied Sciences (Basel, Switzerland)*, *11*(12), 5467. DOI: 10.3390/app11125467

Grassini, S. (2023). Shaping the Future of Education: Exploring the potential and consequences of AI and ChatGPT in educational settings. *Education Sciences*, *13*(7), 692. DOI: 10.3390/educsci13070692

Grech, A., & Camilleri, A. F. (2017). *Blockchain in education*. Publications Office of the European Union.

Grech, A., Sood, I., & Ariño, L. (2021). Blockchain, self-sovereign identity and digital credentials: Promise versus praxis in education. *Frontiers in Blockchain*, *4*, 616779.

Grover, S., & Pea, R. (2013). Computational thinking in K–12: A review of the state of the field. *Educational Researcher*, *42*(1), 38–43. DOI: 10.3102/0013189X12463051

Gruenhagen, J. H., Sinclair, P. M., Carroll, J.-A., Baker, P. R. A., Wilson, A., & Demant, D. (2024). *The rapid rise of generative AI and its implications for academic integrity: Students' perceptions and use of chatbots for assistance with assessments*. ScienceDirect., DOI: 10.1016/j.caeai.2024.100273

Gülen, K. (2023, February 3). *Introduction to artificial intelligence in education*. Data Economy. https://octaedro.com/libro/introduction-to-artificial-intelligence-in-education/

Gupta, A., & Ladiwal, O. (2021). Digital education in India: Future perspective and challenges. *SKIT Research Journal, 11*(2), 87–92. DOI: 10.47904/IJSKIT.11.2.2021.87-92

Gurram, A. (2025). Demystifying Generative AI for Financial Services. *European Journal of Computer Science and Information Technology, 13*(16), 73–86. DOI: 10.37745/ejcsit.2013/vol13n167386

Gustilo, L., Ong, E., & Lapinid, M. R. (2024). Algorithmically-driven writing and academic integrity: Exploring educators' practices, perceptions, and policies in AI era. *International Journal for Educational Integrity, 20*(1), 3. Advance online publication. DOI: 10.1007/s40979-024-00153-8

Hakimi, M., Katebzadah, S., & Fazil, A. W. (2024). Comprehensive Insights into E-Learning in contemporary Education: Analyzing trends, challenges, and best practices. [JETL]. *Journal of Education and Teaching Learning, 6*(1), 86–105. DOI: 10.51178/jetl.v6i1.1720

Häkli, J. (2018). The subject of citizenship–Can there be a posthuman civil society? *Political Geography, 67*, 166–175. DOI: 10.1016/j.polgeo.2017.08.006

Hallahan, D. E., Kauffman, J. M., & Pullen, P. C. (2013). *Exceptional Learners: An Introduction to Special Education: Pearson New International Edition*. Pearson Higher Ed.

Hamilton, I. (2024, June 6). Artificial intelligence in Education: Teachers' opinions on AI in the classroom. Forbes Advisor. https://www.forbes.com/advisor/education/it-and-tech/artificial-intelligence-in-school/

Haoyang, D. L., & Towne, J. (2025, January 9). *AI in education: Real-world success stories*. World Economic Forum. https://tinyurl.com/2s4xkphn

Haque MdA. Sonal D, Haque, S., Rahman, M., & Kumar, K. (2022). Learning management system empowered by machine learning. *AIP Conference Proceedings, 2381*, 020085. DOI: 10.1063/5.0074278

Haque, S., Zeba, S., Haque, M. A., Kumar, K., & Basha, M. P. A. (2023). An IoT model for securing examinations from malpractices. *Materials Today: Proceedings, 81*, 371–376. DOI: 10.1016/j.matpr.2021.03.413

Harun, H. N., & Sallehuddin, Q. (2024, March 25). AI basics to be integrated into primary school curriculum by 2027. *New Straits Times*. https://www.nst.com.my/news/nation/2024/03/1030434/ai-basics-be-integrated-primary-school-curriculum-2027

Hehir, T., Grindal, T., Freeman, B., Lamoreau, R., Borquaye, Y., & Burke, S. (2016). *A summary of the evidence on inclusive education*. Abt Associates.

Hemachandran, K., Verma, P., Pareek, P., Arora, N., Kumar, K. V. R., Ahanger, T. A., Pise, A. A., & Ratna, R. (2022). Artificial intelligence: A universal virtual tool to augment tutoring in higher education. *Computational Intelligence and Neuroscience*, *2022*, 1–8. DOI: 10.1155/2022/1410448 PMID: 35586099

Henry, J., Hernalesteen, A., & Collard, A.-S. (2021). Teaching artificial intelligence to K-12 through a role-playing game questioning the intelligence concept. *Kunstliche Intelligenz*, *35*(2), 171–179. DOI: 10.1007/s13218-021-00733-7

Hess, F. M., & Henig, J. R. (Eds.). (2015). *The new education philanthropy: Politics, policy, and reform*. Harvard Education Press.

Hidayat, M. T. J. J. L. D. (2024).. . *Effectiveness of AI-Based Personalised Reading Platforms in Enhancing Reading Comprehension.*, *11*(1), 115–125.

Hitron, T., Wald, I., Erel, H., & Zuckerman, O. (2018, June). Introducing children to machine learning concepts through hands-on experience. In *Proceedings of the 17th ACM conference on interaction design and children* (pp. 563-568). DOI: 10.1145/3202185.3210776

Hogan, A., Sellar, S., & Lingard, B. (2016). Commercialising comparison: Pearson puts the TLC in soft capitalism. *Journal of Education Policy*, *31*(3), 243–258. DOI: 10.1080/02680939.2015.1112922

Holmes, W., Bialik, M., & Fadel, C. (2021). Artificial Intelligence in Education: Promises and Implications for Teaching and Learning. *OECD Education Working Papers*, 188.

Holmes, W., Bialik, M., & Fadel, C. (2019). *Artificial intelligence in education promises and implications for teaching and learning*. Center for Curriculum Redesign.

Holmes, W., Bialik, M., & Fadel, C. (2023). *Artificial intelligence in education*. Globethics Publications.

Holmes, W., & Tuomi, I. (2022). State of the art and practice in AI in education. *European Journal of Education*, *57*(4), 542–570. DOI: 10.1111/ejed.12533

Holstein, K., & Aleven, V. (2022). Designing for human–AI complementarity in K-12 education. *AI Magazine*, *43*(2), 239–248. DOI: 10.1002/aaai.12058

Holstein, K., McLaren, B. M., & Aleven, V. (2019). Student-Centered AI in Education: Bringing Context and Policy Considerations into Design and Implementation. *AI Magazine*, *40*(2), 54–63.

Hooda, M., & Chandan, . (2023). Opportunities and challenges for artificial intelligence in Indian education. *Scholarly Research Journal for Humanity Science & English Language, 11/57*, 124–135.

Hooda, M., Rana, C., Dahiya, O., Rizwan, A., & Hossain, M. S. (2022). Artificial intelligence for assessment and feedback to enhance student success in higher education. *Mathematical Problems in Engineering, 2022*, 1–19. DOI: 10.1155/2022/5215722

Hossain, Z. (2022). University freshmen recollect their academic integrity literacy experience during their K-12 years: Results of an empirical study. *International Journal for Educational Integrity, 18*(1), 4. Advance online publication. DOI: 10.1007/s40979-021-00096-4

Hossain, Z., Çelik, Ö., & Hertel, C. (2022). Academic Integrity Policy and Instruction in K-12 schools in Australia, Canada, England and the United States. *IASL Annual Conference Proceedings*. DOI: 10.29173/iasl8548

Huang, L. (2023). Ethics of artificial intelligence in education: Student privacy and data protection. *Science Insights Education Frontiers, 16*(2), 2577–2587. DOI: 10.15354/sief.23.re202

Huang, X. (2021). Aims for cultivating students' key competencies based on artificial intelligence education in China. *Education and Information Technologies, 26*(5), 5127–5147. DOI: 10.1007/s10639-021-10530-2

Huk, T. (2021). From Education 1.0 to Education 4.0 - Challenges for the Contemporary School. opus.us.edu.pl. https://doi.org/DOI: 10.15804/tner.2021.66.4.03

Hunter, D., McCallum, J., & Howes, D. (2019). Defining Exploratory-Descriptive Qualitative (EDQ) research and considering its application to healthcare. *Journal of Nursing and Health Care, 4*(1). http://eprints.gla.ac.uk/180272

Huong, X. V. (2024). The implications of artificial intelligence for educational systems: Challenges, opportunities, and transformative potential. *The American Journal of Social Science and Education Innovations, 06*(03), 101–111. DOI: 10.37547/tajssei/Volume06Issue03-17

Hurst, A. (2021). *Developing future-ready skills with peer coaching. The Future of Workplace Learning*. MIT Sloan Management Review., https://f.hubspotusercontent10.net/hubfs/3046411/MITSMR-Future-of-Workplace-Learning-Executive-Guide-2021.pdf#page=7

Ikumapayi, J. O. (2025). The Convergence of FinTech Innovations, AI, And Risk Management: Transforming Traditional Banking, Accounting, And Financial Services. *International Research Journal of Modernization in Engineering Technology and Science*, *7*(2). Advance online publication. DOI: 10.56726/IRJMETS67253

India's AI teacher Iris, a promise for intelligent workforce. (n.d.). INDIAai. https://indiaai.gov.in/article/india-s-ai-teacher-iris-a-promise-for-intelligent-workforce

Injadat, M., Moubayed, A., Nassif, A. B., & Shami, A. (2021). Machine learning towards intelligent Systems: applications, challenges, and opportunities. *Artificial Intelligence Review*. https://arxiv.org/pdf/2101.03655

Intel. (2020). *AI for Youth Program*. https://www.intel.com/content/www/us/en/corporate/artificial-intelligence/digital-readiness-ai-for-youth.html

Ivanitskaya, L., Clark, D., Montgomery, G., & Primeau, R. (2002). Interdisciplinary learning: Process and outcomes. Innovative Higher Education. *Innovative Higher Education*, *27*(2), 95–111. DOI: 10.1023/A:1021105309984

Iwasiuk, D. (2016). Key challenges, opportunities for tech startups in emerging markets. *Moneycontrol.com*.

Jafri, J. A., Mohd Amin, S. I., Abdul Rahman, A., & Mohd Nor, S. (2024). A systematic literature review of the role of trust and security on FinTech adoption in banking. *Heliyon*, *10*(1), e22980. DOI: 10.1016/j.heliyon.2023.e22980 PMID: 38163181

Jaiswal, A., & Arun, C. J. (2021). "Potential of artificial intelligence for transformation of the education system in India". *International Journal of Education and Development using Information and Communication Technology* (*IJEDICT*), 17 (1), pp. 142-158.

Jamro, M. Y., Jamro, F. A., & Print, O. (2024). *AI Matters: Chatbot Integration in Holistic STEM Education*. https://researchprofiles.herts.ac.uk/en/publications/ai-matters-chatbot-integration-in-holistic-stem-education

Jaskie, K., Larson, J., Johnson, M., Turner, K., O'Donnell, M., Christen, J. B., & Spanias, A. (2021). Research experiences for teachers in machine learning. In *IEEE Frontiers in Education Conference (FIE)* (pp. 1–5). Lincoln, NE, USA. DOI: 10.1109/FIE49875.2021.9637132

Javed, T., Nawale, J. A., George, E. I., Joshi, S., Bhogale, K. S., Mehendale, D., Sethi, I. V., Ananthanarayanan, A., Faquih, H., Palit, P., Ravishankar, S., Sukumaran, S., Panchangnula, T., Murali, S., Gandhi, K. S., Ambujavali, R., Manickam, K. M., Vaijayanthi, C. V., Kaunganni, K. S. R., . . . Khapra, M. M. (2024). "IndicVoices: Towards building an inclusive multilingual speech dataset for Indian languages". Retrieved from: https://arxiv.org/pdf/2403.01926

Jiang, S., Tang, H., Tatar, C., Rosé, C. P., & Chao, J. (2023). High school students' data modeling practices and processes: From modeling unstructured data to evaluating automated decisions. *Learning, Media and Technology*, *48*(2), 350–368. DOI: 10.1080/17439884.2023.2189735

Jian, H., Li, G., & Wang, W. (2020). Perceptions, contexts, attitudes, and academic dishonesty in Chinese senior college students: A qualitative content-based analysis. *Ethics & Behavior*, *30*(7), 543–555. DOI: 10.1080/10508422.2020.1711758

Jindal, A., & Bansal, M. (2023). Knowledge and education about artificial intelligence among medical students from teaching institutions of India: A brief survey. *MedEdPublish*, *2020*, 1–9.

Johansen, M. W., Goddiksen, M. P., Centa, M., Clavien, C., Gefenas, E., Globokar, R., Hogan, L., Merit, M. T., Nielsen, S. S., Olsson, I. S., Poškutė, M., Quinn, U., Santos, J. B., Santos, R., Schöpfer, C., Strahovnik, V., Wall, P. J., Sandøe, P., & Lund, T. B. (2022). Lack of ethics or lack of knowledge? European upper secondary students' doubts and misconceptions about integrity issues. *International Journal for Educational Integrity*, *18*(1), 20. Advance online publication. DOI: 10.1007/s40979-022-00113-0

Josyula, H. P. (2023). *Fraud Detection in FinTech Leveraging Machine Learning and Behavioral Analytics*. DOI: 10.21203/rs.3.rs-3548343/v1

Kabudi, T., Pappas, I. O., & Olsen, D. H. (2021). AI-enabled adaptive learning systems: A systematic mapping of the literature. *Computers and Education Artificial Intelligence*, *2*, 100017. DOI: 10.1016/j.caeai.2021.100017

Kajiwara, Y., Matsuoka, A., & Shinbo, F. (2023). Machine learning role-playing game: Instructional design of AI education for age-appropriate in K–12 and beyond. *Computers and Education: Artificial Intelligence*, *5*, 100162. DOI: 10.1016/j.caeai.2023.100162

Kalyanakrishnan, S., Panicker, R. A., Natarajan, S., & Rao, S. (2018). "Opportunities and challenges for artificial intelligence in India". In 2018 *AAAI/ACM Conference on AI, Ethics, and Society* (*AIES '18*), February 2–3, 2018, New Orleans, LA, USA. ACM, New York, NY, USA, pp. 164-170. DOI: 10.1145/3278721.3278738

Kandlhofer, M., Steinbauer, G., Hirschmugl-Gaisch, S., & Huber, P. (2016). Artificial intelligence and computer science in education: From kindergarten to university. In *2016 IEEE Frontiers in Education Conference (FIE)* (pp. 1–9). IEEE.

Kandlhofer, M., & Steinbauer, G. (2021). AI K-12 education service. *Kunstliche Intelligenz, 35*(2), 125–126. DOI: 10.1007/s13218-021-00715-9

Kapoor, N. (2021). *Principles of marketing*. PHI Learning Pvt. Ltd.

Kapron, Z. (2025, March 5). *AI In FinTech: Regulations, Opportunities, Ethical Imperatives*. Forbes. https://www.forbes.com/sites/zennonkapron/2025/03/05/ai-in-FinTech-regulations-opportunities-ethical-imperatives/

Karakose, T., & Tulubas, T. (2024). School leadership and management in the age of Artificial intelligence (AI): Recent developments and future prospects. *Educational Process International Journal, 13*(1). Advance online publication. DOI: 10.22521/edupij.2024.131.1

Karan, B., & Angadi, G. (2024). Potential Risks of Artificial Intelligence Integration into School Education: A Systematic Review. *Bulletin of Science, Technology & Society; Sage Publications.*

Kasneci, E., Sessler, K., Küchemann, S., Bannert, M., Dementieva, D., Fischer, F., Gasser, U., Groh, G., Günnemann, S., Hüllermeier, E., Krusche, S., Kutyniok, G., Michaeli, T., Nerdel, C., Pfeffer, J., Poquet, O., Sailer, M., Schmidt, A., Seidel, T., & Kasneci, G. (2023). ChatGPT for good? On opportunities and challenges of large language models for education. *Learning and Individual Differences, 103*, 102274. DOI: 10.1016/j.lindif.2023.102274

Kauffman, J. M. (1997). *Characteristics of emotional and behavioral disorders of children and youth*. ERIC.

Kaur, S., Tandon, N., & Matharou, G. S. (2020). Contemporary Trends in education transformation using Artificial Intelligence. In *CRC Press eBooks* (pp. 89–103). DOI: 10.1201/9781003032410-7

Kay, J. (2001). Learner control. *User Modeling and User-Adapted Interaction, 11*(1), 111–127. DOI: 10.1023/A:1011194803800

Kelly, A. (2009). The curriculum. *Theory into Practice.*

Kementerian Pendidikan Malaysia. (2023). *Dasar pendidikan digital*. Kementerian Pendidikan Malaysia. https://www.moe.gov.my/storage/files/shares/Dasar/Dasar%20Pendidikan%20Digital/Dasar%20Pendidikan%20Digital.pdf?_t=1709571105

Khalil, M., & Er, E. (2023). Will ChatGPT get you caught? Rethinking of plagiarism detection. In *Lecture notes in computer science* (pp. 475–487). DOI: 10.1007/978-3-031-34411-4_32

Khan Academy. (n.d.). https://www.khanacademy.org/

Khan, M. S. U. R., Mehta, P., Sankar, A., Kumaravelan, U., Doddapaneni, S., Suriyaprasad, G., & Balan, G. V., Jain, S., Kunchukuttan, A., Kumar, P, Dabre, R., and Khapra, M. M. (2024). "IndicLLMSuite: A blueprint for creating pre-training and fine-tuning datasets for Indian languages". Retrieved from: https://arxiv.org/pdf/2403.06350

Khan, A. (2023). ICT and digital revolution: implications for teacher education. In Ahmad, J., & Masih, A. (Eds.), *Teaching and Teacher Education in India*. Springer., DOI: 10.1007/978-981-99-4985-4_17

Khanna, P., Sehgal, R., Malviya, M., Khanna, A., & Dubey, A. M. (2023). "EdTech start-ups: A mode of transformation in teaching and learning". *Asia-Pacific Business Series| Indian SMEs and Start-Ups*, pp. 177-202.

Khan, S. (2012). *The one world schoolhouse: Education reimagined*. Twelve.

Khor, E. T., & Muthulakshmi, K. (2024). A systematic review of the role of learning analytics in supporting personalized learning. *Education Sciences*, *14*(1), 51. DOI: 10.3390/educsci14010051

Kim, H., Park, J., Hong, S., Park, Y., Kim, E., Cho, J., & Kim, Y. (2020). Teachers' perceptions of AI in school education. *Journal of Educational Technology*, *36*(3), 905–930. DOI: 10.17232/KSET.36.3.905

Kim, J., Lee, H., & Cho, Y. H. (2022). Learning design to support student-AI collaboration: Perspectives of leading teachers for AI in education. *Education and Information Technologies*, *27*(5), 6069–6104. DOI: 10.1007/s10639-021-10831-6

Kim, K., Kwon, K., Ottenbreit-Leftwich, A., Bae, H., & Glazewski, K. (2023). Exploring middle school students' common naive conceptions of Artificial Intelligence concepts, and the evolution of these ideas. *Education and Information Technologies*, *28*(8), 9827–9854. Advance online publication. DOI: 10.1007/s10639-023-11600-3

Kim, S., Jang, Y., Kim, W., Choi, S., Jung, H., Kim, S., & Kim, H. (2021). Why and What to Teach: AI Curriculum for Elementary School. *Proceedings of the AAAI Conference on Artificial Intelligence*, *35*(17), 15569–15576. DOI: 10.1609/aaai.v35i17.17833

Kitchenham, B., Brereton, O. P., Budgen, D., Turner, M., & Bailey, J. (2009). Systematic literature reviews in software engineering – A systematic literature review. *Information &amp. Information and Software Technology*, *51*(1), 7–15. DOI: 10.1016/j.infsof.2008.09.009

Kjær Bilstrup, K.-E., Kaspersen, M. H., & Petersen, M. G. (2020). Staging Reflections on Ethical Dilemmas in Machine Learning: A Card-Based Design Workshop for High School Students. In Proceedings of the 2020 ACM Designing Interactive Systems Conference (pp. 1211–1222).

Knyazeva, N., Mikhailova, I., Usmanova, N., & Shindina, T. (2022). Overcoming barriers in developing digital skills for higher education teachers: Challenges and solutions. Review of Artificial Intelligence in Education, 3, e024. Researchgate. https://www.researchgate.net/publication/378165747_Overcoming_Barriers_in_Developing_Digital_Skills_for_Higher_Education_Teachers_Challenges_and_Solutions

Kohler, M., Feldmann, N., Kimbrough, S. O., & Fromm, H. (2014). Service innovation analytics: Leveraging existing unstructured data to assess service innovation capability. *International Journal of Information System Modeling and Design*, *5*(2), 1–21. DOI: 10.4018/ijismd.2014040101

Kooli, C. (2023). Chatbots in Education and Research: A Critical Examination of ethical implications and solutions. *Sustainability (Basel)*, *15*(7), 5614. DOI: 10.3390/su15075614

Kou, G., & Lu, Y. (2025). FinTech: A literature review of emerging financial technologies and applications. *Financial Innovation*, *11*(1), 1. DOI: 10.1186/s40854-024-00668-6

KPMG. (2024). *Ten Key Regulatory Challenges of 2025*. https://kpmg.com/us/en/articles/2024/ten-key-regulatory-challenges-of-2025.html

Kuleto, V., Ilić, M., Dumangiu, M. A., Ranković, M., Martins, O., Păun, D., & Mihoreanu, L. (2021, September 18). Exploring Opportunities and Challenges of Artificial Intelligence and Machine Learning in Higher Education Institutions. *Sustainability (Basel)*, *13*(18), 10424. Advance online publication. DOI: 10.3390/su131810424

Kumar, A. (2021). "New education policy (NEP) 2020: A roadmap for India 2.0". In W. B. James, C. Cobanoglu, & M. Cavusoglu (Eds.), *Advances in global education and research*, 4, pp. 1–8. USF M3 Publishing.

Kumar, R., & Kumari, S. (2020). Digital Divide and AI in Indian Education. *Asian Journal of Educational Research*, 55-67.

Kumar, R., Eaton, S. E., Mindzak, M., & Morrison, R. (2024). Academic integrity and artificial intelligence: An overview. In Springer international handbooks of education (pp. 1583–1596). DOI: 10.1007/978-3-031-54144-5_153

Kumar, D., Haque, A., Mishra, K., Islam, F., Mishra, B. K., & Ahmad, S. (2023). Exploring the transformative role of artificial intelligence and metaverse in education: A comprehensive review. *Metaverse Basic and Applied Research, 2*, 55–55. DOI: 10.56294/mr202355

Kumar, D., & Lal, R. (2023). Technological advancements in the media industry and the current job market in India. In Naim, A. (Ed.), *Accreditation processes and frameworks in higher education* (pp. 289–314). Nova Science Publishers.

Kumar, D., & Lal, R. (2023). Technological Advancements in the Media Industry and the Current Job Market in India. In Naim, A. (Ed.), *Accreditation Processes and Frameworks in Higher Education* (pp. 289–314). Nova Science Publishers.

Kumar, K. S., Prabu, M. M., Kalaiyarasan, G., Selvan, A., Ramnath, R., & Kumar, N. S. (2022). Exploring artificial intelligence and robotics in Indian education: Potential for teacher substitution? *International Journal of Emerging Knowledge Studies, 1*(1), 14–19. DOI: 10.70333/ijeks-01-12-003

Kwangmuang, P., Somabut, A., Duangngern, P., Changpetch, S., Dhithjaroen, C., Techapornpong, O., Sarakan, P., Chaijaroen, S., & Samat, C. (2025a). Designing an AI-enhanced blockchain and FinTech curriculum for youth: A case study of educational and industrial collaboration. *Education and Information Technologies, 30*(10), 13961–13997. Advance online publication. DOI: 10.1007/s10639-025-13384-0

Labadze, L., Grigolia, M., & Machaidze, L. (2023). *Role of AI chatbots in Education: Systematic literature review*. Researchgate., DOI: 10.1186/s41239-023-00426-1

Lai, C.-L. (2021). Exploring University Students' Preferences for AI-Assisted Learning Environment on JSTOR. www.jstor.org. https://www.jstor.org/stable/48629241?searchText=chatbot%20and%20academic%20integrity

Lai, C. Y., Cheung, K. Y., & Chan, C. S. (2023). Exploring the role of intrinsic motivation in ChatGPT adoption to support active learning: An extension of the technology acceptance model. *Computers and Education Artificial Intelligence, 5*, 100178. DOI: 10.1016/j.caeai.2023.100178

Lal, R., & Sharma, G. (2021). Social media influencers for online purchase behaviour: Mediation by brand consciousness. *Journal of Content. Community & Communication, 13*(7), 83–94.

Leading Online Learning Platform & EdTech for Schools. (2026). Schoolnetindia.com. https://www.schoolnetindia.com/offerings/digital-classrooms/k-yan.php

Leal, A. A. (2024). *Algorithms, Creditworthiness, and Lending Decisions*, 321–353. DOI: 10.1007/978-3-031-47946-5_17

Lee, D. K. C., Lim, J., Phoon, K. F., & Wang, Y. (2022). *Applications and Trends in FinTech I* (Vol. 04). WORLD SCIENTIFIC., DOI: 10.1142/12578

Lee, H. S., & Lee, J. (2021). Applying artificial intelligence in physical education and future perspectives. *Sustainability (Basel), 13*(1), 351. DOI: 10.3390/su13010351

Lee, I., & Perret, B. (2022). Preparing High School Teachers to Integrate AI Methods into STEM Classrooms. *Proceedings of the AAAI Conference on Artificial Intelligence, 36*(11), 12783–12791. DOI: 10.1609/aaai.v36i11.21557

Lee, S. J., & Kwon, K. (2024). A systematic review of AI education in K-12 classrooms from 2018 to 2023: Topics, strategies, and learning outcomes. *Computers and Education Artificial Intelligence, 100211*, 100211. Advance online publication. DOI: 10.1016/j.caeai.2024.100211

Lee, V. R., Pope, D., Miles, S., & Zárate, R. C. (2024). Cheating in the age of generative AI: A high school survey study of cheating behaviors before and after the release of ChatGPT. *Computers and Education Artificial Intelligence, 7*, 100253. DOI: 10.1016/j.caeai.2024.100253

Leiblein, M. J. (2018). Platform innovation. In Augier, M., & Teece, D. J. (Eds.), *The Palgrave encyclopedia of strategic management*. DOI: 10.1057/978-1-137-00772-8_363

Levantesi, S., & Zacchia, G. (2021). Machine Learning and Financial Literacy: An Exploration of Factors Influencing Financial Knowledge in Italy. *Journal of Risk and Financial Management, 14*(3), 120. DOI: 10.3390/jrfm14030120

Liang, X., Haiping, L., Liu, J., & Lin, L. (2021). Reform of English interactive teaching mode based on cloud computing artificial intelligence – a practice analysis. *Journal of Intelligent & Fuzzy Systems, 40*(2), 3617–3629. DOI: 10.3233/JIFS-189397

Li, L., Fengchao, Y., & Zhang, E. (2024). A systematic review of learning task design for K-12 AI education: Trends, challenges, and opportunities. *Computers and Education Artificial Intelligence, 6*, 100217. DOI: 10.1016/j.caeai.2024.100217

Lim, W. M., Gunasekara, A., Pallant, J. L., Pallant, J. I., & Pechenkina, E. (2023). Generative AI and the future of education: Ragnarök or reformation? A paradoxical perspective from management educators. *International Journal of Management Education, 21*(2), 100790. DOI: 10.1016/j.ijme.2023.100790

Lin, P., & Van Brummelen, J. (2021, May). Engaging teachers to co-design integrated AI curriculum for K-12 classrooms. In *Proceedings of the 2021 CHI conference on human factors in computing systems* (pp. 1-12). DOI: 10.1145/3411764.3445377

Li, R. (2020). *Artificial Intelligence Revolution: How AI will change our society, economy, and culture*. Skyhorse Publishing.

Liu, C., Chen, Y., & Mo, F. (2023). Transforming organic chemistry research paradigms: Moving from manual efforts to the intersection of automation and artificial intelligence. *National Science Open, 20230037*, 20230037. Advance online publication. DOI: 10.1360/nso/20230037

Liu, M., & Yu, D. (2022). Towards intelligent E-learning systems. *Education and Information Technologies*, *28*(7), 7845–7876. DOI: 10.1007/s10639-022-11479-6 PMID: 36532790

Liu, X., Wang, C., Zhao, S., Ding, J., & Jia, Y. (2024). Role of FinTech adoption in the impact of sustainable policy intervention on enterprise transformation in resource-based cities: Evidence from China. *Resources Policy*, *88*, 104443. DOI: 10.1016/j.resourpol.2023.104443

Li, X., Chen, W., & Alrasheedi, M. (2023). Challenges of the collaborative innovation system in public higher education in the era of industry 4.0 using an integrated framework. *Journal of Innovation & Knowledge*, *8*(4), 100430. DOI: 10.1016/j.jik.2023.100430

Lord, C., Elsabbagh, M., Baird, G., & Veenstra-Vanderweele, J. J. T. l. (2018). Autism spectrum disorder. *392*(10146), 508-520.

Lozi, A. E., Alfityani, A., & Alsmadi, A. A., Al_Hazimeh, A. M., & Al-Gasawneh, J. A. (. (2022). The role of big data in financial sector: A review paper. *International Journal of Data and Network Science*, *6*(4), 1319–1330. DOI: 10.5267/j.ijdns.2022.6.003

Ltd, H. I. P. (n.d.). *School ERP | Campus Management System | Education ERP*. MyClassCampus. https://myclasscampus.com/home

Luckin, R., Cukurova, M., Kent, C., & Du Boulay, B. (2022). Empowering educators to be AI-ready. *Computers and Education: Artificial Intelligence*, *3*, 100076. DOI: 10.1016/j.caeai.2022.100076

Luckin, R., Holmes, M., Griffiths, B., & Forcier, L. (2016).. . *Intelligence*.

Luckin, R., Holmes, W., Griffiths, M., & Forcier, L. B. (2016). *Intelligence Unleashed: An Argument for AI in Education*. Pearson.

Lusardi, A., & Messy, F.-A. (2023). The importance of financial literacy and its impact on financial wellbeing. *Journal of Financial Literacy and Wellbeing*, *1*(1), 1–11. DOI: 10.1017/flw.2023.8

Madhani, Y., Parthan, S., Bedekar, P., Gokul, N. C., Khapra, R., Kunchukuttan, A., Kumar, P., & Khapra, M. M. (2022). "Aksharantar: Open Indic-language transliteration datasets and models for the next billion users". Retrieved from: https://arxiv.org/pdf/2205.03018

Magaldi, D., & Berler, M. (2020). Semi-structured interviews. In Zeigler-Hill, V., & Shackelford, T. K. (Eds.), *Encyclopedia of personality and individual differences*. Springer., DOI: 10.1007/978-3-319-24612-3_857

Mahalingam, T. (2024). Bridging the gap between academia and industry: A case study of collaborative curriculum development. *International Journal of Business Performance Management*, *25*(4), 589–603. DOI: 10.1504/IJBPM.2024.139482

Maiseli, B., Abdalla, A. T., Massawe, L. V., Mbise, M., Mkocha, K., Nassor, N. A., Ismail, M., Michael, J., & Kimambo, S. (2023). Brain–computer interface: Trend, challenges, and threats. *Brain Informatics*, *10*(1), 20. Advance online publication. DOI: 10.1186/s40708-023-00199-3 PMID: 37540385

Majorana, C. D. B., Gonçalves, R. B., Neto, F. L. A., & Camargo, R. Z. (2022). Enhancing Administrative Efficiency in Higher Education with AI: A Chatbot Solution. Review of Artificial Intelligence in Education, 3, e023. Researchgate. https://www.researchgate.net/publication/378170981_Enhancing_Administrative_Efficiency_in_Higher_Education_with_AI_A_Chatbot_Solution

Makhambetova, A., Zhiyenbayeva, N., & Ergesheva, E. (2021). Personalized learning strategy as a tool to improve academic performance and motivation of students. [IJWLTT]. *International Journal of Web-Based Learning and Teaching Technologies*, *16*(6), 1–17. DOI: 10.4018/IJWLTT.286743

Malhotra, C. (2024). Digital India: Past, present and future. In Müller, M. H. P. (Ed.), *Indien im 21. Jahrhundert – Auf dem Weg zur postindustriellen Ökonomie*. Ökonomien und Gesellschaften im Wandel. Springer Gabler., DOI: 10.1007/978-3-658-43014-6_19

Mandal, R., & Mete, J. (2023). Teachers' and students' perception towards integration of Artificial Intelligence in school curriculum: A survey. *International Journal of Multidisciplinary Educational Research, 12*(5), 95–103. http://ijmer.in.doi./2023/12.07.93

Marques, L. S., Gresse von Wangenheim, C., & Hauck, J. C. (2020). Teaching machine learning in school: A systematic mapping of the state of the art. *Informatics in Education, 19*(2), 283–321. DOI: 10.15388/infedu.2020.14

Marrone, R., Taddeo, V., & Hill, G. (2022). Creativity and Artificial Intelligence—A student perspective. *Journal of Intelligence, 10*(3), 65. DOI: 10.3390/jintelligence10030065 PMID: 36135606

Martin, F., Zhuang, M., & Schaefer, D. (2023). Systematic review of research on artificial intelligence in K–12 education (2017–2022). *Computers and Education: Artificial Intelligence*, 100195.

Mason, J., Peoples, B. E., & Lee, J. (2020). Questioning the scope of AI standardization in learning, education, and training. *Journal of ICT Standardisation*, •••, 107–122. DOI: 10.13052/jicts2245-800X.822

Mata, F. J., & Quesada, A. (2014). Web 2.0, social networks and e-commerce as marketing tools. *Journal of Theoretical and Applied Electronic Commerce Research, 9*(1), 56–69. DOI: 10.4067/S0718-18762014000100006

McLaren, B. M., Richey, J. E., Nguyen, H., Hou, X. J. C., & education. (2022). How instructional context can impact learning with educational technology: Lessons from a study with a digital learning game. *178*, 104366.

Mengist, W., Soromessa, T., & Legese, G. (2020). Method for conducting systematic literature review and meta-analysis for environmental science research. *MethodsX, 7*, 100777. DOI: 10.1016/j.mex.2019.100777 PMID: 31993339

Meritnation. (2019). *Meritnation: The No.1 Education Site with Study Material & Live Classes for CBSE, ICSE, CPT, IITJEE, AIPMT & more*. Meritnation.com. https://www.meritnation.com/

Meyer, A., Rose, D. H., & Gordon, D. J. (2014). Universal design for learning. *Theory into Practice*.

Miao, F., Holmes, W., Huang, R., & Zhang, H. (2021). *AI and education: A guidance for policymakers*. UNESCO Publishing.

Microsoft. (2024). *Microsoft Designer - Stunning designs in a flash*. Designer.microsoft.com. https://designer.microsoft.com/

Microsoft. (2024). *Technology Solutions for Schools | Microsoft Education*. Microsoft.com. https://www.microsoft.com/en-in/education

Mikeladze, T. (2023). Creating teaching materials with ChatGPT. In 13th International Research Conference on Education, Language and Literature. https://www.academia.edu/110954212/Creating_teaching_materials_with_ChatGPT

Miles, H., & Ari, F. J. T. (2022). Implementing Personalized Reading Plans with an E-Book Library to Support First-Grade Students'. *Reading Engagement and Comprehension.*, *66*(6), 914–922.

Miller, D. (2024, October 24). *AI and FinTech: Revolutionizing Education Finance*. Future Skills. https://futureskillsacademy.com/blog/ai-and-FinTech-in-education-finance-planning/?form=MG0AV3

Milner, A. E., Thomas, M., Kobbe, E., Fowler, B., Cardon, P., & Marshall, B. (2023). FinTech curricula: A survey of is, accounting, and finance department chairs. *Issues in Information Systems*. Advance online publication. DOI: 10.48009/2_iis_2023_119

Ministry of Education Malaysia. (2024, February). *Education system*. Kementerian Pendidikan. https://www.moe.gov.my/en/dasarmenu/sistem-pendidikan

Mintz, J., Holmes, W., Liu, L., & Ortiz, M. P. (2023, November 28). *Artificial Intelligence and K-12 Education: Possibilities, Pedagogies and Risks*. https://www.tandfonline.com/doi/full/10.1080/07380569.2023.2279870

Mintz, J., Holmes, W., Liu, L., & Perez-Ortiz, M. (2023). Artificial Intelligence and K-12 Education: Possibilities, Pedagogies and Risks. *Computers in the Schools*, *40*(4), 325–333. DOI: 10.1080/07380569.2023.2279870

Mitra, S. (2018). The Future of Learning: AI in Indian Classrooms. *Indian Journal of Educational Technology*, 97 - 109.

Mo, H., & Ouyang, S. (2025). *(Generative) AI in Financial Economics* *. https://papers.ssrn.com/sol3/papers.cfm?abstract_id=5287110

Mohammadkarimi, E. (2023). Teachers' reflections on academic dishonesty in EFL students' writings in the era of artificial intelligence. *Journal of Applied Learning & Teaching*, *6*(2). Advance online publication. DOI: 10.37074/jalt.2023.6.2.10

Mohammed, M. M., & Aysan, A. F. (2024). *Ascent of Regtech: A Bibliometric Analysis of Regulatory Technology*. Eurasian Studies in Business and Economics., DOI: 10.1007/978-3-031-55813-9_9

Mohri, M., Rostamizadeh, A., & Talwalkar, A. (2018). *Foundations of machine learning*. MIT press.

Mollick, E. R., & Mollick, L. (2023). Using AI to Implement Effective Teaching Strategies in Classrooms: Five Strategies, Including Prompts. Social Science Research Network. DOI: 10.2139/ssrn.4391243

Moraes, E. B., Kipper, L. M., Kellermann, A. C. H., Austria, L., Leivas, P., Moraes, J. R., & Witczak, M. (2022). Integration of Industry 4.0 technologies with Education 4.0: Advantages for improvements in learning. *Interactive Technology and Smart Education, 20*(2), 271–287. DOI: 10.1108/ITSE-11-2021-0201

Mousa, A. (2022). Detecting Financial Fraud Using Data Mining Techniques: A Decade Review from 2004 to 2015. *Journal of Data Science : JDS, 14*(3), 553–570. DOI: 10.6339/JDS.201607_14(3).0010

Moustaghfir, S., & Brigui, H. (2024). Navigating Critical Thinking in the Digital Era: An Informative Exploration. International Journal of Linguistics. *Literature and Translation, 7*(1), 137–143.

Mshelia, Y. U., Apeh, S. T., Ikerionwu, C., Blamah, N. V., Erike, A. I., & Elei, F. (2022). A Design-to-Test Technique for Inclusion Coefficients in AI-Driven Systems. 2022 IEEE Nigeria 4th International Conference on Disruptive Technologies for Sustainable Development (NIGERCON)

Muhammad, M. H. (2022). *Culturally Responsive Teaching with High School Teachers Walden University.*

Mukhamediev, R. I., Popova, Y., Kuchin, Y., Zaitseva, E., Kalimoldayev, A., Symagulov, A., Levashenko, V., Abdoldina, F., Gopejenko, V., Yakunin, K., Muhamedijeva, E., & Yelis, M. (2022). Review of artificial intelligence and machine learning technologies: Classification, restrictions, opportunities and challenges. *Mathematics, 10*(15), 2552. DOI: 10.3390/math10152552

Muralidharan, K., Shanmugan, K., & Klochkov, Y. (2022). The new education policy 2020, digitalization and quality of life in India: Some reflections. *Education Sciences, 12*(2), 75. DOI: 10.3390/educsci12020075

Murphy, R. F. (2019). Artificial intelligence applications to support K-12 teachers and teaching: A review of promising applications, opportunities, and challenges. *Rand Corporation, 10*, 1–21.

Nalluri, V., & Chen, L.-S. (2024). Modelling the FinTech adoption barriers in the context of emerging economies—An integrated Fuzzy hybrid approach. *Technological Forecasting and Social Change, 199*, 123049. DOI: 10.1016/j.techfore.2023.123049

Naqvi, A. (2020). *Artificial intelligence for audit, forensic accounting, and valuation: a strategic perspective*. John Wiley & Sons. DOI: 10.1002/9781119601906

Nashwan, S. A., Sadallah, M., & Bouteraa, M. (2023). Use of ChatGPT in academia: Academic integrity hangs in the balance. *Technology in Society*, *75*, 102370. DOI: 10.1016/j.techsoc.2023.102370

Nasim, S. M., Mujeeba, S., AlShraah, S. M., Khan, I. A., Amir, N., & Ali, Z. (2024). Exploring pedagogical perspectives of EFL instructors: Advantages, disadvantages, and implications of Blackboard as an LMS for language instruction. *Cogent Social Sciences*, *10*(1), 2312659. Advance online publication. DOI: 10.1080/23311886.2024.2312659

National Digital Library of India. (2015). Iitkgp.ac.in. https://ndl.iitkgp.ac.in/

National Education Policy. (2020). Policy Document released by Government of India, pp. 56-58. Retrieved from https://www.education.gov.in/sites/upload_files/mhrd/files/NEP_Final_English_0.pdf

Nazaretsky, T., Ariely, M., Cukurova, M., & Alexandron, G. (2022, July). Teachers' trust in AI -powered educational technology and a professional development program to improve it. *British Journal of Educational Technology*, *53*(4), 914–931. Advance online publication. DOI: 10.1111/bjet.13232

Nemorin, S. (2021). Fair-AI. Project Update #6. Preliminary Findings. Retrieved February 4, 2021, from https://www.fair-ai.com/projectupdate-6

NextEducation. (2024). *Next Education - India's Leading K-12 B2B EdTech Company*. Nexteducation.in. https://www.nexteducation.in/

Ng, D. T. K., Leung, J. K. L., Chu, K. W. S., & Qiao, M. S. (2021). AI literacy: Definition, teaching, evaluation and ethical issues. *Proceedings of the Association for Information Science and Technology*, *58*(1), 504–509. DOI: 10.1002/pra2.487

Nguyen, A., Ngo, H. N., Hong, Y., Dang, B., & Nguyen, B. P. T. (2023). Ethical principles for artificial intelligence in education. *Education and Information Technologies*, *28*(4), 4221–4241. DOI: 10.1007/s10639-022-11316-w PMID: 36254344

NIIT - Leading Online Course Provider | PG & Certificate Course. (2022). In *niit.com*. https://www.niit.com/india/

Nkambou, R., Mizoguchi, R., & Bourdeau, J. (2010). *Advances in intelligent tutoring systems* (Vol. 308). Springer Science & Business Media. DOI: 10.1007/978-3-642-14363-2

Noonoo, S. (2018, June 28). All the upgrades and updates from Apple, Google and more at ISTE 2018. *EdSurge*. https://www.edsurge.com/news/2018-06-28-all-the-upgrades-and-updates-from-apple-google-and-more-at-iste-2018

Novick, P. A., Lee, J., Wei, S., Mundorff, E. C., Santangelo, J. R., & Sonbuchner, T. M. (2022). Maximizing academic integrity while minimizing stress in the virtual classroom. *Journal of Microbiology & Biology Education*, *23*(1), e00292-21. Advance online publication. DOI: 10.1128/jmbe.00292-21 PMID: 35496711

O'Dea, X., & O'Dea, M. (2023). Is artificial intelligence really the next big thing in learning and teaching in higher education? A conceptual paper. *Journal of University Teaching & Learning Practice*, *20*(5). Advance online publication. DOI: 10.53761/1.20.5.06

Ojiaku, O. C., Ezenwafor, E. C., & Osarenkhoe, A. (2024). Integrating TTF and UTAUT models to illuminate factors that influence consumers' intentions to adopt financial technologies in an emerging country context. *International Journal of Technology Marketing*, *18*(1), 113–135. DOI: 10.1504/IJTMKT.2024.135674

Ojo, O. (2024). *Promoting artificial intelligence education in K–12 through pre-service teachers' development* (Master's thesis, Itä-Suomen yliopisto).

Okoli, C., & Schabram, K. (2015). A guide to conducting a systematic literature review of information systems research.

Olari, V., & Romeike, R. (2024). Data-related concepts for Artificial Intelligence education in K-12. *Computers and Education Open*, *100196*, 100196. Advance online publication. DOI: 10.1016/j.caeo.2024.100196

Oliveira, K. K. D. S., & Souza, R. C. (2021). *Digital Transformation towards Education 4.0*. Informatics in Education., DOI: 10.15388/infedu.2022.13

Omae, Y., Furuya, T., Matsushita, M., Mizukoshi, K., Yatsushiro, K., & Takahashi, H. (2023). Artificial intelligence education in an elementary school and its evaluation by career development, motivation and rubrics. *Information and Technology in Education and Learning*, *3*(1), Trans-p002. DOI: 10.12937/itel.3.1.Trans.p002

Omar Jian, M. J. K. (2023). Personalized learning through AI. Researchgate. https://www.researchgate.net/publication/376814707_Personalized_learning_through_AI

Onesi-Ozigagun, O., Ololade, Y. J., Eyo-Udo, N. L., & Ogundipe, D. O. (2024). Revolutionizing education through AI: A comprehensive review of enhancing learning experiences. *International Journal of Applied Research in Social Sciences*, *6*(4), 589–607. DOI: 10.51594/ijarss.v6i4.1011

Ouyang, F., & Jiao, P. (2021). Artificial intelligence in education: The three paradigms. *Computers and Education: Artificial Intelligence*, *2*, 100020. DOI: 10.1016/j.caeai.2021.100020

Paek, S., & Kim, N. (2021). Analysis of worldwide research trends on the impact of artificial intelligence in education. *Sustainability (Basel)*, *13*(14), 7941. DOI: 10.3390/su13147941

Pandey, B., & Prasad, S. (2024). USING BRAIN-COMPUTER INTERFACES (BCI) IN EDUCATION. In *THE FUTURE OF EDUCATION IN THE DIGITAL AGE*. IMRF INTERNATIONAL PUBLICATIONS.

Papadopoulos, D., & Hossain, M. M. (2023). Education in the age of analytics: Maximizing student success through big data-driven personalized learning. *Emerging Trends in Machine Intelligence and Big Data*, *15*(9), 20–36.

Park, W., & Kwon, H. (2023). Implementing artificial intelligence education for middle school technology education in Republic of Korea. *International Journal of Technology and Design Education*, *34*(1), 109–135. DOI: 10.1007/s10798-023-09812-2 PMID: 36844448

Pataranutaporn, P., Danry, V., Leong, J., Punpongsanon, P., Novy, D., Maes, P., & Sra, M. (2021). AI-generated characters for supporting personalized learning and well-being. *Nature Machine Intelligence*, *3*(12), 1013–1022. DOI: 10.1038/s42256-021-00417-9

Patel, M. (2024, September 24). *AI in FinTech: How Artificial Intelligence Will Change the Financial Industry*. Linearloop. https://www.linearloop.io/blog/ai-in-FinTech-how-artificial-intelligence-will-change-financial-industry?form=MG0AV3

Patil, S., & Kumar, P. (2023). "Case studies on artificial intelligence for sustainable education in 21st century". pp. 303-310. Retrieved from: https://www.researchgate.net/publication/378683480

Patterson, C. (2023, March 1). *ChatGPT Used by Teachers More Than Students*. Walton Family Foundation. https://www.waltonfamilyfoundation.org/chatgpt-used-by-teachers-more-than-students-new-survey-from-walton-family-foundation-finds?utm_source=chatgpt.com

Paudel, R. (2024). The Impact of Automation and Artificial Intelligence (AI) on Leadership and the Workforce. *Indonesian Journal of Banking and Financial Technology*, *2*(2), 109–124. DOI: 10.55927/fintech.v2i2.8904

Paullet, K., & Morris, R. (2020). STUDENT AND FACULTY PERCEPTIONS OF ACADEMIC DISHONESTY IN ONLINE CLASSES. *Issues in Information Systems*. Advance online publication. DOI: 10.48009/3_iis_2020_327-333

Paul, P. (2022). Digital Education: The Aspects and Growth in Socio-Economic Development—Towards sophisticated Education 4.0 Practice. *Economic Affairs*, *67*(5). Advance online publication. DOI: 10.46852/0424-2513.5.2022.32

Pawlychka, C. (2023). AI as part of the pedagogy: A restorative justice approach. *Canadian Perspectives on Academic Integrity*, *6*(1). Advance online publication. DOI: 10.55016/ojs/cpai.v6i1.76903

Payne, B. H. (2019). An ethics of artificial intelligence curriculum for middle school students. MIT Media Lab Personal Robots Group., Retrieved October 10, 2019, from.

Pedro, F. (2019). Artificial intelligence in education: challenges and opportunities for sustainable development.

Perkins, M., Gezgin, U. B., & Roe, J. (2020). Reducing plagiarism through academic misconduct education. *International Journal for Educational Integrity*, *16*(1), 3. Advance online publication. DOI: 10.1007/s40979-020-00052-8

Peruzzo, F., Ball, S. J., & Grimaldi, E. (2022). Peopling the crowded education state: Heterarchical spaces, EdTech markets and new modes of governing during the COVID-19 pandemic. *International Journal of Educational Research*, *114*, 1–14. DOI: 10.1016/j.ijer.2022.102006

Peterson, D. (2016). Edtech and student privacy: California law as a model. *Berkeley Technology Law Journal*, *31*(2).

Pflugfelder, E. H., & Reeves, J. (2024). Surveillance work in (and) teaching technical writing with AI. *Journal of Technical Writing and Communication*, *54*(4), 419–438. Advance online publication. DOI: 10.1177/00472816241260028

Placide, E. (2024). *The Integration of Artificial Intelligence in Education*. University College of the Cayman Islands.

Player-Koro, C., Rensfeldt, A. B., & Selwyn, N. (2018). Selling tech to teachers: Education trade shows as policy events. *Journal of Education Policy*, *33*(5), 682–703. DOI: 10.1080/02680939.2017.1380232

Plus, b. (2025, April 25). *AI education for FinTech in 2025: A comprehensive guide*. Byteplus. https://www.byteplus.com/en/topic/394296?title=ai-education-for-FinTech-in-2025-a-comprehensive-guide

PM e-Vidya. (n.d.). Pmevidya.education.gov.in. https://pmevidya.education.gov.in/

Pradhan Mantri Gramin Digital Saksharta Abhiyan. (n.d.). Www.pmgdisha.in. https://www.pmgdisha.in/

Prakash, A., Haque, A., Islam, F., & Sonal, D. (2023). Exploring the Potential of Metaverse for Higher Education: Opportunities, Challenges, and Implications. *Metaverse Basic and Applied Research*, *2*, 40. DOI: 10.56294/mr202340

Priya, S., Bhadra, S., Chimalakonda, S., & Venigalla, A. S. M. (2022). ML-Quest: A game for introducing machine learning concepts to K-12 students. *Interactive Learning Environments*, *32*(1), 229–244. DOI: 10.1080/10494820.2022.2084115

Project Sangam: Enabling skilling at scale for a better tomorrow. (n.d.). Microsoft Stories India. https://news.microsoft.com/en-in/features/project-sangam-skilling-anil-bhansali/

Radanliev, P. (2025). AI Ethics: Integrating Transparency, Fairness, and Privacy in AI Development. *Applied Artificial Intelligence*, *39*(1), 2463722. Advance online publication. DOI: 10.1080/08839514.2025.2463722

Rahman, B., Ahmed, O., & Shakil, S. (2021). FinTech in Bangladesh: Ecosystem, Opportunities and Challenges. *International Journal of Business and Technopreneurship*, *l*(11). https://www.researchgate.net/publication/350849277

Rahman, Z. T., Lal, R., & Ratna, R. (2022). An analytical study on the significance of folk and fairytales on the psychology of young children. *International Journal of Early Childhood Special Education*, *14*(5).

Rahman, Z. T., Lal, R., & Ratna, R. (2022). An Analytical Study on the Significance of Folk and Fairytales on the Psychology of Young Children. *International Journal of Early Childhood Special Education*, *14*(5).

Rahman, Z. T., Lal, R., & Rena, R. (2024). Challenges of communication with Gen-Z in the era of artificial intelligence-interceded digital economy. In *AI-oriented competency framework for talent management in the digital economy* (pp. 76–94). CRC Press. DOI: 10.1201/9781003440901-5

Rajpal, S., & Manglani, A. (2023).. . *The Impact of FinTech on Accounting Education.*, *7*(5). Advance online publication. DOI: 10.55041/IJSREM22599

Ramien, D. (2019). *Augmenting Education: Ethical Considerations for Incorporating Artificial Intelligence in Education*. Instructional Design Capstones Collection.

Ramya, P., & Manju, M. (2019). Artificial intelligence for sustainable education in India: Problems and prospects [*IJPTM*]. *International Journal of Production Technology and Management*, *10*(1), 135–143.

Rane, N., Choudhary, S., & Rane, J. (2023). "Education 4.0 and 5.0: Integrating artificial intelligence (AI) for personalized and adaptive learning". DOI: 10.2139/ssrn.4638365

Rastogi, H. (2019). Digitalization of education in India- an analysis. *International Journal of Research and Analytical Reviews*, *6*(1), 160–167.

Reckhow, S. (2013). *Follow the money: How foundation dollars change public school politics*. Oxford University Press.

Reidenberg, J., Russell, N. C., Kovnot, J., et al. (2013). *Privacy and cloud computing in public schools*. Fordham Law School, Center on Law and Information Policy.

Reis, P., Serra, A. P., & Gama, J. (2025). The Role of Deep Learning in Financial Asset Management: A Systematic Review. *Cornell University*. https://arxiv.org/abs/2503.01591

Rizvi, S., Waite, J., & Sentance, S. (2023). Artificial Intelligence teaching and learning in K-12 from 2019 to 2022: A systematic literature review. *Computers and Education: Artificial Intelligence*.

Roberts-Mahoney, H., Means, A. J., & Garrison, M. J. (2016). Netflixing human capital development: Personalized learning technology and the corporatization of K–12 education. *Journal of Education Policy*, *31*(4), 405–420. DOI: 10.1080/02680939.2015.1132774

Robles, V. C., Rivas, M. R., & Campos, J. a. S. (2020). Study of the reasons for and measures to avoid plagiarism in young students of education. *Profesorado Revista De Currículum Y Formación Del Profesorado, 24*(1), 50–74. DOI: 10.30827/profesorado.v24i1.8572

robomateplus_admin. (2016). *Robomate Plus*. Robomate Plus. https://robomateplus.com/

Rogers, E. M. (1962). *Diffusion of innovations* (1st ed.). Free Press.

Ronquillo, C. E., Peltonen, L. M., Pruinelli, L., Chu, C. H., Bakken, S., Beduschi, A., Cato, K., Hardiker, N., Junger, A., Michalowski, M., Nyrup, R., Rahimi, S., Reed, D. N., Salakoski, T., Salanterä, S., Walton, N., Weber, P., Wiegand, T., & Topaz, M. (2021). Artificial intelligence in nursing: Priorities and opportunities from an international invitational think-tank of the Nursing and Artificial Intelligence Leadership Collaborative. *Journal of Advanced Nursing*, *77*(9), 3707–3717. DOI: 10.1111/jan.14855 PMID: 34003504

Ross, J. (2024). *Guidance for developing policies to govern the adoption and use of artificial intelligence in K-12 schools.* https://eric.ed.gov/?id=ED655341

Rotherham, A. J., & Willingham, D. J. E. l. (2009). 21st century. *67*(1), 16-21.

Roy, M. (2020). AI intervention in education systems of India: An analysis. *Solid State Technology*, *63*(2s), 1395–1402.

Rudman, R., & Bruwer, R. (2016). Defining Web 3.0: Opportunities and challenges. *The Electronic Library*, *34*(1), 132–154. DOI: 10.1108/EL-08-2014-0140

Russell, S. (2021). The history and future of AI. *Oxford Review of Economic Policy*, *37*(3), 509–520. DOI: 10.1093/oxrep/grab013

Saha, B., Ahsan, A., Hasliza Muhd Yusuf, D., Aminul Islam, M., Huda, N., & Suryani, I. (2025). Exploring the Drivers of FinTech Adoption in SMEs: A Study from Bangladesh. *International Journal of Business and Technology Management*, *7*(1), 59–71. https://tinyurl.com/peh4bdx9

Sakulkueakulsuk, B., Witoon, S., Ngarmkajornwiwat, P., Pataranutaporn, P., Surareungchai, W., Pataranutaporn, P., & Subsoontorn, P. (2018, December). Kids making AI: Integrating machine learning, gamification, and social context in STEM education. *2018 IEEE international conference on teaching, assessment, and learning for engineering (TALE)* (pp. 1005-1010). IEEE.

Saluja, A. (2023). *Public-private partnerships in EdTech for transforming rural India: How start-ups are shaping the post-COVID landscape*. India's Technology-Led Development., Retrieved from https://www.worldscientific.com/doi/abs/10.1142/9789811271786_0006

Salvadore, S., & Buck, R. H. (2021). Moving from plagiarism police to integrity Coaches: Assisting novice students in understanding the relationship between research and ownership. *International Journal for Educational Integrity*, *17*(1), 20. Advance online publication. DOI: 10.1007/s40979-021-00085-7

Sandu, N., & Gide, E. (2019). "Adoption of AI-Chatbots to Enhance Student Learning Experience in Higher Education in India". *18th International Conference on Information Technology Based Higher Education and Training* (*ITHET*), Magdeburg, Germany, pp. 1-5. DOI: 10.1109/ITHET46829.2019.8937382

Sanusi, I. T., Oyelere, S. S., Agbo, F. J., & Suhonen, J. (2021, October). Survey of resources for introducing machine learning in K-12 context. In 2021 IEEE frontiers in education conference (FIE) (pp. 1-9). IEEE.

Sanusi, I. T., Olaleye, S. A., Agbo, F. J., & Chiu, T. K. (2022). The role of learners' competencies in artificial intelligence education. *Computers and Education Artificial Intelligence*, *3*, 100098. DOI: 10.1016/j.caeai.2022.100098

Sanusi, I. T., Oyelere, S. S., Vartiainen, H., Suhonen, J., & Tukiainen, M. (2023). A systematic review of teaching and learning machine learning in K-12 education. *Education and Information Technologies*, *28*(5), 5967–5997. DOI: 10.1007/s10639-022-11416-7

Saputra, I., Astuti, M., Sayuti, M., & Kusumastuti, D. (2021). Integration of Artificial intelligence in Education: Opportunities, Challenges, Threats and obstacles. A literature review. Researchgate. https://www.researchgate.net/publication/373530759_Integration_of_Artificial_Intelligence_in_Education_Opportunities_Challenges_Threats_and_Obstacles_A_Literature_Review

Sarkar, N., & Lal, R. (2023). Changing Trends of Media Ownership: Marketing Through Community Engagement in Hindi Television News Channels. In Global Applications of the Internet of Things in Digital Marketing (pp. 290-309). IGI Global.

Schiff, D. (2022). Education for AI, not AI for education: The role of education and ethics in national AI policy strategies. *International Journal of Artificial Intelligence in Education*, *32*(3), 527–563. DOI: 10.1007/s40593-021-00270-2

Seo, K., Yoo, M., Dodson, S., & Jin, S.-H. J. J. o. R. o. T. i. E. (2024). Augmented teachers: K–12 teachers' needs for artificial intelligence's complementary role in personalized learning. 1-18.

Shaika, S., Lal, R., & Jonjua, M. (2021). Sustainable Development Goal 3: Case Study of using Folk media as a Potent tool in India. *Journal of Contemporary Issues in Business and Government*, *27*(1), •••.

Shaikh, A. A., Glavee-Geo, R., Karjaluoto, H., & Hinson, R. E. (2023). Mobile money as a driver of digital financial inclusion. *Technological Forecasting and Social Change*, *186*, 122158. DOI: 10.1016/j.techfore.2022.122158

Sharma, P. (2019). Digital revolution of education 4.0. [IJEAT]. *International Journal of Engineering and Advanced Technology*, *9*(2), 3558–3564. DOI: 10.35940/ijeat.A1293.129219

Sharma, S., & Kumar, N. (2024). Navigating the ethical landscape of AI Based resources in Education: Implications for Learning, Proper Usage and Course Design Enhancement. *The Online Journal of Distance Education and e-Learning : TOJDEL.*

Sheetlani, J., & Jadimath, S. S. (2022). Effectiveness of digital India and artificial intelligence in Indian education system. *NeuroQuantology : An Interdisciplinary Journal of Neuroscience and Quantum Physics, 20*(10), 5312–5318.

Shet, A. (2024). Transforming traditional education with PHP: Building an Online classroom. *Amit Shet Al. International Journal of Recent Research Aspects, 11*(2). https://ijrra.net/Vol11issue2/IJRRA-11-02-01.pdf

Shirin, A. (2022). Artificial Intelligence technology on teaching-learning: Exploring Bangladeshi teachers' perceptions. *Embedded Self Organizing Systems, 9*(4), 3–9. DOI: 10.14464/ess.v9i4.553

Siddiqui, Z., & Rivera, C. A. (2023). Embedding FinTech-specific content in higher education. *Risk Governance and Control: Financial Markets and Institutions, 13*(4), 18–29. DOI: 10.22495/rgcv13i4p2

Siemens, G., & Baker, R. S. d. (2012). Learning analytics and educational data mining: towards communication and collaboration. Proceedings of the 2nd international conference on learning analytics and knowledge, Smith, D. D. J. (2010). Introduction to special education: Making a difference. DOI: 10.1145/2330601.2330661

Sikandar, M. A. (2022). The rise of EdTech start-ups in India. *Recent Trends in Management & Social Sciences, 2*, 24–32.

Singer, N. (2015, January 11). Silicon Valley turns its eye to education. *The New York Times*. https://www.nytimes.com/2015/01/12/technology/silicon-valley-turns-its-eye-to-education.html

Singer, N., & Ivory, D. (2017). How Silicon Valley plans to conquer the classroom. *The New York Times*.

Singha, S., & Singha, R. (2024). Revolutionizing content creation and curriculum development through generative AI. In *Advances in educational technologies and instructional design book series* (pp. 261–280). DOI: 10.4018/979-8-3693-1351-0.ch013

Singh, B., & Malhotra, M. (2020). The role of artificial intelligence in the Indian education sector. *OORJA, 18*(1), 21–30. DOI: 10.55399/WGQO2090

Singh, R. K., Prakash, R., & Lal, R. (2021). Adoption of CAB model for instrument development of effectiveness of crime-based reality-shows. *Journal of Content Community and Communication, 14*(7), 230–239. DOI: 10.31620/JCCC.12.21/19

Singh, R. K., Prakash, R., Lal, R., & Nanda, V. (2022). Mediation Role of Crime-Show Impact Between Creating Awareness About Crime and Novelty in Crime. *Journal of Pharmaceutical Negative Results*, •••, 1255–1262.

Skinner, B. F. (1965). *Science and human behavior (No. 92904)*. Simon and Schuster.

Snyder, J. (2025, January 19). *Beyond The Illusion - The Real Threat Of AI: WEF Global Risks Report 2025*. Forbes. https://www.forbes.com/sites/jasonsnyder/2025/01/19/beyond-the-illusionthe-real-threat-of-ai-wef-global-risks-report-2025/

Sophokleous, A., Christodoulou, P., Doitsidis, L., & Chatzichristofis, S. A. (2021, March 19). Computer Vision Meets Educational Robotics. *Electronics (Basel)*, *10*(6), 730. Advance online publication. DOI: 10.3390/electronics10060730

Sreedhar, J., Kumar, M. V. P., Karthik, D. S., Ibrahim, M., Prakash, G. H., Ibrahim, S. K., & Sandeep, P. (2023). The future of AI in education: A review analysis [*IJSREM*]. *International Journal of Scientific Research in Engineering and Management*, *7*(11), 1–10.

Startuptalky. (n.d.). https://startuptalky.com/edtech-startups-using-ar-vr/

Stephens, J. M., St John Watson, P. W., Alansari, M., Lee, G., & Turnbull, S. M. (2021). Can online academic integrity instruction affect university students' perceptions of and engagement in academic dishonesty? Results from a natural experiment in New Zealand. *Frontiers in Psychology*, *12*, 569133. Advance online publication. DOI: 10.3389/fpsyg.2021.569133 PMID: 33679506

Storyweaver. (n.d.). *Digital Library of Stories for Kids | Stories* | Https://Storyweaver.org.in/. https://storyweaver.org.in/en/

Suh, W., & Ahn, S. (2022). Development and validation of a scale measuring student attitudes toward artificial intelligence. *SAGE Open*, *12*(2), 1–12. DOI: 10.1177/21582440221100463

Su, J., & Yang, W. (2023). Unlocking the power of ChatGPT: A framework for applying generative AI in education. *ECNU Review of Education*, *6*(3), 355–366. DOI: 10.1177/20965311231168423

Su, J., & Zhong, Y. (2022). Artificial intelligence (AI) in early childhood education: Curriculum design and future directions. *Computers and Education: Artificial Intelligence*, *3*, 100072. DOI: 10.1016/j.caeai.2022.100072

Su, J., Zhong, Y., & Ng, D. T. K. (2022). A meta-review of literature on educational approaches for teaching AI at the K-12 levels in the Asia-Pacific region. *Computers and Education: Artificial Intelligence*, *3*, 100065. DOI: 10.1016/j.caeai.2022.100065

Sujatmika, S., Masykuri, M., Prayitno, B. A., & Sutarno. (2024). Cultivating students' critical thinking: A comprehensive approach with the integrative collaborative problem-solving (ICoPS) conceptual model. KnE Social Sciences. DOI: 10.18502/kss.v9i19.16502

Swayam Central. (n.d.). Swayam.gov.in. https://swayam.gov.in/

Sytnyk, L., & Podlinyayeva, O. (2024). AI in education: Main possibilities and challenges. *InterConf, 45*(201), 569–579. DOI: 10.51582/interconf.19-20.05.2024.058

Tag-hive. (n.d.) .https://tag-hive.com/class-saathi/

Tahiru, F. (2021). AI in education: A systematic literature review. In *Journal of Cases on Information Technology,* 23 (1),1–20. IGI Global. DOI: 10.4018/JCIT.2021010101

Tandon, R., & Tandon, S. (2020). Education 4.0: A new paradigm in transforming the future of education in India [*IJISET*]. *International Journal of Innovative Science, Engineering & Technology*, *7*(2), 32–54.

Tang, Q. (2024). "A case study on the application of artificial intelligence in education industry". Proceedings of the 2023 3rd International Conference on Modern Educational Technology and Social Sciences (ICMETSS 2023). *Advances in Social Science, Education and Humanities Research, 784*, 99–109. DOI: 10.2991/978-2-38476-128-9_12

Tapalova, O., & Zhiyenbayeva, N. (2022). *Artificial Intelligence in Education: AIED for Personalised Learning Pathways.* https://eric.ed.gov/?id=EJ1373006

Tayade, M. (2021). "Women entrepreneurs in education sector". *Role of Women in Nation Development* (Book of Conference Proceedings of NIT Jamshedpur 2020), 22, 184-191. DOI: 10.47531/MANTECH.2021.22

Teachmint. (n.d.). *Smart Learning Management System (LMS) & Integrated ERP Solution Compatible with Desktop & Mobile App.* https://www.teachmint.com/

Techflow. (2022, January 11). *AI in Education: Global Success Stories Unveiled.* https://teachflow.ai/ai-in-education-global-success-stories-unveiled/?form=MG0AV3

Tedre, M., Toivonen, T., Kahila, J., Vartiainen, H., Valtonen, T., Jormanainen, I., & Pears, A. (2021). Teaching machine learning in K–12 classroom: Pedagogical and technological trajectories for artificial intelligence education. *IEEE Access : Practical Innovations, Open Solutions*, *9*, 110558–110572. DOI: 10.1109/ACCESS.2021.3097962

Teece, D. J. (2017). Dynamic capabilities and (digital) platform lifecycles. In *Entrepreneurship, innovation, and platforms*.

Teichler, U. (2020). Higher education system differentiation, horizontal and vertical. In *Springer eBooks* (pp. 772–778). DOI: 10.1007/978-94-017-8905-9_36

Terzopoulos, G., & Satratzemi, M. (2019). Voice Assistants and Artificial Intelligence in Education. *Proceedings of the 9th Balkan Conference on Informatics*, 1–6. DOI: 10.1145/3351556.3351588

Thakor, A. V. (2020). FinTech and banking: What do we know? *Journal of Financial Intermediation*, *41*, 100833. DOI: 10.1016/j.jfi.2019.100833

The National AI Portal of India. (n.d.). INDIAai. https://indiaai.gov.in/

Thimmanna, Sharma, A. V. N. S., Naik, M. S., Radhakrishnan, S., & Sharma, A. (2023). Personalized Learning Paths: Adapting Education with AI-Driven Curriculum. *European Economic Letters*. DOI: 10.52783/eel.v14i1.993

Thottoli, M. M., Islam, M., Ahsan, A., Yusof, M. F., Hassan, M. S., & Chowdhury, R. S. (2024). Exploring mediating and moderating factors of FinTech adoption for innovations in SMEs. *Cogent Economics & Finance*, *12*(1), 2387443. Advance online publication. DOI: 10.1080/23322039.2024.2387443

Tigges, M., Mestwerdt, S., Tschirner, S., & Mauer, R. (2024). Who gets the money? A qualitative analysis of FinTech lending and credit scoring through the adoption of AI and alternative data. *Technological Forecasting and Social Change*, *205*, 123491. DOI: 10.1016/j.techfore.2024.123491

Timms, M. J. (2016). Letting Artificial Intelligence in Education Out of the Box: Educational Cobots and Smart Classrooms. *International Journal of Artificial Intelligence in Education*, *26*(2), 701–712. DOI: 10.1007/s40593-016-0095-y

Tomlinson, C. A. (2014). *The differentiated classroom: Responding to the needs of all learners*. Ascd.

Topal, A. D., Eren, C. D., & Geçer, A. K. (2021). Chatbot application in a 5th grade science course. *Education and Information Technologies*, *26*(5), 6241–6265. DOI: 10.1007/s10639-021-10627-8 PMID: 34177344

Toppr Answr - Get Help With Homework. (2023). Toppr Ask. https://www.toppr.com/ask/

Touretzky, D., Gardner-McCune, C., Breazeal, C., Martin, F., & Seehorn, D. (2019). A year in K–12 AI education. *AI Magazine*, *40*(4), 88–90. DOI: 10.1609/aimag.v40i4.5289

Unacademy. (2018). *India's largest learning platform*. Unacademy. https://unacademy.com/

Unal, A., & Unal, Z. (2024). Evaluating the integration of artificial intelligence (AI) in K–12 education. *Journal of Interactive Learning Research, 35*(3), 353–387. DOI: 10.70725/546995xiatpy

Van Brummelen, J., Heng, T., & Tabunshchyk, V. (2021). Teaching Tech to Talk: K-12 Conversational Artificial intelligence literacy curriculum and development tools. In *Proceedings of the . . . AAAI Conference on Artificial Intelligence* (Vol. 35, Issue 17, pp. 15655–15663). DOI: 10.1609/aaai.v35i17.17844

Vargas, V. R., Lawthom, R., Prowse, A., Randles, S., & Tzoulas, K. (2020). Implications of vertical policy integration for sustainable development implementation in higher education institutions. *Journal of Cleaner Production, 235*, 733–740. DOI: 10.1016/j.jclepro.2019.07.022

Vartiainen, H., Toivonen, T., Jormanainen, I., Kahila, J., Tedre, M., & Valtonen, T. (2021). Machine learning for middle schoolers: Learning through data-driven design. *International Journal of Child-Computer Interaction, 29*, 100281. DOI: 10.1016/j.ijcci.2021.100281

Velander, J., Taiye, M. A., Otero, N., & Milrad, M. (2023). Artificial Intelligence in K-12 Education: Eliciting and reflecting on Swedish teachers' understanding of AI and its implications for teaching & learning. *Education and Information Technologies, 29*(4), 4085–4105. DOI: 10.1007/s10639-023-11990-4

Vidergor, H. E., & Amram, P. B. (2020). Khan academy effectiveness: The case of math secondary students' perceptions. *Computers & Education, 157*, 157. DOI: 10.1016/j.compedu.2020.103985

Vij, A., & Agarwal, P. (2024). Assessing the challenges and opportunities of artificial intelligence in Indian education [IJGSAR]. *International Journal for Global Academic & Scientific Research, 3*(1), 36–44. DOI: 10.55938/ijgasr.v3i1.71

Vishwanath, M. (2023). The intelligent solution: automation, the skills shortage and cyber-security. *International Conference on Artificial Intelligence*. https://doi.org/DOI: 10.31219/osf.io/8t9sa

Vučković, D., Peković, S., Blečić, M., & Đoković, R. (2020). Attitudes towards cheating behavior during assessing students performance: Student and teacher perspectives. *International Journal for Educational Integrity, 16*(1), 13. Advance online publication. DOI: 10.1007/s40979-020-00065-3

Wang, N., & Wang, K. (2022). Internet Financial Risk Management in the Context of Big Data and Artificial Intelligence. *Mathematical Problems in Engineering*, *2022*, 1–6. DOI: 10.1155/2022/6219489

Wang, S., Christensen, C., Cui, W., Tong, R., Yarnall, L., Shear, L., & Feng, M. (2020). When adaptive learning is effective learning: Comparison of an adaptive learning system to teacher-led instruction. *Interactive Learning Environments*, *31*(2), 793–803. DOI: 10.1080/10494820.2020.1808794

Wang, T., & Cheng, E. C. K. (2021). An investigation of barriers to Hong Kong K-12 schools incorporating Artificial Intelligence in education. *Computers and Education: Artificial Intelligence*, *2*, 100031. DOI: 10.1016/j.caeai.2021.100031

Wang, Y. (2021). When artificial intelligence meets educational leaders' data-informed decision-making: A cautionary tale. *Studies in Educational Evaluation*, *69*, 100872. DOI: 10.1016/j.stueduc.2020.100872

Wang, Z. (2025). A time-series stock price prediction and asset portfolio optimization model based on long- and short-term memory networks. *Journal of Combinatorial Mathematics and Combinatorial Computing*, *124*, 243–258. DOI: 10.61091/jcmcc124-17

Watters, A. (2023). *Teaching machines: The History of Personalized Learning*. MIT Press.

Weber, P., Carl, K. V., & Hinz, O. (2024). Applications of Explainable Artificial Intelligence in Finance—A systematic review of Finance, Information Systems, and Computer Science literature. *Management Review Quarterly*, *74*(2), 867–907. DOI: 10.1007/s11301-023-00320-0

Wikipedia contributors. (n.d.). Start-up company. In *Wikipedia*. https://en.wikipedia.org/wiki/Start-up_company

Williams, R. (2024). Impact. AI: Democratizing AI through K-12 Artificial Intelligence Education (Doctoral dissertation, Massachusetts Institute of Technology).

Williams, R. (2024, February 1). Impact.AI: Democratizing AI through K-12 Artificial Intelligence Education. Dspace.mit.edu. https://dspace.mit.edu/handle/1721.1/153676

Williams, A. R., Windle, R., & Wharrad, H. (2020c). How will Education 4.0 influence learning in higher education? *Journal of Learning Development in Higher Education*, *17*(17). Advance online publication. DOI: 10.47408/jldhe.vi17.572

Williams, R., Ali, S., Devasia, N., DiPaola, D., Hong, J., Kaputsos, S. P., Jordan, B., & Breazeal, C. (2023). AI+ ethics curricula for middle school youth: Lessons learned from three project-based curricula. *International Journal of Artificial Intelligence in Education, 33*(2), 325–383. DOI: 10.1007/s40593-022-00298-y PMID: 35935456

Williams, R., Park, H. W., & Breazeal, C. (2019, May). A is for artificial intelligence: the impact of artificial intelligence activities on young children's perceptions of robots. In *Proceedings of the 2019 CHI conference on human factors in computing systems* (pp. 1-11). DOI: 10.1145/3290605.3300677

Wilson, S. M. (2011, May). Effective STEM teacher preparation, induction, and professional development. In *NRC Workshop on Highly Successful STEM Schools or Programs. Available:* http://www7.nationalacademies. org/bose/Successful_STEM_ Schools_Homepage. html *[May 2011]*.

Wong, G. K. W., Ma, X., Dillenbourg, P., & Huan, J. (2020). Broadening artificial intelligence education in K-12. *ACM Inroads, 11*(1), 20–29. DOI: 10.1145/3381884

Woodruff, K., Hutson, J., & Arnone, K. (2023). Perceptions and barriers to adopting artificial intelligence in K–12 education: A survey of educators in fifty states.

Xiao, C., Xu, S. X., Zhang, K., Wang, Y., & Xia, L. (2023). Evaluating Reading Comprehension Exercises Generated by LLMs: A Showcase of ChatGPT in Education Applications. DOI: 10.18653/v1/2023.bea-1.52

Xia, Q., Chiu, T. K., & Chai, C. S. (2022). The moderating effects of gender and need satisfaction on self-regulated learning through Artificial Intelligence (AI). *Education and Information Technologies*. Advance online publication. DOI: 10.1007/ s10639-022-11547x

Yablonsky, S. (2018b). *Multi-sided platforms (MSPs) and sharing strategies in the digital economy: Emerging research and opportunities*.

Yablonsky, S. (2018a). A multidimensional framework for digital platform innovation and management: From business to technological platforms. *Systems Research and Behavioral Science, 35*(4), 485–501. DOI: 10.1002/sres.2544

Yadav, H., Kar, A. K., & Kashiramka, S. (2022). *Artificial Intelligence Adoption for FinTech Industries - An Exploratory Study About the Disruptions*. Antecedents and Consequences., DOI: 10.1007/978-3-031-15342-6_1

Yandong, Q. (2024). *A case study of the technology acceptance model of FinTech companies using AI in FinTech innovations.* Siam University. https://tinyurl.com/ nh5ehzp9

Yang, W. (2022). Artificial Intelligence education for young children: Why, what, and how in curriculum design and implementation. *Computers and Education: Artificial Intelligence*, *3*, 100061. DOI: 10.1016/j.caeai.2022.100061

Yang, X. (2019). Accelerated move for AI education in China. *ECNU Review of Education*, *2*(3), 347–352. DOI: 10.1177/2096531119878590

Yao, X., Ma, N., Zhang, J., Wang, K., Yang, E., & Faccio, M. (2022). Enhancing wisdom manufacturing as industrial metaverse for industry and society 5.0. *Journal of Intelligent Manufacturing*, •••, 1–21.

Yau, K. W., Chai, C. S., Chiu, T. K., Meng, H., King, I., Wong, S. W. H., & Yam, Y. (2022). Co-designing artificial intelligence curriculum for secondary schools: A grounded theory of teachers' experience. In *2022 International Symposium on Educational Technology (ISET)* (pp. 58–62). DOI: 10.1109/ISET55194.2022.00020

Yau, K. W., Chai, C. S., Chiu, T. K., Meng, H., King, I., & Yam, Y. (2023). A phenomenographic approach on teacher conceptions of teaching Artificial Intelligence (AI) in K-12 schools. *Education and Information Technologies*, *28*(1), 1041–1064. DOI: 10.1007/s10639-022-11161-x

Yeo, W. J., Van Der Heever, W., Mao, R., Cambria, E., Satapathy, R., & Mengaldo, G. (2025). A comprehensive review on financial explainable AI. *Artificial Intelligence Review*, *58*(6), 189. DOI: 10.1007/s10462-024-11077-7

Yin, J., Goh, T., Yang, B., & Hu, Y. (2024). Using a chatbot to provide formative feedback: A longitudinal study of intrinsic motivation, cognitive load, and learning performance. *IEEE Transactions on Learning Technologies*, *17*, 1–13. DOI: 10.1109/TLT.2024.3364015

Yue, M., Jong, M. S. Y., & Dai, Y. (2022). Pedagogical design of K–12 artificial intelligence education: A systematic review. *Sustainability (Basel)*, *14*(23), 15620. DOI: 10.3390/su142315620

Yue, M., Jong, M. S. Y., & Ng, D. T. K. (2024). Understanding K–12 teachers' technological pedagogical content knowledge readiness and attitudes toward artificial intelligence education. *Education and Information Technologies*, *29*(15), 1–32. DOI: 10.1007/s10639-024-12621-2

Yu, Z. (2020, October). Visualizing Artificial Intelligence Used in Education Over Two Decades. *Journal of Information Technology Research*, *13*(4), 32–46. DOI: 10.4018/JITR.2020100103

Zafari, M., Bazargani, J. S., Sadeghi-Niaraki, A., & Choi, S. M. (2022). [Education: A Systematic Literature Review. *IEEE Access*]. *Artificial Intelligence and Applications (Commerce, Calif.)*, •••, K-12.

Zawacki-Richter, O., Marín, V. I., Bond, M., & Gouverneur, F. (2019). Systematic review of research on artificial intelligence applications in higher education – where are the educators? *International Journal of Educational Technology in Higher Education*, *16*(1), 39. Advance online publication. DOI: 10.1186/s41239-019-0171-0

Zeide, E. (2017). The limits of student purpose limitations. *University of Miami Law Review*, *71*(2).

Zhai, X., Chu, X., Chai, C. S., Jong, M. S. Y., Istenic, A., Spector, M., Liu, J.-B., Yuan, J., & Li, Y. (2021). A Review of Artificial Intelligence (AI) in Education from 2010 to 2020. *Complexity*, *2021*(1), 1–18. DOI: 10.1155/2021/8812542

Zhang, W., Aliannejadi, M., Yuan, Y., Pei, J., Huang, J.-H., & Kanoulas, E. (2024). Towards Fine-Grained Citation Evaluation in Generated Text: A Comparative Analysis of Faithfulness Metrics. https://arxiv.org/pdf/2406.15264

Zhang, H., Lee, I., Ali, S., DiPaola, D., Cheng, Y., & Breazeal, C. (2023). Integrating ethics and career futures with technical learning to promote AI literacy for middle school students: An exploratory study. *International Journal of Artificial Intelligence in Education*, *33*(2), 290–324. DOI: 10.1007/s40593-022-00293-3 PMID: 35573722

Zhang, K., & Aslan, A. B. (2021). AI technologies for education: Recent research & future directions. *Computers and Education: Artificial Intelligence*, *2*, 100025. DOI: 10.1016/j.caeai.2021.100025

Zhang, Y., & Cui, X. (2024). FinTech, business regulations, and urbanization: Shaping the landscape of natural resource rent in G10 countries. *Resources Policy*, *89*, 104551. DOI: 10.1016/j.resourpol.2023.104551

Zhou, Z., Ning, M., Wang, Q., Yao, J., Wang, W., Huang, X., & Huang, K. (2023). Learning by Analogy: Diverse Questions Generation in Math Word Problem. DOI: 10.18653/v1/2023.findings-acl.705

Zohuri, B., & Rahmani, F. M. (2024). Revolutionizing Education: The dynamic synergy of personalized learning and artificial intelligence. *International Journal of Advanced Engineering and Management Research*, *9*(1), 143–153. DOI: 10.51505/ijaemr.2024.9111

Zoting, S. (2024, August 9). *AI in Education Market*. Precedence Research. https://www.precedenceresearch.com/ai-in-education-market

About the Contributors

Syed Far Abid Hossain is currently working as an Assistant Professor at BRAC Business School, BRAC University. He has obtained PhD in Management Science from the School of Management (AACSB Accredited), Xi'an Jiaotong University, PRC. He holds an MBA degree from the University of Sunderland, UK and a BBA (Marketing) degree from Dhaka University. During his Ph.D., he received the best publication award by the local government. In addition, he was awarded the best CSC scholar award from the Chinese Government in 2018. He was the top CGPA scorer in his PhD batch. Before joining BRACU, he served as an Asst. Professor and Coordinator, MBA Program at IUBAT – International University of Business Agriculture and Technology where he was awarded the Miyan Publication Award and selected one of the top researchers in 2021 for his outstanding research publications. Also, Dr. Abid received the best presenter award in the international seminar on emerging challenges and opportunities in business and economy in 2021. Dr. Abid also has professional work experience in different national & multinational organizations such as ACI, Robi Axiata Ltd. etc. Mr. Abid authored more than 60+ academic journal articles, conference papers and book chapters in internationally recognized, peer reviewed and well-indexed Journals (ISI, Scopus, SSCI, SCIE, ABDC, ESCI, EI) from Elsevier, Springer, SAGE, Taylor and Francis, Frontiers, Science Direct, Emerald, MDPI and IGI global. Some of the renowned journals are: Interactive Learning Environments (Q1), Plos One (Q1), Technology, Pedagogy and Education (Q1), International Journal of Gender and Entrepreneurship (Q1), International Journal of Environmental Research and Public Health (Q1), PeerJ (Q1), F1000 Research (Q1), Frontiers in Psychiatry (Q1), Heliyon (Q1), Asia Pacific Journal of Business administration (Q2), SAGE Open (Q2), Journal of Public Health Research (Q2), The Chinese Economy (Q2), Cogent Education (Q2) and so on. Till date, Dr. Abid has 2100+ citations in Google scholar. Dr. Abid has published numerous books, book chapters and conference proceedings with famous publishers like Springer Nature and IGI global. His research interests include academic performance, education psychology, education management, technology in education, women entrepreneurship, innovation and media entrepreneurship. Apart from his current roles at BRAC Business School, Dr. Abid serves as a regular reviewer of famous journals from reputed publishers including Elsevier, Wiley, Springer, SAGE, Taylor and Francis, Frontiers, Emerald, IGI Global. Dr. Abid severed as an editorial board member of 16th South Asian Management Forum in 2021. Dr. Abid also served as a session chair in various conferences. Dr. Abid is strongly involved with GEPN (Global Education Policy network) for international research collaboration. Till date, Dr. Abid is proudly co-authored with renowned professors and researchers from University of Oxford, UK and many other recognized higher educational institutions from different parts of the world.

Walton Wider s a Professor at INTI International University, Malaysia. He holds a PhD in Psychology and specialises in educational psychology, higher education, and organisational behaviour. He has published extensively in Web of Science-indexed SSCI and SCIE journals, including the International Journal of Human–Computer Interaction, Business Process Management Journal, Applied Research in Quality of Life, School Mental Health, Sustainable Development, Journal of Studies in International Education, and International Journal of Inclusive Education. His research adopts a data-driven, interdisciplinary approach, with a strong focus on bibliometric and science-mapping methodologies. His work addresses key issues in digital transformation, mental health, and innovation in education and organisations..

***

Juraini Zainol Abidin is a senior lecturer in Accounting and Finance at Universiti Malaysia Perlis (UniMAP) with over 20 years of professional experience in banking and finance. Her research focuses on corporate failure, corporate governance, risk management, environmental economics, public policy, and SME financing, particularly within the Malaysian context. She has published interdisciplinary studies on SME failure, and co co-authored ELV policy, and water quality analysis for sustainable aquaculture, contributing to research that bridges economic analysis with policy innovation.

Arif Ahsan is a full-time doctoral researcher at the Department of Business, Universiti Malaysia Perlis (UniMAP), Malaysia, currently on study leave from his role as Assistant Professor at IUBAT, Bangladesh. His academic journey spans Bangladesh, the United Kingdom, and Malaysia, with degrees from AIUB, Kent Business School (UK), and UniMAP. His research focuses on the adoption of

FinTech, AI integration, financial inclusion, and SME development in emerging economies. He has published in peer-reviewed journals on topics such as digital finance, financial literacy, and AI-driven innovation. Arif actively engages in international academic workshops and welcomes collaboration on FinTech and inclusive finance.

Khaled Arafat is an aspiring student with an interest in research work. Graduated from BRAC University, majoring in Human Resources and Computer Information Management (CIM), he actively spends his time in research works and projects. Currently, he has two research articles and papers on IGI Global and The Business Standard.

Tanjila Azad is a graduate of English, majoring in Literature, from BRAC University. She has a strong foundation in communication, research, and creative writing, complemented by experience in content development, editorial work, and team coordination. Notably, as a Resonance Team Member, she contributed to producing cohesive and high-quality publications through effective collaboration.

Anika Zarin Chowdhury is a graduate of BRAC Business School, BRAC University, with a degree in Human Resource Management. Her work lies at the intersection of organizational behavior and emerging technologies, with a particular focus on the transformative potential of Artificial Intelligence. She has authored a book chapter on AI and contributed to the academic community by peer reviewing four research papers for IGI Global Scientific Publishing. With nearly a year of experience in Organizational Development and Excellence (ODE), she applies theoretical insights to practical organizational challenges. Committed to lifelong learning, she aims to bridge the gap between human capabilities and AI, approaching research with a thoughtful, interdisciplinary perspective.

Nandini Deb is Assistant Professor at Manav Rachna International Institute of Research and studies .

Deep Moni Gogoi is an Assistant Professor at Manav Rachna International Institute of Research and studies.

Puan Juliazilah Binti Junit is an Associate Dean and Lecturer at the Department of Languages, Faculty of Social Science and Humanities at Tunku Abdul Rahman University of Management and Technology (TAR UMT). She holds a Bachelor of Education (Hons) and a Master of Linguistics and is currently pursuing her PhD. Her major areas of study and specialization include Teaching English as a Second Language (TESL) and Linguistics. Puan Juliazilah's research interests encompass

Systemic Functional Linguistics, Applied Linguistics, Sociolinguistics, Discourse Analysis, and the teaching and learning English as a Second Language (ESL) and English as a Foreign Language (EFL).

Khadijatul Labannya holds a Bachelor's degree in Human Resource Management with a minor in Marketing from BRAC University and is currently pursuing her MBA in HRM at the same institution. She is actively working on two research articles for IGI Global. Her academic interests lie at the intersection of HRM and marketing, with a focus on strategies that enhance organizational effectiveness. Alongside her graduate studies, she remains engaged in research projects that support her professional growth and future academic endeavors.

Ruhi Lal is Head of the department and Professor at Manav Rachna International Institute of Research and studies .

Chee Seong Low, commonly known as Lawrence, is an accomplished academic and researcher specialising in psychology. With a Master of Science in Occupational Psychology from the University of Nottingham and a Bachelor of Psychology from Murdoch University, Lawrence has developed a robust foundation in the psychological sciences. Currently serving as the Associate Dean for Quality Assurance at Tunku Abdul Rahman University of Management and Technology in Kuala Lumpur, Malaysia, Lawrence oversees the quality assurance processes for academic programmes. His role ensures the maintenance of academic standards and compliance with regulatory bodies, contributing significantly to the university's educational excellence. In addition to his research, Lawrence has been an active lecturer since 2013, imparting knowledge in various psychology courses, including Industrial and Organisational Psychology, Health Psychology, and Research Methods. His dedication to teaching excellence earned him the Outstanding Lecturer Award in 2019. Lawrence's commitment to advancing the field of psychology through rigorous research and quality education continues to inspire his students and peers alike. His contributions to academia, coupled with his leadership in quality assurance, underscore his pivotal role in shaping the future of psychological education and research.

Sayada Mollika earned a Bachelor of Arts and a Master of Arts in English from BRAC University in 2021 and 2023, respectively, with a focus on ELT and Applied Linguistics. She works as a Teaching Assistant at the English and Humanities Department at the moment. She was a YouTube content creator and a beginner-level WordPress developer from 2017 to 2019. Her entrepreneurial endeavors included crafting and selling handmade artificial flowers online. Sayada Mollika's diverse experiences reflect her multifaceted skills, as does her keen interest in online entrepreneurship. Her research interests include teaching English as a foreign and second language, the integration of technological gadgets and AI assistance in English teaching, syllabus and materials design, barriers to ESOL learners mastering English in urban and rural contexts, English for specific purposes, Second language acquisition, The art of sophisticated language and persuasion in business, English education policy and practice and ELT in religious seminaries.

Dayang Hasliza Muhd Yusuf is a faculty member at the Faculty of Business & Communication, Universiti Malaysia Perlis (UniMAP), Malaysia. Her research spans business innovation, entrepreneurship, technology management, and SME development, with a strong emphasis on digital transformation and e-government adoption. She has co-authored numerous peer-reviewed publications, including highly cited works on SME success factors, workplace behaviour, and financial technology adoption. Dr. Dayang is affiliated with the Centre of Excellence for Social Innovation & Sustainability and actively contributes to advancing inclusive and innovation-driven business practices in Malaysia.

Hasanat Fariha Noon is an engineer specializing in renewable energy, with a growing focus on interdisciplinary research that bridges technology, sustainability, and intelligent systems. Her research interests include the application of machine learning in air filtration systems to address air quality challenges, and the integration of artificial intelligence in educational contexts. Driven by a data-driven and adaptive mindset, she is committed to developing solutions that are both technically grounded and environmentally meaningful.

Anna Wen Huey Ong obtained her Master's in Education (Psychology) from National Chiao Tung University and a Bachelor of Social Science (Hons) in Psychology from Universiti Tunku Abdul Rahman. She is currently pursuing a Doctorate in Education at the Open University Malaysia. She has over 9 years of teaching experience across different age groups. Her dedication to teaching excellence earned her the Outstanding Lecturer Award in 2023. She is interested in exploring various research topics, including psychometrics, family relationships, education, and mental health.

P. Sharimila Bai Pandurenga Rao is an Associate Dean and Lecturer at the Department of English Studies, Faculty of Social Science and Humanities at Tunku Abdul Rahman University of Management and Technology (TAR UMT). She holds a Bachelor of Arts English Language Studies (Hons) from Universiti Kebangsaan Malaysia (UKM) and a Master of Linguistics from the University of Malaya. Her major areas of study and specialization include English Studies and Applied Linguistics. Ms P Sharimila Bai's research interests focus on Sociolinguistics and

Discourse Analysis. She is dedicated to teaching and research, aiming to contribute significantly to her fields of interest.

Saimah Kamal Promee is a graduate in Electrical Engineering from Stony Brook University, with a second major in Applied Mathematics and Science, and is currently pursuing her PhD. As a Research Assistant in the Opto-electronic Sensors and Systems Lab, she develops electrical grid monitoring systems and analyzes circuit behavior to improve power efficiency. Her experience spans teaching, lab assistance, technical support, and electrical system design. Combining interdisciplinary expertise, Saimah is committed to innovative research, collaborative problem-solving, and advancing practical solutions to complex engineering challenges.

Iffat Sahira Ramisha holds a Bachelor's degree in Human Resource Management with a minor in Marketing. Her scholarship interrogates the dynamic interplay between organizational behavior, employee relations, and strategic marketing, with an emphasis on translating HR insights into innovative organizational practices. This paper represents her inaugural academic contribution, signaling a commitment to advancing original, theory-informed perspectives. Ramisha is dedicated to bridging human resource principles with creative marketing strategies, striving to generate research that is both conceptually rigorous and practically transformative within contemporary organizational contexts.

Rezuana Tabassum completed her Bachelor of Arts in English from BRAC University in 2022 with two majors, 'ELT and Applied linguistics' and 'Human Resource Management'. She is currently pursuing her Master of Arts in English from BRAC University as well. She is working there as a Teaching Assistant in the English and Humanities Department. Her research interest includes various sectors related to English as well as the business sector.

Yong Wei Yap obtained her Bachelor of Arts (Honours) English Language from Universiti Tunku Abdul Rahman and Master of Education (Teaching of English as Second Language, TESL) from Universiti Putra Malaysia. She has over 10 years of experience in teaching English courses to learners from various backgrounds since joining Tunku Abdul Rahman University of Management and Technology (TAR UMT) in 2013.

Index

A

F

H

I

K

T

U

V

www.ingramcontent.com/pod-product-compliance
Lightning Source LLC
LaVergne TN
LVHW081537300926
849161LV00006B/1467